D1714711

REEXAMINING THE EISENHOWER PRESIDENCY

Recent Titles in
Contributions in American History

News in the Mail: The Press, Post Office, and Public Information, 1700–1860s
Richard B. Kielbowicz

North from Mexico: The Spanish-Speaking People of the United States. New Edition, Updated by Matt S. Meier
Carey McWilliams

Reagan and the World
David E. Kyvig, editor

The American Consul: A History of the United States Consular Service, 1776–1914
Charles Stuart Kennedy

Reform and Reaction in Twentieth Century American Politics
John J. Broesamle

A Quest for Security: The Life of Samuel Parris, 1653–1720
Larry Gragg

Anti-Racism in U.S. History: The First Two Hundred Years
Herbert Aptheker

James Kirke Paulding: The Last Republican
Lorman Ratner

New York at Mid-Century: The Impellitteri Years
Salvatore J. LaGumina

Alternative Constitutions for the United States: A Documentary History
Steven R. Boyd

Racism, Dissent, and Asian Americans from 1850 to the Present: A Documentary History
Philip S. Foner and Daniel Rosenberg, editors

The American Grocery Store: The Business Evolution of an Architectural Space
James M. Mayo

REEXAMINING THE EISENHOWER PRESIDENCY

Edited by Shirley Anne Warshaw

Foreword by Louis Galambos

CONTRIBUTIONS IN AMERICAN HISTORY, NUMBER 149
David E. Kyvig, Series Adviser

Greenwood Press
Westport, Connecticut • London

56364

Library of Congress Cataloging-in-Publication Data

Reexamining the Eisenhower presidency / edited by Shirley Anne Warshaw ;
    foreword by Louis Galambos.
       p. ; cm. — (Contributions in American history, ISSN 0084–9219 ;
    no. 149)
       Includes bibliographical references and index.
       ISBN 0–313–28792–9
       1. United States—Politics and government—1953–1961.
    2. Eisenhower, Dwight D. (Dwight David), 1890-1969. I. Warshaw,
    Shirley Anne, 1950– . II. Series.
    E835.R424   1993
    973.921′092—dc20   92–42430

British Library Cataloguing in Publication Data is available.

Library of Congress Catalog Card Number: 92–42430
ISBN: 0–313–28792–9
ISSN: 0084–9219

First published in 1993

Greenwood Press, 88 Post Road West, Westport, CT 06881
An imprint of Greenwood Publishing Group, Inc.

Printed in the United States of America

The paper used in this book complies with the
Permanent Paper Standard issued by the National
Information Standards Organization (Z39.48–1984).

10 9 8 7 6 5 4 3 2 1

CONTENTS

FOREWORD

Louis Galambos

Dwight David Eisenhower helped lead this country through three of the most important transitions in world politics during the twentieth century. The first was World War II, in which Eisenhower played a vital part as a military leader. The second was in great measure a product of that war: it involved the dual processes of the rise to power of the Soviet Union and the communist movement it led, and of the collapse of the colonial empires. Eisenhower—as both a military and a political leader—had a major role in helping the United States work out and implement its responses to these two changes in global politics. As the United States devised new policies dependent upon heavy engagement in world affairs and defined the basic strategy and tactics of containment, Eisenhower was in a crucial position to influence national policy and to secure the public support it needed.

The third transition was less well understood at the time and is still largely misinterpreted by many Americans, including some of the most distinguished historians. That was the transition away from a political system in which the central dynamic was a drive to enlarge the administrative state in an effort to provide greater security and equity to the country's citizens. The shift was toward a system oriented more to efficiency and innovation in the private sector as a means of providing greater income and the consumer goods and services most of the nation's citizens seemed to want. Today we frequently discuss that transition as part of the post–1970 response to heightened global economic competition. But in reality the change began long before 1970. Its origins were much broader than our current effort to compete with Japan and Germany. While this transition began rather early in the United States—in the 1950s, I contend—it has in the years since World War II spread around the world. Today it is sweeping through eastern Europe, the former Soviet Union, Latin America, and Africa, accompanied by a powerful supporting drive to introduce or improve democratic procedures in those societies.

Those who read this volume carefully will have an exciting opportunity to stand with America's leaders at two of these important crossroads in twentieth-century history. This volume focuses on aspects of the presidency of Dwight David Eisenhower that are important and of enduring value largely because of what they tell us about those crossroads and about the complex choices the United States and its leaders made at that trying time in the development of our nation and of its role in the world. The reader will be able to make up her or his own mind as to how effectively Eisenhower coped with these challenges.

Consider for a moment some of the choices. In its foreign relations during the 1950s, the United States had to decide whether it could maintain over the long run the policy of containing Soviet expansion—a policy Eisenhower had helped to devise and then implement as the first Supreme Commander of the military forces of the North Atlantic Treaty Organization (NATO). The Korean War had raised serious questions about the viability of that policy and, in particular, about its long-term impact on America's capitalist economy. There were problems emerging in other parts of the world as well: problems stemming from the breakup of the old colonial empires and problems stemming from the rise of socialist and nationalist regimes that in many cases were hostile to the United States and its objectives.

Eisenhower was as convinced in 1953 as he had been in the late 1940s that the United States had to stand as the bulwark against Soviet expansionism and the development of new communist regimes. During his NATO years he actually refined his commitment to the fundamentals of containment, adding to his geo-political analysis a new emphasis upon America's need for trading partners over the long haul. Our economy could not succeed, he decided, if it became increasingly isolated from the markets and raw materials it needed overseas. The health of the U.S. economy was the foundation stone of his foreign policy, and the long view was his constant refrain. If we could maintain a healthy, productive capitalist economy while maintaining a steady pressure against the expansive forces of communism around the world, we could, Eisenhower thought, eventually outlast our opponents. If, however, we decided to buy so much security that we weakened the economy, we would lose in the long run. This was the essence in foreign policy of the "middle way," and he recognized that to sell that policy to the American people and then to hold the government on that course would be no small task. Within the country and without, powerful forces worked against the restraint embodied in the middle way. However, as the events of 1991 in the former Soviet Union indicated, Eisenhower had charted a brilliant course for the nation.

At home too there were vital decisions that had to be made and new policies that had to be implemented. For many decades the central feature of politics in

America had been a multifaceted effort to provide through government greater security for particular groups in the society and to introduce a greater measure of equity. Great pulses of reform in local, state, and national politics had over the years since the late nineteenth century given the United States its first formidable administrative state. Americans for the first time had been introduced to peacetime, public bureaucracy—an institution long familiar in Europe and Asia. Meanwhile, interest-group politics, by slowly eroding the support for the traditional political parties, had changed the basic nature of the nation's democratic system.

Eisenhower was convinced that Americans did not want and did not need another pulse of domestic reform. He therefore sought to reduce the size and intrusive nature of the administrative state. He did not want to get rid of the successful programs and policies developed over the years—Social Security, for example—and after some hesitation he became convinced that new measures were needed to ensure civil rights for black Americans. But he did sincerely want to reverse the trend toward the growth of government. He was opposed to regulation where the market would suffice; he was opposed to public authority where private action could achieve our common goals. Along the way, he wanted to balance the federal budget and reduce the inflationary pressures on American society.

In the 1950s it was not at all clear that either the domestic or foreign policies sought by Eisenhower could be successfully implemented or that either would constitute a major crossroads in world history. In the 1960s many Americans considered his policies to have been nostalgic failures. How different this appears today. In foreign policy the basic containment strategy that Eisenhower maintained has succeeded. Throughout the world communist regimes have been forced by their own failures to abandon the command economies they had long contended were the wave of the future. The polyglot Soviet empire has disintegrated, as Eisenhower had predicted. In country after country the driving force of politics has become an effort to introduce a market-oriented system resembling in fundamental ways the capitalist economy on which Eisenhower pinned his faith. The expansive force has gone out of state socialism, just as the architects of the containment policy prophesied it would.

Similarly, in domestic policy the Republican Eisenhower administrations appear to have represented a distinct turning point in the nation's political development. Before 1952 the Democratic Party had controlled the White House for thirty years. From the 1952 election to the present day, the Republican Party has captured the presidency in seven out of ten elections. For most of the last four decades, a conservative coalition in Congress has dominated the legislative process almost as completely as the Republicans have controlled the White House.

As the force of liberalism waned, a formidable effort to replace political controls with market controls has become a major force in our society. Equity and security, once our nation's watchwords, have yielded to efficiency and innovation—themselves now proclaimed to be the best ways to protect the equity and security of all the people over the long run. The Eisenhower administrations of the 1950s were part of the first wave of this dramatic change in our polity—a change which has gradually spread to most of the industrial nations. That movement and the accompanying drive to democratize have become the New Deal of the 1980s and 1990s just as surely as liberalism was the keynote of the New Deal in the 1930s.

In the 1950s, when these issues first arose, they all seemed to be primarily matters of domestic concern. But in Eisenhower's mind, the questions of political economy were always tightly interwoven with the central elements of U.S. foreign policy. Many years later these interconnections would become obvious to most Americans. But before that happened, the nation would experience a determined effort in the 1960s to go far beyond what Eisenhower thought the country could afford either in domestic or foreign affairs. The effort to expand social welfare—the "butter" of domestic reform—and simultaneously to adopt a more aggressive foreign policy—the "guns" of Vietnam—would create so many economic problems for the nation that the United States would in the late 1960s try to revert with a dramatic heave to a more Eisenhower-like approach. The experience of the 1960s would foster a growing recognition of the tight links between matters foreign and domestic. Out of that experience too would come the beginnings of the revisionism that would change for the better Eisenhower's historical standing as a president.

By the time the swing toward Eisenhower revisionism was well underway, the United States was hotly engaged in deregulation. Liberals and conservatives were joining hands to promote the sort of policies Eisenhower had begun advocating in the 1952 campaign and continued during his subsequent years in office. The market now reigned supreme. Suspicion about the regulatory state has become an article of faith in the United States and has in recent years spread, nation by nation, throughout the western world. Then, as the capstone of this movement, world communism fractured. Suddenly the strongest condemnations of the state could be heard coming from some of those very nations that earlier in this century had done the most to enhance the power of the state. Eisenhower would be excused a chuckle if he were alive today.

From our perspective today his role in history seems secure, determined in large part by where he stood relative to these two major shifts in global politics and economic life: the development of a polarized world polity experiencing dramatic change stemming primarily from the twin forces of nationalism and socialism and the shift in world focus from equity/security in a governmental setting to efficiency/innovation in a competitive setting. In each case Eisenhower's vindication came many years after he delivered his 1961 Farewell Address—years, in fact, after he died in 1969.

Thus history has changed in vital ways the historical evaluation of Dwight Eisenhower's presidency. How different it looked in the 1950s and 1960s. In the 1950s most intellectuals and academicians were dedicated—in varying degrees of commitment—to those well-established goals of the liberal society: equity and security. They were as well convinced that government planning could in most regards do a better job than the market could in allocating resources and evaluating performances. Most wanted the traditional reform movements to continue unabated. Eisenhower stood against their most cherished beliefs, and they responded with scorn to both the rhetoric and policy of his administrations.

He was in many ways an easy target. There were the fumbled press conferences—not all of which were products of calculated obfuscation. There were the wealthy friends—a few of whom did indeed take advantage of their privileged positions. There was his slowness to move against the demagogue Joseph McCarthy. His slowness to speak out for civil rights. His lowbrow reading habits. His bridge games and, above all, his golf. What more did a clever journalist or a clever journalist posing as a historian need to caricature the man?

So we had to wait some years until all of that had settled down. Not until world history had ground another few decades into the dust were we able to get a more accurate appraisal of Eisenhower's leadership. If today that appraisal threatens to err on the side of praise almost as much as the earlier evaluations did on the side of criticism, we can perhaps excuse that with reference to the enthusiasm that normally accompanies conversion. And we can also feed into our personal conclusions a discount factor that acknowledges that the analytical pendulum's swing to the right today has something to do with how far it swung to the left yesterday.

In Eisenhower's case the scholarly and publishing communities that have contributed to the reappraisal of his role in the history of this country can surely take pride in what they have accomplished. We are today in a much better position to understand the man and his times because of the work these communities have done. Much of that work is reflected in this volume. Many of the contributions are by those who have done the most to promulgate a clearer understanding of Ike. They in turn have benefited from the efforts of all of those—in government service and in private life—who have worked to make the documentary record of the Eisenhower administrations available for research. This required prodigious efforts in declassification, historical editing, and archival work. Eisenhower himself wanted as full a historical record available to as many researchers as possible. He had confidence that serious historians and biographers would get it right, and now, some decades after the fact, his faith in scholarship seems to be vindicated, as does his faith in American democracy and in the capitalist system he worked so hard to preserve.

INTRODUCTION

Shirley Anne Warshaw

During the past decade, scholars have started to reassess the Eisenhower presidency, due in large part to the work of Princeton University scholar Fred Greenstein. Greenstein, in his carefully researched work on Eisenhower as president entitled *The Hidden-Hand Presidency* (New York: Basic Books, 1982), provides detailed analyses of Eisenhower as a skillful politician who used "hidden-hand" leadership to manage controversial issues. The view of Eisenhower as a detached president, easily persuaded by his staff and often manipulated by Sherman Adams and John Foster Dulles, is dispelled by Greenstein's work. Greenstein's later work, *How Presidents Test Reality* (San Francisco: Russell Sage Foundation, 1989), written with John P. Burke, provides further support for Eisenhower's activist management style.

The availability of the presidential papers in Abilene, Kansas, many of which have been recently opened, has provided scholars with fresh sources of material on the Eisenhower administrations. These documents reveal a president totally involved in decision making and in command of every facet of the decision-making process. He was clearly not, as some have suggested in earlier writings, a figurehead president.

President Eisenhower demanded a broad range of policy options and discussed those options in Cabinet and staff meetings. Participants in these discussions were never deferential to the president or reticent to offer their views. Often these meetings were lively, even heated exchanges of proposals. However, each participant was keenly aware that the president would make the final decision. Eisenhower respected the views of his advisers but demanded their loyalty in implementing policy decisions, regardless of the extent of their personal support.

This volume examines how President Eisenhower used a hidden-hand leadership style to direct not only policy development but crisis management. The chapters included here are part of the rapidly growing body of "revisionist" literature that has emerged during the past decade and focuses on this presidential activism. All of the material included in this volume was presented at the Eisenhower Symposium held at Gettysburg College in Gettysburg, Pennsylvania, in October 1990. The purpose of this international symposium was to examine the Eisenhower presidency as part of the nation's centennial celebration of Eisenhower's birth.

The Gettysburg symposium drew over 100 contributors and hundreds of participants from around the world. This volume includes selected contributions from the symposium involving both domestic and foreign policy. Each of the chapters highlights a critical issue during the Eisenhower administration and illustrates how the president managed the players and the outcome of the decision-making process.

It should be noted that the symposium actively solicited the broadest spectrum of research on the Eisenhower presidency and did not attempt to include only those authors who supported the hidden-hand thesis. However, the research presented at the symposium almost exclusively focused on Eisenhower's activism in the policy process. This research involves authors not only from the United States but also from Germany, the United Kingdom, and Australia. Their conclusions, regardless of discipline, academic training, or geographic orientation, support the activist-president theory. The revisionist literature of the 1980s has become the mainstream literature of the 1990s.

It should also be noted that this is the second volume to be produced from the Eisenhower Symposium. The first volume, entitled *The Eisenhower Legacy*, edited by Shirley Anne Warshaw (Silver Spring, Md.: Bartleby Press, 1992), includes a series of discussions by the major speakers at the symposium on President Eisenhower's leadership style. These speakers were primarily members of the Eisenhower White House staff and Cabinet and members of the press. Also in *The Eisenhower Legacy*, many of the key Eisenhower scholars, including Louis Galambos, Fred Greenstein, Stephen Ambrose, and David Eisenhower, discuss their view of the Eisenhower presidency.

THE GETTYSBURG CONNECTION

Gettysburg College's affiliation with President Eisenhower began in 1915, when, as a senior cadet at West Point, he traveled to Gettysburg to study the battlefield. He returned to Gettysburg three years later to command a training center for the Tank Corps next to the battlefield named Camp Colt. During part of his assignment at Camp Colt he lived in housing on the Gettysburg College campus.

General Eisenhower returned to the Gettysburg College campus in 1946 to accept an honorary Doctor of Laws degree from the college. Four years later, the Eisenhowers purchased a 190-acre farm on the battlefield, just west of Seminary Ridge. The Eisenhowers remained at the farm throughout their lives and deeded the land to the National Park Service upon their death.

Throughout his administration, President Eisenhower used the facilities of Gettysburg College for numerous official activities. After his term of office ended in 1961, President Eisenhower retired to his farm and used the offices of Gettysburg College for meetings and to write his memoirs. The college gave the president and his staff the use of a building on campus, which is known today as Eisenhower House. During the next eight years, Eisenhower wrote three volumes: *The White House Years: Mandate for Change, 1953–1956* (Garden City, N.Y.: Doubleday, 1963); *Waging Peace, 1956–1963* (Garden City, N.Y.: Doubleday, 1965); and *At Ease, Stories I Tell to Friends* (Garden City, N.Y.: Doubleday, 1967). He was also a member of the college's board of trustees from 1961 until his death in 1969 and was an active participant in college decisions.

As a result of this long relationship, Gettysburg College held an international symposium October 10–14, 1990, to commemorate President Eisenhower's one-hundredth birthday. This was part of a national celebration that included numerous celebrations throughout the nation, a White House reception for Eisenhower family and friends, a joint resolution by Congress honoring President Eisenhower, and a resolution in the Pennsylvania House of Representatives honoring the president.

The Eisenhower Symposium brought together several hundred scholars, members of the Eisenhower Cabinet and staff, and reporters who covered the Eisenhower administration. The scholarly papers presented at the symposium all had a common thread: an administration far more active in domestic and foreign policy—and, in particular, a president far more active in the policy-making process—than previously cited.

THE EISENHOWER CONNECTION

This volume includes ten chapters presented at the Eisenhower Symposium at Gettysburg College. *Reexamining the Eisenhower Presidency* begins with a chapter by Michael Wala and another by Travis Beal Jacobs focusing on the period between the end of Eisenhower's military career following World War II and the beginning of his political career in 1952 when he was president of Columbia University. During this brief period Eisenhower honed his expertise in domestic, economic, and diplomatic policy and established a wide network of wealthy supporters through two key activities: the American Assembly and the Council on Foreign Relations.

During his tenure at Columbia University he established a conference center called the American Assembly designed to examine new ways of promoting democratic principles. Much to Eisenhower's delight, W. Averell Harriman donated his family's estate to the university to house the American Assembly endeavors. Throughout his brief term at Columbia, Eisenhower devoted a significant portion of his time to raising funds from corporations and Columbia alumni for the American Assembly.

In addition to the American Assembly, Eisenhower spent a considerable amount of time with members of the Council on Foreign Relations to discuss the rebuilding of Europe. Members of the Council included many of the nation's most prominent political and corporate leaders whose goal was to provide a plan for the rapid economic revitalization of Europe. Eisenhower had been asked to join the council to provide military expertise on issues of geopolitical stability. His involvement with the council, however, proved to be extremely educational to him for it broadened his knowledge of economic and political matters and provided a framework for informed discussions during the 1952 presidential campaign.

It is also worth noting that Eisenhower's contacts from the American Assembly and the Council on Foreign Relations later became key financial backers of the 1952 presidential campaign. Eisenhower skillfully brought the backers of the American Assembly and the council into his campaign. It is doubtful that Eisenhower would have proceeded with his campaign without their financial connections and their own personal contributions. Eisenhower's adroitness in the political world was clearly unfolding long before he announced his candidacy for the presidency.

Once in office, Eisenhower established a White House staff structure designed to provide him with a broad range of policy options. The complexity of managing the nation's national and international objectives required the president to be well briefed in military, diplomatic, intelligence, and economic affairs. The linkages in these policies also mandated a strong coordination effort within the White House. Eisenhower replaced the informality of previous administrations with a more orderly and systematic process of decision making. Bradley H. Patterson's picture of the White House staff is one of a well-oiled machine providing detailed policy options for the president and coordinating presidential directives.

The administration's handling of civil rights has been characterized as dismal by several Eisenhower scholars, including Stephen Ambrose (*Eisenhower: The President* [New York: Simon and Schuster, 1984]). Ambrose argues that President Eisenhower did not aggressively pursue civil rights legislation or enforcement throughout his eight years in office. However, this view has been repeatedly challenged by Eisenhower staff, former Attorney General Herbert Brownell, and a host of scholars. Brownell and others note that Eisenhower's record in civil rights included efforts to end discrimination in federal employment and in employment by federal contractors; to end segregation in Washington, D.C.; to make the desegregation of the armed forces a reality; and to appoint unprecedented numbers of blacks to positions in the Executive Branch.

Two chapters in this volume support Brownell and his colleagues and shed new light on the efforts by the Eisenhower administration to aggressively pursue civil rights initiatives. In chapter 5, Donald W. Jackson and James W. Riddlesperger, Jr., argue that the 1957 Civil Rights Act was carefully crafted by Attorney General Brownell and maneuvered through Congress by the president. Eisenhower is portrayed by Jackson and Riddlesperger as engaged, active, and far more involved in day-to-day legislative leadership than many accounts of his presidency suggest. His success in winning congressional support for the 1957 Civil Rights Bill was even more significant in light of Lyndon Johnson's opposition in the Senate to major portions of the bill.

Similarly, another chapter on civil rights by Michael Mayer chronicles the skill that President Eisenhower used to dismantle the system of segregation in the south. According to Mayer, he appointed moderates and liberals to the Fourth and Fifth Circuit Courts of Appeal, which enforced the Supreme Court's *Brown v. Board of Education of Topeka* decision. One case is discussed at length by Mayer, that of the nomination of his solicitor general, Simon E. Sobeloff, to sit on the Fourth Circuit Court of Appeals. Sobeloff had been a longstanding opponent of racial inequality and had testified before the Senate Judiciary Committee on behalf of a federal antilynching bill in 1933. Eisenhower's nomination and strong defense of Sobeloff throughout the Senate confirmation process were part of his aggressive approach to civil rights. In spite of the strong political backlash within the south and within Congress, Eisenhower sought to move the full weight of the federal judiciary toward the complete integration of the nation's school systems.

President Eisenhower's vision for a just educational system was mirrored by his vision for a space program whose priority was to benefit the scientific community. Eisenhower supported the development of spacecraft that would yield new scientific knowledge about the earth, the moon, and the entire galaxy. He firmly withstood, according to Giles Alston in chapter 6, the protestations of the military community to proceed with a rapid deployment in space of military hardware to compete with the Soviet deployment of Sputnik. Under Eisenhower's stewardship, the National Aeronautics and Space Administration (NASA) was launched in 1958 with scientific, rather than military, goals.

Following this theme of an activist president, Iwan W. Morgan examines the role of President Eisenhower in achieving three balanced budgets during his two terms in office. Since 1932, only seven budgets have been balanced: three under Truman, three under Eisenhower, and one under Johnson. Eisenhower's concern for a balanced budget was predicated on two concerns, according to Morgan. First, he saw the reestablishment of fiscal responsibility as the essential prerequisite for halting the burgeoning role of the federal government. Eisenhower viewed big government as a threat to free enterprise and to a strong system of dual federalism. Second, he feared that a constantly expanding military budget would eventually require an excessive level of national resources. By masterful use of the presidential podium, he convinced the public that deficits were ruinous and that the Democrats were constant spenders. He was named *Time* magazine's Man of the Year in 1959 for performing "the political miracle of making economy popular."

President Eisenhower's political expertise is further evidenced in Henry Z. Scheele's analysis of the relationship between Eisenhower and House Majority and Minority Leader Charles A. Halleck. Although quite aware of the institutional conflicts between the executive and legislative branches, Eisenhower sought to ameliorate some of these institutional differences by cultivating a warm relationship with Charles Halleck. At Halleck's urging, Eisenhower met regularly with the leaders of both houses and periodically invited every one of the 531 members of Congress to the White House. He adroitly sought to personalize his relationship with members to mitigate the inevitable institutional conflicts.

During his run for a second term, Scheele notes, Eisenhower asked Halleck to give the nominating speech at the Republican National Convention held in San Francisco's Cow Palace. Halleck eagerly accepted and at the convention praised Eisenhower's accomplishments while in office, assuring the nation that Eisenhower's illness would not jeopardize his presidency. The skill with which Eisenhower brought Halleck into his fold was a clear indicator of the political acumen of the thirty-fourth president.

Finally, the volume includes two chapters on President Eisenhower's leadership style in foreign policy. Michael Graham Fry examines the course of action followed by Eisenhower during the 1956 Suez crisis. Eisenhower's decision to handle the Suez affair principally on substantive rather than political grounds gave Adlai Stevenson a formidable weapon in the 1956 elections.

Yet Eisenhower masterfully kept the Suez crisis from deteriorating into a domestic political crisis by focusing on the need to keep America out of war. His solution was to approach all sides with diplomatic and economic pressure rather than military pressure. Eisenhower not only kept the nation out of a Middle East war but neutralized Stevenson's attacks.

The final chapter in the volume, by Kenneth Kitts and Betty Glad, examines crisis management during the 1956 Hungarian rebellion. Given the constraints on the American capacity to act within the Soviet sphere of influence, President Eisenhower decided on a policy of nonintervention. He narrowed access to the decision-making process so that he could control the results and preempt any possible momentum in favor of a more aggressive military response. This hidden-hand decision-making process, moreover, enabled him to escape the negative political fallout from a policy that reversed the commitment of the Republican Party to the rollback of Soviet power in eastern Europe.

In conclusion, each of the ten chapters included in this volume presents President Eisenhower as an activist president, totally versed in policy options, and carefully weighing the outcome of each option. He was a thoroughly involved president, cognizant of both the political and policy ramifications of each of his decisions. He was not, as has often been asserted, maneuvered by members of his Cabinet and staff into their chosen positions. The Eisenhower legacy is one of a president with a clear agenda for domestic and foreign policy and skilled at moving those policies through the labyrinth of congressional and public demands.

REEXAMINING THE EISENHOWER PRESIDENCY

1

AN "EDUCATION IN FOREIGN AFFAIRS FOR THE FUTURE PRESIDENT": THE COUNCIL ON FOREIGN RELATIONS AND DWIGHT D. EISENHOWER

Michael Wala

Dwight D. Eisenhower seems to be one of the presidents of the United States who has received significant biographical attention. But then, Eisenhower was not only president but was also a hero of World War II. His career as a soldier has been well mapped, and his administration has been more closely studied as more and more documents in the National Archives and in the Eisenhower Library, Abilene, Kansas, have become available to researchers in recent years. Surprisingly, however, the interlude between his service as Army general and his appointment on December 19, 1950, as Supreme Allied Commander in Europe has received very little attention.

This may be explained because his service as president of Columbia University—from June 1948 to December 1950—does not really fit into the picture of Eisenhower as general and U.S. president. Also, his time at Columbia was a less happier episode in Eisenhower's life. "Eisenhower did not cut much of a figure," historian Robert H. Ferrell says of his tenure. The general had to entertain and serve as fund-raiser, and "his calendar quickly filled with luncheons, dinners, and meetings."[1] There are strong indications, however, that suggest that this period may have served, in the broadest sense, as part of "the political education of General Eisenhower," as one of his biographers has termed it.[2] He had to deal with an environment that was not comparable with his experiences as soldier and with a military setting. As the former provost at Columbia noted, Eisenhower was not a peer in intellectual discussions with the faculty, and as a result, a "gulf between the president's office and the academic disciplines" might well have existed. This gulf never seemed to be bridged during his tenure as president. Eisenhower, nevertheless, learned to function in a civilian environment and to head an administration in the nonmilitary sector of the public sphere, and surely broadened his perspectives.[3]

Also at this time, when the opportunity arose, Eisenhower grasped the chance to learn more about economics and foreign policy, specifically about the interdependency of military, economic, and political matters in foreign affairs: for two years, from January 1949 until December 1950, he led a Council on Foreign Relations (CFR) group that studied the political and military implications of the Marshall Plan. The general, although occupied with his duties as president of the university, missed only two of twenty meetings of the group. "Whatever General Eisenhower knows about economics," one member of the Aid to Europe group later claimed, "he has learned at the study group meetings." The Rockefeller Foundation, a sponsor of the council's meeting and research program, went even further and suggested the study group had "served as a sort of education in foreign affairs for the future President of the United States."[4]

With about 2,500 members today, the Council on Foreign Relations, like many other organizations concerned with international policy, had been founded in the first quarter of this century as a counterpart of what is today the Royal Institute for International Affairs in London.[5] From the council's inception, its members supported an internationalist and antiisolationist attitude toward foreign affairs. They perceived the American decision to refrain from joining the League of Nations as a grave error, an error that had made the developments of the 1930s and World War II possible. They hoped the newly founded United Nations organization would provide a stable system of defined and enforceable rules. Its stability would further international trade, and all countries would benefit. The council believed that the United States should play a major role in the world that would pay tribute to the military, economic, and moral strength of the nation. From the council's founding until the end of World War II, it had developed from an elitist men's club to a renowned forum for high-level discussions by experts on international affairs.[6] During this period, the council grew into the role of respected adviser in matters of foreign policy.[7]

The study group Eisenhower was to head was founded when Franklin A. Lindsay, assistant to Paul G. Hoffman, administrator of the Economic Cooperation Administration (ECA), asked his friends at the council on May 1, 1948, to set up a large-scale research program on the European Recovery Program (ERP). The ERP was hardly a month old, but Lindsay did not believe the administration would launch such a study in the immediate future. Guidelines and evaluations with the broader picture in mind, not hampered by the pressure of the day-to-day work the ECA faced, were highly desirable. Lindsay counted on council president Allen W. Dulles and the council's staff to help the ECA formulate long-range plans. Immediately, discussions and planning began on how such a study group could be organized and conducted and what aspects should receive primary attention. However, another six months passed before all preparatory discussions and difficulties in organizing the study group had been resolved.[8]

Dulles had his reservations about the envisioned program, and he was not certain if the State Department would react favorably to this possibly vast undertaking. During World War II, the council had organized a program similar to what the studies program for the ECA might turn out to be. Only a few days after Germany had attacked Poland, the council's executive director, Walter H. Mallory, and *Foreign Affairs* editor, Hamilton F. Armstrong, offered the State Department help in developing the war and peace aims of the United States. War and Peace Studies were set up in close cooperation with the Department of State and remained operative until August 1945. This effort resulted in more than 680 confidential memoranda, reports, and digests of discussion on questions of security, armaments, and peace aims and on political, territorial, economic, and financial problems for the use of government officials.[9]

With the War and Peace Studies terminated shortly after V-J Day, the council continued its weekly discussion and study group meetings, occasional dinner meetings, and a few full-membership meetings at the Harold Pratt House in New York City, activities that had been somewhat cut back during the war. These meetings were often used as forums: speakers could transmit their ideas to an interested public, advocate their causes, and further the development of public opinion. Council members received information and could, in turn, convey their impressions through multiple channels of communication.[10] Through this function as a forum the council was influential—differently from case to case, and very seldom exclusively and directly. It participated in a network of government agencies and private organizations bound together through formal and informal ties. Council members cooperated to devise foreign policy through self-regulation and by attempting to mediate a consensus supported in large part by societal elites. The council played an important role in this strategy: it helped to possibly facilitate agreement even before a policy was decided upon. Additionally it served as an important base for recruitment for high-level posts in the State Department and in other governmental agencies.[11]

It is likely that Franklin Lindsay contemplated this when he asked the council's help in studying long-term implications of the European Recovery Program. He may even have considered a program comparable to the War and Peace Studies. As a result, the council contacted Richard M. Bissell, Jr. (assistant administrator of the ECA), Theodore Geiger (special assistant to Bissell for policy), and Lincoln Gordon (head of the ECA's internal study department) to discuss the plan with them.[12] All three supported the idea of a council investigation and proclaimed "keen interest," and ECA's administrator Paul Hoffman in mid-June wrote in support of the council's idea. The Council on Foreign Relations' Committee on Studies approached the whole notion with much more caution than some council members and their friends at ECA may have hoped. A memorandum on the plan, together with a copy of Hoffman's letter, was sent to all members of the committee and was discussed during one of the next meetings.[13]

During these preliminary discussions, John H. Williams of the Federal Reserve Bank argued against an "inside job" for the ECA. He feared that the council could later serve as a scapegoat for mistakes the administration had made. Nevertheless, he agreed to consider serving as chairman of the group. A subcommittee of the Committee on Studies was to select and invite members to participate in the group's work. Background material would be provided by members of the council's staff, but the group, the Committee on Studies maintained, should primarily depend on the "wisdom and judgment" of its members.[14]

At the Committee on Studies meeting on October 7, 1948, the plan for the study group received its final approval. It was decided that the council would work completely independently of the ECA and that a book, based on the group's research, should be published.[15] When Percy W. Bidwell proposed that the group would need a "shrewd and capable person with political wisdom as well as economic knowledge to serve it," Winfield Riefler, economist at the Institute of Advanced Studies at Princeton University, suggested that Dwight D. Eisenhower was the "obvious chairman." The committee "strongly endorsed" his suggestion because it "believed that a distinguished nonpartisan investigation of the most important problem before our country today might give the general just the type of connection with public affairs which would be most useful to him, as well as close contact with some of the individuals whom he must get to know as president of Columbia." After considerable discussion, the committee requested Allen Dulles, Henry M. Wriston, and John W. Davis to ask Eisenhower to accept the chair.[16]

Dulles, Wriston, and Davis were well-chosen representatives to sway Eisenhower to become chairman of the group: Dulles, well-known Republican and former chief of mission of the Office of Strategic Services (OSS) in Switzerland and Germany, was the highest representative of the council; Davis, a former president of the council, had been a (unsuccessful) Democratic candidate for U.S. president; and Wriston, as president of Brown University and president of the Association of American Universities, was a colleague of Eisenhower. This truly bipartisan and eminent group of men was able to persuade the general when they met with him on the afternoon of November 3, 1948, in his office at Columbia.[17]

Eisenhower, however, carefully considered the scope of his involvement and had his assistant Kevin C. McCann check out the council. Arrangements could not be made before November 18, for McCann to meet with Dulles, Wriston, and Walter Mallory. Mallory wrote to McCann that they would have ample opportunity to discuss the plans.[18] With McCann the schedule for meetings could be laid out, and it was agreed that the group would start working in January 1949. There is no account of what was said at these meetings, but Eisenhower must have been duly impressed. The council emissaries had indicated that the State Department was deeply interested in his work at the Council on Foreign Relations.[19]

The agenda the group was to research was extensive, involving economic as well as military aspects. Originally, the group was to research the economic situation in Europe at the end of postwar American aid. It was assumed that

Europe would still have major economic problems at that time.[20] Determinants for an economic independence of Europe were discussed as well as the question of military support to ensure the safety of Europe. Under Eisenhower's chairmanship the discussions rapidly turned to military aspects and to the problems military buildup might cause for the effort of economic reconstruction of Europe. Bissell had sent the council a long list of possible research topics of primary interest to the ECA, such as trade and economic relationships between the European states and their economic relations with the world market. But the twenty topics were of an exclusively economic nature, and thorough research would certainly have overtaxed the council's normal conduct of study groups. At the first group meeting, it became obvious that discussion of military aspects would dominate the meetings. Economic matters were discussed at subsequent meetings, but Eisenhower usually dominated the discussion and routinely turned the attention to political and military matters.[21]

Eisenhower's difficulty in following deliberations and theoretical arguments of economists and bankers and the more technical aspects of investment, inflation, and devaluation was one reason for this emphasis on military aspects. The general knew his shortcomings and, on one occasion, freely admitted that he knew so little about such things that his opinion was essentially worthless.[22] Another reason for the emphasis on military matters, however, was the change in American aid policy toward Europe during the preceding few years. The Marshall Plan originally had been envisioned as "political economy in the literal sense of the term," to use George F. Kennan's expression. It was a measure that was to pay tribute to American interests and American ideas about political constellations in Europe without, at the same time, actively provoking an open clash with the USSR. But even before the European Recovery Program had passed Congress, American and European military leaders realized that economic aid would not suffice and that a defense community would have to be established to deter possible Soviet aggression.

The British and French foreign ministers, even by 1947 (during the first discussions on the Marshall Plan), had raised the issue of a defense treaty. Together with their American partners, they negotiated during the remainder of the year how such a military program could be established. In the meantime, it had become obvious that cooperation with the USSR in Europe was hardly possible. The Communist coup in Czechoslovakia in February 1948—which prompted Congress to a swift passage of the Economic Assistance Act—added to the difficulties. Lucius D. Clay cabled in the beginning of March from Berlin that the situation over the last few weeks had become dangerous and that now a serious, and possibly military, conflict with the USSR seemed imminent.

In the United States, negotiations and discussions between Secretary Marshall and Under Secretary Robert M. Lovett, on the one side, and Senators Arthur S. Vandenberg and Tom Connally, on the other side, began in the first weeks of April 1948.[23] After deliberations by the Senate Committee on Foreign Relations, Senator Vandenberg, on May 19, 1948, proposed a resolution to Congress asking for a defense treaty between the United States and the western European nations in accordance with Article 51 of the United Nations' charter. By the time Vandenberg asked the Senate on June 11 to vote on his resolution, the relations between the USSR and the United States had deteriorated further. The USSR had already for some time disturbed access of the western allies to the Soviet sector in Berlin. After the currency reform in the three western zones of Germany had been announced on June 19, the blockade of the city, which was to last for thirteen months, began.[24]

The main problem politicians in Washington discussed in the following months regarding the North Atlantic Treaty Organization (NATO) was if rearmament of European countries might prevent effective economic rehabilitation. When President Truman, in his famous quotation, called the Marshall Plan and the Truman Doctrine "two halves of the same walnut," the military alliance, undoubtedly, was the third "half." The Communist coup in Czechoslovakia in February, the Vandenberg Resolution and the Berlin Blockade in June 1948, and the beginnings of official consultations about a European Defense Community and NATO had shifted the attention away from economic issues. With General Eisenhower as chairman of the group, the discussion rapidly moved away from the economic and political emphasis to deliberations on military aspects.

The members of the study group were well informed about the latest developments when they discussed the very strong interdependence between the Marshall Plan and the Alliance at their first meeting on January 10, 1949. Eisenhower maintained that both the Marshall Plan and NATO were directed to ensure "democracy in the enterprise system." But J. P. Morgan partner Russell C. Leffingwell, although agreeing in general with Eisenhower, had doubts if simultaneous economic reconstruction and rearmament would be possible. Eisenhower was much more positive: the Europeans would maintain that this was infeasible, but the supply of raw materials and the right impetus would show what was really possible. A buildup of armed forces was imminent, Eisenhower maintained, and it was certain that possible Soviet aggression could, at this time, only be stopped at the Pyrenees and the English Channel. This evaluation was not to be mentioned in public, he warned, because it would take away every hope for western Europeans and might endanger the economic success of the ERP.[25]

The members of the group did not believe that war with the Soviet Union was imminent, at least not until the European Recovery Program had been completed. Asked for a vote if they believed that the USSR, even accidentally, would unleash a war, Leffingwell told the other group members that George Kennan had argued that the Soviets might, to reach their political aims, create a crisis that could not be controlled. A majority of the group members regarded that this danger was great or considerable.[26] Psychological support and security the Europeans would receive through the conclusion of the defense treaty, Hamilton Armstrong maintained, would be much more important than any weapon they might receive.

Eisenhower himself reported that the Truman administration was willing to do everything possible to support and strengthen a western European defense community. This was the case despite the reluctancy of some members of the administration to restrain the United States' freedom of action by such an alliance. Eisenhower shocked his audience by stating that if western Europe were overrun by the Soviets, the United States would be on its way to extinction. The general proposed, in a rough outline of the domino theory, that, without western European nations as allies, the United States could eventually be surrounded by enemies. He continued his analogy by arguing that if western Europe were to go, Africa would be in danger and so would South America. He further noted that he believed that Asia was already lost or in jeopardy. This made economic recovery of western Europe all the more pressing, for it would serve to strengthen the war potential of these countries against a military attack. In addition, Eisenhower argued, it would keep their economies strong enough to keep them from being susceptible to communist infiltration from within.[27]

Additionally, Eisenhower reminded the group members that the region did possess a great and competent potential of skilled labor and industrial capacity. It would also have, through its colonies, influence on large regions in the world. A political community of the western European nations would be of greatest importance and would have implications far beyond successful economic aid through the Marshall Plan.[28]

While there still remained a heated discussion within the administration on whether Spain and Germany should be members of the envisioned military alliance, the CFR members quite easily found a consensus on this problem. General Eisenhower argued that Spain was of major military importance to the United States, for it controlled the entrance to the Mediterranean and was protected on the north by the Pyrenees. He urged the members to consider the military importance of Spain over its internal politics.[29]

The Soviet Union and communism, the most dangerous enemies Eisenhower had referred to, supposedly not only endangered the western European countries from the outside but from the inside as well. The council members were convinced that the Marshall Plan and NATO would ensure domestic security in the participating countries and would prevent Communist coups. Particularly in France and Italy, it seemed possible that Communists could come to power through elections. Council members were certain that a better standard of living and stable political institutions could serve as a vaccine.[30]

This scenario not only applied to Europe but to the world at large. The group members agreed that NATO should only be one part of a whole system of military alliances with the United States spanning the globe. At a meeting on March 7, 1949, Eisenhower proposed to draft a memorandum on the subject. It was supposed to show government officials and politicians, shortly before the

North Atlantic Treaty was to be signed, that similar treaties or agreements would be necessary in other regions. He suggested forwarding such a memorandum to Secretary of the Navy James F. Forrestal for the National Security Council or to Dean Acheson, who had been recently named Secretary of State. The memorandum called upon the president to extend the Truman Doctrine "to include a flat warning that aggression in any form, in any part of the world, will always be considered as 'dangerous to our peace and safety.' This is the language of James Monroe, and we believe that it now applies to the whole world." Only three days later, on March 10, 1949, Eisenhower handed the memorandum to Under Secretary of State James Webb.[31]

Even the rearmament of Germany was considered reasonable to avert this danger. McGeorge Bundy, assistant to Henry L. Stimson and "ghostwriter" of his memoirs *Active Service in War and Peace*, had prepared a working paper on the political equilibrium in western Europe. Rearmament of Germany, Bundy had written, was being proposed only by "irresponsible men." Hanson Baldwin, military editor of the *New York Times*, believed that this evaluation was hardly realistic. The Federal Republic of Germany had just been established, and Baldwin thought it inconceivable that an independent nation could be prevented from having an army.[32]

Eisenhower pursued a somewhat different line of argument in this respect. He stated that the pivotal question was who the United States feared more: the Germans or the Russians. Treating Germany as a neutral power would drive it into the arms of the Soviet Union and thus would, unnecessarily, increase the number of potential enemies. When Baldwin mentioned political means to check Germany's drive for yet another war, Bundy somewhat sarcastically referred to the 1930s, when political guarantees had existed to no avail. Economist Jacob Viner of Princeton University summarized the whole problem by saying that the nation feared a German menace but was also concerned about Germany as a potential ally. In this, Eisenhower counseled patience: the danger a strong and reunited Germany certainly posed to the security of all nations was "a reason not to hurry the unification of Germany." But if, in some time, the emotional background of fear of the Germans had eased, everyone would agree to embrace Germany as an ally. While group members Allen Dulles and Hamilton Armstrong advised a slower pace in shifting the political attitude toward the former enemy, and economist Emile Després could hardly envision Germany as a loyal ally to the United States at all, Ford International Corporation manager Graeme K. Howard wanted West Germany immediately accepted as a member of NATO, "part and parcel."[33]

The great moment for the study group came on December 11, 1950. North Korean troops had, after some clashes in the demilitarized zone on the thirty-eighth parallel, overrun almost all of South Korea within two months. After the deployment of U.N. troops in August—consisting mostly of American units and commanded by General Douglas MacArthur—North Korean troops were pushed back toward the Chinese border. On November 26, Chinese troops attacked, and a long and painful retreat to the south of Seoul began.

Eisenhower, at Truman's request, flew to Washington, D.C., and met with the president on October 28. Eisenhower was informed that the American Chiefs of Staff were convinced that a commander-in-chief for the North Atlantic Pact forces should be named immediately, with him as the primary choice. He came away from this meeting with the impression that, "at this moment, I would estimate that the chances are about nine out of ten that I will be back in uniform in a short time."[34]

By December 11, the date of the last meeting of the Aid to Europe group that Eisenhower chaired, he knew that official announcement of his assignment as Supreme Allied Commander in Europe was only a matter of days. It had been planned that Eisenhower's authority in his new position would be more restricted than he would have wished. He was supposed to go through "channels" and would have to submit his reports via the Department of State to the military headquarters in Washington. Neither this setting nor the weakness of military forces in Europe added to Eisenhower's fondness for the job.[35]

Henry Wriston met Eisenhower on the steps to the council on December 11, 1950, and raised the subject.[36] Wriston proposed that it would be a good idea to draft, together with the council group, a letter to President Truman. They could let the president know what problems the group members foresaw in connection with Allied forces in Europe.[37]

Memoranda prepared by the group's staff or outside experts were discussed, as during many of the preceding meetings. Nevins delineated in his report the military weakness of the French forces, and Lindsay Rogers discussed the possibility that Europe might develop into a neutral and third power, independent of the United States and the Soviet Union. The strength of the USSR and the relative weakness of NATO countries were made drastically clear to the members present. The group members agreed that the European allies had an insignificant defense if the Soviet Union chose to attack. All they could possibly count on was the hope of a will for peace in the eastern bloc, clashes between party leaders of the individual socialist countries, the generally better fighting power of NATO troops, and the atomic bomb—not a very suitable weapon in a conventional war and in a situation where the USSR had detonated its first atomic bomb in 1949.[38]

In the face of these grave prospects, Wriston's idea to write a letter to the president to convey the group's impressions about the importance of military readiness was well received. While the other group members enjoyed the customary study group dinner, Eisenhower sketched out the letter to Truman. Averell Harriman, then special assistant to the president, had participated in an earlier meeting. Now he was called upon to help with last-minute corrections and delivery of the council memorandum.[39] Eisenhower's manuscript was revised and modified, and Allen Dulles discussed the draft with Harriman to help finalize the letter to President Truman.[40]

In his first draft Eisenhower had been quite outspoken and drastic. His evaluation that the United States and the free world were in critical danger of defeat and of "the extinction of our treasured ideals" was mellowed and rephrased in the subsequent revision to say that the United States and other countries still free were in critical danger. Both Eisenhower and the group members agreed that the United States and its friends should rapidly produce powerful military forces. The group members agreed, however, on Eisenhower's call for strategic air strength, which was equal to an effective bombing attack against Russia and further agreed that about twenty U.S. divisions should be deployed in Europe. In his discussion with Dulles, Harriman suggested that they delete the reference to twenty divisions, and they changed the mention of capabilities from an effective bombing attack against Russia to "an effective bombing attack in the event of war."[41]

In his cover letter to Truman, Harriman—now with official knowledge of the council's letter—stressed the importance of the council in mobilizing public opinion. But Harriman somewhat deceived Truman by maintaining that General Eisenhower, although active in the group, had not been involved in the letter.[42]

In the final version that Truman received, Eisenhower and the group members claimed that the United States would face disastrous consequences if the nation's enemies were to attack. The letter argued that national security was at stake, that the military forces had to be built up speedily and effectively with minimal costs, that all government spending not related to military buildup should be minimized, and that a large number of American troops should be stationed in Europe. The last paragraph of the letter argued for a military strength that would carry the nation through the future without war, but which would be prepared to wage it if it were thrust upon us. Truman's comment to Harriman, in the face of this dramatic analysis, was rather calm. He simply thanked Harriman for the memorandum and noted that it was an interesting document that he read with much pleasure.[43]

It would be futile—amd well beyond the scope of this short chapter—to examine all of Eisenhower's actions and speeches, internal memoranda, and statements made before 1949 and then compare them to expressions made after 1951 and when he was president of the United States. Eisenhower cannot be put into an experimental setting in a sort of before-and-after study to find out just how much his perceptions of the world encompassed the complexity of economic and political aspects in foreign affairs, and how this had changed over the two-year period he served as chairman of the Aid to Europe group.

Claims that Eisenhower learned everything he knew about economics at the council and that he received an education in foreign affairs at the corner of 68th Street and Park Avenue are highly exaggerated. As Supreme Commander of the Allied Forces in Europe during World War II, he had handled the political management of this military effort. His later responsibilities as Chief of Staff of the Army and as member of the Joint Chiefs of Staff had involved him in political as well as foreign affairs. At the council, Eisenhower clearly dominated the discussions on military aspects; this was his field of expertise, and at times his fellow council members were a captive audience. But at the same time, he was not spared a sometimes confusing discussion of a variety of aspects of foreign policy and economy, of the interdependency of military and economic, political, and even psychological factors in international relations. For example, in the case of devaluation of the pound sterling, Eisenhower wrote to a friend that he had his doubts about the propriety of such actions, doubts which were enhanced by the disagreement among the economists themselves.[44] But he may have learned that such was a part, if not the essence, of a nonmilitary world.

All available evidence suggests that Eisenhower had a great capacity to understand and utilize information provided in the group meetings—if they were not too technical. Certainly, the council's study group was not his only source of information, and Eisenhower discussed all important foreign policy issues with a variety of people—experts and friends. The assertion that Eisenhower gained all his knowledge about economics from study group meetings and the Rockefeller Foundation's claims that these meetings served as Eisenhower's education in foreign policy are certainly embroidered exaggerations. Nevertheless, it is quite likely that his two-year stint at the Council on Foreign Relations— in the broad sense of an educational as well as a social experience—helped in the preparation of Dwight D. Eisenhower for the presidency of the United States.

NOTES

The author would like to thank McGeorge Bundy, William Diebold, Tomas Jaehn, Franklin Lindsay, and Grayson Kirk for their comments on an earlier version of this chapter. Research for this study was aided by financial support provided by the German Marshall Fund of the United States.

1. Robert H. Ferrell, ed., *The Eisenhower Diaries* (New York: W. W. Norton, 1981), 148.

2. Blanche Wiesen Cook, *The Declassified Eisenhower: A Divided Legacy* (Garden City, N.Y.: Doubleday, 1981), reports that Eisenhower's friends in New York "invited him to join their clubs and the policy sessions at the Council on Foreign Relations," 61.

3. Louis Galambos, ed., *The Papers of Dwight David Eisenhower: Columbia University*, vol. X (Baltimore: Johns Hopkins University Press, 1984), xviii. Grayson Kirk's responsibilities as the provost of Columbia were not made easier by Eisenhower's inexperience with problems of academic administration. See Kirk to Michael Wala, October 1, 1990.

4. Eisenhower did not attend meetings during his convalescence at Key West, March 28, 1948, to April 12, 1949 (he had fallen ill on March 21), and during his vacation at Augusta National Golf Club, Augusta, Ga., January 20, 1950, to January 26, 1950. During the 21 working days in February, his office received 2,100 pieces of mail—100 per day. Joseph Kraft, "School for Statesmen,"*Harper's* 248 (July 1958): 64–68. Excerpts from Trustees Confidential Monthly Report, January 1, 1953, 39–40, Rockefeller Foundation Records (RFR) 1.2/57/440, Rockefeller Foundation Archives, Rockefeller Archives Center, North Tarrytown, N.Y.

5. M. L. Dockrill, "Historical Note: The Foreign Office and the 'Proposed Institute

of International Affairs 1919,' '' *International Affairs* (London) 56 (Fall 1980): 665–72; Whitney H. Shepardson, *Early History of the Council on Foreign Relations* (Stamford, Conn.: Overbrook Press, 1960), 1–8; Hamilton Fish Armstrong, *Peace and Counterpeace: From Wilson to Hitler* (New York: Harper & Row, 1971).

6. Women were not admitted to council membership until 1970.

7. Among the very few accounts of the council's history are: Robert D. Schulzinger, *The Wise Men of Foreign Affairs: The History of the Council on Foreign Relations* (New York: Columbia University Press, 1984); Elisabeth Jakab, "The Council on Foreign Relations," *Book Forum* 3 (1978): 418–72; and G. William Domhoff, *The Power Elite and the State: How Policy Is Made in America* (New York: de Gruyter, 1990), 113–44. The most recent study is Michael Wala, *Winning the Peace: Amerikanische Außenpolitik und der Council on Foreign Relations, 1945–1950* (Stuttgart: Steiner, 1990).

8. Lindsay to Dulles, May 1, 1948, Allen W. Dulles Papers (AWDP), box 36, Seeley G. Mudd Manuscript Library, Princeton, N.J. Dulles and Lindsay had met earlier that week in Washington. Dulles is much better known for his service with the OSS in Bern, Switzerland, during World War II and for his stint as director of the CIA from 1953 to 1961. For his interest in foreign policy, see also Allen W. Dulles, *The Marshall Plan* (Oxford: Berg Publishers, 1993), edited and with an introduction by Michael Wala.

9. The best source on the council for the World War II period is Laurence H. Shoup and William Minter, *Imperial Brain Trust: The Council on Foreign Relations and United States Foreign Policy* (New York: Monthly Review Press, 1977). Official accounts are: CFR, *The War and Peace Studies of the Council on Foreign Relations* (New York: CFR, 1946); and U.S. Department of State, Harley Notter, ed., *Postwar Foreign Policy Preparations, 1939–1945* (Washington, D.C.: U.S. Government Printing Office, 1949).

10. Probably more influential than speeches were informal discussions at dinner or over a cocktail after the formal part of these meetings.

11. Of the higher positions (from assistant secretary level on up) of State Department and related agencies of the Truman administration, 42 percent were filled by council members. During the Eisenhower years, however, this portion declined to 40 percent, only to again increase to 51 percent under Kennedy and to 57 percent under Johnson. See William M. Minter, "The Council on Foreign Relations: A Case Study in the Societal Bases of Foreign Policy Formulation," Ph.D. dissertation, University of Wisconsin–Madison, 1973, 122. "Whenever we needed a man," John J. McCloy, high commissioner for Germany, recalls somewhat exaggeratedly, "we thumbed through the roll of Council members and put through a call to New York." See Kraft, "School for Statesmen," 67.

12. Bissell was to join the study group in May 1950 after leaving the ECA; Mallory to Eisenhower, May 10, 1950, Dwight D. Eisenhower Pre-Presidential Papers (EPP), box 28, Eisenhower Library, Abilene, Kan.; Bissell to Eisenhower, May 15, 1950, *ibid.*

13. Memorandum, Dulles to Mallory, May 4, 1948, study group on Aid to Europe (AE), Records of Groups, volume XXXA, Council on Foreign Relations Archives, Harold Pratt House (hereafter cited as RGCFR with the appropriate volume number); Geiger (Special Assistant for Programming Policy and Procedures) to Dulles, June 3, 1948, *ibid.*; Dulles to Hoffman (copy), June 15, 1948, *ibid.*; Hoffman to Dulles, June 22, 1948, *ibid.*; Bissell to Dulles, July 7, 1948, *ibid.*; Dulles to Bissell, July 12, 1948, *ibid.* Copies of all these letters are in RGCFR, 1.2/57/440.

14. Minutes of meeting of Subcommittee of the Committee on Studies of the CFR, August 4, 1948, AE/RGCFR-XXXA; Committee on Studies meeting, October 7, 1948, *ibid.*; Committee on Studies meeting, November 29, 1948, RFR, 1.2/58/444. To cover

the expenses for the study group, Executive Director Walter Mallory had asked Henry Ford II for a Ford Foundation grant. In May 1948, the Rockefeller Foundation supplied $50,000; no further attempts in this direction were made thereafter. Mallory to Eisenhower, December 31, 1948, AE/RGCFR-XXXA; Bidwell to Mallory, May 3, 1949, *ibid.*; Resolution 49010, RFR, 1.2/57/440.

15. On the basis of the study group's deliberations and background papers, Howard S. Ellis later wrote *The Economics of Freedom: The Progress and Future of Aid to Europe* (New York: Harper, 1950).

16. Committee on Studies Meeting, October 7, 1948, AE/RGCFR-XXXA, 7. It is very likely that the possibility of Eisenhower eventually running for president of the United States was addressed during the lengthy discussion. Some members of the Democratic Party had tried to draft Eisenhower in the spring of 1948 for nomination as candidate. Only after insisting on his nomination could the incumbent Truman run for a second term in office.

17. Wriston recalled in 1968 that he, Davis, and Mallory visited Eisenhower. See Wriston, Columbia University Oral History Interview, 4. It is far more likely that the CFR stuck to its original plan and sent Davis, Wriston, and Dulles. These names appear on Eisenhower's desk calendar for the November 3, 1948, meeting. See Galambos, *Papers of Dwight David Eisenhower: Columbia University*, volume 11 (Baltimore: Johns Hopkins University Press, 1984), 1575.

18. Mallory to McCann, November 8, 1948, EPP, box 183. McCann did not make a good impression on the council members he met: he drank just water and would not have anything to eat for lunch; Diebold interview with Michael Wala, August 23, 1990.

19. Eisenhower, *Papers of Dwight David Eisenhower*, volume 11, 1578; Mallory to Eisenhower, November 26, 1948, EPP, box 183. In this letter Mallory also asked Eisenhower for ''any suggestion about staff—particularly on the military side.'' Eisenhower immediately sent a telegram to Brigadier General Arthur S. Nevins and offered him a ''splendid prospect for New York position.'' See telegram, Eisenhower to Nevins, November 29, 1948, EPP, box 86. Nevins, who had helped Eisenhower with his wartime memoirs, took the job. See Eisenhower to Nevins, January 3, 1948, *ibid.*; and Eisenhower to Lovett, December 20, 1948, EPP, box 72.

20. William Diebold to Michael Wala, October 2, 1990.

21. ''Suggestions for the Council on Foreign Relations' Research Project,'' signed ''TG/dg,'' n.d., enclosure, Bissell to Dulles, July 7, 1948, AE/RGCFR-XXXA. Bissell wrote that this list was only to serve as a suggestion and that he did not expect the group to prepare studies on all topics. Kirk to Wala, October 1, 1990. Economic aspects were mostly discussed in the background material and memoranda the council staff provided.

22. Excerpts from Trustees' Confidential Monthly Report, January 1, 1953, RFR, 1.2/57/440, 40. See also Eisenhower to Philip D. Reed (chairman of the board of General Electric), April 3, 1950, EPP, box 97. He was usually picked up at Columbia by Nevins or council staff members and was briefed on the way to the council's headquarters at the corner of 68th Street and Park Avenue. Eisenhower to Leffingwell, July 11, 1949, EPP, box 71.

23. Herbert Feis, *From Trust to Terror: The Onset of the Cold War, 1945–1950* (New York: Norton, 1970), 306–8; Robert A. Lovett, Diary and Daily Log Sheet, entries April 21 and 28, 1948 (New York: Brown Brothers, Harriman, and Co. Records, New York Historical Society); memorandum of conversation between Marshall, Lovett, Vandenberg,

and John F. Dulles, April 27, 1948, John Foster Dulles Papers (JFDP), box 37, Mudd Manuscript Library, Princeton, NJ.

24. The Senate voted 64 to 4 in favor of the resolution (Senate Resolution 239).

25. Memorandum, "Studies on Aid to Europe," n.d., enclosure, Mallory to Eisenhower, November 26, 1948, RFR, 1.2/57/440; Digest of Discussion (DD), January 10, 1949, AE/RGCFR-XXXA, 5, 4, 13. William Diebold wrote most of these digests. They are not verbatim transcriptions of what was said but very elaborate reports of the discussions, sometimes consisting of as many as twenty single-spaced pages. Statements are attributed to specific members of the group, and every member received a copy of a draft for corrections.

26. DD, March 7, 1949, AE/RGCFR-XXXA, 3.

27. Memorandum, "Studies on Aid to Europe"; DD, January 10, 1949, AE/RGCFR-XXXA, 5, 4, 11, 13.

28. DD, January 10, 1949, AE/RGCFR-XXXA, 6, 7–10.

29. DD, January 10, 1949, AE/RGCFR-XXXA, 7; DD, March 7, 1949, AE/RGCFR-XXXA, 10.

30. DD, January 10, 1949, AE/RGCFR-XXXA, 11.

31. DD, March 7, 1949, AE/RGCFR-XXXA, 12; "S–2," March 9, 1949, *ibid.*

32. DD, June 27, 1949, AE/RGCFR-XXXA, 14–17; McGeorge Bundy, "Working Paper on the Problem of Political Equilibrium," memorandum M–13, June 16, 1949, AE/RGCFR-XXXIIA.

33. DD, June 27, 1949, AE/RGCFR-XXXA, 14–17. Després taught at Williams College. In a *New York Times* article on December 29, 1949, Baldwin displayed more concern about a revival of German militarism: "The moment we put arms in the hands of any great numbers of Germans," he wrote, "that moment Germany will be calling the tune, not we. The moment Germany is rearmed, she holds the balance of power—not we." In his *Economics of Freedom*, Ellis is much more critical about German rearmament than the members of the study group. He concludes his chapter "Should Western Germany Be Rearmed" with the sentence: "For security against the revival of militarism and an aggressive policy in Western Germany, the allies should rely on enforcement of disarmament and demilitarization," 233.

34. Robert Ferrell, *The Eisenhower Diaries*, entry October 28, 1950 (New York: W. W. Norton, 1981), 178–80.

35. Memorandum, Lincoln Gordon (assistant to the president) to Harriman, "Subject: Immediate Dispatch of General Eisenhower to Europe," December 4, 1950, marked "Top Secret and Urgent"; W. Averell Harriman Papers (hereafter WAHP), box 284, Library of Congress, Washington, D.C. Eisenhower actually did find a way to communicate with Truman without going through channels: he sent frequent informal reports to Harriman who in turn would pass them on to the president. Eisenhower to Harriman, February 24, 1951, WAHP, box 284; Truman to Eisenhower, March 9, 1951, *ibid.*

36. At about the same time, the Committee on the Present Danger had been founded in the United States, fully supported by George C. Marshall, who had become Secretary of Defense. The committee advocated universal military training and preparedness of American and North Atlantic defenses. Wriston had been one of the founding members of this organization.

37. Henry M. Wriston, "Eisenhower Study Group Letter to President Truman December 12, 1950," April 22, 1968, AE/RGCFR-XXXIA.

38. DD, December 11, 1950, AE/RGCFR-XXXIA; Nevins, "Limitations on Use of

Available French Military Manpower Due to Lack of Equipment or Fiscal Difficulties,''
M–29, December 4, 1950, AE/RGCFR-XXXIIIA; Lindsay Rogers, "Europe as a 'Neutral' or 'Third' Force,'' M–28, December 4, 1950, *ibid*.

39. Wriston, "Eisenhower Study Group Letter,'' AE/RGCFR-XXXIA, 7; Dulles to
Wriston, December 29, 1950, AWDP, box 44.

40. Wriston, "Eisenhower Study Group Letter,'' AE/RGCFR-XXXIA, 6–7; Memorandum on the occasion of a study group "reunion'' on October 30, 1962, Hamilton
Armstrong, November 1, 1962, Hamilton F. Armstrong Papers (HFAP), box 24, Seeley
G. Mudd Manuscript Library, Princeton, N.J. Wriston recalls that Dulles made an ap-
pointment with Harriman for breakfast the next morning and that he took the sleeper to
Washington. See Wriston, Columbia University Oral History Interview, 8. William Die-
bold confirmed that this was very likely what happened; Diebold interview with Michael
Wala, Council on Foreign Relations, New York, October 16, 1990.

41. Wriston, "Eisenhower Study Group Letter,'' AE/RGCFR-XXXIA; Armstrong et
al. to President Truman, December 12, 1950, President's Secretary's File (PSF), box
114, Harry S. Truman Papers, Truman Library, Independence, Mo.; Draft, n.d., handwritten note: "Received from Allen Dulles,'' WAHP, box 283.

42. It is very doubtful that Dulles did not tell Harriman of Eisenhower's involvement.
In addition to sending a note and a copy of Truman's reply to Armstrong, Harriman sent
a note and copy of the president's comment to Eisenhower. See Harriman to Eisenhower,
December 16, 1950, marked "Confidential,'' WAHP, box 282.

43. DD, December 11, 1950, AE/RGCFR-XXXIA; Armstrong et al. to President
Truman, December 12, 1950, PSF, box 114; Memorandum for the President, Averell
Harriman, December 13, 1950, *ibid*.; Memorandum for: Averell Harriman, From: The
President, December 15, 1950, signed "H.S.T.'', *ibid*.; the original is in WAHP, box
290. On October 31, 1962, a reunion of the Aid to Europe group took place. See
Eisenhower to McCloy, May 30, 1962, Dwight D. Eisenhower, Post-presidential Papers,
1962, Principal Files, box 21, DDEL.

44. Eisenhower to Leffingwell, July 11, 1949, EPP, box 71.

Appendix: Members of the "Aid to Europe" Group Meetings at the Council on Foreign Relations

Research Staff:

Howard S. Ellis, director
Philip W. Bell
McGeorge Bundy
Emile Després
William Diebold, Jr.
Edwin C. Hoyd
Brig. Gen. Arthur S. Nevins
Maxwell Obst
Lindsay Rodgers

Council Staff:

Percy Bidwell
George S. Franklin, Jr.
Walter H. Mallory

Members:

Hamilton F. Armstrong	CFR
Hanson Baldwin	military editor, *New York Times*
Richard M. Bissell	formerly with ECA
McGeorge Bundy	Harvard University
James B. Carey	Congress of Industrial Organization (CIO)
William L. Clayton	Anderson, Clayton & Co., Houston, Texas
Allen W. Dulles	CFR
Edward Mead Earle	Princeton University
Graeme K. Howard	Ford International
George F. Kennan	Princeton University
Grayson Kirk	Columbia University
Russell C. Leffingwell	J. P. Morgan and Company
Stacy May	International Basic Economy Corporation
Isidor I. Rabi	department of physics, Columbia University
Philip D. Reed	General Electric
Jacob Viner	department of economics, Princeton University
John H. Williams	vice president, Federal Reserve Bank; Harvard University
Henry M. Wriston	Brown University

2

EISENHOWER, THE AMERICAN ASSEMBLY, AND THE 1952 ELECTIONS

Travis Beal Jacobs

In 1952 Dwight D. Eisenhower entered politics and scored an impressive victory in the presidential campaign. In recent years scholars have written excellent accounts of Eisenhower and the 1952 election and published perceptive articles on Eisenhower and Eisenhower revisionism. The political opportunities Eisenhower had and rejected in the postwar period are well known. They range from President Harry Truman's offer in 1945 at Potsdam to support the general in 1948 to his renewed effort in November 1951. In the interim, Truman had proposed in 1947 to run as vice president if Eisenhower accepted the 1948 Democratic nomination, and in 1948 Democrats and Republicans alike sought Eisenhower as a candidate. Indeed, the Eisenhower "boom" in 1948 prompted biographer Stephen Ambrose to write, "It stretches the truth, perhaps, but only slightly, to say that Eisenhower, in 1948, turned down the Presidency of the United States."[1]

There is, however, more to the story of Eisenhower's road to the White House than has appeared so far. These accounts overlook or minimize important mileage markers on his trip to 1600 Pennsylvania Avenue, and in doing so they miss certain signs that help explain his success at the Chicago convention in the bitter struggle with Senator Robert A. Taft for the Republican Party nomination in 1952. The story, moreover, helps one to understand the depth and intensity of the opposition in the intellectual community to his candidacy, especially at Columbia University, from which he had been given an indefinite leave of absence as president to go to NATO in December 1950. It may also at least partially explain why the assessments of Eisenhower's post–World War II career were negative for so many years. As Louis Galambos wrote in his introduction to volumes ten and eleven of *The Papers of Dwight David Eisenhower*, the general's "activities as president of Columbia University seem to have received far less attention than they deserve."[2]

The reasons for Eisenhower accepting the presidency of the university in June 1947 would lead to the creation of the American Assembly and play a vital role in his willingness to seek the Republican nomination in 1952. Columbia was not, as biographer Peter Lyon asserted, "a most peculiar decision." Trustee Tom Watson, the president of IBM, may have painted for Eisenhower "the rosiest picture" of Columbia, but the general saw an opportunity to express convictions he held fervently. While Eisenhower later referred to Watson's pressure as "a 'stampeding' process," the general acknowledged that the stampede took over a year; moreover, if there were a stampede, he was encouraged in making the Columbia decision by his brother Milton, the president of Kansas State University.[3]

He convinced himself that "acceptance was a duty" and that he was merely "changing the method by which I will continue to strive for the same goals." He would take to Columbia University his fanatic belief "in the American form of democracy" and in "the practice of true cooperation among sovereign nations . . . until an effective world order is achieved." He informed the trustees that his main purpose was "to promote basic concepts of education in a democracy." Two and a half years later, in January 1950, he recorded in his diary that he believed he could do more at Columbia "than anywhere else to further the cause to which I am devoted, the reawakening of intense interest in the basis of the American system."[4]

Eisenhower's acceptance is significant for more than his reasons for going to Morningside Heights. It reveals the way in which he would approach his appointment to NATO and, initially, the Republican Party nomination in 1952. He had to be persuaded that it was his duty and that his selection received unanimous support; moreover, he would outline his position "so that I may at least be sure that these points have been considered by you and your advisers." Thus, on the eve of the official vote by the Board of Trustees, and after it was widely reported in the press that he would be Columbia's next president, he wrote a remarkable letter to Tom Parkinson, the chairman of the Search Committee and president of the Equitable Life Assurance Society. He expressed bluntly and specifically his terms; he issued, essentially, an ultimatum, as he knew his letter would arrive only hours before the trustees meeting. He informed Parkinson that he wanted "no misunderstanding of any kind," and if there were any problems, the board meeting should be postponed. A few days earlier he had written: "Under no circumstance could I go into such a venture unless I felt assured that there was practically unanimous conviction among those responsible."

The trustees had little choice. Similarly, he wrote President Truman on the even of the announcement of his NATO appointment in December 1950. This time, however, he did not mail the letter and, instead, conveyed his position verbally to W. Averell Harriman, President Truman's Special Assistant on Foreign Affairs, and to the president. Finally, his supporters, who argued that he had to return home in early 1952 to seek actively the Republican nomination, received this Eisenhower response. The general approached these three challenges between World War II and his election in 1952 in the same way. He had been called to duty; his position would be clear, and he expected full support; and he would keep his options open.[5]

Columbia had offered Eisenhower a forum, and he quickly seized the opportunity. In mid-twentieth-century America no other public figure expressed such a fervent interest in citizenship in a liberal democratic society, and he did so much more than any president of the United States since Woodrow Wilson, also a university president. Eisenhower delivered his Installation Address on October 12, 1948, and he conveyed his passionate concerns about the challenge America faced in the cold war and outlined his goals.

In "today's challenge to freedom," he asserted, "every institution within our national structure must contribute to the advancement" of "democratic citizenship." Some 20,000 persons heard him emphasize the importance of academic freedom, as he declared that "the truth about communism is today an indispensable requirement if the true values of our democratic system are to be properly assessed." He observed that scholars, statesmen, skilled professionals, and great leaders in every area would come from the university, "but Columbia shall count it failure, whatever their success, if they are not all their lives a heaven of better citizenship."[6]

He had launched his crusade for youth and democratic citizenship but, within a few months, he was called to Washington. The administration wanted him to advise Secretary of Defense James Forrestal on unification of the armed services. In January 1949, he began serving as the informal chairman of the Joint Chiefs of Staff at the Pentagon. On March 21, 1949, he suffered an acute intestinal attack; after a week in bed he went to President Truman's Little White House in Key West for two and a half weeks and then spent a month recuperating at the Augusta National Golf Club with his close friends. He did not return to Columbia until mid-May, and in July he left for a two-month vacation in Colorado.[7]

When Eisenhower returned to Morningside Heights in September 1949, he took a different approach to fulfilling his purpose at Columbia. Whereas he had gone to Columbia with the belief that its primary task was to educate better citizens, most of the university community believed that the goals were scholarship and the pursuit of knowledge. Eisenhower concluded that, if the university would not or could not respond to his view, new vehicles would be necessary for his crusade. And, in the process, he seemed less and less concerned with the day-to-day affairs of the university, though he maintained a close interest in the activities of Columbia College and worked hard on behalf of the university.

Eisenhower recalled in *At Ease* that he "began to elaborate the idea of a truly national assembly where we could mobilize in addition to the University's educational and intellectual resources other experts from every walk of life." He held "the vision of a great cultural center where business, professional, and governmental leaders could meet from time to time to discuss and reach conclusions concerning problems of a social and political nature." These discussions, he believed, would produce "some clearly agreed upon truths and observations." He thought about the idea "almost incessantly," but he "got no farther than a name—the American Assembly." Then W. Averell Harriman's offer to give to Columbia Arden House, the magnificent Harriman family estate fifty miles from New York City, enabled Eisenhower to create the American Assembly. He reminded his close friend and adviser Bill Robinson, executive vice president of the New York *Herald-Tribune*, that he had gone to Columbia in the hope that through his presidency he could be of some service to his country.[8]

Even before the trustees formally accepted the gift, Eisenhower had started raising funds for the project. He had been talking about his ideas with Bill Burnham, a Wall Street investment banker who knew industrialists and financiers throughout the country, and Burnham proposed to introduce him to Leonard "Mc" McCollum, president of Continental Oil. The general's commitment to stressing the American way of life was persuasive, and he learned that the Texas oilman had gained "an entirely different conception" of his presidency. According to Burnham, McCollum believed that hardly anyone understood Columbia's president's aims for the university and the nation. Soon, Eisenhower described his views at length, asserting that "the chief responsibility of our educational institutions is to establish a sharper understanding of the American system, a sharper appreciation of its values and a more intense devotion to its fundamental purposes." Columbia, moreover, had "an outstanding faculty capable of taking the initiative in the study and analysis, from a national viewpoint, of the great social, political, and economic problems."[9]

On June 6, 1950, the sixth anniversary of D-Day, Eisenhower invited McCollum, Burnham, and Phil Young, dean of the School of Business, to his home at 60 Morningside to plan for a fund-raising luncheon McCollum and Burnham would give at the University Club. Dean Young, the son of Owen D. Young, would administer the American Assembly. At the luncheon Eisenhower enthusiastically discussed his conference proposal and sought support from Frank Abrams, chairman of Standard Oil of New Jersey; Bob Woodruff, the president of Coca-Cola and one of the general's golfing and hunting companions; Clarence Francis, General Foods chairman; and the presidents of Kennecott Copper, National City Bank, and AT&T.[10]

A few weeks later, McCollum arranged a special trip for six very wealthy Texans to fly to New York for a luncheon with the general at Bill Burnham's apartment. Burnham told Eisenhower that "Mc" knew the project needed some $250,000 for a strong start. Since the general would not want to be under any obligation to anyone by asking for money, Burnham suggested that Eisenhower give him and "Mc" a letter requesting or authorizing them to solicit funds. The group included Bob Kleberg, the president of the King Ranch who had offered to devote his money and efforts on behalf of Columbia, and H. J. "Jack" Porter, an oil producer and Republican Party leader in Texas. Porter had only known the general for a few months, but he strongly supported the American Assembly concept and would play a prominent role in the controversy over delegates for the Republican convention in 1952.[11]

In early July 1950, Harry Bullis, the General Mills chairman, gave an informal dinner for Eisenhower in Minneapolis. Bullis recently had met the general through Burnham, and Eisenhower traveled on the company's executive plane. The Korean War had started in late June, and the general's visit received front-page attention. He discussed the war at a press conference, and he added that "universities—and we want Columbia to take the lead—can be of more use to the world today." During the dinner he hoped he "did not bore the assembly with my convictions and enthusiasm," and afterwards he sent notes to most of the guests, a "Who's Who" of Minnesota leaders. "Like Julius Caesar," Bullis wrote, "you came, you saw, you conquered." The General Mills executive added, "You not only sold us on your Columbia project, but you made a sale of far greater potentialities—one that only you can close when the proper time comes."[12]

Eisenhower began his summer vacation with a trip to California and the Bohemian Grove before going to Denver for six weeks. He attended an American Assembly luncheon in San Francisco, given by the president of Standard Oil of California who soon sent $25,000 from his company to sponsor an American Assembly session. When McCollum arranged in Denver another "Texas" luncheon, the guests contributed over $11,500 for the Assembly, and Porter personally gave Eisenhower a $10,000 check from Kleberg. With Eisenhower's "personal interest and guidance," Kleberg wrote, the conferences might provide "some worthwhile answers to the vast and complicated problems with which our country is faced." The previous noon, ten top Phillips Petroleum executives met with him for lunch; Chairman K. S. "Boots" Adams contributed $50,000 and, later, another $25,000.[13]

Several of McCollum's Texas friends had asked the general specifically to "outline in writing the country's need for this program and the method of operation." Eisenhower replied in a long letter on September 14 that he had come "out of World War II" with "a profound conviction that America was in danger for two reasons." The first was "The Communist threat from without," and the second was "The failure of most of us to remember that the basic values of democracy were won only through sacrifice and to recognize the dangers of indifference and of ignorance." Emphasizing "that democracy could be destroyed by creeping paralysis from within," he added that, since America was "at war" in Korea, it was "even more important . . . that a greater effort be made to study these problems, in conjunction with the mess we face abroad." The Korean War, indeed, enhanced his appeal. The American Assembly, he concluded, "is action, not just words." Soon, similar letters would go to Porter and other friends of the general. Porter, meanwhile, had sent some 600 letters to solicit funds from Texans.[14]

Before leaving Denver Eisenhower launched the "Crusade for Freedom" in a nationwide radio address Labor Day weekend to raise funds for the National Committee for a Free Europe. He had objected to a proposed draft and prepared one himself, and he made extensive changes on a revised draft and read paragraphs over the telephone to the Deputy Secretary of Defense. "Eisenhower Opens Crusade for Freedom; His Charge," the *Denver Post* front-page headline read, "REDS PLOT TO ENSLAVE U.S." Underneath four photographs of Eisenhower at the podium, a two-column headline added: "General Urges 'Big Truth' to Fight 'Big Lie.' " Across the rest of the page came the headline "BIG HOLE TORN IN U.S. LINE; 45-MILE FRONT PERILED." The "Crusade for Freedom" speech received an enthusiastic response from Bullis, and it unquestionably appealed to many of his American Assembly supporters; indeed, Eisenhower saw a connection between his appeals for the "Crusade" and the Assembly.[15]

The New York luncheons and Eisenhower's trips to Minnesota, California, and Colorado provided the initial financial support for the American Assembly, and in September 1950, Harriman offered to contribute several hundred thousand dollars for the rehabilitation and maintenance of Arden House. Eisenhower, thus, was in position to present the proposal to the Columbia Board of Trustees. On October 2, 1950, the board formally approved the plan and accepted the Arden Estate. Eisenhower informed the university's deans, directors, and executive officers and then publicly announced the American Assembly at a special Columbia Associates luncheon on October 18. This prominent alumni development group agreed to sponsor the proposal and to give Eisenhower all the support needed to bring the project to fruition. The members and many special guests constituted an impressive list, and they heard Eisenhower describe what he saw "not only as a great vision but something that can come into being instantly and effectively." The Associates suggested that contributions be sent directly to Eisenhower at his Columbia office. After the Associates luncheon he took the evening train to Pittsburgh and carried his message to alumni in western Pennsylvania. A *New York Herald-Tribune* editorial concluded: "A bold and imaginative appeal to rationality and informed good will, the Assembly is a fine example of educational statesmanship."[16]

Eisenhower returned to Columbia for Homecoming Weekend and then left for a series of appearances in Chicago, St. Louis, Indianapolis, Cincinnati, and Charleston. He stressed his Assembly plan to alumni groups and, as the *Alumni Magazine* noted, "press conferences were an important part of the trip." Neil McElroy, president of Procter & Gamble, soon reported that after Eisenhower's Cincinnati visit he had "rounded up" $25,000.[17]

As Eisenhower campaigned that fall for the American Assembly, he was thrust again into the arena of national politics and foreign affairs. First, Governor Thomas E. Dewey of New York declared that he would not run again for the presidency and that the Republican Party had Dwight D. Eisenhower. Second, after the start of the Korean War, the question of NATO and the rearming of West Germany became vital. President Truman called Eisenhower during his midwestern trip, and the general went directly to Washington at the end of the trip. Press reports soon indicated that he would become commander of the NATO forces. "I am convinced," the general wrote to a Denver oilman after seeing Truman, "that there is so much for us to do here in the interest of our country that I am anxious that the great work [the American Assembly] go ahead regardless of the location of my particular port of duty."[18]

On November 6, 1950, he recorded in his diary that he started "on a trip to Chicago, Dallas, Texas Agricultural and Mechanical College, Houston, Oklahoma City, Chicago, home. I travel in interests of American Assembly. . . . It has appealed mightily to businessmen, and support, both moral and material, has been fine." He listed specifically the major contributors and the amounts, adding "so, I'm encouraged." Arguing that "the concept of the American Assembly will increase in importance according to the duration and intensity of the tensions under which we live," he wrote to Cliff Roberts that if he returned to active duty, he must "depend upon my friends even more completely than I have in the past." He added that "it will be a wonderful thing to know that all its adherents are more than ever determined upon its success." Indeed, they were, and on the eve of his departure they surprised him. Roberts, an investment banker and chairman at Augusta National, gave a dinner for the Eisenhowers and presented him with pledges for the Assembly totaling $50,800. The solicitors were friends and members of Augusta, and they included, in addition to Roberts, W. Alton "Pete" Jones, Ellis "Slats" Slater, Bill Robinson, Douglas Black, and Bob Woodruff.[19]

The trip itself proved successful. It began with a luncheon in Chicago for leading businessmen, given by Ed Bermingham, an influential investment broker and Eisenhower adviser, and ended with contributions of $10,000 from Amon Carter and $15,000 from Sid Richardson. Carter, president and publisher of the *Fort Worth Star-Telegram*, and Richardson, a multimillionaire oilman, were two of his oldest friends in Texas. Carter saw that this "great work you are carrying on" could "be a blessing to our country and humanity in general." Texas newspapers gave front-page attention to the general's visit and his American Assembly proposal. "Thoughtful citizens," the *Houston Post* concluded, "will find much nourishing food for reflection in Gen. Eisenhower's message."[20]

He continued his demanding schedule. He traveled to Boston to promote his plan, and the *Boston Herald* saw the Assembly as "a fine complement to the New England tradition of free discussion in town meeting." Robert Cutler, president of the Old Colony Trust Company, in his words, "invited a dozen gold-plated magnates" to meet Eisenhower, "who won them all to his side, for the American Assembly or anything else." During the overnight trip the general avoided all questions about politics and NATO.[21]

Perhaps the dinner arranged a week later by Clarence Dillon, head of Dillon, Reed, illustrated well Eisenhower's position that fall. Dillon invited prominent financiers in New York to give Eisenhower a chance to describe the Assembly, so that the Columbia Associates could go after the men for money. Actually, the general recorded in his diary, since "everyone was in such a blue funk over the tragic news from Korea" with the massive and devastating Chinese Communist offensive, Dillon suggested he discuss "the Korean debacle." Eisenhower showed "the additional problems it imposed upon us as citizens. . . . And so, finally, I ended up arguing for the American Assembly idea." Or, as he wrote Bermingham, he had the task of helping pick the group up from the floor.[22]

Eisenhower continued to push the Assembly, even after Truman in mid-December officially assigned him the command of American forces in Europe. When Cutler declined to serve as Eisenhower's "personal representative" for the proposal, the Bostonian asserted that his enthusiasm for the Assembly had waned because of the Korean setback and his fear that the project would falter without Eisenhower's "constant, daily force to breathe life into it." On his last day in his Columbia office, December 31, 1950, Eisenhower replied that the Korean situation made it "more important than ever before to push the plan." He had tried "to reserve a day" to write "all those individuals who have jumped in so enthusiastically" on the Assembly, but "the calendar has defeated me." Consequently, he asked Burnham to thank personally the "many, many others" supporting the plan, and he extended invitations to visit him in Europe. He had, meanwhile, personally thanked the first eighty contributors, even some who had given only ten to twenty-five dollars.[23]

Eisenhower's conviction, enthusiasm, and dynamism raised the funds for Columbia's American Assembly, and its organization proceeded so smoothly that the first conference would be held as early as spring 1951. The topic, appropriately, would be "The Relationship of the United States to Western Europe," and he planned to return from NATO for it. He and Phil Young persuaded Lewis Douglas, the former ambassador to Great Britain, to become chairman of the Policy Board. The initial members represented business, labor, and agriculture and included Bullis; McCollum; John Cowles of the *Minneapolis Morning Tribune*; Oveta Culp Hobby of the *Houston Post*; Robert Wood of Sears, Roebuck; former Postmaster General James Farley; William Green of the American Federation of Labor; the dean of the Cornell Agriculture School; the president of the Farm Bureau Federation; and the president of the Amalgamated Clothing Workers of America.[24]

At the American Assembly dedication ceremonies in May 1951, Harriman presented Arden House to the university and expressed his "highest hopes" for this "1951 version of the old-fashioned town meeting." He saw Arden House as "a national meeting place" that would continue "this great experiment . . . so that our country, and our way of life can be strengthened. . . . That is our heritage." He urged its preservation "at all costs." The purpose of the Assembly, according to its charter, was "to arrive at and disseminate impartial and authoritative findings on questions of national and international importance, and thus stimulate the growth of informed opinion with a view to the preservation

and strengthening of the democratic processes and principles of freedom.'' The *New York Herald-Tribune* described the opening session in a prominent front-page article, and the lead editorial saw ''the beginning of an experiment which may have wide and fruitful significance.''[25]

The next day Harriman wrote on White House stationery to Eisenhower, who had stayed in Europe, that the general had conveyed his real hope and enthusiasm for the important role the Assembly would play. Harriman's unwavering support for the American Assembly proposal demonstrated his conviction that Eisenhower was sincerely committed to methods that were useful to the country in its forthcoming struggles. Harriman's hopes would be fulfilled. Indeed, Arden House took great pride in introducing and developing the ''conference-center concept.'' The American Assembly, Eisenhower asserted in 1967, had held ''scores of meetings concerned with almost every aspect of human society. Throughout the years, its influence, although difficult to measure, has been far reaching beyond my dreams of almost two decades ago. Much of the time,'' he added, ''I think its beginnings were my principal success as University President.'' A few years later Harriman emphasized Eisenhower's ''very fine motivations'' and recalled with ''tremendous satisfaction'' that the American Assembly had been ''remarkably successful.'' What Eisenhower established has had a long and influential history; the Assembly held its eighty-first conference on April 1992, on ''After the Soviet Union: Implications for U.S. Policy.''[26]

Harriman's important role, Eisenhower's commitment to democratic citizenship and his project, and the success of the American Assembly seriously challenge assertions by several historians that Eisenhower had partisan political ambitions in establishing the conference center. ''The eventual values of these assemblies, if any,'' Peter Lyon argues, ''were never estimated to be as great as the benefit to Eisenhower from raising the money to support them. . . . There was a good deal of window dressing, but the aroma of politics hung over the whole enterprise, acrid and unmistakable.'' Blanche Wiesen Cook indicates that Eisenhower created the Assembly in order to communicate ''his developing political positions'' and to express his fears ''that certain social and economic changes would destroy America's traditional values.'' Stephen Ambrose asserts that, when Eisenhower toured the country in 1950 ''to meet with such men'' as H. L. Hunt, Robert Cutler, and Harry Bullis, it was ''presumably on behalf of the American Assembly.''[27]

Eisenhower's determination to launch the American Assembly, though, did have extremely important consequences that would be crucial when he decided to run for the presidency in 1952. Indeed, it is conceivable that his nomination would have been impossible without his Assembly friends. In the fund-raising he met rich and influential persons throughout the country. Since his arrival at Columbia he had emphasized themes of individual liberty, democratic citizenship, the American way of life, nonpartisanship, cooperation, and the danger of centralization and statism. As he stressed the need for service to his country and a ''middle way,'' he said what they wanted to hear, especially during the somber

Korean War, and he was persuasive. He created a vast network of support. As Phil Young recalled, if you wanted to meet Eisenhower you had to go to the Assembly dinners, and the general knew who had contributed. In an era of increasing political partisanship and bitterness with the Korean stalemate and McCarthyism, his personal appeal was welcomed and assuring.[28]

While at NATO Eisenhower continued his activities on behalf of the Assembly. He did not return for the Arden House dedication ceremonies in May 1951, in order to avoid becoming involved in the controversy over Truman's firing of General Douglas MacArthur. During 1951 he worried increasingly about the dangers of inflation, and the second Assembly topic would be on that important and timely subject. He knew, moreover, it would appeal to the major donors, such as "Boots" Adams of Phillips Petroleum.[29]

During his first year at NATO his friends formed and, with the help of many of his Assembly contributors, financed "Citizens for Eisenhower." The general, though, continued to refuse to "get tangled up in any kind of political activity" unless there were a genuine draft. He took this position, even though Milton Eisenhower argued that if the choice in 1952 were Truman or Senator Taft, "any personal sacrifice . . . is wholly justified." As Ambrose observed, Eisenhower wanted the Republican Party nomination by acclamation. Senator Taft, however, was winning the convention delegates and making that impossible. Still, when Eisenhower's name was entered in the New Hampshire primary, the general said he would not "ask for relief" from NATO or seek the nomination. His victory in New Hampshire on March 11, 1952, "astonished" and "moved" him but did not change his position.[30]

The Minnesota primary results a week later were even more "astonishing," and the "Minnesota Miracle" forced him publicly "to re-examine my personal position and past decisions." Although the delegation would be pledged to favorite son Harold Stassen, Eisenhower's success can be partially attributed to his American Assembly efforts. Harry Bullis, a member of its board, served as the Eisenhower National Committee's financial representative in the state. Brad Mintener, a prominent Pillsbury Mills executive, had attended the successful Assembly dinner in Minneapolis, and he and Eisenhower's friends organized a last-minute write-in campaign. John Cowles's *Minneapolis Morning Tribune* declared it "An Amazing Vote." The more than 100,000 write-in voters forced Eisenhower to admit that "the mounting numbers of my fellow citizens" meant that he "could not much longer remain actively in command" at NATO. As Ellis Slater later recorded, Eisenhower's close friends "drew courage" from his "strong advocates" in Minnesota. On April 2, 1952, he requested relief as Supreme Commander effective June 1.[31]

Eisenhower's earlier activities on behalf of the American Assembly paid even greater dividends in Texas. Jack Porter led the Eisenhower challengers to the Taft-dominated Republican organization, and he received important support from Sid Richardson and from McCollum and Oveta Culp Hobby, both members of the Assembly's board. Mrs. Hobby, executive vice president of the *Houston*

Post, effectively used her newspaper and its TV station to partisan advantage. In a complicated delegate selection process, Porter's people were victorious on the percent level, but the Taft forces blocked them at the state convention and chose a Taft delegation. The ensuing fight over the contested Texas delegation became a *cause célèbre*. The *Post* focused daily on the need for "Fair Play," "the voice of the people," "the Taft 'Steal,' " and Eisenhower's subsequent trip to Texas and his charge that the "Old Guard's 'Steal' " was a betrayal. The controversy quickly received nationwide attention. At the Chicago convention the Eisenhower forces skillfully used the issue of "Fair Play" and won the crucial battle for the contested delegates. The defeat badly hurt Taft, and Eisenhower gained momentum. When Eisenhower fell just short on the first ballot for the nomination, his "strong advocates" in Minnesota led the delegation to switch and make him the Republican nominee.[32]

His American Assembly activities had contributed to his victory in Chicago, but these activities also had contributed to the growing resentments against Eisenhower at Columbia University. His emphasis on "general education for citizenship" and interest in the Citizenship Education Project at Teachers College were antiintellectual to many on the Morningside Heights campus. The Columbia faculties did not care for a military man as president and disliked his military assistants, who kept him inaccessible and had little sense of the academic world. He had presided at his first University Council meeting, but it did not go well and, thereafter, he delegated the task to the provost. His frequent absences, for the Army, his illness, or on behalf of the American Assembly, further weakened his leadership on campus. Douglas Black, who was his publisher for *Crusade in Europe*, a close friend, and an active Columbia Trustee, believed that the general "never had the feeling or understanding" of Columbia.[33]

This negative reaction intensified as Eisenhower devoted more and more of his time and energies to the American Assembly concept. The efforts, according to economist Eli Ginzberg, "added to the marginality of his administration." His fund-raising for the Assembly, moreover, did not help the university's financial plight, and the more he appealed to donors for the Assembly, the more conservative he sounded. For example, he told a Houston audience: "If all that Americans want is security, they can go to prison." Years later Eisenhower acknowledged that most of the Columbia faculties opposed the Assembly and considered it silly. The reaction, however, was more serious than that.[34]

For many at Columbia, the American Assembly came to illustrate, months before he departed for NATO in January 1951, his lack of interest in the university itself as well as the gap between him and the academic community. While he had been "the practical favorite of liberals" in America in 1948 and, according to historian Alonzo Hamby, many were willing to accept him as late as early 1952, liberals at Columbia thought otherwise. They disliked his association with oilmen and businessmen, and, increasingly, they saw him as using the university for his interests. Few knew that the trustees had refused to accept his resignation when he went to NATO.[35]

The faculties of Columbia University could be expected to oppose in 1952 any Republican nominee, but the depth of the opposition to Eisenhower had deep roots. The nomination by the Democrats of Adlai Stevenson and the events of the campaign, from Richard Nixon through Joe McCarthy, served to harden their position. Their intensity increased when Eisenhower in September welcomed Senator Taft to the President's House at 60 Morningside and accepted the senator's prepared statement. Taft "represented a good deal of what was unacceptable to the university faculty people," economist Raymond Saulnier recalls, "and to have Eisenhower sit down and make peace was, of course, a surrender." The meeting became known as "The Surrender of Morningside Heights,'" and many saw it as an embarrassment for them and the university.[36]

In mid-September Peter Gay, an instructor in government at Columbia College, protested the *New York Times'* endorsement of Eisenhower, and for the rest of the campaign Columbia would be associated with partisan politics. The frustration grew because Arthur Hays Sulzberger, owner and publisher of the *Times*, was a Columbia trustee, and it was widely believed that at least a majority of the editorial board favored Stevenson. A few days later six prominent Columbia intellectuals joined other city intellectuals in sending a long letter of protest to the *Times*.[37]

The pace quickened, and reaction produced further reaction. Both the Stevenson and Eisenhower supporters realized that their association with Eisenhower at Columbia guaranteed publicity. On October 1, 1952, the Columbia *Spectator* endorsed Stevenson, and nearly 100 faculty members elected Pulitzer-Prize-winning historian Allan Nevins chairman of a faculty-for-Stevenson group and named a prominent executive committee. In reply, the Columbia Alumni for Eisenhower promised to mail to 15,000 alumni a brochure celebrating Eisenhower's achievements at the university. Soon theologian Reinhold Niebuhr criticized Eisenhower in a letter to the *New York Times*. On October 5 historians Nevins and Richard Morris issued a statement on behalf of 23 professors analyzing and criticizing Richard Nixon's secret fund, and the president of the College's Alumni Association quickly denounced their motives. On October 16 over 300 "Volunteers for Stevenson on the Columbia University Faculties and Staff" published a full-page advertisement in the *Times*, prepared by historian Richard Hofstadter. When the *New York Daily News* and California's Governor Earl Warren claimed that Columbia harbored more communists than any other university, fears of an Eisenhower-Nixon-McCarthy victory grew on Morningside Heights. Meanwhile, the university's administrative leaders had agreed not to be involved publicly in the growing controversy, but the dean of the School of Journalism soon broke ranks and bitterly criticized Columbia. He accused the administration of violating academic freedom and of indirectly subsidizing Eisenhower's campaign by allowing him to use the President's House. Not surprisingly, the dean's remarks received extensive newspaper coverage.[38]

The controversy continued to escalate. The Eisenhower forces retaliated with advertisements in the *Times* and the Republican *Herald-Tribune*—Bill Robinson's newspaper—which offered a reduced rate. The Stevenson group immediately charged that 455 of the 714 persons on the Eisenhower list had no academic or administrative function at Columbia and that it was a "deliberate misrepresentation intended to mislead the readers" about faculty opinion at Columbia. Moreover, the Stevenson group noted that the Eisenhower people had not solicited money for the ads.[39]

The frustrations of the Eisenhower years at Columbia had been unleashed and received nationwide publicity. As the controversy degenerated, professional friendships were badly strained. Historian Harry J. Carman, the widely respected Dean Emeritus of Columbia College, led the Eisenhower group on campus and was one of the very few liberal arts faculty members to support the general. Years later he sadly recalled the way his colleagues in the department looked at him with disbelief. Only one or two had agreed with him, while the Stevenson supporters among the Americanists, besides Nevins, Hofstadter, and Morris, included the prominent or soon-to-be prominent Henry Steele Commager, Lawrence Cremin, David Donald, Henry Graff, William Leuchtenburg, Dumas Malone, James Shenton, and Harold Syrett. On January 16, 1953, Eisenhower made his farewell appearance at Columbia, and Carman had to introduce the president-elect; it was one of the hardest and most difficult moments of his life. For many years, Carman emphasized, his colleagues reminded him of how little they thought of Eisenhower and of his presidency of the United States.[40]

Columbia University played an important role on Eisenhower's road to the White House. The university presidency, his first civilian position, gave him the chance to develop and express his views on contemporary society. It also gave him the opportunity to create the American Assembly, and his Assembly supporters would have a profound influence on his career. In establishing the Assembly, he would broaden his horizons and demonstrate his commitment to democratic citizenship. The Columbia experience would make him better prepared for the presidency of the United States; it would also contribute to the sharp intellectual criticism of him for many years.

NOTES

1. Stephen E. Ambrose, *Eisenhower: Soldier, General of the Army, President-Elect, 1890–1952* (New York: Simon and Schuster, 1983), p. 464; David McCullough, *Truman* (New York: Simon and Schuster, 1992), pp. 430, 584, 887–88. Earlier versions of this chapter were presented at Gettysburg College's "The Eisenhower Legacy: A Centennial Symposium" on October 13, 1990, and appeared in *Presidential Studies Quarterly* in 1992. I am grateful for assistance from the Middlebury College Research Fund and the Earhart Foundation.

2. Arthur M. Schlesginer, Jr., has written that Eisenhower's reputation declined, "at least among intellectuals," much sooner than the reputation of presidents generally. "The Ike Age Revisited,"*Reviews in American History* 11 (March 1983): 1–2; Louis Galambos, ed., *The Papers of Dwight David Eisenhower* (PDDE), vol. X, (Baltimore: Johns Hopkins University Press, 1984), xxiii. Robert F. Burk added that "considerable fleshing out is

still needed" for "the period of Eisenhower's life from the end of World War II to his decision to run for the presidency in 1952." "Eisenhower Revisionism Revisited: Reflections on Eisenhower Scholarship," *The Historian* 50 (February 1988): 206–7.

3. Peter Lyon, *Eisenhower: Portrait of the Hero* (Boston: Little, Brown and Co., 1974), 373; Robert H. Ferrell, ed., *The Eisenhower Diaries* July 24, 1947 (New York: W. W. Norton, 1981), 143; Eisenhower to Milton Eisenhower, May 29, 1947, *PDDE*, VIII (Baltimore: Johns Hopkins University Press, 1978), 1737–38; Milton Eisenhower to Eisenhower, June 10, 1947, *ibid.*, 1759, n.2; Milton Eisenhower to Eisenhower, June 17, 1947, Dwight D. Eisenhower Library (DDEL), Abilene, Kan.

4. Eisenhower to Walter Bedell Smith, July 3, 1947, *PDDE*, VIII, 1799–1800; Eisenhower to Edward Everett Hazlett, Jr., July 19, 1947, *ibid.*, 1836–38; and Eisenhower to Thomas I. Parkinson, June 23, 1947, *ibid.*, 1775–76; Ferrell, *Eisenhower Diaries*, c. January 1, 1950, 169.

5. Eisenhower to Parkinson, June 23, 1947, *PDDE*, VIII, 1775–76; Eisenhower to Thomas Watson, June 14, 1947, *ibid.*, 1757–58; Eisenhower to Truman, December 16, 1950, *PDDE*, XI (Baltimore: Johns Hopkins University Press, 1984), 1488–93.

6. *New York Times*, October 13, 1948, 1, 21.

7. Dwight D. Eisenhower, *At Ease: Stories I Tell to Friends* (Garden City, N.Y.: Doubleday, 1967), 329; "Chronology," *PDDE*, XI, 1587–93.

8. Eisenhower, *At Ease*, 350; Eisenhower to W. Averell Harriman, November 30, 1949, *PDDE*, X, 843–45; Eisenhower to Adolphus Andrews, Jr., September 29, 1950, DDEL; Eisenhower to Robinson, June 9, 1950, *ibid.*

9. William H. Burnham to Eisenhower, May 15, 1950, DDEL; Eisenhower to Leonard McCollum, May 31, 1950, and September 12, 1950, *PDDE*, XI, 1144–48, 1305–10.

10. *Ibid.*, 1148, n.9.

11. Burnham memo to Eisenhower, July 10, 1950, DDEL.

12. *Minneapolis Morning Tribune*, July 8, 1950, 1; Eisenhower to Bullis, July 11, 1950, *PDDE*, XI, 1218–19.

13. Eisenhower to John A. Krout, August 10, 1950, *PDDE*, XI, 1269–70; Eisenhower to Kleberg, August 14, 1950, *ibid.*, 1273–74; the Trustees of Columbia University in the City of New York, *Minutes*, January 8, 1951, and February 4, 1952, Central Archives, Columbia University (CACU).

14. Eisenhower to McCollum, September 12, 1950, *PDDE*, XI, 1305–10.

15. Eisenhower to Burnham, August 21, 1950, *ibid.*, 1280–81; *Denver Post*, September 5, 1950, 1; Eisenhower to Bullis, September 5, 1950, DDEL.

16. Robert Schulz memo for Eisenhower, "Phil Young Conference with Harriman," September 8, 1950, DDEL; Trustees of Columbia, *Minutes*, October 2, 1950, CACU; Memo to Deans, Directors, and Departmental Executives, October 12, 1950, *PDDE*, XI, 1379–82; Columbia Associates Policy Committee, Meeting, October 4, 1950, and Eisenhower's Remarks, "The American Assembly, 1950–59: General and Administrative Papers," vol. I, Columbia Associates Luncheon on the American Assembly Plan, October 18, 1950, American Assembly, Columbia University (AACU). The previous evening Eisenhower had met with Porter, Burnham, and McCollum in Connecticut. Editorial, "The American Assembly," *New York Herald-Tribune*, October 20, 1950, 24.

17. "The American Assembly," vol. III; McElroy to Eisenhower, November 24, 1950, *PDDE*, XI, 1443, n.2.

18. Ferrell, *Eisenhower Diaries*, October 13, 28, and November 6, 1950, 177–82;

Eisenhower to Robert Harron, October 16, 1950, and Eisenhower to Fred Manning, November 3, 1950, *PDDE*, XI, 1383–84, 1405–1406.

19. Ferrell, *Eisenhower Diaries*, November 6, 1950, 180–81; Eisenhower to Roberts, November 6 and November 7, 1950, *PDDE*, XI, 1141–42, 1416–17.

20. Eisenhower to Bermingham, November 18, 1950, DDEL; Eisenhower to Carter, November 29, 1950, and Eisenhower to Richardson, November 29, 1950, *PDDE*, XI, 1447–49; *Houston Post*, November 11, 1950, 1, and editorial, "The Eisenhower Plan," 8; *Dallas Morning News*, November 12, 1950, 1.

21. Editorial, "Back to New England," *Boston Herald*, October 20, 1950; *Boston Daily Globe*, November 23, 1950; *Rochester Times Union*, October 18, 1966; "The American Assembly," vol. III, AACU.

22. Ferrell, *Eisenhower Diaries*, November 29, 1950, 182; Eisenhower to Bermingham, December 12, 1950, DDEL.

23. Eisenhower to Cutler, December 31, 1950, *PDDE*, XI, 1477–78; Eisenhower to Burnham, December 31, 1950, *ibid.*, 1517–18; Eisenhower to Bermingham, December 31, 1950, DDEL; "The American Assembly," vol. III, AACU. Eisenhower left for Washington on January 1, 1951, and for Paris on January 6.

24. "The American Assembly," vols. II and IV, AACU.

25. *Ibid.*, vol. II; *New York Herald-Tribune*, May 23, 1951, 1, 12, and editorial, "The American Assembly," 22.

26. Harriman to Eisenhower, May 22, 1951, DDEL; "The American Assembly," pamphlet (n.d.), AACU; W. Averell Harriman, personal interview, Washington, D.C., October 13, 1977; Phil Young, personal interview, Van Hornesville, N.Y., June 15, 1977.

27. Lyon, *Eisenhower*, 407; Blanche Wiesen Cook, *The Declassified Eisenhower: A Divided Legacy* (Garden City, N.Y.: Doubleday, 1981), 82–83; Ambrose, *Eisenhower*, 493.

28. Ferrell, *Eisenhower Diaries*, January 14, 1949, 153–54; Young, interview. Robert Griffith has argued that during these years Eisenhower developed a concept of corporate liberalism. "Dwight D. Eisenhower and the Corporate Commonwealth," *American Historical Review* 89 (February 1982): 87–123. The general's speeches and letters, though, seem to reflect essentially the values of small-town America and his commitment to internationalism.

29. Eisenhower to Roberts, November 1, 1951, DDEL; Eisenhower to K. S. Adams, November 20, 1951, *ibid.* At the second Assembly in the spring of 1952, according to participant Raymond J. Saulnier, many thought that Eisenhower would return from Europe dramatically just for the conference. Personal interview, New York, June 13, 1991.

30. Ambrose, *Eisenhower*, 518–22; John Robert Greene, *The Crusade: The Presidential Election of 1952* (Lanham, Md.: University Press of America, 1985), 78–82; Ellis D. Slater, personal interview, Edgartown, Mass., September 1, 1972; Eisenhower to Sherman Adams, March 12, 1952, *PDDE*, XIII, 1059–60.

31. *New York Times*, March 21, 1952; Herbert S. Parmet, *Eisenhower and the American Crusades* (New York: Macmillan, 1972), 41; *Minneapolis Morning Tribune*, editorial, "Eisenhower in the Primary: An Amazing Vote," March 20, 1952, 6; Eisenhower to Mintener, March 20, 1952, *PDDE*, XIII, 1097; Eisenhower to Truman, April 2, 1952, *ibid.*, 1154–55; Ellis D. Slater, *The Ike I Knew* (Baltimore: Johns Hopkins University Press, 1980), 21; Dwight D. Eisenhower, *Mandate for Change* (New York: Simon and Schuster, 1963), p. 22.

32   REEXAMINING THE EISENHOWER PRESIDENCY

32. Paul T. David, Malcolm Moos, and Ralph M. Goldman, eds., *Presidential Nominating Politics in 1952: The South*, vol. III (Baltimore: Johns Hopkins University Press, 1954), 318–31; Burnham to Eisenhower, January 20, 1952, *PDDE*, XIII, 914–15. For examples of front-page coverage by the *Houston Post*, see May 2, 5, 25, 27, and 29, and June 22, 1952. Mrs. Hobby's husband had been president of the newspaper since 1924. Parmet, *Eisenhower*, 76; Greene, *Crusade*, 91–94, 107–15.

33. Douglas Black, personal interview, New York, June 6, 1973.

34. Eli Ginzberg, personal interview, New York, December 11, 1990; Eisenhower to McCollum, September 12, 1950, *PDDE*, XI, 1305–10; *New York Times*, December 9, 1949; Dwight D. Eisenhower, Oral History Project, 1967, DDEL; Saulnier, interview.

35. Alonzo L. Hamby, *Beyond the New Deal* (New York: Columbia University Press, 1973), 229, 492. The trustees did decide to close the President's House, and it was reopened when he returned to the United States in 1952. Trustees of Columbia, *Minutes*, February 8, 1951, CACU.

36. Saulnier, interview.

37. *New York Times*, September 13 and October 11, 1952; *Newsweek*, October 27, 1952. Doug Black, a close colleague of Sulzberger at Columbia, later stated that the entire editorial board opposed Eisenhower. Mrs. Sulzberger, a Barnard trustee, supported Stevenson. Interview, New York, June 6, 1973.

38. The executive committee included Richard Hofstadter, Peter Gay, David Truman, Justus Buchler, Irwin Edman, and Oscar J. Campbell. *New York Times*, October 2, 3, 6, 15, and 16, 1952; Columbia *Spectator*, October 1, 2, 3, 8, 10, 15, and 16, 1952.

39. *New York Times*, October 23, 1952; *New York Herald-Tribune*, October 23, 1952; Harry J. Carman, personal interview, New York, December 1, 1961.

40. Carman, interview; Henry F. Gaff, personal interview, New York, June 13, 1991.

3

Eisenhower's Innovations in White House Staff Structure and Operations

Bradley H. Patterson, Jr.

After the war in Europe, the former Supreme Commander looked back and wrote: "the teams and staffs through which the modern commander absorbs information and exercises his authority must be a beautifully interlocked, smooth-working mechanism. Ideally, the whole should be practically a single mind. . . . ''[1] It was no surprise then, that as president, Eisenhower carried this principle of organization with him into the White House. He applied that principle by inaugurating new White House staff units, most of which, by now, have proven their worth as lasting parts of the contemporary presidency.[2]

The setting of the Eisenhower White House staff inaugurations, however, is significant—especially the influences that were intersecting at the apex of American public administration in the years just before Eisenhower's accession to the Oval Office. There were three such influences: (a) the tremendously expanded American role in the world following World War II, (b) the work of the first Hoover Commission, and (c) the success of the secretariat idea in the seniormost Cabinet department.

As George Elsey, a senior aide to President Harry S. Truman, notes, the American government over which Harry Truman and Dwight Eisenhower presided faced daunting demands on its administrative capabilities.[3] In the late 1940s the indispensable linkages among the military, diplomatic, intelligence, economic, and information aspects of our foreign relations—in fact the intertwining of foreign and domestic affairs generally—were at last being recognized. With that recognition new institutions (the National Military Establishment, the State-War-Navy Coordinating Committee, the National Security Council, the Central Intelligence Agency, the National Security Resources Board, the Council of

Economic Advisers, the Psychological Strategy Board) were being created to shape a newly minted coordination out of the dross of old bureaucratic dynasties. America's vastly changed role in the world of "cold war" (the Marshall Plan, NATO) thus bred a changed government; the Executive Office was transformed and the White House itself was forced to supplement the intimacy and informality of earlier years with more systematic and orderly processes of public administration.

The first Hoover Commission turned its attention to these challenges and specifically to how the White House itself should be modernized. It recommended that "The President should be given funds to provide a staff secretary, in addition to his principal Secretaries, to assist him by clearing information on the major problems on which staff work is being done in the President's office, or by the Cabinet or interdepartmental committees."[4] Truman did not accept this recommendation, but as his administration ended, that commission proposal still stood out boldly on the public administration horizon as a totally new concept in White House structure.

The vice chairman of the first Hoover Commission was Dean Acheson. As Under Secretary of State, he had assisted George Marshall in instituting the Executive Secretariat at the top of the department, in the Office of the Secretary. When Acheson himself became Secretary, he and Under Secretary James E. Webb built the then-experimental Executive Secretariat into the most sophisticated and successful coordination apparatus anywhere in Washington at that time. There was a subunit that produced for the department's top officers a daily "Secret" and a daily "Top Secret" digest of all State's cable traffic, plus a summary of the decisions that were just being made by assistant secretaries. There was also a subunit that provided fast, professional, central secretariat services for all of the department's many internal task forces and committees and for those interdepartmental committees chaired by State. There were subunits for correspondence review and for assembling all the policy records of the Office of the Secretary. Under the leadership of Carlisle H. Humelsine, the director of the Executive Secretariat from 1948 to 1950, the secretariat ("S/S") and its energetic but publicity-shunning career officers (of which the author was one) proved how a small staff unit in the immediate office of a department head could quietly but toughly—and without second-guessing the substantive judgments of line officers—aid and, when necessary, enforce coordination across a big institution's typical tangle of egos and bureaucracies. State's Executive Secretariat was thus one of the principal precedents for the Hoover Commission recommendation and a template for the new staff units that Eisenhower, five years later, would bring into the White House itself.

Pressed and helped by these three conjoining influences and, most importantly, spurred by his own lifelong commitment to orderly administration, President Eisenhower inaugurated some twenty-one new mini-instruments within the White House.

THE WHITE HOUSE ROLE OF THE VICE PRESIDENT

When President Truman absented himself from meetings of the National Security Council (as he did for most of its first three years, attending only twelve
of the NSC's first fifty-seven sessions), he decided that Secretary Acheson should
preside, even though Vice President Alben Barkley had been added as a statutory
member of the council in August 1949. Eisenhower, however, believed that if
he had to be absent from NSC or Cabinet meetings (and he missed very few of
either), a constitutional rather than a departmental officer should be in the chair.
Vice President Richard Nixon was therefore given this responsibility. (The decision-making role of approving the NSC and Cabinet Records of Action was,
of course, reserved for the president alone.) NSC and Cabinet papers were sent
to the vice president's office on Capitol Hill, and a senior vice presidential aide
was invited to the White House Cabinet Room for the post-Cabinet oral debriefings given by the Secretary to the Cabinet to the group of departmental representatives known as the Cabinet assistants.

THE SPECIAL ASSISTANT TO THE PRESIDENT FOR
NATIONAL SECURITY AFFAIRS

Since its inception in 1947, the National Security Council's staff had been
headed by an Executive Secretary, as provided by law. On March 23, 1953,
President Eisenhower inaugurated a new position on his personal White House
staff: Special Assistant to the President for National Security Affairs, to whom
the NSC Executive Secretary, and the latter's entire staff group, would henceforth
report. The president elevated Robert Cutler, previously an administrative assistant, to this post. (Others who later served in it during the Eisenhower years
were Dillon Anderson, William H. Jackson, and Gordon Gray.)

A 1960 memorandum by the National Security Council's Executive Secretary,
James S. Lay, described the Special Assistant's responsibilities:

The Special Assistant was made responsible for determination, subject to the President's
desires, of the Council agenda, for briefing the President in advance of Council meetings,
and for presenting matters for discussion at the Council meetings. As Chairman of the
[NSC] Planning Board he was responsible for scheduling Planning Board work and for
the manner of presentation and quality of such work. He was to appoint (subject where
necessary to the President's approval) such ad hoc committees, such consultants from
outside the Government and such mixed governmental-non-governmental committees as
might be required. He supervised the work of the NSC staff through the Executive
Secretary.

Finally, the Special Assistant was charged with bringing to the attention of the President,
with recommendations for appropriate action, lack of progress by an agency in carrying
out any policy assigned to it; . . . the role of the Special Assistant was, on behalf of the
President, to inspect, not to evaluate or to direct.[5]

Equipped with these broad instructions and backed by a staff of (by 1956) twenty-eight or more, Cutler powered the National Security Council into precisely what Eisenhower wanted it to be: his chosen collegial instrument for national security advice.

THE SPECIAL ASSISTANT TO THE PRESIDENT FOR CONGRESSIONAL LIAISON

President Eisenhower identified the strategic duty of building a bridge to Congress and created a special White House office to do so. From the first days after inauguration, retired Major General Wilton B. Persons, a veteran in legislative liaison from Pentagon years, led and strengthened this area of White House operations. Several senior officers (Gerald Morgan, Bryce Harlow, Jack Anderson, I. Jack Martin, Clyde Wheeler, Earle Chesney, and Homer Gruenther) were, at one time or another, on Persons's staff (Fred Seaton also assisted occasionally). It was very clearly understood: no other staff officers were to stray into the business of making commitments to congressmen unless under instructions from Persons and Co., while he and his colleagues could of course call on any office in the entire staff to assist with the tasks of explaining and defending the president's policies to members or staff on the Hill.

On nearly every Tuesday morning, the Persons group arranged and Eisenhower chaired meetings of the legislative leaders who came from the Hill to the Cabinet Room; on nearly every Saturday morning the Liaison Seven would host a meeting in the Cabinet Room of the various departmental congressional liaison officers— thus tying them into a Cabinetwide network of intelligence sources and expediters. What Eisenhower inaugurated in elevating and strengthening this strategic part of the White House staff has been continued by every succeeding president.

THE SPECIAL ASSISTANT TO THE PRESIDENT FOR INTERGOVERNMENTAL RELATIONS

Before two months of his administration had elapsed, Eisenhower moved to emphasize his interest in intergovernmental relations. On March 30, 1953, he proposed that Congress authorize a temporary "Commission to Study Federal, State and Local Relations." Congress agreed; the Commission on Intergovernmental Relations was established on the following July 10. Meyer Kestnbaum, chairman of the Board of Hart, Schaffner and Marx, was appointed chairman.

The commission's report of June 20, 1955, included the proposal that each president have "a Special Assistant in the Executive Office . . . to serve with a small staff as the President's chief aide and adviser on State and local relationships. He should give his exclusive attention to these matters throughout the government. He would be the coordinating center."[6]

Eisenhower did not wait for this recommendation to come to him; on February 1, 1955, he appointed Howard Pyle, a former governor of Arizona, to be an administrative assistant to the president. One of Pyle's principal areas of concentration was intergovernmental relations.

The Kestnbaum Commission and the Second Hoover Commission both reported later in 1955. On October 10 Eisenhower pulled Kestnbaum himself into the White House as a Special Assistant for Intergovernmental Relations—with the assignment to handle the followup on the recommendations stemming from both of those prestigious advisory bodies.

Thus began yet another major unit of the White House staff. Two of the later presidents (Johnson and Nixon) experimented with assigning the intergovernmental liaison function to their respective vice presidents; today the office is a firmly recognized division of the personal staff of the president.

THE OPERATIONS COORDINATING BOARD AND THE SPECIAL ASSISTANTS TO THE PRESIDENT FOR COLD WAR PLANNING AND FOR SECURITY OPERATIONS COORDINATION

Only four days into his administration, Eisenhower established an ad hoc committee chaired by William H. Jackson, chairman of the President's Committee on International Information Activities, to review the capabilities of the Psychological Strategy Board, which had been created by President Truman on June 20, 1951. The Jackson Committee stressed that "psychological strategy" could not be divorced from official policies and actions; it recommended that the Psychological Strategy Board be replaced by an Operations Coordinating Board (OCB) to be composed of under secretaries plus a "representative of the President."

Eisenhower agreed, and the Operations Coordinating Board was created by Executive Order 10483 of September 2, 1953. The board was to oversee the agencies' "detailed operational planning responsibilities" and "the coordination of the interdepartmental aspects of the detailed operational plans" to achieve "timely and coordinated execution." The board could also "initiate new proposals for action." There was a senior group of board assistants, and there were many interagency working groups, all served by an OCB staff that was headed by an executive officer (Elmer B. Staats).

The presidential representative was C. D. Jackson, who at that time had the title of Special Assistant to the President for Cold War Planning. Later presidential representatives were Nelson Rockefeller (December 1954–December 1955) and William H. Jackson (March 1956–December 1956).

By early 1957 the two national security coordinating bodies, the NSC and the OCB, were becoming so closely interwoven that Eisenhower decided to formalize the union. In Executive Order 10700 of February 25, 1957, he placed the Operations Coordinating Board completely within the National Security Council's bailiwick and three months later established a White House Special Assistant for Security Operations Coordination who would be the presidential representative to the board and also its vice chairman. (Fred Dearborn was the first incumbent of this position; Karl Harr succeeded him in 1958.) Eisenhower's final action in the NSC/OCB conjunction took place January 13, 1960, when he made his Special Assistant for National Security Affairs (by this time, Gordon Gray) the chairman of the Operations Coordinating Board and gave new, complementary instructions to the Special Assistant for Security Operations Coordination.

(In its 1960 report, Senator Jackson's special Government Operations Subcommittee on National Policy Machinery complained about the formalistic and complicated nature of the OCB. The newly inaugurated President Kennedy agreed, and abolished it. However Kennedy immediately strengthened the role of the NSC staff itself under Security Adviser McGeorge Bundy, and not long thereafter created, right in the basement of the White House, one of the most potent and intrusive operations-tracking units of any presidency: the first Situation Room. Reagan, while proclaiming "Cabinet Government," built a second one.)

Eisenhower and Kennedy were both right: there is no separation between policy formulation and coordinated execution; a unified NSC staff now oversees both. But the original NSC-OCB union spawned children and grandchildren: at the end of the Reagan presidency the combined NSC staff numbered 190 persons.

THE PRESIDENT'S ADVISORY COMMITTEE ON GOVERNMENT ORGANIZATION

Within a few days of his election in November 1952, President Eisenhower asked his brother, Milton, and two other senior officers seasoned in government affairs, Nelson Rockefeller and Arthur Flemming, to advise him on the organizational issues he would confront in January.[7] The three dug out the recommendations of the first Hoover Commission and reviewed reorganization studies that had been prepared at Temple University in Philadelphia. They met almost daily, briefing the president-elect and also the newly designated Cabinet officers on immediate organizational questions.

Four days after inauguration, Eisenhower by executive order formalized the threesome into the President's Advisory Committee on Government Organization, thereafter known as PACGO. Budget Bureau Director Joseph M. Dodge and his management division assisted them, but the three advisers knew that it was essential to have their own small but private and independent staff (principally Jarold Kieffer and Arthur Kimball).

Milton Eisenhower summed up PACGO's record:

In the eight years of the Eisenhower administration, our committee met about one hundred and twenty times. Informal and formal conferences with the President were numerous—in all probability ninety meetings, sometimes for as much as an hour for the consideration of a single proposal. . . . The score card of our endeavors was this: Fourteen plans became effective under the Reorganization Act. . . . Seven reorganization measures were put into effect by executive order.... Two became law through congressional enactments. In addition many helpful changes in working procedures were brought about by presidential letters addressed to appropriate agency heads.[8]

Kennedy abolished PACGO, but Johnson drew both policy and structural advice from an impressive series of task forces from the private sector. Nixon created a special council under Roy Ash to help him with his reorganization proposals, while Carter injected a large temporary staff into the Office of Management and Budget to develop an ambitious but relatively unsuccessful set of reorganization initiatives. Nothing quite like PACGO has been created since the Eisenhower years, however, and its archives still await the enterprising scholar who will tell its story in the detail it deserves.

THE WHITE HOUSE STAFF SECRETARY

As summarized earlier in this chapter, the First Hoover Commission in 1949 recommended the creation of a position of staff secretary. Said the commission:

At present there is no one place in the President's Office to which the President can look for a current summary of the principal issues with which he may have to deal in the near future; nor is a current summary of the staff work available on problems that have been assigned to his advisers, his staff agencies or the heads of departments and agencies. To meet this deficiency, the Commission proposes the addition of a staff secretary. He would not himself be an adviser to the President on any issue of policy, nor would he review (in a supervisory capacity) the substance of any recommendation made to the President by any part of his staff.[9]

These cautions were the lessons from the experience of the Department of State's Executive Secretariat, then only two years old.

The day after he became president, Eisenhower created and filled this new position; its first incumbent was Brigadier General Paul T. Carroll who had been military assistant to General Eisenhower at the Supreme Headquarters of the Allied Powers in Europe (SHAPE) in Paris. Ike described the staff secretary's duties in his own words: "If a document was incomplete, 'Pete' Carroll would ask for additional facts to complete it. If coordination with other pertinent agencies was required, he would see to it that the matter was brought to their attention."[10]

When General Carroll died in September 1954, Ike immediately replaced him with Colonel (later General) Andrew J. Goodpaster. As part of their staff secretary functions, Carroll and Goodpaster were especially involved in handling day-to-day liaison between the Oval Office and the Department of Defense. Andy Goodpaster was assisted by the late L. Arthur Minnich and, beginning in October 1958, by Lieutenant Colonel John S. D. Eisenhower, the president's distinguished son. In the same suite, in those years, sat William J. Hopkins, the immensely skilled but self-effacing executive clerk whose White House career spanned four decades. Together with the Assistant for National Security Affairs (see above) and the Cabinet Secretariat (see below) the men in the staff secretary's office were indeed the nerve center of the Eisenhower White House, precisely as the Hoover Commission intended.

Their duties and status were more formally set out and then called to the attention of the rest of the Executive Branch in the fall of 1954, as discussed in the next section. With some hiatus in the Kennedy, Johnson, and Carter years, the function of staff secretary has now become an established part of the modern White House team.

THE CABINET SECRETARIAT

Just as the war ended, a debate was in progress at senior levels around government and later at the staff level within the first Hoover Commission. Eisenhower as Army Chief of Staff sent the Secretary of War a memorandum on January 8, 1946, making the following recommendation:

A system of committees similar to the State-War-Navy Coordinating Committee, with a common secretariat to integrate the work of the committees, appears to be the most practicable method of coordinating the functions of the executive departments and agencies for the formulation of policy and for planning, and of insuring coordinated executive action. . . . It is therefore proposed that (a) A Cabinet secretariat be established as a separate division of the Executive Office of the President to provide the necessary secretarial services to committees charged with coordinating functions. (b) A Cabinet Secretary be appointed by the President to direct the activities of the Cabinet Secretariat, to act as Secretary to the President at Cabinet meetings. . . . Through the intimate relationship of the members of this interlocking secretariat organization, their common methods of procedure and their knowledge of the cognizance and interests of the departments and agencies of the Executive Branch of the Government, the machinery of coordination would be bound into an integrated whole.[11]

In December 1946, Vannevar Bush, chairman of the Joint Research and Development Board of the Department of Defense, made the same recommendation to President Truman, pointing out that a secretariat in the White House could "Prepare in advance the matters which are to be taken up at Cabinet meetings. . . . The preparation of the agenda . . . should include not only the subjects on which the President wishes Cabinet advice, and matters which the Cabinet members themselves desire to raise, but also matters which the Secretariat wishes to raise on its own initiative."[12]

However, the eminent political scientist Harold Stein and the senior Hoover Commission staff officer, Don K. Price, were very skeptical of such talk of a Cabinet secretariat; they were afraid it would assume a British-style model of decision making in the American White House. Price warned Chairman Herbert Hoover in December 1947:

The principal arguments advanced against the "cabinet secretariat" idea . . . are: The President should not be required to handle a policy problem through any set procedure, or to consult any fixed group of officials, or take up problems except at the time he chooses. A Cabinet secretariat might reduce the flexibility with which he could direct his subordinates. . . . To formalize Cabinet procedure could invite legislative interference with the method by which the President directs his department heads.[13]

True to his earlier convictions, Eisenhower did initiate a modest Cabinet secretariat operation soon after inauguration; at first it was simply an instruction to one of his senior assistants, Gabriel Hauge, to collect items for the Cabinet agenda. In the summer of 1953, following an internal study of White House operations by a former SHAPE associate, Carter L. Burgess, Eisenhower formalized the procedure a bit further and appointed Maxwell M. Rabb as the Secretary to the Cabinet.

In the summer of 1954, Burgess was asked to do a second study (the author was his assistant). A presentation, with charts, was made to the president in the Oval Office on August 3, 1954.[14] Burgess and the author stressed that "nothing should restrict the President's direct contact with his Cabinet and Agency heads," that the staff and Cabinet secretariat that they were recommending "must not be an institution by itself."

To emphasize to Eisenhower that he recognized the differences between the British/Cabinet and the American/presidential decision-making systems, Burgess included in his set of charts a special display board that made the comparison completely clear. To help guarantee that he would never be accused of not understanding that difference, or of aping the British system, Ike ordered that same special display chart deleted from the set that was later to be printed and circulated to his Cabinet associates.

In their presentation to the president, Burgess and the author recommended that each Cabinet officer designate a trusted senior staff person to be a Cabinet assistant and that together this group would form a nerve network that the staff secretary and the Cabinet secretary could use to pass information and requests. Specific formats were suggested for staff secretary instructions; a system of formal Cabinet papers was proposed, with oral debriefings to be given to the assembled Cabinet assistants by the Cabinet secretary immediately after Cabinet meetings.

Eisenhower found in these recommendations precisely the system he was looking for; he approved them immediately. He further ordered that the presentation be (a) repeated to the Cabinet at its meeting in Laurel Lodge at Camp David on August 13, 1954, at which time Ike confirmed to the Cabinet members his strong endorsement of this strengthened system; (b) put in the form of a booklet (entitled "Staff Work for the President and the Executive Branch") which, under cover of a Sherman Adams memorandum of August 20, 1954, was distributed to all the departments and agencies; and (c) taken, together with its charts, around to senior staff meetings in each of the Cabinet departments to let all of their senior officers know that this was the way Ike was henceforth going to manage his other-than-NSC decision procedures.[15]

Rabb asked the author to join the White House staff as the assistant Cabinet Secretary, and together they initiated a nearly seven-year period of orderly and systematic domestic affairs decision-making processes in the Eisenhower presidency.

In his eight years, there were 236 meetings of Ike's full Cabinet; they discussed 1,236 items (some recurrent). Following that 1954 formalization, 112 Cabinet papers were distributed by the secretariat for discussion and decision; 72 others were circulated in a separate Information Series. A total of 160 Records of Action were written up, approved by the president, and then dispatched to all Cabinet members. There were never any Cabinet votes; Ike made all the decisions.

The five-person Cabinet Secretariat (two officers and three secretaries) also served a sub-Cabinet of Under Secretaries, kept an eye on the meetings of Cabinet committees (the author often sat with them), and periodically made up Cabinet Action Status Reports, flagging instances of poor departmental compliance to the Chief of Staff.

Robert Gray succeeded Maxwell Rabb as Cabinet Secretary in the spring of 1958.

For the American presidency, Ike's new Cabinet Secretariat was a first, and successful, experiment in public administration support for the Cabinet as a group. The only reasons for its success were that (a) it fitted Eisenhower's own decision style and (b) the White House officers who managed it, like their colleagues in the staff secretary's group, abided strictly by the prescription that had been laid down by the Brownlow Committee in 1936: while doing their work energetically, they never interposed themselves between the president and his Cabinet members.

These nuances and limitations were lost on most outside observers. The October 21, 1954, headline taking up the front half-page in the *Washington Daily News* ran: "IKE IS SETTING UP WHITE HOUSE LIKE A MILITARY STAFF." The 1960 edition of Richard Neustadt's *Presidential Power* termed Eisenhower's "staffs and interagency committees and paper-flows" "pernicious" because they made him "typically the last man in his office to know tangible details and the last to come to grips with acts of choice." The workings of Ike's system, Neustadt pontificated, "often were disastrous for his hold on personal power."[16] It was not until Princeton University scholar Fred Greenstein published his work based on the actual Eisenhower papers that scholars got a more balanced view of the Eisenhower White House.[17]

"STAFF NOTES"

In early 1956 the much-respected Carter Burgess was called in for a third review of White House operations. Again Burgess looked to the Department of State's secretariat as a model. In an April 23, 1956, report, he recommended that a research staff be added to the staff secretary's office to prepare an overnight White House Staff Summary to include "digests of the most significant developments during your off-duty hours in the Executive Branch, the Congress, the United States, and the rest of the world."[18] Ike approved that recommendation with alacrity, and General Goodpaster hired another State Department secretariat veteran, Albert P. Toner, to put such a summary together. Others who later assisted Toner were Phillip E. Areeda and Christopher H. Russell. With typical understatement, Goodpaster gave the potent new summary a modest title: "Staff Notes."

On July 5, 1956, a Goodpaster instruction was sent to all the Executive departments and agencies: the White House wanted "brief informational notes on items within your field of interest which may bear upon past presidential decisions or which may flag especially important up-coming problems."[19] Toner passed the word that interpreted Goodpaster's diplomatic request: "One of our criteria for rejection would be that it was in the New York *Times* yesterday morning. Once something would appear in the public domain, by our standards it was declared legally dead."[20]

But it was often difficult to wrest these tidbits of presidentially significant information from the possessive departments. Some sent their press releases; others deluged the editors with insignificant material. Toner and his associates would keep emphasizing to Cabinet officers the benefit of having a guarantee that vital information would go straight into the Oval Office; they would waylay Cabinet secretaries as they entered the White House Mess, and they kept fever charts of every agency's submissions. Goodpaster would notify Chief of Staff Sherman Adams if the line on any chart took a nose-dive; Adams would then telephone a pungent prod to the foot-dragger. On at least one occasion the president had Goodpaster speak up at a Cabinet meeting to remind the members of the high value Ike placed on these Staff Notes reports.

Slowly the system took hold. The submissions multiplied; the White House staffers' editing was always severe, but in each item they kept in the essence of the information. Every night, and sometimes during the day, a page and a half went in to Eisenhower (with copies to Nixon and to seven of the White House seniors). Ike would occasionally scratch notations in the margins and ask for supplemental data; of course that was one of the purposes of the whole procedure.

In four and a half years, 9,694 items were submitted as raw material and 7,429 went to the president as Staff Notes paragraphs. Ike read every one of them; thus, there were 7,429 instances where the president avoided being surprised by events or decisions within his own Executive Branch.[21]

Kennedy disparaged much of Eisenhower's staff system, but he kept this element of it (on a once-a-week basis), and so has every succeeding president. Thus did Ike's 1956 innovation prove its worth: now daily or weekly reports of this kind are a standard requirement from within the White House as well as from the departments and agencies.

VERY SPECIAL ASSISTANTS FOR VERY SPECIAL PROBLEMS

From time to time every president is presented with a public policy issue of extraordinary messiness: an aroused public demanding action, many departments involved, political opponents charging that he is asleep when he should be grabbing the wheel. Substantive responses may require billions; thorough reorganizations take years—and the president has neither. He does, however, have an instant option that will portray himself as taking charge and as jolting stodgy governmental machinery to move faster: he can appoint a White House "czar." No Senate confirmation is needed, and a suite can always be found in the Executive Office Building next door. It is a legitimate presidential gambit; the "czar" sometimes achieves real success (although often being a thorn in the Cabinet's side). Roosevelt and Truman had few such officers in the White House; Eisenhower created a full dozen of them.

Four have already been mentioned: Meyer Kestnbaum (preceded by Howard Pyle) for intergovernmental relations, C. D. Jackson (followed by Nelson Rockefeller and William H. Jackson) for "cold war planning," Fred Dearborn (followed by Karl Harr) for security operations coordination, and the PACGO trio for government organization issues.

There were eight others. The creation of each of them grew out of unique circumstances and urgencies. Some of them resulted in lasting structures in the White House environment; others were present no longer than the Eisenhower administration.

The Special Assistant to the President for Science and Technology

On November 7, Eisenhower created a "missile czar"—summoning James R. Killian, Jr., to Washington from his post as president of the Massachusetts Institute of Technology. Said Ike in an address to the nation: "Through him, I intend to be assured that the entire program is carried forward in closely-integrated fashion."[22] Killian was heard to comment: "Apparently I had been hired as a miracle worker."[23]

Killian was invited to sit with the Cabinet, with the National Security Council, and in other specialized meetings. He played a central role in wading into what he called the "anvil chorus of contestants" as to which agency would run the forthcoming space program; he won the president's backing for a civilian rather than a military leadership. Whether or not to support an international nuclear test ban was another issue in which Killian supplied independent analysis and advice. He and later his successor, George Kistiakowsky, chaired the interdepartmental Federal Committee on Science and Technology, which in Kistiakowsky's words "remained a gathering of individuals who represented frequently opposing agency positions and just were unable, unwilling . . . to think on a national, federal level."[24] The Killian-Kistiakowsky operation later grew into the Office of Science and Technology Policy, which in 1976 was made a statutory part of the Executive Office of the president. Killian himself described his White House experiences in a revealing book: *Sputnik, Scientists and Eisenhower*.

The Special Assistant to the President for Aviation Facilities Planning and Airways Modernization

By 1956 the advent of large, commercial jet aircraft was bringing consternation to the managers of U.S. airports and aviation safety systems. The Departments of Commerce and Defense (housing the Civil Aviation Administration and the Air Force respectively) were still debating about how to divvy up responsibility for air traffic control; the interdepartmental coordinating machinery for aviation matters (the Air Coordinating Committee [ACC], chaired in the Department of Commerce) was a constipated outfit.[25] Eisenhower recognized a need that would not wait, bypassed the ACC, created an ad hoc position on the White House staff of Special Assistant for Aviation Facilities Planning, and summoned into service Edward P. Curtis from Kodak (he had been Chief of Staff of the Strategic Air Force in Europe). Curtis produced a comprehensive report that was discussed at a Cabinet meeting.

In the spring of 1957, just as Curtis was finishing his work, two civilian planes collided over the Grand Canyon—the worst civil air disaster in the nation up to that time. What had been urgent now became critical; the Curtis report had to be transformed into legislation and speeded through Congress. Again Ike reached out to a wartime USAF colleague and brought in retired Lieutenant General Elwood R. "Pete" Quesada to handle precisely that mission. When Quesada needed top-level White House muscle with the Commerce and Air Force contestants, he got it; with a staff of eight, he drafted and shepherded through Congress the legislation that was needed to create a new Federal Aviation Agency.

Whom did Eisenhower send over to be the first head of that agency? It was "Pete" Quesada himself—a move which has been repeated a number of times as presidents pick some of their top-level White House associates to move over from senior staff to senior line responsibilities.

The Special Assistant for Public Works Planning

Eisenhower had long been suspicious of "pork-barrel" public works projects: costly enterprises mandated by Congress that bypassed economic or cost-benefit analysis by state or by federal executive branch officials. He backed up his suspicions with vetoes of several rivers-and-harbors and public works appropriations. At the same time he wanted to strengthen his own resources for that cost-benefit analysis above and beyond his institutional capabilities—resources that were in the Bureau of Reclamation, the Corps of Engineers, and the Bureau of the Budget. By strength he meant White House strength.

Once more Ike reached into his reservoir of wartime talent and in August of 1955 elevated a West Point classmate and former Deputy Chief of Army Engineers, retired Major General John S. Bragdon, to the new post of Special Assistant to the President for Public Works Planning. Bragdon headed a small staff that included Floyd D. Peterson, who succeeded him in July 1960.[26]

The Special Assistant to the President for Disarmament

To demonstrate his personal commitment to press ahead and try to diminish the threat of the use of nuclear weapons in the world, Eisenhower on March 19, 1955, created this special position on his White House Staff and appointed Harold Stassen to the post. (Stassen had most recently been the director of the Foreign Operations Administration, the organization which succeeded the Mutual Security Administration.) This experiment in the use of personal White House staff proved much less successful than the others catalogued in this chapter.

In July 1955 came Eisenhower's first summit conference with the new leaders of the Soviet Union—Bulganin and Khrushchev. Stassen and his colleague on the staff, Nelson Rockefeller, insisted on being in the delegation.[27]

On the day before he was to make the speech unveiling his "Open Skies" proposal, Eisenhower finally did invite Stassen and Rockefeller to Geneva to help him polish his remarks. The Russian leaders, however, rejected Ike's proposal.

Just a year later, with Eisenhower out of the country in Panama, Stassen held a press conference announcing that Eisenhower had approved the concept of an open Republican Convention that summer and further stated that he, Stassen, was supporting not Nixon but Governor Christian Herter of Massachusetts as the vice presidential running mate. "When Eisenhower was told," biographer Stephen Ambrose recounted, "he instructed [Press Secretary James] Hagerty to issue a statement stressing Stassen's right as an American to campaign for whomever he wished, but that he could not conduct independent political activity and remain a member of the 'official family.' Eisenhower was therefore giving Stassen a leave of absence without pay until after the convention."[28]

In January 1957, Eisenhower had become so concerned with Stassen's growing independence that he cut off Stassen's direct access to the White House and insisted that he report to the president through the Secretary of State. At the London Disarmament Conference the following spring, Stassen disobeyed his instructions, began to deal directly with the Russians, and infuriated Prime Minister Macmillan. Eisenhower told Macmillan that he was "astonished and chagrined," called Stassen home, and reprimanded him. Ten months later he asked for Stassen's resignation as disarmament adviser, suggesting another post in the administration. Stassen refused, left the government entirely, and went to Pennsylvania to run unsuccessfully for governor.

The Stassen case illustrates the danger a president runs when he places a person into a senior Cabinet or White House post who has—or imagines he has—an independent political following. That independence, which at first seems attractive, turns out to be the temptation to abandon the very teamwork that the president most of all requires.

The Special Consultant for Agricultural Surplus Disposal

One of the earliest and also most persistent policy issues faced by Eisenhower was how to get rid of the billions of dollars of surplus farm commodities the government had bought from U.S. farmers under its price support program. This was a foreign trade as well as a domestic agricultural problem; the Departments of Commerce, State, Agriculture, and Treasury were all involved in it. After conferring with Secretaries Dulles and Benson and with the president, Chief of Staff Sherman Adams, on March 8, 1954, arranged the creation of a new special consultantship on the White House staff and persuaded Clarence Francis, the chairman of the board of General Foods, to take the job.

In his book, Adams described both Francis's accomplishments and frustrations: "Francis wasted no time in putting together an interagency committee and it proceeded to get something done. One of the results was the Agricultural Trade and Development Act, better known as PL 480, which was designed to expand foreign markets for our agricultural goods."[29]

Adams recounts the policy disputes with Secretary Dulles, who did not want to see the United States' disposals undermining the agricultural export markets of allies like Canada and Australia.

But a year later, when Francis took stock, he found that he had programmed the disposal of $500 million worth of surplus commodities. In 1955, it was over $100 million in actual disposals and in 1956 $350 million. In the next four years $1.5 billion worth of goods went overseas. Within two years Francis and his co-operators pushed 330 million pounds of surplus butter onto the market and an inventory of 570 million pounds of dried milk almost completely disappeared. But Francis could not keep up with the ingenuity of the American farmer. . . . And there was always Dulles, keeping careful watch over any trespass on the traditional markets of our friends. Francis found it hard going.[30]

Francis stayed on the job all through the rest of the Eisenhower administration; under Kennedy the post was changed to "The Food for Peace Coordinator," and it was held by George McGovern.

The Special Assistant to the President for Foreign Economic Policy

Among the several multidimensional and therefore multijurisdictional issue-areas facing an American president, foreign economic policy is one of the most complex. All the national security departments and half the domestic agencies are directly concerned in one or more of the interwoven subareas in this arena: trade, east-west controls, tariffs, stockpiling, commodity exports and imports (especially farm products, timber, minerals), shipping, financing, credit, currency convertibility, investments, loans, development objectives, telecommunications, tax policy, and more. As in every recent presidency, Eisenhower and his aides stewed over this problem. In June 1954 economic counsellor Gabriel Hauge and trade adviser Clarence Randall met with the PACGO and urged that trio to look for an answer. A memorandum went to the president on July 12 suggesting that he authorize a "high priority" PACGO study. He approved it, agreed to ask former Budget Director Joseph Dodge to "direct the staff work of this project" and aired the matter at Cabinet.

By October Dodge had a draft that set out three options for foreign economic policy coordination: (1) create an Executive Office (or White House) unit with a senior aide at its head and a small staff; (2) in addition, establish a new, formal Council on Foreign Economic Policy, chaired by an Executive Office/White House representative; or (3) expand the responsibility of the existing Operations Coordinating Board to include foreign economic policy. The PACGO members endorsed option 2 but with its chairman to be in the White House; in a November 17 luncheon discussion Eisenhower approved this recommendation. All the participants also agreed that the "obvious choice" for the senior White House staff officer was Dodge himself.

Ike's December 1 letter to Dodge included the following mission statement:

Effective immediately I am designating you a Special Assistant to the President to assist and advise me in accomplishing an orderly development of foreign economic policies and programs and to assure the effective coordination of foreign economic matters of concern to the several departments and agencies of the Executive Branch.

More particularly, in respect to foreign economic matters, I shall look to you to provide for the anticipation of problems and issues, ensure advance preparation, analyze information for the purpose of clarifying and defining issues, and determine the primary responsibilities of the executive agencies for the preparation of original documents and for any other steps necessary to produce a coordinated and agreed upon governmental position.[31]

In the same letter, the president established the Council on Foreign Economic Policy (CFEP), designated Dodge as its chairman, and expressed the hope that his work would "lead to a substantial simplification of the present structure" of ad hoc mechanisms.

When Dodge returned to private life some months later, the president appointed Clarence Randall to succeed him as Special Assistant and as chairman of the council. Randall stayed until the end of the Eisenhower administration.

It was relatively easy (at that time) to establish a Cabinet-level interdepartmental committee, designate a high-ranking chairman (other than the president himself), and then trust, or hope, that when the chairman called meetings the

Cabinet officers would show up. But there is an iron law of meeting attendance: Cabinet members can be counted on to come only to those conclaves that the president personally chairs. The author attended several of Randall's CFEP sessions at which the sole Cabinet-level officer was George Humphrey.

In more recent years, Ford, Reagan, and Bush all used an Economic Policy Council for coordination in this area, with backstop staff in the White House—but the president himself was *de jure* the council's chairman.

The Special Assistant to the President on Atomic Energy

Lewis Strauss had been a member of the Atomic Energy Commission (AEC) after the war, and on July 2, 1953, he was sworn in as its chairman, serving until June 30, 1958. But from March 9, 1953, until November 12, 1958, Strauss wore a second hat: as Special Assistant to the President on Atomic Energy matters.

As chairman of the AEC, Admiral Strauss had offices a few blocks from the White House, and he had AEC staff who supported him in his chairmanship role. In that capacity he attended National Security Council meetings (but rarely, if ever, Cabinet sessions) and had staff representation on the NSC Planning Board and at the OCB. As a White House assistant, however, Strauss operated on his own; he had neither office space within the White House perimeter nor aid of any kind to help him in his White House duties. He came into senior policy meetings ad hoc to advise the president whenever Eisenhower asked—which was often—on such matters as Ike's Atoms for Peace speech at the United Nations, disarmament questions, and atomic weapons development and the test ban negotiations.

Eisenhower's biographer Stephen Ambrose is critical of what he described as "Strauss's ability to keep the President from consulting with a broad spectrum of the scientific community and limiting him to contact with such convinced atomic scientists as [Ernest] Lawrence and [Edward] Teller."[32] This changed in October 1957, after Sputnik went up and after James Killian became the Science Adviser (discussed in the section on the Special Assistant to the President for Science and Technology). In November of 1958, Strauss left the White House to accept a recess appointment as Secretary of Commerce; later the Senate refused to confirm him for that post.

This Special Assistantship was unique to the Eisenhower administration. Succeeding presidents simply used their AEC chairmen and their science and technology advisers for counsel in the atomic energy area.

Advisor to the President/Special Assistant to the President for Personnel Management

There are twenty-four different and separate personnel systems in the Executive Branch (for example, the Civil Service, the military services, the Foreign Service,

Customs, the FBI, the Secret Service, the Public Health Service, and so on). While each is governed by its own statutes and regulations, there are many issues they face in common: recruitment, testing, executive education, evaluation, affirmative action, pay, retirement, and even, if the winter snow is deep, which of their employees should come to work in the morning.

Presidents have recognized the need for White House support in these common areas of personnel policy and personnel management. In the famous Executive Order 8248 of September 10, 1939, which first established the Executive Office of the president and the beginnings of the White House staff, Franklin Delano Roosevelt initiated a Liaison Office for Personnel Management. His Executive Order specified that the Liaison Office should be headed by one of the newly created administrative assistants to the president; he named William H. Mc-Reynolds to hold that position.

Truman's administrative assistant for personnel issues was Donald Dawson, appointed on August 6, 1947. Dawson, however, combined personnel management functions with the White House patronage operation and in 1948 was also put in charge of all the advance work for the forthcoming presidential election campaign.

Eisenhower thus did not inaugurate the White House Personnel Management office. His innovation, however, was twofold: (a) he sharply separated the White House's personnel management task from its patronage work, and he institutionalized the former office in Executive Order 10452 of May 1, 1953, and specified its title—Advisor to the President on Personnel Management; (b) Ike then put this hat on the head of the man who was already chairman of the Civil Service Commission—Philip Young, the former dean of the Business School at Columbia. Young divided his time between the commission and the White House, and he had a small staff of White House aides (Joseph Winslow and Henry DuFlon) who served him in his Executive Office Building suite. One of the personnel policy issues to which Young gave a great deal of attention was the idea of a career executive service—a proposal on which Young and the PACGO group collaborated but of which the Congress eventually disapproved.

In March 1957 Young was appointed the ambassador to the Netherlands. On September 16, Eisenhower issued a new Executive Order (number 10729) reconstituting the Personnel Management Office once more. This time, Ike brought Rocco C. Siciliano from the Department of Labor into the White House as Special Assistant to the president. The divorce from the patronage business was reconfirmed and another separation also made: Siciliano was a White House officer only; the Civil Service Commission chairmanship was left in independent hands.

Executive Order 10729's mission statement was an almost word-for-word copy of the 1953 Order, including this paragraph:

Undertake on behalf of the President, and in collaboration with the Bureau of the Budget, a program designed to raise the level of effectiveness of personnel management in the executive departments and agencies, to improve steadily all personnel management systems, and to bring about the proper coordination in personnel management among the executive departments and agencies.[33]

When Siciliano left the White House at the end of November 1959, Eisenhower continued the post and on December 3, appointed Eugene J. Lyons, formerly an assistant postmaster general (for personnel) to be this Special Assistant.

President Johnson combined all three duties: chairmanship of the Civil Service Commission, White House patronage boss, and personnel management adviser in one person—John W. Macy, Jr. In its Civil Service Reform Act of 1978, however, Congress specified that the first two of that threesome shall never be combined again.[34]

CHIEF OF STAFF

The most significant innovation that President Eisenhower brought to the organization of the American presidency was the office of Chief of Staff.

The modern White House, no matter how well lubricated by informal relationships, is a precisely organized assemblage of some twenty principal offices or functions.[35] Fourteen help the president handle rather specific areas of policy or operations: national security, domestic affairs, counsel, legislative affairs, political affairs, intergovernmental affairs, communications, press secretary, public liaison, speechwriting and research, scheduling, presidential personnel, advance and ad hoc "czars." Two others are less directly controlled by the president but are major players in the White House environment: the vice president and the first lady. These sixteen offices are not only distinct in duties but extremely protective of turf; each proudly serves the president in its separate domain.

In the Eisenhower White House the fourteen were more like ten: the vice president was not physically part of the immediate White House environment, and the first lady, unlike some of her successors, was not a major White House policy participant. Even in the Eisenhower years, however, that broad variety of functions and offices was already present, and, as we have seen in the preceding pages, there was an impressive number of individual "czars." There was specialization, and there was turf.

In Ike's own words: "The White House Staff, operating under approved policies, is responsible for these and other classes of duties. Obviously, to be successful the staff must be coordinated within itself by a responsible head."[36]

Who coordinates? Who schedules the work assignments? Who makes sure that memoranda on the same subject reach the Oval Office at the same time, and in time to prepare the president for his decision deadlines? Who insists that these proud, brainy individualists talk to each other, sharpening their policy disagreements while smoothing down their *ad hominem* edges? Whose antennae are everywhere in the White House to identify next week's problems while keeping today's manageable?

The president absolutely requires that such a magic man be at the White House center—not the man in the center of the Oval Office (it was Eisenhower who asked "Must I be my own Sergeant-Major?"), but right next door.

Eisenhower specified the title "The Assistant to the President" and named his choice: former New Hampshire governor Sherman Adams.

Many other authors (including Adams himself) wrote about the work of this first Chief of Staff over the five years and eight months of his service; the author has no intent to duplicate that extensive record. Adams had Cabinet status (i.e., he sat at the table during meetings) although he spoke only when a query was addressed to him. His actual duties were not as comprehensive as those of the more recent Regan, Sununu, and Skinner: he concentrated on domestic affairs and spent a heavy slice of his time on patronage. He left most of the legislative liaison business to his deputy, General Persons, and although he could attend NSC meetings whenever he wished, he left most of the coordination duties in national security affairs to Generals Cutler and Goodpaster.

Adams made the decisions as to the Cabinet agenda, and so accurate was his judgment about what were the president's priorities that never once in the author's years in that room did Ike question the agenda. When he was sure of the president's wishes, Adams would often take it upon himself to convey the bad news or the negative answer to the disappointed petitioners. Thus grew his reputation as the "abominable 'no'-man." Outsiders were as misled about the Chief of Staff as they were about the secretariat system. When Adams resigned in the fall of 1958, General Persons took over his duties.

Kennedy and Johnson avoided designating any of their personal officers as a Chief of Staff; Carter held off naming one until his associates pointedly demonstrated to him what a mess his White House system had become (and then he designated a person not well suited to the job).[37]

Today the Chief of Staff position is recognized as an indispensable control point for the coordination of the work of the modern White House. The staff secretary, the Cabinet secretary, and the president's personal assistant are his principal allies—the four together forming a centripetal nexus amidst the very centrifugal universe of the Cabinet and its departments and agencies. It is to Dwight Eisenhower and to Sherman Adams that the nation owes this debt of innovation: helping to bring orderly administration to the very apex of government.

TELEVISION AT PRESS CONFERENCES

Ike had Press Secretary Jim Hagerty tell the press in 1953 that he was considering permitting television cameras into his press conferences. The inauguration of his Eisenhower *glasnost* came by stages. In a press conference of March 10, 1954, Ike answered a question put to him by Roscoe Drummond of the *New York Herald Tribune*, and in his response to the reporter's followup request that his answer be on the record, he promised Drummond that he would authorize the transcript to be released, if Hagerty would clean up any "errors of grammar." The transcript was released, and a new era in White House news conferences had begun.

In 1955 Eisenhower made good on his promise to permit TV cameras into the press conferences—and a second new era in the president-press dialogue had its inception. In all, Eisenhower gave 193 press conferences. Every succeeding president has adopted Ike's innovation; now the whole nation watches while the president is grilled by the fourth estate.

THE FIRST BLACK WHITE HOUSE STAFF OFFICER

In August 1952, E. Frederic Morrow, a public affairs staff officer at CBS, signed on as a consultant in the Eisenhower presidential campaign. Following the election, Sherman Adams informed Morrow that he and the president wanted him to join the new administration in Washington—in fact, to be a member of the White House staff.

As Morrow recounts in his book, the recruitment process turned out to be frustrating and roundabout.[38] His first appointment was in the Department of Commerce; it was not until July 2, 1955, that the initial promise was finally kept and Morrow was made Administrative Officer for Special Projects on the White House staff. Cause for the delay: nobody could come up with a definite answer to the question "what would Morrow do on the White House staff?"

Morrow was in fact given a series of increasingly sensitive responsibilities: at first such administrative chores as security in the Executive Office Building, later much travelling and speaking to both white and black groups, and finally Adams designated Morrow to be the successor to Max Rabb in handling civil rights issues and correspondence.

Morrow's diary-style book is candid in describing the up-and-down experiences he had in the White House: on some occasions feeling exhilarated at small victories and breakthroughs, more frequently ending up discouraged at the glacial pace of progress on civil rights issues. Morrow suffered the well-known and inevitable tensions of a White House public liaison official who tries to balance the pressures from the advocacy groups to which he feels close with defending the president's policies that those same groups consider insufficient. Morrow even endured personal slights within the White House itself.

But he was there, and stayed there—a new symbol in some old territory. His book ends: "I am grateful to President Eisenhower for giving me the privilege and honor of aspiring beyond the former rigid boundaries of caste and class and permitting me to serve in a position formerly beyond the ken of an Afro-American. No other job, situation, period, honor or distinction I ever have will be quite like it."[39]

THE WHITE HOUSE STAFF BOOK

By the end of an administration, a White House staff is more than an ad hoc assemblage of men and women. They are a family, a brotherhood/sisterhood, the surviving soldiers who fought the good fight.

The Eisenhower staff embodied this camaraderie in one extra enterprise that the author believes is unique in the history of the modern White House: a yearbook of their time together, entitled *White House Staff Book, 1953–1961*. Between plain, gray covers, its 170 pages contain pictures and brief biographies of all the staff members who served; the names of all the White House secretaries; pictures of all the senior career support staff, the chauffeurs, the mess-waiters, the Columbine crew; a chronicle of the major events of the eight Eisenhower years; and a color reprint of a National Geographic feature story on the inside of the mansion and its famous rooms.

Two staff members (Frederic E. Fox and James M. Lambie, Jr.) put the *White House Staff Book* together, and every Eisenhower staff veteran treasures his numbered copy. That he authorized the time and funds to prepare the booklet is but another tribute to the graciousness and courtesy that Eisenhower showed to the men and women who served him loyally and well.

On the opening page of the book is a quotation from Ike's own Class of 1915 West Point Yearbook:

If, in the years to come, the perusal of these pages will serve to bridge the gap between us and the past, and to bring to mind pleasant reminiscences, made mellow by the magic touch of time, of our cadet days; if this humble result of our efforts will, when the age of retirement is reached, be the key in an oft-visited vault of memory, then our expectations will be exceeded and we shall be content.[40]

* * * * * * * *

The modern White House was created during the quarter-century following World War II. By 1970 it had evolved to the large and sophisticated structure it constitutes today. Its staff members change, not just every four years but constantly; its operational style of course adapts to fit the preferences of each president. But since 1970, the elements, functions, and offices of the contemporary White House have been kept in place quite similarly from president to president—not out of any statutory obligation but because they in fact meet the actual needs of today's chief executive.

Dwight D. Eisenhower, in the Oval Office from 1953 to 1961—the middle eight years of that quarter-century—was perhaps the president who did the most to shape the structure of the modern White House. On the one hand, he inaugurated an impressive number of specialized units and officers; on the other, he compensated for the resulting internal pluralism by introducing mechanisms of coordination and order. The centrifugal forces of his variegated White House family he harnessed together by the centripetal magnetism from twin Secretariats and from a tough Chief of Staff.

Most of his innovations, furthermore, have endured—compelling evidence that his organizational good sense has matched the personal popularity the nation has accorded him ever since.

NOTES

1. Dwight D. Eisenhower, *Crusade in Europe* (Garden City, N.Y.: Doubleday and Company, 1948), 75.

2. See Bradley H. Patterson, Jr., *Ring of Power: The White House Staff and Its Expanding Role in Government* (New York: Basic Books, 1988).

3. George M. Elsey, interview with the author, Washington, D.C., July 10, 1986.

4. U.S. Congress, "Report on the General Management of the Executive Branch," *Commission on the Organization of the Executive Branch of the Government*, 83rd Congress, First Session, 1949.

5. James S. Lay, Jr., *An Organizational History of the National Security Council*, attachment to Mr. Lay's letter of June 30, 1960, to J. Kenneth Mansfield, Staff Director of the Senate Subcommittee on National Policy Machinery, Washington, D.C., 33–34.

6. Commission on Intergovernmental Relations, *A Report to the President for Transmittal to the Congress* (Washington, D.C.: U.S. Government Printing Office, 1955), 87.

7. Rockefeller had first come into government in 1940 and in 1953 was also serving as Under Secretary of the Department of Health, Education and Welfare; in 1955 he was made Special Assistant to the president. Arthur S. Flemming entered government in July 1939 as a member of the U.S. Civil Service Commission. Eisenhower borrowed him from Ohio Wesleyan University, where he was president, to make him director of the Office of Defense Mobilization in the Executive Office of the president, and later elevated him to the position of Secretary of Health, Education and Welfare.

8. Milton S. Eisenhower, *The President Is Calling* (Garden City, N.Y.: Doubleday, 1974), 261.

9. U.S. Congress, "Report on the General Management of the Executive Branch," 22–23.

10. Dwight D. Eisenhower, *The White House Years: Mandate for Change, 1953–1956* (Garden City, N.Y.: Doubleday, 1963), 117.

11. Dwight D. Eisenhower, memorandum to the Secretary of War, "A System of Coordination in the Executive Branch of Government," January 8, 1946 (author's personal collection).

12. Vannevar Bush and Oscar Cox, memorandum to President Truman, "A Presidential and Cabinet Staff," December 19, 1946 (author's personal collection).

13. Don K. Price, memorandum to Herbert Hoover, "Origins of the 'Cabinet Secretariat' Idea," December 31, 1947, 2–3 (author's personal collection).

It is interesting to note that this warning came at the very time President Truman signed the National Security Act, which, in its creation of the National Security Council, was, frankly, a legislative specification of presidential decision making.

14. The text of this presentation and the set of 30″ × 40″ charts used to accompany it are now at the Eisenhower Library.

15. Upon his appointment as assistant Cabinet secretary, it was one of the author's

first assignments, in the fall of 1954, to take these charts and booklets around to those senior staff meetings and to repeat the same presentation that had been given to the president in August. These presentations, plus Ike's thoroughgoing support of the staff secretariat/Cabinet secretariat system, gave a boost to the idea of creating an executive secretariat at the top level within each of the respective agencies. Today this institutional device has been installed in all of the Cabinet departments.

16. Richard E. Neustadt, *Presidential Power* (New York: John Wiley and Sons, 1960), 158, 159.

17. Fred I. Greenstein, *The Hidden-Hand Presidency: Eisenhower as Leader* (New York: Basic Books, 1982).

18. Carter L. Burgess and W. K. Scott, "A Staff Plan for the President," brochure to accompany a presentation to President Eisenhower, April 23, 1956, 36 (author's personal collection).

19. Patterson, *Ring of Power*.

20. Albert P. Toner, OH 491, 67, Dwight D. Eisenhower Library (DDEL), Abilene, Kan. Used with permission.

21. Draft "Special Staff Note," January 14, 1961, "Review of Operations" file, DDEL.

22. Dwight D. Eisenhower, Address to the Nation, November 7, 1957, *Public Papers of the President, Dwight D. Eisenhower, 1957* (Washington, D.C.: U.S. Government Printing Office, 1960), 796.

23. James R. Killian, Jr., *Sputnik, Scientists and Eisenhower: A Memoir of the First Special Assistant to the President for Science and Technology* (Cambridge, Mass.: MIT Press, 1977), 32.

24. *Ibid.*, 31.

25. Elwood R. Quesada, oral interview with the author, 1986.

26. Eisenhower, Address to the Nation, 390–91.

27. Stephen E. Ambrose, *Eisenhower: The President* (New York: Simon and Schuster, 1984), 261.

28. *Ibid.*, 323.

29. Sherman Adams, *First-hand Report: The Story of the Eisenhower Administration* (New York: Harper and Brothers, 1961), 390.

30. *Ibid.*

31. Dwight D. Eisenhower, *Public Papers of the President, 1954* (Washington, D.C.: U.S. Government Printing Office, 1960), 1097.

32. Ambrose, *Eisenhower: The President*, 400.

33. The quotation is from paragraph (d) of the Executive Order. It is significant to note that in the phrase "to improve steadily all personnel management systems," the limiting adjective "civilian," which had appeared between the words "all" and "personnel" in Executive Order 10452 of 1953 was now being deleted.

34. 5 USC 1102, Public Law 95–454, Title II, 201(a), October 13, 1978.

35. See Patterson, *Ring of Power*.

36. Eisenhower, *Public Papers of the President, 1954*, 88.

37. See Patterson, *Ring of Power*, 302.

38. E. Frederic Morrow, *Black Man in the White House* (New York: Coward-McCann, 1963).

39. *Ibid.*, 302.

40. *White House Staff Book, 1953–1961*, author's personal collection.

4

Eisenhower and the Southern Federal Judiciary: The Soboloff Nomination

Michael Mayer

In the last decade or so, historians have found much to admire in the presidency of Dwight Eisenhower.[1] The thirty-fourth president's record on civil rights, however, continues to receive less credit than it is due.[2] While Eisenhower was no drum major for civil rights, his record compares favorably with that of his immediate predecessor and successor. Eisenhower attempted to end discrimination in federal employment and in employment by federal contractors, took significant steps toward ending segregation in Washington, D.C., began to make the desegregation of the armed forces a reality, and named unprecedented numbers of blacks to positions in the executive branch. In addition, his administration obtained passage of the first civil rights legislation since Reconstruction. Those achievements notwithstanding, Eisenhower's appointments to the federal judiciary in the states most affected by the *Brown v. Board of Education of Topeka* decision constituted his greatest contribution to the cause of civil rights. Especially when compared with comparable appointments of Harry Truman and John Kennedy, Eisenhower's accomplishment stands out in dramatic relief. The moderates and liberals he appointed to the Fourth and Fifth Circuit Courts of Appeal oversaw the dismantling of the system of segregation in the south. On the other hand, Eisenhower was nothing if not a gradualist, which is perhaps why he made his greatest contribution through the appointment of judges. By its very nature, as he well knew, the legal process is a slow one.

In evaluating the civil rights records of federal judges, most historians give the judges Eisenhower appointed to the Fourth and Fifth Circuits high marks. Eisenhower appointed Elbert Parr Tuttle, Warren L. Jones, John R. Brown, John Minor Wisdom, and Ben Cameron to the Fifth Circuit, which covered Georgia,

Alabama, Mississippi, Florida, Louisiana, and Texas. With the notable exception of Cameron, all established fine records on civil rights. Eisenhower named Simon E. Sobeloff, Clement F. Haynsworth, and Herbert S. Boreman to the Fourth Circuit, which comprised Maryland, Virginia, West Virginia, North Carolina, and South Carolina. Eisenhower's appointments to the Fourth Circuit all voted consistently to end segregation. Years later, when Richard Nixon nominated him to the Supreme Court, Haynsworth would come under fire from the NAACP and liberals; but Haynsworth voted repeatedly in the late 1950s and early 1960s for desegregation. Indeed, several southern senators opposed his nomination precisely because he was not a segregationist. As the 1960s progressed and the issue became integration, rather than desegregation, his votes became more conservative. Even then, his position had not changed; the context had.[3]

Some historians have dismissed Eisenhower's appointments of liberals to the bench as accidents—the unexpected results of an inept and bungling presidency. Others have argued that the appointments resulted almost incidentally because Eisenhower appointed Republicans, who, almost by definition in the south of the 1950s, were outside the mainstream.[4] Still others have contended that the appointments were the work of Attorney General Herbert Brownell and that Eisenhower paid little attention to nominees to the federal bench. None of these analyses gives adequate credit to Eisenhower, who in fact paid careful attention to the appointment of federal judges.

Rayman Solomon proposed that presidential administrations are motivated by three considerations in the appointment of federal judges: patronage, policy, and professionalism.[5] According to his model, while each of these factors influences most, if not all, administrations, one factor tends to predominate in the approach of a given administration to making judicial appointments. There can be little doubt that the Eisenhower administration placed primary emphasis on professionalism. Ultimate responsibility for submitting lists of nominees to the president belonged to the attorneys general, Herbert Brownell (1953–1957) and William Rogers (1957–1961). However, developing lists and preliminary screening of potential nominees were the responsibilities of the deputy attorney general. Rogers held this post from 1953 to 1957 and was succeeded by Lawrence Walsh. These men were highly professional lawyers, and they sought out the most highly qualified lawyers and judges for appointment to the federal bench. Moreover, Eisenhower himself placed great faith in professional values. One reflection of this attitude was the weight given to the recommendations of the American Bar Association.[6] It should be noted that the great majority of the Eisenhower administration's appointments went to Republicans, at least in part because twenty years of Democratic rule prior to Eisenhower's administration meant that over 80 percent of federal judges were Democrats in 1952.[7] Nevertheless, professional qualifications dominated the Eisenhower administration's criteria for judges at all levels.

Eisenhower demonstrated his interest in judicial appointments in a memo he sent to Rogers not long after the latter became attorney general. In that memo

Eisenhower affirmed his deep personal commitment to the appointment of federal judges. He also made it clear to Rogers that it was his habit to carefully look over judicial nominations, and he urged Rogers to meet with him before any nominations were sent to the White House for his official approval.[8]

While policy issues took a back seat to professional concerns, Eisenhower and his aides in the Justice Department were well aware of the implications of their appointments to the federal judiciary in the south.[9] In this context, Eisenhower's appointments to the Fourth and Fifth Circuit Courts stand in stark contrast to Truman's and Kennedy's. Several historians and political scientists have argued that because Eisenhower was a Republican and was less beholden to southern Democrats, he could make such appointments with less political cost; but the Democrats controlled Congress for the last six years of Eisenhower's presidency, and that meant that the obstructionist southerners who headed committees while Kennedy was president held the same posts during Eisenhower's administration. Their power to obstruct was no less great during Eisenhower's presidency than it was during Kennedy's. Moreover, Eisenhower made significant inroads in the south in the election of 1952; Allan Shivers of Texas, Robert F. Kennon of Louisiana, and James F. Byrnes of South Carolina, among other leading southern Democrats, had supported Eisenhower in 1952.[10] Eisenhower carried Texas, Tennessee, Virginia, and Florida and came close in Louisiana.[11] Democrats had no monopoly on risking the loss of political support by appointing liberal federal judges to the southern circuits.

Nothing so well demonstrated both Eisenhower's awareness and intent, as well as the political cost he was willing to pay to put liberals on the appellate bench, as the nomination of his solicitor general, Simon E. Sobeloff, to sit on the Fourth Circuit Court of Appeals. An outspoken and active opponent of racial inequality, Sobeloff had opposed segregation and exclusion of blacks from public housing in the 1930s and testified before the Senate Judiciary Committee in behalf of a federal antilynching bill in 1933. He continued his opposition to segregation throughout the 1940s and into the 1950s. In addition, Sobeloff had argued the government's case on the implementation of the school segregation cases. In doing so, he had pushed for a somewhat stronger position than the government eventually took. Eisenhower could not have been unaware of Sobeloff's position; the president himself had toned down Sobeloff's draft of the government's brief.[12]

Thus, it was with full knowledge of Sobeloff's position that, on July 14, 1955, Eisenhower nominated him to succeed Morris A. Soper.[13] Almost immediately, southerners let out a rebel yell of opposition. As was the case with the Civil War, the first sign of trouble came from South Carolina. Senator Strom Thurmond wasted no time in announcing his opposition to Sobeloff's appointment. A ''brief review'' of Sobeloff's record convinced Thurmond that the solicitor general ''could not sit in impartial judgment as a member of the court which may review cases involving the constitutional rights of the States. He has been a strong advocate of integration of the races in the public schools.'' The nomination demonstrated, according to Thurmond, that the administration was "more interested in making political appeals to the bloc votes of minority groups than in adherence to constitutional government."[14] South Carolina's governor, George Bell Timmerman, called the nomination "political chicanery" and branded the appointment "an insult to the nation's intelligence and a slap in the face of the South." "Sobeloff," Timmerman explained, "is an outspoken integrationist." To support his assertion, Timmerman pointed out that Sobeloff had "argued for the administration in favor of mixing the races in the public schools of the South." Timmerman had another complaint as well. Eisenhower had failed to follow the custom of rotating appointments between the states of the Fourth Circuit. Under the custom of rotation, he argued, the appointment should have gone to South Carolina, and Sobeloff was from Maryland. In making this appointment, claimed Timmerman, Eisenhower "has showed complete disregard for established custom and is playing cheap politics with the lives of little children." "The administration," he charged, "has ordained another high priest to preside at the sacrificial offering of the South on the political altar in the effort to convert into the Republican camp the bloc support of ethnic groups in the large industrial cities."[15]

Outside the south, editorial opinion was overwhelmingly and enthusiastically favorable to the nomination of Sobeloff. The *Washington Post* wrote that Sobeloff's appointment would "serve to return to the bench a wise and seasoned judge of the highest caliber; unhappily, it will serve also to take from the Department of Justice a moderating and enlightening influence there."[16] The latter comment referred to Sobeloff's refusal to argue the government's case or to sign the government's brief in a case involving the firing of John Peters under the Loyalty Program. Although the Peters case arose under the Truman administration's Loyalty Program, it reached the Supreme Court after the Eisenhower administration had taken office. Sobeloff objected to procedures that had not allowed Peters to confront or even to know the identity of his accusers. The Supreme Court later decided in favor of Peters. In Sobeloff's own Baltimore, the *Sun* enthused that the nomination was "singularly appropriate."[17] Even in Missouri, another border state, the *St. Louis Post-Dispatch* lauded the nomination in an editorial titled "Splendid Choice for the Bench."[18] Black newspapers also welcomed the nomination. The *Washington Afro-American* praised the nominee as "having one of the best minds in the legal profession" and predicted that "he will be in line as an associate justice of the U.S. Supreme Court."[19]

In reality, southern opposition to the nomination was based exclusively on Sobeloff's publicly stated opposition to segregation. Still, the issue of rotation was a real one. South Carolina had not had a representative on the Fourth Circuit for thirty years. However, South Carolina's legal and political elite had damaged themselves by bickering over possible candidates. Even the so-called Independent Democrats (who had generally supported Eisenhower) could not agree on a candidate. Thurmond fervently supported Robert McC. Figg of Charleston, who had represented the Clarendon County school district in *Brown v. Board of Education* and was his closest political and personal ally. Curiously, while Thurmond maintained that Sobeloff's participation in *Brown II* disqualified the solicitor general for the nomination, Thurmond had no reservation about putting forward Figg, who had participated in the same case on the other side. James Byrnes, another Eisenhower supporter, endorsed David Robinson of Columbia.

Divided loyalties constituted only part of the problem. The Eisenhower administration had difficulty finding a qualified candidate in South Carolina who would enforce the law as stated by the Supreme Court in the *Brown* decision.[20]

South Carolina's other senator, Olin D. Johnston, was a "Regular Democrat" and inveterate foe of the administration. The nomination of Sobeloff "sincerely disappointed" him, but he added that he "did not expect much more from the present administration." He was nonetheless "very sorry" to see the president "choose the man who helped present the Justice Department segregation case before the Supreme Court." Several observers speculated that Old Line Democrats, and Johnston in particular, would benefit politically from the appointment. Johnston was up for reelection in 1956 and, before the Sobeloff nomination, seemed to be in trouble. He had stumped the state in 1954 for Edgar Brown, whom Thurmond had defeated overwhelmingly. Since then, Johnston had been running hard, attacking the administration's farm program and its "liberal foreign trade program." The nomination of Sobeloff, on top of the Supreme Court's decision on segregation, gave Johnston "that much more ammunition to use against the Eisenhower Democrats in 1956." Papers loyal to the Democratic Party played up the threat that Sobeloff's elevation to the circuit court was a step toward nominating him to the Supreme Court. That several northern papers speculated about Sobeloff's chances for the Supreme Court added fuel to the fire.[21]

Old Line Democrats throughout South Carolina joined in Johnston's assault. In a vituperative editorial, the *Anderson* (South Carolina) *Independent* attacked "Brynes, Thurmond, and Company," who had supported the Republican ticket in 1952. Adopting an I-told-you-so attitude, the editorial chided: "We said the Republican Party was 'black' when it was founded; that if Eisenhower were elected and the Republicans took over Washington, then it would be Katie-bar-the-door." As incontrovertible proof of the evil intentions of the Republicans, the paper noted that "it is significant that Ike rewarded Sobeloff in the full knowledge of how he stands on integrating the races. Sobeloff is for mixing 'em, whenever and wherever." The editorial gloated that, even after backing Eisenhower, Byrnes and Thurmond did not have enough influence with the administration to block Sobeloff's nomination.[22]

The Senate Judiciary Committee named a subcommittee consisting of John McClellan (D., Ark.), Estes Kefauver (D., Tenn.), and Herman Welker (R., Idaho) to examine the nomination; hearings were scheduled for July 26. In the meantime, the Virginia League, a statewide prosegregation organization, sent letters to all members of the Judiciary Committee opposing the nomination. Sobeloff, they argued, was "a strong advocate of racial integration and, possibly, mongrelization—a philosophy which . . . can destroy this republic."[23]

Johnston undertook what would be the most determined opposition to Sobeloff's confirmation. He proclaimed that judges who would sit on segregation cases "should be qualified and unbiased." "Sobeloff," he contended, "has already indicated his views on this subject, and therefore, in my opinion, is not qualified."[24]

Maryland's senators, John Marshall Butler and J. Glenn Beall, both Republicans, rallied to Sobeloff's defense. Butler called the nominee "eminently qualified" and predicted that there would not be enough opposition to block confirmation. Beall was equally vigorous in support of the nominee. In fact, Sobeloff's qualifications were beyond credible doubt. He had served with distinction as deputy city solicitor and city solicitor of Baltimore, built a highly successful private practice, served as chief judge of Maryland's Court of Appeals (the state's highest court), and, at the time of his nomination, was solicitor general of the United States.[25]

If the Sobeloff nomination revived Johnston's flagging political fortunes, it presented Thurmond with an awkward political problem. He had won the election in 1954 as a write-in candidate, and, during that campaign, he had promised to resign in 1956 and run in the Democratic primary to fill his vacated seat. Now he faced reelection, and the Regular Democrats could criticize him for bolting from the Democratic Party and, in doing so, contributing to the nomination of Sobeloff. On July 17, 1956, he released a "Special Segregation Statement" in which he declared that recent decisions of the Supreme Court (meaning *Brown*) "hinged on the testimony of sociologists and psychologists." In a thinly veiled reference to the Sobeloff nomination, he chastised the administration's actions. "Even on new appointments to the courts, which require Senate confirmation," he warned ominously, "there is little apparent concern over whether the new members of the courts will follow the Constitution instead of the psychology books."[26]

James Eastland and Johnston sent a joint letter to McClellan, chairman of the subcommittee reviewing the nomination, on July 26. In it, they asked for "a reasonable length of time" to make "a more careful and thorough investigation into Sobeloff's qualifications." The two southern senators claimed to be "engaged in a study" of "the recent Peters case and other aspects of his [Sobeloff's] public record and utterances." The subcommittee granted an indefinite postponement. Johnston crowed: "As far as I'm concerned, Sobeloff will not be confirmed this year." The administration, however, continued to press for a hearing and confirmation. When asked about the postponement in a press conference, Eisenhower defended his choice of Sobeloff. "I thought" said the president, "he was an excellent appointment to the court."[27]

Eastland desperately searched for an issue other than segregation on which to oppose the nomination. Toward that end, his staff told reporters that Sobeloff believed in the usurpation of power by the courts. They cited a speech Sobeloff had given to the Judicial Conference of the Fourth Circuit in 1954, in which he had remarked that the Supreme Court was often the final formulator of public policy.[28] This strategy suffered a severe blow when John Parker, chief judge of the Fourth Circuit Court of Appeals, wrote a letter to the chairman of the Judiciary Committee, Harley Kilgore (D., W. Va.), requesting that the Judiciary Committee quickly confirm Sobeloff. Parker scoffed at the criticism of Sobeloff's remark about the role of the Supreme Court. Sobeloff's idea, wrote Parker, "has been recognized so long that it never occurred to me there could be any doubt about the matter."[29]

The *Sun* probably spoke for much of the nation when it criticized Eastland and Johnston for their action. The southerners, argued an editorial in the Baltimore paper, were "interested primarily in Mr. Sobeloff's views on the school segregation cases." The editorial compared the procrastination on Sobeloff's nomination with the delay of John Marshall Harlan's appointment to the Supreme Court. In both cases, the "investigations" were "piffling and the delays disgraceful." Above all, noted the *Sun*, the holding action was silly; blocking Sobeloff would not alter the Court's decision in *Brown*.[30]

Nevertheless, by July 28, the administration's attempts to push for hearings on Sobeloff's nomination had collapsed. The press speculated about the possibility of a recess appointment, but the Baltimore papers indicated that Sobeloff probably would not accept one. Congress adjourned with the Sobeloff nomination bottled up in subcommittee. If Sobeloff were to take a place on the court, he would have to be nominated again the next session.[31]

Throughout most of the country, editorial opinion condemned the failure to act on Sobeloff's nomination. The *St. Louis Post-Dispatch* dismissed the charges relating to Sobeloff's speech as "sheer humbug." The real reason southerners opposed Sobeloff, the paper asserted, was his role in the segregation cases.[32] From Washington, the *Post* found Sobeloff's speech "unexceptionable" and pointed out that Parker found nothing in it with which to take exception. The Senate's failure to act on the nomination "worked a serious hardship on the heavily overburdened Fourth Circuit Court," and the only real reason for opposition was Sobeloff's role in *Brown II*.[33] Doris Fleeson's column in the *Washington Star* praised Sobeloff's "wisdom" and added that he was "both learned and humane." She dismissed the criticism of Sobeloff and predicted that Sobeloff would eventually be confirmed; in the meantime, however, the delay worked a hardship on the Fourth Circuit Court, and all of this because Sobeloff had argued the government's case in the implementation of *Brown*.[34]

Even from the south came criticism of the delay. The *Raleigh News and Observer* pointed out that the Fourth Circuit desperately needed the new judge and that even Parker, "who is as much a Southerner as any of the objectors, has testified that he sees nothing objectionable in the speech." The paper bluntly stated that the real reason for opposition was Sobeloff's "views on segregation."[35] The *Charlotte Observer* bemoaned the "logjam" in the federal courts, attacked the tactic of delay, and dismissed charges against Sobeloff as a "thin pretext."[36] Perhaps the most striking comment appeared in the *Washington Afro-American*, which ran a cartoon of Eastland and Thurmond filibustering Uncle Sam over the Sobeloff nomination with the simple caption: "We Don't Like It."[37] The true nature of Eisenhower's appointment and of the opposition to it was lost on no one.

After the Congress adjourned, the political stakes involved in the Sobeloff nomination increased. Eisenhower would now have to send up the nomination to the new session—and in an election year. Several newspapers noted that the nomination would face strong opposition from southern Democrats, including some who had supported Eisenhower.[38] Whatever the political cost, the administration unlimbered its big guns in defense of Sobeloff. Eisenhower made a speech to the American Bar Association in which he said that he would not appoint anyone who would not "serve in the tradition of John Marshall."[39] Brownell addressed a B'nai B'rith dinner honoring Sobeloff and made it clear that Sobeloff would again be nominated for the Fourth Circuit. More than that, his glowing praise of Sobeloff's character and qualifications put the full weight of the administration solidly behind the nomination.[40]

Opposition to the nomination was gearing up as well. Olin Johnston gave a talk to the Optimist Club in Rock Hill, South Carolina, in which he blasted the administration and bragged that, as a member of the Judiciary Committee, he had managed to block the Sobeloff nomination. To the discomfort of pro-Eisenhower Democrats, he charged that the administration had not been satisfied with the *Brown* decision; it had to "go one better" by nominating Sobeloff to the appellate court.[41]

Eisenhower resubmitted Sobeloff's name on January 12, 1956, and Johnston immediately announced his opposition. The senator from South Carolina asked for the appointment of a special subcommittee of the Judiciary Committee to look into Sobeloff's qualifications. Having been burned the previous session for his crude, segregationist opposition to Sobeloff, Johnston this time made no mention of integration. He charged that Sobeloff had been guilty of a conflict of interest in a case involving the failure of the Baltimore Trust Company in 1934.[42]

Matters became more complicated when Judge Armistead Dobie of the Fourth Circuit announced his qualified retirement on January 20, leaving Parker as the only active judge on the court.[43] In one sense, Dobie's announcement might have served to eliminate one objection to Sobeloff's confirmation. Now South Carolina could have its appointment.[44] The *Columbia* (South Carolina) *State* bitterly noted that it had been South Carolina's turn when Soper retired but that Eisenhower had picked Sobeloff "on the recommendation of Brownell et al." With a second opening on the Fourth Circuit, however, "it certainly should be South Carolina's turn."[45]

However, South Carolina's Democrats continued to bicker, this time over possibilities to replace Dobie, and several observers speculated that Virginia's congressional delegation, which was solidly united behind District Court Judge Albert V. Bryan, might steal the appointment.[46] Further complicating the issue, Thurmond, facing an election, was desperate to get something from the administration. In late February, Thurmond declared that he had written directly to Eisenhower and that Brownell had promised the next appointment to South Carolina.[47]

The Sobeloff nomination received what appeared to be a fatal blow on February 28, 1956, when Senator Harley M. Kilgore, chairman of the Judiciary Committee, died. With Kilgore's death, Eastland became the ranking Democrat on the Judiciary Committee and was thus in line for the chairmanship. One of the most outspoken critics of integration, the *Brown* decision, and Sobeloff, Eastland now appeared to be in a position to block approval of Sobeloff's nomination. To no avail, the NAACP and Americans for Democratic Action (ADA) opposed Eastland; and Senators Wayne Morse of Oregon and Herbert Lehman of New York led a bitter fight on the Senate floor, during which Lehman called Eastland "a symbol of racism in America." Liberals bitterly denounced the Senate's seniority system, even as the Senate voted to confirm Eastland's inevitable succession on March 2, 1956. The elevation of Eastland seemed to doom Sobeloff's prospects for confirmation.[48]

Fortunately for the administration, the subcommittee of the Judiciary Committee reviewing the nomination had already been chosen before Kilgore's death. Moreover, the seniority system did not always work to the southerners' advantage. Matthew Neely of West Virginia took the seat on the Judiciary Committee left empty by Kilgore's death, frustrating Sam Ervin's attempt to fill the vacancy. Neely got the position because he had more seniority than Ervin.[49]

The Republican Policy Committee met on March 6, 1956, and agreed to take up the Sobeloff nomination with Eastland but could come up with no suggestions for forcing action on the nomination.[50] By the end of the month, the nomination was still stuck in the subcommittee, and hearings had not even been scheduled.

Things seemed to look up for the nomination in early April. The *New York Times* predicted confirmation soon after the session began, and Drew Pearson wrote that Lyndon B. Johnson had approached Eastland and told him that, for the sake of the Democratic Party, Sobeloff must be confirmed. According to Pearson, Eastland had agreed, provided that the confirmation would not damage his friend Johnston's chances for reelection. Not long after the meeting, State Senator John Taylor withdrew from the race against Johnston. Pearson confidently, and erroneously, predicted that there would be no more opposition to the nominee in the Judiciary Committee.[51] Johnston responded to Pearson's column by announcing that he remained as opposed as ever to Sobeloff.[52]

Finally, on April 23, the new subcommittee, chaired by Joseph C. O'Mahoney (D., Wyo.) and consisting of Thomas C. Hennings (D., Mo.), John L. McClellan (D., Ark.), Arthur V. Watkins (R., Utah), and Herman Welker (R., Idaho), announced that hearings on the Sobeloff nomination would be held on May 3.[53] Moreover, pressure was building on the Judiciary Committee to act. Senator

Prescott Bush, a Republican from Connecticut and father of a future president, called the delay on the nomination "an affront to President Eisenhower and those who believe with him in civil rights."[54] Editorials all over the country welcomed the hearings as long overdue.[55]

Any celebrations were premature. The long-awaited hearings were postponed again, this time because of the death of Senator Alben Barkley.[56] Hearings finally began on May 5, largely because of intense pressure brought by the administration and Republican leaders in the Senate as well as Democratic leaders who, as the *Columbia* (South Carolina) *State* put it, "are afraid the Democratic party will lose some liberal support if Sobeloff's nomination is not acted on soon."[57] The hearings lasted five hours. Olin Johnston opened the testimony with an attack on Sobeloff's role in the investigation of the failure of the Baltimore Trust Company during the Great Depression. Both Maryland senators, the leaders of the bar of Baltimore and Maryland, a former Democratic senator from Maryland (who had been involved with the liquidation of the Baltimore Trust Company), and the court-appointed receiver of the company all testified on Sobeloff's behalf. In addition, all three of the sitting judges on the Fourth Circuit testified in support of the nomination.

The charges about conflict of interest proved baseless. The highlight of the hearing came when a seventy-three-year-old, retired, self-described real estate dealer named Charles Shankroff testified in support of Johnston's charges. It turned out that Shankroff was not a lawyer, or even a licensed real estate broker. He was known for hanging around lower courts and attempting to stir up litigation. He was, in short, a troublemaker and something of a crank. O'Mahoney ruled his testimony irrelevant and unsupported. Shankroff persisted, and O'Mahoney ordered him off the stand.[58]

In addition to Shankroff, a string of segregationists testified against the nomination. In spite of the ugly nature of their message, some of the racists gave the proceedings a note of levity, if unintentionally. William Stephenson, a former shipyard clerk who had become president of the Virginia League, asked the Senate to "deliver us from a man with such foreign ideas."[59] He then raised the issue of the Peters case. When O'Mahoney asked him if he knew how the Supreme Court decided that case, Stephenson had to admit that he did not. Bruce Dunston, a real estate agent from Richmond, summed up their argument when he said, "I am proud of my heritage of race," and Sobeloff "expresses the judgment for the forced mixture of races," which "does not assure the existence of the white race." In addition, Sobeloff's approval of "the illegal decision of the Supreme Court" demonstrated that he did not believe in constitutional law.[60] The most impressive testimony against Sobeloff came from O. L. Warr, a farmer from Darlington, South Carolina, and a member of the Citizens Council. He said that he did not question Sobeloff's ability or integrity, but that the nominee's views were so different from those of the people of the Fourth Circuit as to disqualify him. His very nomination was a "contemptuous insult and a gratuitous provocation.'' Sobeloff, according to Warr, was "the man most prominently associated in our minds with the overthrow of our way of life.''[61]

The hearings made absolutely clear the basis for opposition to the nomination; Sobeloff was a threat to segregation. An editorial in the *Washington Post* characterized the testimony against Sobeloff as "a little sputter of prejudice." Witnesses had produced "nothing discreditable in his record.''[62] After examining the testimony, the *St. Louis Post-Dispatch* found no basis for opposing the nomination and urged the Judiciary Committee to act promptly and favorably. Whether or not it did so would be "the first important test of the chairmanship of Senator James O. Eastland.''[63]

O'Mahoney announced on May 17 that the subcommittee had "informally approved" of the Sobeloff nomination. On the same day, however, Johnston launched a verbal attack against Sobeloff on the floor of the Senate and criticized O'Mahoney for cutting off Shankroff. He urged the Judiciary Committee to investigate further Shankroff's charges.[64]

Without any prior announcement, the subcommittee held further hearings on May 21. The hearing was decided on in the meeting of the Judiciary Committee that immediately preceded it. Sam Ervin of North Carolina insisted on testifying before the subcommittee, and he led the charge for the opposition. Ervin testified endlessly about how recent decisions of the Supreme Court usurped the power of the states. O'Mahoney finally asked what any of this had to do with the nomination before the subcommittee, to which Ervin replied that Sobeloff's public statements indicated that his thinking was in line with the Court's. It was a curious argument for a man who fancied himself a constitutional lawyer: Sobeloff was unqualified to sit on an appellate court because he agreed with the decisions of the Supreme Court. O'Mahoney tried to force an immediate vote on the nomination, but he encountered determined obstruction from the southerners. Eastland moved to postpone further hearings for a month. When that failed, Johnston attempted to win delay by objecting to all proposed times for scheduling more hearings. O'Mahoney finally settled matters by announcing that the subcommittee would meet the following morning.[65]

After the hearings on May 22, at which Sobeloff deftly answered Ervin's charges, O'Mahoney, Watkins, and Hennings declared in favor of Sobeloff's confirmation. McClellan and Welker declined to make their intentions known; although, from his questioning, McClellan obviously did not favor the nomination. Welker had his own reasons to be displeased with Sobeloff. An inveterate anticommunist, Welker did not like Sobeloff's role in the Peters case or his liberal views in general.[66]

The administration continued its unequivocal support of the nomination. At a press conference the day after the hearings, Eisenhower expressed his hope that the Senate would confirm Sobeloff "as rapidly as possible" and characterized the nomination as "a fine appointment to the court.''[67]

Later that week, on May 25, the subcommittee voted three to none in favor of Sobeloff. Hennings made the motion and was supported by O'Mahoney and Watkins. McClellan and Welker did not vote. Now, however, the nomination faced an even greater hurdle in the full Judiciary Committee, where, as chairman, Eastland presented a formidable obstacle. Johnston also sat on the Judiciary Committee, and upon learning of the subcommittee's vote, Johnston promised that "they'll hear from me at the full committee meeting." In addition, Ervin promised to lead a fight against the nomination on the floor of the Senate. Despite Ervin's pledge, the real question became whether or not southerners would be able to keep the nomination bottled up in committee until the end of the session. If put to a vote, the Judiciary Committee would most probably vote in favor of the nomination; the entire Senate would almost certainly do so. Delay was the one weapon left to the southerners, but it was one at which they were expert.[68]

Still, some southern observers began to question whether Sobeloff's opponents had botched their strategy. John L. McMillan, a congressman from South Carolina, argued that the opposition would have been more effective if it had focused on the issue of rotation. The various allegations of scandals or unfitness had been decimated in the hearings.[69] The *Charlotte Observer* contended that Johnston's charges "built up sympathy for Sobeloff." Moreover, "their collapse made the entire opposition to the nominee seem slightly ridiculous."[70] Edward H. Simms, a columnist for the *Florence* (South Carolina) *Morning News*, recommended focusing on Sobeloff's supposed inability to judge cases dealing with segregation impartially. In making his argument, Simms betrayed a tinge of antisemitism that tainted much of the opposition to Sobeloff. "It is true," he wrote, that "members of a minority race can become bitter to the point of being incapable of impartial action. Sobeloff has certainly been a strongly-opinionated crusader in this field [segregation] over which he will preside and decide, as a judge."[71]

With the full Judiciary Committee scheduled to meet on May 29, newspapers in several regions once again vigorously urged Sobeloff's confirmation.[72] Both Ervin and Johnston asked to appear before the full committee, and Senator Willis A. Robertson of Virginia announced that he would oppose Sobeloff on the floor if the nomination came out of the Judiciary Committee. Robertson based his opposition on "the fact that he [Sobeloff] had previously been a partisan" in the type of litigation he would be called upon to decide on the bench. The scheduled meeting of the full Judiciary Committee never came about. Voting on a highway bill forced its cancellation.[73]

At the next meeting of the Judiciary Committee, on June 4, Johnston staged a minifilibuster by reading an endless statement at a painfully slow pace. He completed only a quarter of his statement before the Judiciary Committee went into closed session to consider other matters. Johnston offered no new evidence; rather, he argued that South Carolina deserved the appointment and rehashed charges that had been answered and dismissed in the subcommittee's hearings. Seeking to stall in any way possible, Johnston asked for further inquiry into charges relating to the Baltimore Trust Company.[74]

The meeting did produce several developments. O'Mahoney, Everett Dirksen, and Hennings noted that if the second vacancy on the Fourth Circuit went to South Carolina, it would eliminate some of the objections to Sobeloff. O'Mahoney agreed to write to Brownell to inquire into the delay in naming Dobie's successor. On the other side, Senator William E. Jenner, a reactionary Republican from Indiana, announced his opposition to Sobeloff and his intention to persuade his close friend Welker to join him.[75]

Johnston's bid for reelection benefited from his obstructionist role. The *Columbia Record* declared that Johnston "finally got back on the track" in opposing Sobeloff and "gained the fourth delay in as many weeks."[76] Johnston sent a newsletter to his constituents boasting of his success in delaying Sobeloff's confirmation. He charged that the blame for Sobeloff's nomination rested with the Democrats who had supported Eisenhower in 1952.[77] Indeed, the battle over confirmation gave ammunition to Regular Democrats throughout the Palmetto State. The *Florence Morning News* noted that "disregard for accepted custom is a characteristic of the Eisenhower administration" and that the Regular Democrats had warned against this when some of the state's leaders supported Eisenhower. Custom and precedent, the editorial argued, had "allowed the South to capture control of much of the legislative branch." "It has been through the Democratic Party," the *Morning News* reminded its readers, "that this state has gained what national authority it has."[78]

The day after the Judiciary Committee met, the attorney general, speaking at a National Press Club luncheon, denounced Johnston's "rather reckless" charges and said that they had been "completely disproved." He stated his displeasure with the "undue delay" and hoped "that a favorable vote [would] come very soon."[79]

Brownell's desire for a vote was understandable. A majority of the Judiciary Committee favored confirmation. Whether that vote would take place, however, was open to question. If the southerners could delay action on the nomination until the end of the session, they could defeat it—and Eastland was chairman.

The Judiciary Committee scheduled yet another round of hearings for June 11. The committee met at 10:30 A.M. but had to adjourn at noon when the Senate met. With aid from his friends, Johnston easily occupied the entire hour and a half. Eastland read Brownell's response to the committee's inquiry about the second vacancy. Brownell responded that the matter was under "active consideration," but he also "respectfully" reminded the committee that it had not yet acted on Sobeloff. His implication was that there would be no name submitted for Dobie's post until the Judiciary Committee had acted on Sobeloff's nomination. The administration could play hardball too; until the Sobeloff nomination was acted on, South Carolina's claim to the next vacancy on the court would be held in abeyance. As the meeting adjourned, Maryland's John Marshall Butler demanded to know when hearings would resume. Eastland responded that he hoped the group could meet later in the week. When Robertson asked to testify against the nominee, Butler charged the southerners with "filibustering." Butler accurately, if not technically correctly, described the southerners' strategy. They hoped to prevent the nomination from reaching the Senate until near the end of the session. Then they could filibuster on the floor. In their best of all possible worlds, a Democrat would defeat Eisenhower in the fall, and the Sobeloff nomination would never reappear.[80]

Although he opposed Sobeloff's nomination, Eastland assured the administration that there would be a vote. However, he canceled meetings on June 18, for lack of a quorum, and again on June 22, when Johnston objected to meeting while the Senate was in session.[81] Finally, on June 25, the Judiciary Committee voted five to four to act on the Sobeloff nomination on June 28. O'Mahoney made the motion to force a showdown and told the southerners that if they were going to filibuster, to do so on the floor of the Senate.[82]

When the committee met on June 28, they heard more from Johnston followed by Robertson's statement. Unlike Johnston, who persisted in pressing his trumped-up accusations concerning the Baltimore Trust Company, Robertson conceded that Sobeloff was a "highly competent lawyer and an intelligent and honorable man." Nevertheless, Robertson said that the people of Virginia lacked confidence in him and that "faith in public justice would be shaken by his presence on the bench." The nomination, charged Robertson, was politically motivated, engineered by Brownell with an eye to win votes of "interest groups" outside the south. The Fourth Circuit would hear many cases involving segregation in subsequent years. Robertson asked if Virginia would be "compelled to try these cases before a judge who had proclaimed his personal views on the subject from lecture platforms throughout the nation as well as before the Supreme Court itself?"[83]

That afternoon, the Senate was in session debating foreign aid. Lyndon Johnson asked for unanimous consent to allow the Judiciary Committee to meet while the Senate was in session. Johnston objected. O'Mahoney and Butler attempted to override Johnston's objection, which would have taken only a simple majority. However, after checking with the parliamentarian, Johnston informed the majority leader that the motion to override was a debatable point and that he would filibuster if such a motion were made. Rather than lose the foreign aid bill to a filibuster, Johnson persuaded O'Mahoney and Butler not to attempt an override. Johnston's victory was short-lived. O'Mahoney and the pro-Sobeloff majority pushed Eastland to agree to call a meeting of the Judiciary Committee the following day. O'Mahoney announced that he would ask for a vote, and Dirksen promised that "there will be a second to his motion."[84]

This time the vote took place, and, as expected, Sobeloff was overwhelmingly approved by a vote of nine to two; but the southerners had not yet given up. The committee agreed not to report the nomination to the Senate for a week, and Johnston promised to wage a "prolonged" fight against confirmation on the floor. Richard Russell of Georgia, Kerr Scott of North Carolina, and Robertson, among others, promised to help.[85]

Delay remained the lone arrow in the southern quiver, but the Dixiecrats made the most of it. Butler announced that he would file the majority report by July 5, but Johnston announced that he was not sure the minority report would be ready by that time.[86]

The administration lent its full weight to the battle in the Judiciary Committee. Deputy Attorney General William Rogers went to Capitol Hill himself and waited outside the committee room while the committee held an executive session, in what Anthony Lewis called "an unusual gesture of concern."[87] Rogers and members of his staff had been lobbying for a vote on the nomination.

As the Sobeloff nomination awaited action by the full Senate, southern newspapers speculated on the implications of the nomination and the battle to defeat it. The *Charlotte Observer* ran a feature article titled "Who Is Sobeloff?" by Frank Vander Linden. The piece pointed out that many southerners regarded Sobeloff as a "foreigner" from Baltimore, sent down by the Republicans to "preside over cases that could rip apart the whole social fabric" of the south. Sobeloff, whom Vander Linden described as "something of a hero to minority groups and liberals," had "always been more 'liberal' than the usual 'orthodox' Republican." Vander Linden also observed that the action on Sobeloff opened the way for naming a successor to Dobie.[88] The *Richmond Times* also reflected on the meaning of the Judiciary Committee's vote. Southern senators objected to Sobeloff because "they know or are pretty sure he is an integrationist." The Richmond paper pointed out that Sobeloff had refused to argue the Peters case when he disagreed with the government's position, and it therefore concluded that since Sobeloff had argued the government's case in *Brown II*, he must favor integration.[89]

The majority report of the Judiciary Committee came out on July 7. It asserted that "it is doubtful if any judicial nomination has received more minute examination" and pointed out that Sobeloff had been confirmed unanimously by the Senate to be solicitor general less than two and a half years before. It then proceeded to consider and dismiss each of Johnston's points. The minority report repeated the various objections raised in the hearings.[90]

In a desperate attempt to block the Sobeloff nomination, the senators of North Carolina, South Carolina, and Virginia signed a joint statement on July 12 urging the Senate to reject the nominee and declaring Sobeloff "personally obnoxious" to them. The claim that a nominee was "personally obnoxious" had been traditionally asserted by an individual senator when objecting to a nominee from his own state. Its application to a region was novel. The six senators hoped to get William Laird, a Democrat from West Virginia, to join them. Matthew Neely, West Virginia's other senator and also a Democrat, declared in favor of Sobeloff, as did Maryland's two senators. Ervin seemed to be the force behind the maneuver, although Johnston claimed to have suggested it to the Tar Heel.[91]

When the nomination came up on the Senate calendar, the majority leader asked that it be passed over at that time and considered the following week.[92]

During that week, crosses were burned on the front lawns of Sobeloff, Chief Justice Earl Warren, Justice Felix Frankfurter, and the home of the NAACP's chairman in Prince Georges County, Maryland.[93]

Lyndon Johnson finally broke the deadlock. On July 13, he called a marathon session for July 16 to consider the Sobeloff nomination. The Senate would convene at 9:30 in the morning and stay in session until it had acted on the nomination. Finally, shortly after 8:00 in the evening, the Senate overwhelmingly approved the nomination. During the extended debates, southern senators declared that Sobeloff was "offensive to the majority of the people he will serve." Johnston spoke repeatedly. Ervin, Robertson, and Thomas A. Wofford (D., S.C.) joined him in attacking the candidate. Ervin said that the Senate would normally reject a nominee obnoxious to six senators, and it would do so in this case "if it were not for the fact that there is agitation about racial questions in the United States at this time." Robertson called the nomination "an affront" to the people of Virginia, North Carolina, and South Carolina. He charged the administration with "an effort to woo certain political pressure groups in other parts of the nation by an action which is offensive to a majority of the people in the region [Sobeloff] will serve." These interest groups insisted on Sobeloff, he said, "because they like his racial views." Eastland launched what the *Columbia State* described as "a fiery, arm waving attack on the nomination." The solicitor general, he maintained, was "right on the borderline of Red philosophy." And that, he added, was "the kindest thing that can be said about him." Finally, Johnston made a motion to recommit the nomination to the Judiciary Committee, which the Senate rejected by a vote of sixty-three to twenty. Shortly after, the Senate confirmed the nomination sixty-four to nineteen.[94]

Lyndon Johnson played a major role in the confirmation of Sobeloff. He pressed the southerners to abandon obstructionist tactics; his decision to call a marathon session essentially defeated any filibuster.[95] The reasons for Johnson's actions were complex. At the same time he engineered Sobeloff's confirmation, he bottled up the administration's civil rights bill and killed it for the session.[96] Although the two actions might have seemed contradictory, they shared a common goal. Johnson wanted no bloodletting over civil rights in an election year; it could serve no purpose other than splitting the Democratic Party. Even given the eight hours of debate on Sobeloff's nomination, Johnson managed to keep the rhetoric to a relative minimum. He persuaded Johnston to cut an "angry two-hour oration" to twenty minutes.[97]

Liberal and establishment papers from outside the south lauded the long-awaited confirmation. "The Nation is fortunate," wrote the *Washington Post*, "in having so wise and judicious a man seated on an appellate court which is likely to play a key part in the adjustment of racial problems."[98] The *Baltimore Evening Sun* asserted that the vote proved that the allegations by Johnston and Eastland "were just so much ugly window dressing and did not obscure the central and obvious issue [race]."[99] Mary McGrory's column in the *Washington Star* lauded the Senate's action in confirming Sobeloff and Sobeloff himself.

"Mr. Sobeloff's liberal views are well known; so is his skill in articulating them," she wrote.[100] An editorial in the same paper noted that, had Sobeloff been nominated to a judicial post outside the south, no serious opposition would have arisen.[101] The *Baltimore Sun* pointed out that Sobeloff's opponents "simply did not have a case" and that "the real basis of opposition was the identification which Southern senators made between Mr. Sobeloff and the Supreme Court's segregation decision."[102] The *Washington Afro-American* rejoiced at Sobeloff's victory after a "disgraceful delay of twelve months." During that time, the Senate's rules had allowed "an unreconstructed little band of Dixiecrats to make jackasses" out of the majority. With thinly disguised glee, the *Afro-American* speculated that Eisenhower would name Sobeloff to the next vacancy on the Supreme Court. "Certainly," concluded the editorial, "the President could name no man better qualified."[103]

The *Charlotte Observer* soberly reflected on the meaning of the vote on Sobeloff in the Senate. Southern senators "fought bitterly" to keep Sobeloff off the court, and "they lost." The vote had to be regarded as a "set back for the so-called 'Southern position' in national affairs." The vote "points up once again the South's difficulties in the battle over the rights of minorities and the growing interest of the federal government in protecting those rights." Most southerners believed that the Supreme Court was the "sole area of trouble," but the margin in the Senate was three to one. The nomination and battle over confirmation demonstrated conclusively that southerners were "unable to influence a Republican administration." Perhaps even more important, they had been unable to influence senators of their "own party."[104]

The *Columbia State* focused on more immediate causes for concern. With Dobie already retired and Parker near retirement, Sobeloff would become chief judge of the circuit before long. Even worse, Sobeloff was now "in direct line for appointment to the U.S. Supreme Court, if and when a vacancy should occur there."[105]

On its editorial page, the *State* made a more partisan argument. Eisenhower and the Republicans might have "started it," but "the Democrats cannot escape blame." After all, the Democrats controlled the Senate. Lyndon Johnson came in for special criticism. "If he is the South's hope," warned the *State*, "we had better be looking for someone else."[106]

Columbia's other paper, the *Record*, issued the most bitter rebel war cry. The paper sharply criticized Olin Johnston for failing to filibuster. The battle over the nomination on the floor lasted only ten hours; Sobeloff's opponents, charged the *Record*, "were not so much defeated as they surrendered."[107] This ignored the facts that southerners did not have the votes to block cloture and that, because of Lyndon Johnson's decision to call a marathon session, no other business could be conducted until Sobeloff's nomination came to a vote.

The *Florence Morning News* ruminated that Eastland, "one of the most powerful men in the Senate," and Johnston, "a senior member" of the Judiciary Committee, could not stop the Sobeloff nomination. Southerners should reflect on the implication of that for future civil rights legislation.[108] The warning proved prophetic. In the next session of Congress, the Eisenhower administration would gain passage of the first civil rights legislation since Reconstruction.

The nomination of Sobeloff to the Fourth Circuit and the ensuing donnybrook in the Senate reveal much about Eisenhower's commitment to ending segregation. The president knew of Sobeloff's position on segregation and his activism from firsthand experience and still nominated him to one of the two circuit courts most effected by the *Brown* decision. The battle over Sobeloff's confirmation revolved around a single issue—race. Throughout the yearlong contest, the administration steadfastly stood by its nominee. Eisenhower supported the nomination in public; Brownell lent his strong and public support; and Rogers lobbied senators extensively. The administration maintained its position in the face of bitter opposition from the south. After Johnston and Eastland blocked confirmation in 1955, the administration resubmitted the nomination immediately upon the opening of the next session. Thus, there can be no doubt about the administration's intent or commitment.

Moreover, the argument that Eisenhower could make such an appointment without political cost simply will not wash. Democrats who had supported Eisenhower in 1952, particularly in South Carolina, encountered enormous difficulties because of the nomination. Undoubtedly this cost Eisenhower some political support. Eisenhower actively sought support in the south, managed to crack the solid south in 1952, and hoped to establish a real opposition party in the region. The controversy over his nomination of Sobeloff unquestionably hampered these efforts.

If Eisenhower had made only this one appointment, it might be meaningless. But four of his five appointments to the Fifth Circuit and all three of his appointments to the Fourth Circuit fell within the liberal to moderate range. Soon after the battle over Sobeloff, for example, Eisenhower nominated Haynsworth over the objection of Strom Thurmond, a senator from Haynsworth's own state, who was pushing his own segregationist candidate. The Senate ultimately approved Haynsworth, but not without a prolonged struggle.[109]

Sobeloff took his seat on the Fourth Circuit on July 19, 1956. During his seventeen-year tenure, his opinions broke new ground in areas of reform of the criminal justice system, legislative reapportionment, and civil rights. Slightly less than two years after Sobeloff took his seat on the Fourth Circuit, John J. Parker died, and Sobeloff succeeded him as chief judge. Under Sobeloff, the Fourth Circuit established a reputation as one of the most liberal of all federal courts of appeal, and Sobeloff made his greatest mark in the area of civil rights. He led the Fourth Circuit away from Parker's formulation that *Brown* required desegregation, not integration. In 1970, Sobeloff voted to uphold Judge James B. McMillan's use of court-ordered busing in *Swann v. Charlotte-Mecklenburg*. Although he could not persuade a majority of his brethren on the Fourth Circuit, the Supreme Court subsequently affirmed the position Sobeloff took in his dissent. Although Sobeloff was frequently mentioned as a possible nominee to the

Supreme Court in the 1950s, Eisenhower never nominated him. Some of Sobeloff's friends thought that his stand in the Peters case hampered his chances. In fact, it was Felix Frankfurter's determination not to resign until a Democrat occupied the White House that most likely cost Sobeloff a chance to be nominated. The likelihood of any president nominating a second Jew to the Supreme Court was not great.[110]

Eisenhower's appointments to the federal judiciary in the south revealed much about his intentions with respect to civil rights. Eisenhower believed that segregation was wrong and that it was his duty as president to see that the federal government did nothing to support it. At the same time, he believed that segregation could be ended only through a gradual process that allowed time for education and for southern attitudes at least to begin to change. The highly professionalized judges he appointed would uphold the law as declared by the Supreme Court. In doing so, they would desegregate the south. By the very nature of the legal process, however, the change would be a gradual one.

NOTES

1. See, for example, Stephen E. Ambrose, *Eisenhower: The President* (New York: Simon and Schuster, 1984); William Bragg Ewald, Jr., *Eisenhower the President: Crucial Days, 1951–1960* (Englewood Cliffs, N.J.: Prentice-Hall, 1981); Elmo J. Richardson, *The Presidency of Dwight D. Eisenhower* (Lawrence: Regents Press of Kansas, 1979); and Fred I. Greenstein, *The Hidden-Hand Presidency: Eisenhower as Leader* (New York: Basic Books, 1982).

2. Robert Fredrick Burk, *The Eisenhower Administration and Black Civil Rights* (Knoxville: University of Tennessee Press, 1984); David J. Garrow, "Black Civil Rights During the Eisenhower Years," *Constitutional Commentary* 3, no. 2 (Summer 1986): 361–73; William E. Leuchtenburg, "The White House and Black America: From Eisenhower to Carter," in M. V. Namorato, ed., *Have We Overcome?* (Jackson: University Press of Mississippi, 1979), 121–45. Ambrose, in *Eisenhower*, is also critical of Eisenhower's record on civil rights.

3. Harold W. Chase, *Federal Judges: The Appointing Process* (Minneapolis: University of Minnesota Press, 1972), gives generally high marks to Eisenhower's appointments to the Fifth Circuit, with the exception of Ben Cameron. See also "Judicial Performance on the Fifth Circuit," 73 *Yale Law Journal* 90 (1963), which commends Tuttle, Brown, and Wisdom; rates Jones inconsistent; and criticizes Cameron. J. W. Peltason, *Fifty-Eight Lonely Men: Southern Federal Judges and School Desegregation* (New York: Harcourt, Brace and World, 1961), has praise for Sobeloff, Haynsworth, and Boreman on the Fourth Circuit and Tuttle, Brown, Jones, and Wisdom on the Fifth (23–27). Jack Bass, *Unlikely Heroes* (New York: Simon and Schuster, 1981), offers the best account of the Fifth Circuit's struggle with the issue of segregation. Eisenhower's appointments, with the notable exception of Cameron, are among Bass's "unlikely heroes." See also Frank T. Read and Lucy S. McGough, *Let Them Be Judged: The Judicial Integration of the Deep South* (Metuchen, N.J.: Scarecrow Press, 1978). The one notable exception is Mary Curzan, "A Case Study in the Selection of Federal Judges: The Fifth Circuit, 1953–1963," Ph.D. dissertation, Yale University, 1968. Curzan chal-

lenges the idea that Eisenhower's appointments to the Fifth Circuit had better records on civil rights cases than Kennedy's appointments. Aside from the fact that the dissertation is available only in summary form without full scholarly apparatus, her quantitative approach is inadequate. She weights all cases the same, despite the obvious fact that some decisions are more important than others. She also fails to separate out district judges from appellate judges (who have greater impact on the development of law), and Eisenhower's appointments to the appellate bench were especially good. What's more, Curzan's peculiar method of categorizing cases leads her to the startling conclusion that Frank Johnson, one of the civil rights heroes of the bench, was a segregationist. For evidence to the contrary, see Tinsley E. Yarborough, *Judge Frank Johnson and Human Rights in Alabama* (Tuscaloosa: University of Alabama Press, 1981); and Robert F. Kennedy, Jr., *Judge Frank M. Johnson, Jr.* (New York: Putnam, 1978). For an account of the Fourth Circuit's decisions, see Sanford Jay Rosen, "Judge Sobeloff's Public School Race Decisions," 34 *Maryland Law Review* 498 (1974).

4. Burk, *The Eisenhower Administration*, 199–200.

5. Rayman L. Solomon, "The Politics of Appointment and the Federal Courts' Role in Regulating America: U.S. Courts of Appeals Judgeships from T. R. to F.D.R.," *American Bar Foundation Research Journal* 1984, no. 2 (Spring 1984): 285–343.

6. William Rogers, interview with the author, Washington, D.C., March 21, 1990; Lawrence Walsh, interview with the author, Washington, D.C., March 22, 1990; William Rogers, "Judicial Appointments in the Eisenhower Administration," 41 *Journal of the American Judicature Society* 40 (1957); Chase, *Federal Judges*, 89–91, 98, 101; Dwight D. Eisenhower, *The White House Years: Mandate for Change, 1953–1956* (Garden City, N.Y.: Doubleday, 1963), 226–27, 230. See also Dwight Eisenhower to Edgar Eisenhower, March 23, 1956, Eisenhower Diary Series, March 1956, Misc. (2), Whitman File, Dwight D. Eisenhower Library, Abilene, Kansas (hereafter DDEL): "Nothing gives me such a great sense of frustration as to realize that even the lawyers of this country have not come to understand that I do not consider federal judgeships as included in the list of appointments subject to 'patronage.' "

7. Chase, *Federal Judges*, 98, 112; interview with William Rogers, March 21, 1990.

8. William P. Rogers, memorandum to the attorney general, Administration Series, 1958 (5), Whitman File, DDEL. Brownell and Eisenhower met regularly to discuss judgeships. See Brownell to President, March 10, 1955, Administration Series, Herbert Brownell, Jr., 1955–1956 (3), Whitman File, DDEL. Further evidence of Eisenhower's involvement is a long letter to Rogers in which the president expressed displeasure with some of the procedures that had emerged in the process of selecting nominees for federal judgeships. Eisenhower wanted to be more involved at an earlier stage. See Eisenhower to Rogers, February 10, 1959, Administration Series, William P. Rogers, 1959 (4), Whitman File, DDEL. In addition, when Eisenhower met with his legislative leaders on January 10, 1956, one of them pointed out that the Democrats would stall on judicial appointments if they thought they could control the White House after 1956. Eisenhower doubted that they could "find something wrong with" any of his judicial appointments. This, he said, was "something I've personally taken under my own eye. And I've had some big fights. That's one thing—I insist on high qualifications." He said that he put before the Judiciary Committee "the finest possible men." See Notes on Legislative Leaders Meeting, January 10, 1956, L–27 (2), Legislative Series, White House Office, Staff Secretariat, DDEL.

9. William Rogers, interview with the author, March 21, 1990; and Lawrence Walsh, interview with the author, March 22, 1990.

10. Shivers to Eisenhower, July 16, 1953, Official File (hereafter OF) 142-A–4 (1), DDEL; Byrnes to Eisenhower, November 20, 1953, *ibid.*; Kennon to Eisenhower, November 20, 1953, *ibid.*

11. Herbert Parmet, *Eisenhower and the American Crusades* (New York: Macmillan, 1972), 146–47; Richardson, *The Presidency*, 21; Arthur S. Link and William B. Catton, *American Epoch*, 5th ed. (New York: Knopf, 1980), 721.

12. Michael S. Mayer, "With Much Deliberation and Some Speed: Eisenhower and the *Brown* Decision," *Journal of Southern History* 52, no. 1 (February 1986): 63–70.

13. *Baltimore Sun*, July 15, 1955; *Baltimore Evening Sun*, July 15, 1955; *New York Times*, July 15, 1955; *Washington Post*, July 15, 1955; *Washington Star*, July 15, 1955; *St. Louis Post-Dispatch*, July 15, 1955; Soper to Eisenhower, April 15, 1955, OF 100-B-4, DDEL.

14. *Washington Star*, July 16, 1955; *Charlotte Observer*, July 16, 1955.

15. *Charlotte Observer*, July 16, 1955.

16. *Washington Post*, July 17, 1955.

17. *Baltimore Sun*, July 16, 1955. See also the *Baltimore Evening Sun*, July 15, 1955, which praised the nomination as "a welcome one" and predicted quick confirmation.

18. *St. Louis Post-Dispatch*, July 16, 1955.

19. *Washington Afro-American*, July 19, 1955.

20. *Baltimore Sun*, July 16, 1955; William Rogers, interview with the author, March 21, 1990; Thurmond to Eisenhower, May 24, 1955, General File (hereafter GF) 4-C–4, Figg, DDEL; Adams to Thurmond, May 26, 1955, *ibid.*; Charles Willis to Robert Minor, May 26, 1955, *ibid.*; Minor to Willis, June 1, 1955, *ibid.*; Thurmond to Eisenhower, June 28, 1955, *ibid.*; Adams to Thurmond, July 1, 1955, *ibid.*; Edward Tate to Minor, July 1, 1955, *ibid.* Owen Cheatham wrote to Sherman Adams explaining that "Mr. Figg is probably closer to Strom than any other man in the State. . . . [T]hey are close personal friends, they visit each other's homes, and their wives are close friends." See Cheatham to Adams, December 4, 1956, GF 4-C–4, Endorsements, DDEL. The *Washington Afro-American*, July 23, 1955, crowed that "one of the reasons South Carolina has been without a representative on the [Fourth Circuit] court and probably will be for some time is that the state's legal representatives have indicated that they have no regard for Federal laws and in effect, have advocated disobedience of the laws." The same article pointed out that, in his argument before the Supreme Court, Figg had contended that the people of South Carolina would never accept integration and that mixing races would "destroy the public school system."

21. *Baltimore Sun*, July 16, 1955; *Sumter* (South Carolina) *Daily Item*, July 19, 1955; *Anderson* (South Carolina) *Independent*, July 20, 1955; *Columbia* (South Carolina) *Record*, July 19, 1955; *Orangeburg* (South Carolina) *Times and Democrat*, July 20, 1955. In its issue of July 28, 1955, the *Charlestown Evening Post* ran an editorial from the *Greenville* (South Carolina) *Piedmont*, which stated: "However well qualified Simon E. Soboleff may be for the federal bench, his appointment . . . has done the administration and the Republican party no good in the South, especially in South Carolina." The editorial asserted that "the Republicans are making an all-out effort to recapture the Negro vote." Given these circumstances, "confirmation may be delayed, but it almost certainly cannot be withheld."

22. *Anderson Independent*, July 20, 1955. In addition to Soboleff's nomination, the

editorial also cited the appointment of a black to head the Special Projects Group to support its position. The black man to whom the editorial referred (although not by name) was E. Frederic Morrow. The *Independent* pointed out that Morrow had been a "campaign advisor in 1952" and wondered "if he wrote part of the speech Ike delivered in Columbia—and one moreover wonders where he was during the visit!"

23. *Baltimore Evening Sun*, July 21, 1955.

24. *Baltimore Evening Sun*, July 22, 1955.

25. *Baltimore Evening Sun*, July 22, 1955.

26. *Washington Post*, July 17, 1955; *New York Times*, June 17, 1955.

27. *Baltimore Sun*, July 27, 1955; *Washington Star*, July 26, 29, 1955; *New York Times*, July 28, 1955; *Columbia State*, July 27, 1955; *Washington Post*, July 27, 28, 1955; *Columbia Record*, July 26, 1955; *Charleston Evening Post*, July 28, 1955. Subcommittee member McClellan's role seems to have been crucial. Kefauver announced his support for Sobeloff; Welker had no comment.

28. *Baltimore Sun*, July 28, 1955; *Washington Star*, July 29, 1955. The actual phrase from Sobeloff's speech was: "The Court may reject a case, not because the question is unimportant, but because it thinks the time not ripe for decision. In our system the Supreme Court is not merely the adjudicator of controversies, but in the process of adjudication, it is in many instances the final formulator of national policy."

29. *Baltimore Sun*, July 28, 1955; *Washington Post*, July 28, 1955; Sobeloff Hearings, pp. 204–205, *Congressional Record*, United States Senate, Eighty-Fourth Congress, Second Session, July 16, 1956, 11659.

30. *Baltimore Sun*, July 28, 1955.

31. *Baltimore Sun*, July 27, 29, August 5, 1955; *Washington Post*, July 28, August 4, 1955; *Washington Star*, July 29, 1955.

32. *St. Louis Post-Dispatch*, July 30, 1955.

33. *Washington Post*, July 28, 1955.

34. *Washington Star*, July 29, 1955.

35. *Raleigh News and Observer*, July 31, 1955. The *Post* ran another editorial condemning the delay on August 4, 1955. An editorial in the *Baltimore Evening Sun* of August 4, 1955, praised Sobeloff's "impressive qualifications" and attacked southern senators who opposed him only because of his "known views" on segregation.

36. *Charlotte Observer*, October 29, 1955.

37. *Washington Afro-American*, August 9, 1955.

38. *Baltimore Evening Sun*, August 23, 1955; *Washington Star*, August 26, 1955.

39. *New York Times*, August 25, 1955; *Baltimore Sun*, August 25, 1955.

40. *New York Times*, November 9, 1955; *Baltimore Sun*, November 9, 1955; *Washington Post*, November 9, 1955.

41. *Charlotte Observer*, November 22, 1955.

42. *Washington Star*, January 12, 15, 1956; *Washington Post*, January 13, 15, 1956; *New York Times*, January 13, 1956; *Baltimore Evening Sun*, January 14, 1956.

43. *Baltimore Sun*, January 15, 1956; *Washington Star*, January 20, 1956.

44. *Baltimore Sun*, January 25, 1956.

45. *Columbia State*, January 25, 1955.

46. *Greenville* (South Carolina) *News*, February 21, 24, 1956; *Columbia State*, February 22, 1956.

47. *Greenville News*, February 24, 1956; Thurmond to Eisenhower, February 11, 1956, GF 4-C-4, Figg, DDEL; Martin to Thurmond, February 16, 1956, *ibid.*; Tait to

Tom Hogan, February 16, 1956, *ibid.*; Charles E. Daniel to Thurmond, November 26, 1956, GF 4-C-4 Endorsements, DDEL; B. M. Edwards to Alester G. Furman, Jr., November 13, 1956, *ibid.*; Thurmond to Cheatham, November 20, 1956, *ibid.*; *Charlotte Observer*, March 29, 1956.

48. *Baltimore Sun*, February 29 (see both Peter Kumpa's article and the editorial criticizing the seniority system), March 1, 3, 1956; *Wall Street Journal*, February 29, 1956; *Baltimore News*, March 10, 1956. In an editorial on March 3, 1956, the *Washington Post* accused Eastland of "actively fomenting resistance to the law of the land" and said that he had "demonstrated about as much judicial temperament as a prosecutor in a star chamber." According to the *Post*, Eastland got the position only because of seniority and "there ought to be a real vote on the fitness of men for these important posts." See also *Washington Post*, March 3, 1956; *New York Times*, March 3, 1956; *Washington Afro-American*, March 31, 1956.

49. *Baltimore Sun*, March 3, 1956; *Greenville News*, March 3, 1956.

50. *Baltimore Sun*, March 7, 1956; *Washington Daily News*, March 7, 1956.

51. *New York Times*, April 9, 1956; *Washington Post*, April 9, 1956. Rogers said that Eastland never blocked the nomination of any judge (interview with the author, March 21, 1990).

52. *Washington Post*, April 10, 1956.

53. *Baltimore Sun*, April 24, 1956; *Washington Post*, April 24, 1956; *Baltimore Evening Sun*, April 24, 1956. The *Evening Sun* welcomed the hearings as a "break in an unexcusable blockade." Sobeloff had "a distinguished career and deserves better of the committee than he has up to now received."

54. *Washington Post*, April 25, 1956; *Baltimore Sun*, April 25, 1956; *New York Times*, April 25, 1956. Bush conceded that some senators "opposing Mr. Sobeloff because of his liberal views" were, "perhaps, reflecting the sentiments of their constituencies, misguided though they may be." However, the tactic of simply delaying action on the nomination was "wrong."

55. *Washington Post*, April 26, 1956; *St. Louis Post-Dispatch*, April 26, 1956; *Charlotte Observer*, April 30, 1956. The *Observer*'s editorial criticized Johnston and others, who held up the nomination "because they were fearful of the Sobeloff views on the racial situation." In arguing the government's case in *Brown*, Sobeloff was "merely . . . doing his duty" as solicitor general. The administration's policy came from the president and attorney general.

56. *Washington Star*, May 2, 1956; *Charlotte Observer*, May 3, 1956.

57. *Columbia State*, May 4, 1956.

58. Hearings Before the Committee on the Judiciary on the Nomination of Simon E. Sobeloff, of Maryland, To Be United States Circuit Judge, Fourth Circuit, United States Senate, Eighty-Fourth Congress, Second Session, May 5, 21, 22, June 4, 11, 25, and 28, 41-46.

59. Sobeloff Hearings, 58.

60. Sobeloff Hearings, 64.

61. Sobeloff Hearings, 69. For coverage of the hearings on May 5, see Sobeloff Hearings, 1–114; *Baltimore American*, May 6, 1956; *Baltimore Evening Sun*, May 5, 1956; *Baltimore Sun*, May 6, June 5, 1956; *Charlotte Observer*, May 6, 29, 1956; *Charleston News and Courier*, May 6, 1956; *Columbia State*, May 6, 1956; *Columbia Record*, May 5, 1956; *St. Louis Post-Dispatch*, May 6, 1956; *Washington Post*, May 6, 1956; *New York Times*, May 6, 1956; and *Washington Star*, May 5, 1956. The *Charleston*

News and Courier ran a headline: "Sen. Johnston's Case Against Sobeloff Wrecked in Hearing." The article pointed out that Johnston had subpoenaed John D. Hospelhorn, who had been a receiver for the Baltimore Trust Company, and that Hospelhorn had testified that Sobeloff had done nothing wrong and had conducted himself honorably. As the paper put it, the "final blow" came when "Johnston's own chief witness joined the denials."

62. *Washington Post*, May 7, 1956. The *Post* concluded that southerners opposed Sobeloff because they associated "Mr. Sobeloff with the crumbling of the walls that have separated the white and Negro races in schools, restaurants, and other public places." The *Baltimore Sun* arrived at a similar conclusion: "the main objection to Mr. Sobeloff comes from Southerners who resent his part in arguing the Government's cause in the segregation cases" (May 8, 1956). An editorial in the *New York Times* of May 18, 1956, stated that the reason for delay on Sobeloff's nomination was "obvious." "Southern segregationists fear, doubtless correctly, that Mr. Sobeloff believes in the Supreme Court's decision on the public schools and in the procedures laid down to implement it." Although the hearings had provided segregationists with a "field day," they had produced nothing that "could in any way diminish [Sobeloff's] ability, his integrity or his fitness" for the court.

63. *St. Louis Post-Dispatch*, May 11, 1956.

64. *Washington Post*, May 18, 1956; *Columbia State*, May 18, 1956; *Baltimore Sun*, May 18, 1956; *Greenville News*, May 18, 1956.

65. Sobeloff Hearings, 115–40; *Baltimore Sun*, May 22, 1956; *Columbia State*, May 22, 1956; *Baltimore Evening Sun*, May 21, 1956; *Washington Star*, May 21, 1956; *Charlotte Observer*, May 22, 1956; *Columbia Record*, May 22, 1956.

66. Sobeloff Hearings, 141–213; *Columbia Record*, May 22, 1956; *Washington Post*, May 23, 1956; *Washington Star*, May 22, 1956; *Columbia State*, May 23, 1956; *New York Times*, May 23, 1956; *Baltimore Evening Sun*, May 22, 1956; *Washington Afro-American*, May 26, 1956; *Baltimore Sun*, May 23, 1956.

67. *Public Papers of the President: Dwight D. Eisenhower, 1956* (Washington, D.C.: U.S. Government Printing Office, 1957), 519; *Washington Star*, May 23, 1956; *Columbia State*, May 24, 1956; Press Conference Notes, May 27, 1956, Papers of James C. Hagerty, DDEL. Notes, May 23, 1956, President's Press Conference, *ibid.*

68. *New York Times*, May 24, 1956; *Washington Post*, May 25, 1956; *Columbia State*, May 25, 1956; *Greenville News*, May 25, 1956; *Baltimore Sun*, May 25, 1956.

69. *Florence Morning News*, May 25, 1956.

70. *Charlotte Observer*, May 29, 1956.

71. *Florence Morning News*, May 25, 1956.

72. *Washington Post*, May 26, 1956; *Baltimore Evening Sun*, May 26, 1956; *St. Louis Post-Dispatch*, May 26, 1956; *New York Times*, May 29, 1956.

73. *Washington Star*, May 25, 29, 1956; *Baltimore Sun*, May 25, 30, 1956; *St. Louis Post-Dispatch*, May 25, 1956.

74. *Baltimore Evening Sun*, June 4, 1956; *Baltimore Sun*, June 5, 1956; Sobeloff Hearings, 215–29.

75. *Baltimore Sun*, June 5, 1956; Sobeloff Hearings, 226–27; *Washington Post*, June 5, 1956; *Greenville News*, June 4, 1956; *Columbia Record*, June 6, 1956.

76. *Columbia Record*, June 6, 1956.

77. Johnston newsletter, June 8, 1956, clipping books, Papers of Simon E. Sobeloff, Library of Congress.

78. *Florence Morning News*, June 8, 1956.

79. *Baltimore Sun*, June 6, 1956; *Washington Afro-American*, June 9, 1956; *New York Times*, June 6, 1956.

80. *Washington Afro-American*, June 9, 1956; *Columbia Record*, June 9, 1956; *Florence Morning News*, June 10, 1956; *Baltimore Evening Sun*, June 11, 1956; *Baltimore Sun*, June 12, 1956; *New York Times*, June 12, 1956; *Greenville News*, June 12, 1956; *Charlotte Observer*, June 12, 1956; *Washington Afro-American*, June 12, 1956. An editorial in the *Afro-American* of June 12, 1956, charged that the southerners opposed Sobeloff because "they fear him because as a Federal judge he would enforce the Constitution requiring the integration of public schools." Sobeloff, continued the editorial, was "eminently qualified," and every accusation against him had been "discredited and disproved." Aside from his role in the school segregation cases, the Dixiecrats objected to "the fact that he is a Jew and a Republican." The editorial concluded that, if the Democrats could not put through "deserved nominations," they had no right to ask to be returned to power in November. "Already the cry is in the air that a vote for any Democratic Senator or Representative is a vote for the Eastlands and Talmadges to keep their present stranglehold on the business of Congress." A week later, the *Afro-American* ran a column by Louis Lautier, which criticized the "farcical" hearings and accused opponents of the nomination of "both racial and religious prejudices" (June 19, 1956).

81. *Columbia State*, June 23, 1956.

82. Sobeloff Hearings, 245–46; *Washington Star*, June 25, 1956; *Baltimore Evening Sun*, June 25, 1956; *Greenville News*, June 26, 1956; *Baltimore Sun*, June 26, 1956; *Columbia State*, June 26, 1956; *Washington Post*, June 26, 1956. Voting for the motion were: Butler (R., Md.), Kefauver (D., Tenn.), Watkins (R., Utah), and Dirksen (R., Ill.). Voting against were: Eastland (D., Miss.), Johnston (D., S.C.), Langer (R., N.D.), and Daniel (D., Va.).

83. Sobeloff Hearings, 249–72; *Washington Star*, June 28, 1956; *Richmond News Leader*, June 28, 1956; *Baltimore Evening Sun*, June 28, 1956.

84. *Baltimore Evening Sun*, June 28, 1956; *Columbia State*, June 29, 1956; *Columbia Record*, June 28, 1956; *Washington Post*, June 29, 1956.

85. *Baltimore Evening Sun*, June 29, 1956; *Washington Post*, June 30, 1956; *Baltimore Sun*, June 30, 1956; *Columbia Record*, June 29, 1956; *Washington Star*, July 5, 1956; *New York Times*, June 30, 1956; *Charlotte Observer*, June 30, 1956. The original vote was eight to two. The majority consisted of four Republicans and four Democrats. Voting for were: John Marshall Butler (R., Md.), Dirksen (R., Ill.), Watkins (R., Utah), Langer (R., N.D.), O'Mahoney (D., Wyo.), Hennings (D., Mo.), Kefauver (D., Tenn.), and Neely (D.,W. Va.). The votes of four members of the Judiciary Committee were not immediately recorded—Price Daniel (D., Va.), Alexander Wiley (R., Wis.), Herman Welker (R., Idaho), and William Jenner (R., Ind.). Wiley later voted for confirmation, making the final vote nine to two. The two dissenters were Eastland and Johnston.

86. *Columbia Record*, June 29, 1956.

87. *New York Times*, June 30, 1956.

88. *Charlotte Observer*, June 30, 1956.

89. *Richmond Times*, July 3, 1956.

90. Report of the Committee on the Judiciary on the Nomination of Simon E. Sobeloff, Executive Report No. 8, United States Senate, Eighty-fourth Congress, Second Session, July 6, 1956 (the majority report covers 1–11; the minority report is on 12–24); *Baltimore Sun*, July 7, 1956; *New York Times*, July 7, 1956; *Richmond Times-Dispatch*,

July 7, 1956; *Charlotte News*, July 7, 1956; *Washington Star*, July 7, 1956; *Columbia State*, July 7, 1956; *Washington Post*, July 7, 1956. The minority report asserted South Carolina's right to the appointment (12–16), claimed that Sobeloff did not have an "open mind" on issues of segregation (16–18), charged that Sobeloff believed in judicial usurpation (18–22), and argued that Sobeloff was "repugnant to the people in the area served" (22–24).

91. *Columbia State*, July 7, 14, 1956; *Greenville News*, July 10, 15, 1956; *Baltimore Sun*, July 13, 1956; *Washington Star*, July 11, 1956; *Charlotte Observer*, July 15, 1956; *Washington Post*, July 15, 1956.

92. *Washington Star*, July 11, 1956.

93. *Washington Star*, July 14, 1956; *New York Times*, July 15, 1956; *Greenville News*, July 15, 1956.

94. *Congressional Record*, United States Senate, Eighty-fourth Congress, Second Session, July 16, 1956, 11642–89. Robertson's speech appears on 11647–54. Johnston's remarks appear throughout. Ervin's speech is on 11664–67. Wofford's speech is on 11669–74. See also *Columbia State*, July 14, 16, 1956; *Washington Post*, July 17, 1956; *Washington Star*, July 22, 1956; *New York Times*, July 17, 1956; *Baltimore Evening Sun*, July 16, 17, 1956; *Columbia Record*, July 17, 1956; *Baltimore Sun*, July 17, 1956; and *St. Louis Post-Dispatch*, July 17, 20, 1956. Speaking for Sobeloff were Butler, O'Mahoney, Dirksen, and Lehman. The difference in the vote to recommit and the vote to confirm was Carl Hayden (D., Ariz.), who voted with the southerners to recommit and then voted with the majority to confirm. The vote for Sobeloff broke down as follows. Thirty-five Republicans and twenty-nine Democrats voted for. Four Republicans and fifteen Democrats voted against. Three of the four Republicans voting against the nomination made up a who's who of neanderthal Republicanism: William F. Jenner (Ind.), Joseph R. McCarthy (Wis.), Herman Welker (Idaho), and John J. Williams (Del.). The fifteen Democratic votes against came exclusively from the south. Delaware's other senator, Frear, was the lone Democratic vote against from north of the Mason-Dixon Line.

95. *Washington Post*, July 18, 1956; *Columbia State*, July 18, 1956; *New York Times*, July 18, 1956.

96. See Michael S. Mayer, "The Eisenhower Administration and the Civil Rights Act of 1957," *Congress and the Presidency* 16, no. 2 (Autumn 1989): 143–44.

97. Joseph and Stewart Alsop column, *New York Herald Tribune*, July 18, 1956.

98. *Washington Post*, July 18, 1956.

99. *Baltimore Evening Sun*, July 17, 1956.

100. *Washington Star*, July 17, 1956.

101. *Washington Star*, July 20, 1956.

102. *Baltimore Sun*, July 18, 1956.

103. *Washington Afro-American*, July 24, 1956.

104. *Charlotte Observer*, July 19, 1956.

105. *Columbia State*, July 19, 1956.

106. *Columbia State*, July 18, 1956. The *Greenville News* of July 22, 1956, saw the vote to confirm as "a vote against the South" and noted bitterly that Sobeloff may have been appointed by a Republican president, but the vote to confirm was "aided and abetted by Democrats." It also pointed out that Johnson called the Senate into session unusually early and kept it in session until it acted on the nomination.

107. *Columbia Record*, July 19, 1956.

108. *Florence Morning News*, July 20, 1956.

109. Report of Proceedings, Hearings held before Special Subcommittee of the Committee on the Judiciary, Nomination of Clement F. Haynsworth, Junior, to Be United States Circuit Judge for the Fourth District, March 7, 1957, Files of the Senate Judiciary Committee, Washington, D.C.; Thurmond to Owen R. Cheatham, November 20, 1956, GF 4-C–4, DDEL; Cheatham to Sherman Adams, December 4, 1956, *ibid.*; Thurmond to Adams, November 27, 1956, *ibid.*; Adams to Cheatham, December 6, 1956, *ibid.*; Thurmond to Eisenhower, July 7, 1956, Alpha File, Administration Series, DDEL; memo of telephone conversation between Thurmond and Adams, November 27, 1956, *ibid.*; memo of telephone conversation between Adams and Thurmond, November 29, 1956, *ibid.*; memo of telephone conversation between Thurmond and Adams, December 8, 1956, *ibid.*; *Richmond Times Dispatch*, February 20, 1957.

110. Michael S. Mayer, *Simon E. Sobeloff* (Baltimore: University of Maryland School of Law, 1980), 18–28; Sanford J. Rosen, ''Judge Sobeloff's Public School Race Decisions,'' 34 *Maryland Law Review*, 498–531; Bernard Schwartz, *Swann's Way: The School Busing Case and the Supreme Court* (New York: Oxford University Press, 1986), 21–24; Peltason, *Fifty-Eight Lonely Men*, 23–25, 129, 217; *School Board of Charlottesville v. Allen*, 263 F. 2d 295 (4th Cir. 1959); *Duckworth v. James*, 267 F. 2d 224 (4th Cir. 1959); *Dodson v. School Board of Charlottesville*, 289 F. 2d 439 (4th Cir. 1961); *Green v. School Board of Roanoke*, 304 F. 2d 118 (4th Cir. 1962); *March v. County School Board of Roanoke City*, 305 F. 2d 94 (4th Cir. 1962); *Jackson v. School Board of Lynchburg*, 321 F. 2d 230 (4th Cir. 1963); *Bell v. School Board of Powhatan County*, 321 F. 2d 494 (4th Cir. 1963); *Buckner v. County School Board of Greene County*, 332 F. 2d 452 (4th Cir. 1964); *Wanner v. County School Board of Arlington County*, 357 F. 2d 452 (4th Cir. 1965); *Bowman v. County School Board of Charles City County*, 382 F. 2d 613 (4th Cir. 1967); *Brunson v. Board of Trustees of School District No. 1 of Clarendon County*, 429 F. 2d 820 (4th Cir. 1970); *Swann v. Charlotte-Mecklenburg Board of Education*, 431 F. 2d 138 (4th Cir. 1970); *United States v. Scotland Neck City Board of Education*, 442 F. 2d 575 (4th Cir. 1971).

5

THE EISENHOWER ADMINISTRATION AND THE 1957 CIVIL RIGHTS ACT

Donald W. Jackson and
James W. Riddlesperger, Jr.

Often, the seeds of potential public policies are easily conceived and planted but exceedingly slow to sprout. The full bloom of maturity and the bearing of good fruit of the expected type are sometimes so far removed from the conception that only the most attentive and long-lived progenitors can witness the harvest. The Civil Rights Act of 1957 offers an excellent example. This chapter recounts the long and slow sequence of events, beginning in the 1940s, that led eventually to enactment of that statute. Our chief purpose is to show how fundamentally different were the perceptions of the political controversy and predicted consequences of the act in 1957, relative to those that may be formed with the convenient assistance of hindsight today. It is equally interesting to view the perspectives of the political controversy over the 1957 Civil Rights Act from the different vantage points of the Eisenhower administration and of the Democratic leadership in the Congress. To be more specific, consider the following points:

1. Viewed from the perspective of the proponents of civil rights legislation within the Eisenhower administration, the Republican Party in 1955 had the opportunity to seize the high ground by proposing moderate legislation that would attract minority voters and contribute to the emergence of the Republican Party as a moderately progressive majority party in American politics. Seen from that perspective, the enactment of civil rights legislation would have contributed to that result.

2. Viewed from the somewhat more cynical perspective of some Republican politicians, the proposal by the Eisenhower administration of civil rights legislation presented the prospect for casting the largely southern Democratic leadership in the Congress as

advocates of racism and reaction. Seen from that perspective, the defeat of the proposed civil rights legislation would have contributed to that result.

3. Viewed from the perspective of the Eisenhower administration's proponents of civil rights legislation, the Senate-imposed amendments to the act stripped the moderate measure of its teeth and largely destroyed its vitality.

4. Viewed from the perspective of the Democratic leadership in the Congress, most notably that of Majority Leader Lyndon Johnson, the Eisenhower administration was either inept or cynical in its proposal and espousal of civil rights legislation.

5. Viewed from the perspective of Senator Johnson and his allies, the compromises that led to Senate amendments enabled the enactment of the first civil rights legislation since Reconstruction. But for those compromises and the efforts of the Democratic leadership, no bill could have been passed in the Senate.

6. Viewed from the perspective of all the participants, the controversy over the 1957 act centered on the provision of jury trials in contempt cases and on the possibility of aggressive federal enforcement of civil rights in the south, including the possible use of federal troops. The creation of the U.S. Commission on Civil Rights was largely noncontroversial.

7. Viewed from today's perspective, the creation of the Civil Rights Commission, the hearings it conducted in the south (particularly with respect to infringement on the right to vote), and the facts that it fed to the media and to political decision makers were probably much more important than were the more controversial aspects of the 1957 act.

BACKGROUND

What key events led to the Civil Rights Act of 1957? On December 5, 1946, President Truman created his President's Committee on Civil Rights by Executive Order 9808. The committee was charged with the task of assessing the "civil rights goal of the American people," "our achievements and shortcomings," and the "government's responsibility" for success or failure. The committee's objective was to recommend steps to help the country reach its goals.[1]

The idea for such a committee had been circulating around Washington at least since the wartime race riots of 1943.[2] Following some particularly nasty and vivid racially motivated killings in the south in connection with the 1946 election, in September 1946, Truman's administrative assistant, David Niles, discussed with the president the possibility of creating a commission to study mob violence and civil rights. At a subsequent meeting, after hearing that Congress might be reluctant to act, President Truman said that he would create such a commission by executive order. A few days later Tom Clark, then the attorney general, had the order drafted.[3]

The committee's report, *To Secure These Rights*, was published in 1947. Among its recommendations were the reorganization of the Civil Rights Section and its enhancement to full divisional status within the Department of Justice, the creation by Congress of a permanent Commission on Civil Rights, and the enactment of various federal laws that would serve to strengthen the protection of the right to vote.[4] These were roughly the same provisions that were proposed by the Eisenhower administration in 1956–1957.

The Civil Rights Section of the Criminal Division of the Department of Justice had been created by then Attorney General Frank Murphy in 1939.[5] In 1947, when the report of the President's Committee was issued, it consisted of seven attorneys, all stationed in Washington. It depended entirely on the FBI for its investigatory work and on local U.S. attorneys for prosecution of cases.[6]

Another of the recommendations of the President's Committee was an anti-poll-tax measure. When an effort was made in the Senate in 1949 to bring the measure to a vote, the then two-thirds cloture requirement was applied to the motion to bring the bill to a vote. In the following session, on March 11, 1949, the two-thirds Senate cloture rule was continued by a vote of forty-six to forty-one. Among those voting to protect cloture was the newly elected Senator Lyndon Johnson, who made his maiden Senate speech in defense of cloture, urging that its loss would leave a Senate minority defenseless. That marked the end of any prospect for civil rights legislation during the Truman presidency.[7]

THE EISENHOWER ADMINISTRATION, 1952–1956

Even under the most lenient current standards for judging accomplishments, the first term of the Eisenhower presidency achieved little in the civil rights arena other than to offer largely symbolic reassurances. The standards of the day were, however, even more lenient. Thus, Mark Stern reports that the NAACP was pleased with the administration's first-term record,[8] specifically with its Committee on Government Contracts (on equal employment for government contracts), its briefs in the school desegregation cases, its abolition of segregated schools and other facilities on military installations, its efforts to desegregate public accommodations in the District of Columbia, and its appointments of blacks to government positions.[9]

The 1952 Republican platform had contained only the most general endorsement of civil rights, but, to be fair, so had the Democratic platform. However, the events of 1954 and 1955 had brought civil rights to the front burner. In November 1955, E. Frederic Morrow had written Cabinet Secretary Maxwell Rabb that the south was "on the verge of a dangerous racial confrontation."[10] It is important to remember for the context of the time that *Brown v. Board of Education of Topeka* had been initially decided on May 17, 1954, and that 1955 was the year that witnessed both the "all deliberate speed" enforcement decision in the *Brown* case and the beginning of the Montgomery bus boycott, when Rosa Parks refused to relinquish her bus seat.

On December 2, 1955, the Cabinet met to consider civil rights language for the forthcoming State of the Union message. The administration was caught between the White Citizens Councils and the Klan, on one side, and a burgeoning civil rights movement, on the other. Attorney General Herbert Brownell presented the Justice Department's recommendations, which included a bipartisan commission to investigate violent racial incidents, raising the Civil Rights Section to a Division, strengthening the laws protecting voting rights, and providing for injunctive relief. Then Vice President Nixon, apparently acting with the penchant for hardball politics that he was to exhibit so many times in his career, suggested that were the administration simply to toss the civil rights controversy to the Congress, southern Democrats could probably be relied upon to drag their feet and to block remedial legislation, to the eventual political credit of the Republican Party.[11]

However, at a meeting of legislative leaders held on December 8, 1955, a memorandum prepared by White House Counsel Gerald Morgan proposed that the president take positive action by recommending legislation to prevent interference with voting on the basis of race, religion, or national origin—to include prohibition of the poll tax—so as to redeem his broad 1952 Republican platform pledge.[12] In January 1956, a number of meetings were held in connection with the drafting of the president's State of the Union message. His message of February 5, 1956, included the recommendations that Brownell had outlined at the December 2, 1955, Cabinet meeting.

To carry out the references to civil rights in the president's message, Attorney General Brownell prepared a Cabinet paper on his program, which was first presented at a Cabinet meeting on March 9, 1956. Prior to the attorney general's presentation to the Cabinet, J. Edgar Hoover delivered a twenty-four-page cautionary report on "Racial Tension and Civil Rights," in which he identified and summarized the activities of civil rights proponents and opponents since *Brown v. Board of Education* in 1954. Brownell's presentation followed Hoover's. The Cabinet minutes indicate that Brownell stressed that the program would be the recommendation of the Justice Department, rather than that of the president. Several expressed their concerns over the timing and the manner of presentation, so the president instructed Brownell to bring the program back to the Cabinet for final review before submitting it to Congress.[13]

On March 11, the president, Sherman Adams, Morgan, and Brownell met to review the entire civil rights program. The president authorized Brownell to submit the provision regarding the Civil Rights Commission as an administration proposal but wanted to submit the remaining provisions as Justice Department suggestions. Brownell submitted the proposals to Congress on April 9 and testified before the House Judiciary Committee on the following day.[14] Speaker Sam Rayburn worked successfully with House Republican Leader Joe Martin to get the administration's bill out of the House Rules Committee. The House passed the bill before adjourning in July for the 1956 election campaign, but it was not brought to a vote in the Senate, largely due to Senator Johnson's sending it to the Judiciary Committee, then chaired by Senator Eastland of Mississippi.[15] Newspaper columnist Joe Alsop suggested that the Eisenhower administration had not been serious in its proposal or in its efforts to enact the bill but had intended the bill only as political fodder for the forthcoming election.[16]

THE CRITICAL YEAR, 1957

In the second volume of his memoirs, *Waging Peace*, President Eisenhower duly noted both the gains for the Republican ticket in the south and his increased support among black voters in the 1956 election. He interpreted this as a solid gain for his centrist Republican politics. In his January 1957 State of the Union message he endorsed all four sections of the civil rights legislation introduced the previous year, and his 1957 recommendation to the Congress was clear and simple: enact the proposed legislation in its *entirety*.[17]

IN THE HOUSE

In February, the House Judiciary Committee began hearings on the bill. Rayburn had to contend again with Howard Smith of Virginia, the chairman of the House Rules Committee. Smith refused to call a meeting of the committee and then left town to avoid pressure from Rayburn. His committee eventually did report the bill, however, and it came to a vote in the House on June 18, 1957. President Eisenhower could not understand how any Republican could possibly oppose proposals as mild as these, and the administration consistently opposed efforts in the House to add a jury trial amendment.[18] An amendment to recommit the bill, so that a provision for jury trials in criminal contempt actions could be inserted, was rejected by a vote of 158 to 251, with only 45 Republicans opposing the administration's position. The entire bill passed by a vote of 286 to 126; 118 Democrats voted in favor, while 107 Democrats voted against the bill. Of those who opposed, 98 were southern Democrats, including the entire Texas delegation, save for Speaker Rayburn himself, who, as presiding officer, cast no vote. No southern Democrat voted for the bill. On the Republican side the vote was 168 to 19.[19]

IN THE SENATE

The vote in the House was only a prelude to the intricate politics of the U.S. Senate. Debate on the Senate floor was scheduled to begin on July 8, 1957, once the Senate had rejected Georgia Senator Russell's point of order, the acceptance of which would have sent the bill to committee. In his letters to constituents, Senator Johnson referred to the pending legislation as the "so-called Civil Rights bill" and noted that he had voted with Senator Russell to send the bill to committee "but that we lost that fight." The sense of his correspondence with conservative constituents was that he fought off the efforts of the Eisenhower administration to pass a stronger measure. With more liberal constituents, he expressed firm support for the right to vote. As we will show in the next several pages, he sensed that the right to vote was the provision around which a majority in the Senate could be formed.[20] Most observers agree that it was Johnson's behind-the-scenes work that led to passage of a bill, when otherwise none would have been possible.[21]

The bill that passed the House and came to the Senate floor for debate on July 8, 1957, was, as we have noted, largely consistent with the recommendations of the 1947 report of President Truman's committee. The conflict in the Senate probably had more to do with the way the legislation was characterized and perceived than with its substantive content. The battle lines for that conflict had been drawn during hearings before the Senate Judiciary Committee. In his testimony before that committee on February 14, Attorney General Brownell had admitted that the Justice Department's request for authority to bring injunction suits under Section III of the proposed legislation would include the possibility of injunctive relief against all civil rights violations, not merely the denial of voting rights. Senator Sam Ervin of North Carolina attempted to connect that authority with the possible use of federal troops to enforce injunctions in the south. Following that, southern Democrats, including Lyndon Johnson, began to call Section III the "force bill" provision.[22]

Senator Russell of Georgia raised the "force bill" theme again in an attack on the Senate floor on July 2. Russell called for a national referendum on the bill. Following Russell's remarks, President Eisenhower's understanding of the bill and his purposes were perhaps unclear and certainly have been variously interpreted. In his memoirs, Eisenhower entirely omits discussion of his seeming vacillation. But, for whatever reasons, the president admitted publicly on July 4, after rereading the bill, that Section III contained "certain phrases I didn't completely understand," and he said that he would have to talk with the attorney general about its meaning. The Justice Department's response was that while the issue of voting rights was the primary object of Section III, even under existing law federal troops could be used, if necessary, to enforce federal court orders.[23] Two weeks later, the president commented at a press conference that, "If you try to go too far too fast . . . you are making a mistake." Because of such words, Emmet John Hughes characterized Eisenhower's leadership at the time as "limp" and concluded that his weakness "served almost as a pathetic and inviting prologue to Little Rock."[24] However, other sources, including the president's correspondence and the minutes of his meetings with Republican legislative leaders, give a somewhat different impression.

In his letter of July 23, 1957, to former Supreme Court justice and South Carolina Governor James Byrnes, Eisenhower explained his remarks on July 4, which had suggested his confusion about Section III. In that letter he noted that he had been accused in the press conference of not fully understanding some of the language of the bill, but in fact he had been referring to conflicting legal opinions that had been given him regarding Section III. One of these opinions had been that the authority sought would be circumscribed and limited by other existing laws. The other opinion provided him was that the authority could, in ambitious hands, be expanded to constitute a virtual police state procedure. He emphasized in the letter to Byrnes that he wanted to ensure that no one was persecuted by the law.[25]

The minutes of the president's meetings also reflect something less than confusion over the meaning of the bill. On July 6, 1957, only two days after having expressed his puzzlement over Section III, Eisenhower met with Attorney General Brownell; Vice President Nixon; Senators Knowland, Dirksen, and Saltonstall; House Minority Leader Martin; and House Majority Leader Charles Halleck. Knowland and Dirksen suggested that Section III might be struck from the bill by a narrow margin and that a substitute provision would be more acceptable. Saltonstall said that Lyndon Johnson was trying to work out a compromise. The president said that it would be best for him to keep out of the details at this stage but to speak in favor of four things: the proposed Civil Rights Commission and the establishment of the Civil Rights Division, voting rights, and the support of the federal judiciary. He said that he intended to stay on principle and out of detail and that the purpose of Section III was simply that the "orders of federal courts will be supported." In the minutes he said that the present bill was intended to support district judges and school boards in their responsibility to complete the Supreme Court's decision "with all deliberate speed." Eisenhower conceded, however, that the modification and clarification of Part III would not be harmful.[26]

The next meeting of legislative leaders was three days later on July 9. The attorney general reported that the use of federal troops to enforce the law had always been a possibility but that it had been the custom since 1870 to include specific authorization of troops in new legislation. Brownell supposed that a provision might be included specifically to exclude the use of troops. Halleck then asked how important Section III was to the administration. The attorney general responded that it would serve to extend civil rights to things other than the right to vote.

The President said that the only new thing in the picture was the Supreme Court decision [in *Brown v. Board of Education*], and the Administration wanted to make certain that Federal court orders are not flouted. He thought there was a need to show that the Courts can be upheld in their decisions. The President asserted the Administration approach was designed to be very moderate, because the more you stir up passions, the more you set back the whole process of improvement in this subject.

The President thought that this should all be cleared up quickly, for the Executive has a constitutional responsibility to support the Courts.[27]

The next day the president met with Senator Richard B. Russell. Eisenhower assured Russell that the primary purpose of the bill was to protect the right to vote, and Russell privately assured the president that he agreed with the justice of the president's position and with his assessment of the need for the provision. Shortly thereafter, an amendment to Section III, which purported to repeal prior statutory authority for the use of federal troops, was adopted by the Senate ninety to zero.[28]

Eisenhower's public position now was to stress the importance of protecting the right to vote, which was set out in Section IV of the bill. Frederic Morrow wrote to Sherman Adams on July 12, expressing his grave concern over reports that the administration might soften the requirement of the bill, but for all practical purposes the deed was already done. Many concluded at the time that Eisenhower jettisoned Section III to protect Section IV.[29] At a news conference on July 17, the president indicated that it would be unwise for the attorney general to bring suit on his own to enforce school integration.[30]

On July 24, the Senate eliminated Section III from the bill by a vote of fifty-two to thirty-eight. In his memoirs, Eisenhower said that this amendment "was a blow" and reported that Brownell was bitterly disappointed. He noted, however, that he had been warned by the Republican leadership that an attempt to renew Section III would destroy the possibility of any legislation. Eisenhower reported that he agreed to "push no farther."[31] Attention now turned to efforts by southern Senators to amend Section IV to include a jury trial requirement.

Now we will see the critical intervention of Lyndon Johnson, both in the passage of the bill in the Senate and in the eventual agreement reached between Congress and the Eisenhower administration. George Reedy was Johnson's principal adviser on the civil rights bill. In a series of memos written in July 1957, Reedy counselled Johnson to find some way for the Senate to act on the bill. "The one inescapable necessity of the current Senate debate over civil rights," Reedy wrote, "is that it must end in meaningful action." "It is reasonable," Reedy suggested, "to protect the Negro's right to vote." "It is unreasonable to deprive men of the right to a jury trial when they are being tried on criminal charges." On the other hand, Reedy suggested, it was reasonable "to permit a judge to punish overt contempt of court." According to Reedy, only the northern "liberal" Democrats would be the losers were such a bill to pass. The Republicans would get the credit for sponsoring the bill and bringing it to the floor for a vote. The southern Democrats would get credit for removing the "force" provision of Section III. Moderates of both parties would get credit for the compromise bill. Reedy then appealed to Johnson to play the leadership role in bringing these results about. Johnson was, he said, the "only bridge between the South and the moderate elements of the North." Johnson was "the only force" that could "check the extremists of the North."[32]

However, while Eisenhower had reluctantly conceded Section III, he was prepared to stand firm against amending Section IV to include any jury trial provision. Proponents of the bill, including the president, were quite unwilling to cede to southern juries the virtual power to nullify civil rights enforcement. Reedy writes that the confrontation between the Eisenhower and Johnson positions looked very much like the proverbial irresistible force running up against an immovable object:

There was no apparent "give" on either side. The Southerners were not going to permit the passage of a bill without a guarantee of jury trials—and they had the force to prevent passage. The civil rights bloc of senators were not going to permit the passage of a bill with a guarantee of jury trials—and they had the force to prevent passage. It appeared as though many months of planning and careful work were going down the drain.[33]

The way out lurked in what to laymen would seem like an obscure point of law, but that point, coupled with Johnson's willingness to exploit it and to cajole his colleagues, allowed Johnson to reach what Reedy called his "greatest height" and to produce a "legislative miracle."[34]

According to Lawson, former Roosevelt aide Ben Cohen had seen an article by Carl Auerbach, then a University of Wisconsin law professor, in the April 29 issue of the *New Leader*. Auerbach's article describes the distinction between civil and criminal attempt. In civil contempt, a person who is in violation of a court order, and thereby in contempt, may be confined to jail until he or she gains release by agreeing to comply with the court order. No jury trial is offered in such circumstances because the purpose of the contempt order is remedial, and the contempt is a matter directly between the judge and the person who willfully and continuously refuses to obey a court order. Criminal contempt, on the other hand, is for the purpose of punishing someone who has previously been contemptuous of a court order. Since it is punitive, it is very much like a criminal proceeding, though obviously not an ordinary crime. Auerbach writes that jury trials could be reserved for criminal contempts while leaving judges ample contempt powers in civil proceedings. Cohen approached Johnson directly with this suggestion, and he, Abe Fortas, and Dean Acheson drew up the plan. It was introduced in July as an amendment in the Senate. When Johnson seized upon it as his compromise measure, he made it the key to the deadlock that he had already been battering compulsively. George Reedy's description can't be bettered:

He pleaded and threatened and stormed and cajoled. He prowled the corridors of the Senate grabbing Senators and staff members indiscriminately, probing them for some sign of amenability to compromise. He spent hours on the phone in nonstop conversations with the most ingenious legal minds he knew—Corcoran, Rowe, Cohen, Clifford, Fortas, Acheson—pleading with them for something to break the log jam. Virtually single-handed, he kept a large body of very strong-minded and willful men concentrating on a purpose which most of them thought could not be achieved.[35]

President Eisenhower, however, was unpersuaded, and he was not alone. On July 27 a statement of eleven law school deans and thirty-four law professors who opposed the jury trial amendment was released.[36] At his meeting with Republican legislative leaders on July 30, the president reaffirmed his opposition to any jury trial amendment,[37] and at a press conference the following day he reported that his advisers had found thirty-six different federal laws where contempt citations were not subject to jury trials.[38] All this was in vain, for the jury trial amendment was passed in the Senate by a vote of fifty-one to forty-two on August 1.

Val Washington, director of minorities for the Republican National Committee, wrote Lyndon Johnson on August 6 that the adoption of the jury trial amendment had been "one of the blackest days in American history . . . for Negroes and other dark races, not only in the United States, but around the world." "I am positive, Senator, that neither you, nor any of your Southern colleagues would vote for this Bill unless you know it is meaningless and ineffective," Washington concluded.[39]

At the meeting of Republican legislative leaders on August 6, Deputy Attorney General William Rogers called the amended bill a "monstrosity—the most irresponsible act he had seen during his time in Washington."[40]

THE FINAL COMPROMISE

The House voted not to accept the Senate amendments. This caused the bill to be lodged in the House Rules Committee, where the chairman, Judge Smith of Virginia, was quite content to leave it. At this point, Speaker Rayburn intervened as the mediator between the House and the Senate. He called the White House and said that the "Democrats are willing to talk it over."[41] Rayburn's role in getting the act out of Smith's committee was critical, leading to the conclusion that it "was a law that could have easily been defeated in the House Rules Committee if Rayburn had not chosen to support it."[42]

Eisenhower had to determine whether to support the weakened bill or to let it die in its current form. Vice President Nixon urged that the administration reject the Senate version, and the president threatened to veto any bill containing the Senate's jury trial amendment. Minority Leader Martin was also willing to let the bill die in its Senate form. Eisenhower quotes in his memoirs from a letter he wrote to a friend at about this time: "the week had been a depressing one," and the "Country took an awful beating."[43] At a meeting with Republican legislative leaders on August 13, the president said that he found it ironic that the Democrats had made it seem that the civil rights bill was their project and that the Republicans might get the blame now, were there to be no bill.[44] The president chose, however, to fight against the current Senate version. To that end, White House Counsel Morgan, working with the Justice Department, proposed a compromise to the president and to the Senate conferees on August 16 to the effect that the right to trial by jury in contempt cases would obtain only when the penalty might be in excess of 90 days or when the fine might be in excess of $300. On August 23, Lyndon Johnson called the president and reported that he could get the southern leadership to agree to $300 and 45 days. Eisenhower asked for 10 minutes, and called Knowland and Martin from the floor. Both agreed to the compromise; according to the notes of the telephone calls, Knowland was more enthusiastic than Martin. Eisenhower encouraged Martin by saying that it would be a "Great victory." The president then called Johnson back, and the deal was struck. On August 26, President Eisenhower and Senator Johnson had a private breakfast at which Johnson summed up the legislative year and expressed the hope that the 12 Republican senators who had previously voted against the bill would support the compromise. The following day, August 27, presidential aide Bryce Harlow wrote a memo to Eisenhower reporting a call from Lyndon Johnson. Johnson wanted the president to know that while no member of the Texas House delegation had voted for the civil rights bill the first time, this time a total of 12 Texans in the House voted for the civil rights bill and only 5 voted against it. Johnson called this a victory for moderation and reasonableness.[45] The House had passed the compromise by a vote of 279 to 97, and on August 29 the Senate voted in its favor 60 to 15.

After passage of the bill, Lyndon Johnson wrote to a black constituent that the legislation was a "right to vote" bill, which "while not perfect is the best that we were able to pass at this time." To a white constituent he wrote that he "would not have voted for the bill in its original form" and argued that "we knocked out the force bill provision" and added an amendment guaranteeing the right to trial by jury. Finally, Johnson argued that if the bill had died, he was certain that in the next session, someone would have pushed through a much more drastic bill which would have included provisions as bad as, if not worse than, the ones in the Senate. To a constituent who supported the bill, Johnson wrote that his vote was the first time that a Texas senator had supported such legislation since Reconstruction days.[46]

On August 13, Dean Acheson wrote a letter to Senator Johnson to challenge the journalistic impression that the bill was merely a compromise. Acheson urged Johnson to say that the bill was among the great achievements since the war in the field of civil rights.[47]

On August 30, Martin Luther King, Jr., wrote Vice President Nixon. In addition to congratulating Nixon for his support and courage in seeking to make the civil rights bill a reality, Reverend King concluded that the compromise bill was far better than no bill at all.[48]

President Eisenhower signed the 1957 Civil Rights Act into law on September 9, 1957.

SHORT- AND LONG-TERM CONSEQUENCES, LARGELY UNFORESEEN TANGIBLE RESULTS

In one of his July 1957 memos to Lyndon Johnson, George Reedy attempted to assess and summarize the attitudes of the journalists who were covering the civil rights debates in Congress. Reedy concluded that most journalists didn't even know that a provision for a fact-finding civil rights commission was in the bill, and those who did "care even less."[49] The creation of the U.S. Commission on Civil Rights and the elevation of civil rights from sectional to divisional status within the Justice Department were both noncontroversial and uninteresting to the media. As we have seen, the attention of political actors was focused almost entirely on the authority of the Justice Department to bring injunctive suits on its own initiative (which was limited by Senate amendment to injunctive suits involving the right to vote) and on the question of whether those who might violate a federal injunction would be entitled to a jury trial on their contempt (juries being required by Senate amendment only for criminal contempts where the punishment was greater than $300 or the jail term greater than forty-five days).

Yet when the U.S. Commission on Civil Rights issued its first report in September 1959, it included the following:

Nearly two years after the passage of the [1957] Act the Department of Justice had brought only three actions under its new powers to seek preventive civil relief. . . . In a presentation to a subcommittee of the House Appropriations Committee it was revealed that of 32 Civil Rights Division cases pending at the end of fiscal 1958, only 7 were properly in the category of "civil rights" as that term is generally understood, 3 were in the field of voting and elections, and no more than 4 were racial cases.[50]

In his book, *Black Ballots*, Steven F. Lawson reports that from 1958 to 1960 the Civil Rights Division received twenty-three complaints alleging racial disenfranchisement in the south.[51] In its 1961 report, the Civil Rights Commission noted somewhat greater activity by the Department of Justice. While no clear count of cases brought under the 1957 act was set out in the report, it appears that about fourteen suits had been filed; several of them proved to be time-consuming test cases on the constitutionality of the 1957 act.[52] In its 1963 report, the commission found that during 1962 and 1963 the Justice Department had filed twenty-two voting suits, eight of which involved "reprisals or intimidation."[53]

Lawson concluded from such evidence that it was the work of the Civil Rights Commission that exposed both the "manifold instances of disenfranchisement" in the south and the failure of the Department of Justice to deal effectively with it.[54] The fair inference is that political controversy over Sections III and IV of the 1957 act was much ado about little. The fact-finding work of the U.S. Commission on Civil Rights was no doubt far more important than anything accomplished by the Civil Rights Division of the Department of Justice under the 1957 act. Indeed, it can fairly be argued that it was the fact finding of the Civil Rights Commission (within the federal government), the witness of the Civil Rights Movement led by Martin Luther King, Jr. (outside of government), and the intransigence of southern leaders like Bull Connor, Ross Barnett, and George Wallace that combined with extensive media coverage of events in the south to lead proximately to the enactment of the 1960 and 1964 Civil Rights Acts and to the Voting Rights Act of 1965. Only when the authority contained in those acts was in the hands of the U.S. government was there a decent prospect for federal enforcement of civil rights. This is simply another way of saying that the politics involved in the enactment of the 1957 act were largely symbolic.

SYMBOLIC RESULTS

In his memoir of Lyndon Johnson, George Reedy wrote that the 1957 act "gave Southern senators only a mythical claim that they had preserved jury trial rights for their constituents."[55] "Johnson had tossed them a real olive branch, the sort of thing where they could go home and say, 'Yes, they rolled over us, but we fought and at least we fixed it up so that them goddamn Yankee carpetbaggers couldn't come back and also they couldn't brand you as a criminal without a trial by jury.' "[56]

Strong civil rights proponents in the Congress saw even the original administration bill as a very modest measure and the Senate-amended version as weak and tepid, even if it was the best that could be passed. Reedy said that they missed the point of it all. While the enforcement provisions of the 1957 act were weak, and the utilization of them by the Justice Department was modest at best, this was the first civil rights legislation passed since Reconstruction. As Reedy put it: "A major branch of the American government that had been closed to minority members of the population seeking redress for wrongs was suddenly opened. The civil rights battle could now be fought out legislatively in an arena that previously had provided nothing but a sounding board for speeches."[57]

Reedy claims that Johnson "assessed the forces at work," "correctly forecast the reactions of protagonists to the world outside," and "selected the time to move." He claims that Johnson saw in advance that the 1957 act would open the door to more substantive civil rights legislation.[58] Reedy's retrospective analysis of the symbolic consequences of the 1957 act seems to be correct and well founded, but his claims for Johnson's foresight are probably extravagant.[59]

The proposal and passage of the 1957 Civil Rights Act did offer the Republican Party under President Eisenhower's leadership a chance to occupy a moderately progressive position in American politics. To Eisenhower's credit, that position seems quite consistent with his own political world view, but for whatever reasons, he was unable, in the long run, to keep the Republican Party moving in that direction. Eventually, the Democratic Party, and especially Lyndon Johnson, seized civil rights issues and made the movement its own—at least symbolically.

A CONCLUDING INTERPRETATION OF EISENHOWER'S LEADERSHIP

Eisenhower's letter to Captain Hazlett reflecting his understanding of the relations among law, popular attitudes, and social change probably illustrates quite well his fundamental reticence about dealing with public issues in an emotional or provocative way, as well as his views on the limits of federal authority.[60] Yet, at another level lay his resolve to uphold and respect the Constitution and the federal courts—as Little Rock eventually would demonstrate.

Mark Stern's article on civil rights strategies during the first two years of the

Eisenhower administration reviews the revisionist literature on the Eisenhower presidency. That literature largely describes President Eisenhower as being more engaged and more proactive in the policies of his administration than did earlier reviews. Stern himself concludes that with respect to civil rights policy "overall, Eisenhower's stewardship as party leader and President appeared to be a very successful and well-crafted balancing act of party building and policy leadership."[61] Privately, he seems mostly to have mastered his paperwork and to have been well-informed and in charge, even if publicly on some occasions he may have either stumbled or dissembled for his own political purposes.

Eisenhower's leadership strategy was far more active than some have suggested. It included comprehensive discussions with his advisers on all major aspects of the bill and active engagement with congressional leadership during the critical conference committee stage. But Eisenhower's leadership fell short of the role that many modern presidents have played in that he was willing to leave the cajoling and detailed negotiation to his administrative assistants and to congressional leaders. This follows from Eisenhower's general view of the presidency as one where through institutionalized procedures, alternatives are presented to the president. Once the president's decision is made, it is the duty of the administrative team to carry out policy making so that the president may move on to other tasks.[62] Modern presidents move directly from decision making to coalition building, relying on more than party ties and institutionalized support. They engage in personal leadership to cajole individual members of Congress to support the president's position in developing an issue-specific coalition.[63]

Eisenhower took an active policy leadership role in helping to pass the 1957 Civil Rights Act, and he provided moral leadership to the cause of the Civil Rights Movement. However, he left the personalized leadership in the passing of the act to congressional leaders Johnson and Rayburn.

NOTES

1. Probably the most important preceding presidential initiative in civil rights was the creation of the Fair Employment Practice Committee by President Franklin D. Roosevelt in 1941. President Truman continued and supported that initiative. Then presidential candidate Eisenhower opposed a federal Fair Employment Practices Commission at a 1952 press conference. See Mark Stern, "Presidential Strategies and Civil Rights: Eisenhower, the Early Years, 1952–54," *Presidential Studies Quarterly* 19 (1989): 773.

2. In Detroit in the summer of 1943, riots broke out over the admission of blacks to a federally financed housing project and over the promotion of blacks at a Packard plant. Thirty-four were killed; twenty-five of them were blacks, seventeen of whom were killed by the police. Richard Kluger, *Simple Justice: The History of* Brown v. Board of Education *and Black America's Struggle for Equality* (New York: Alfred Knopf, 1975), 284.

3. Robert J. Donovan, *Conflict and Crisis: The Presidency of Harry S. Truman, 1945–48* (New York: W. W. Norton, 1977), 245.

4. U.S. President's Committee on Civil Rights, *To Secure These Rights: The Report*

of the President's Committee on Civil Rights (New York: Simon and Schuster, 1947), 151.

5. Murphy became a justice of the U.S. Supreme Court only a year later and served until his death in 1949. He often voted with the liberal wing of the Court, most notably Black and Douglas.

6. U.S. President's Committee, *To Secure These Rights*, 119.

7. Robert J. Donovan, *Tumultuous Years: The Presidency of Harry S. Truman, 1949–53* (New York: W. W. Norton, 1982), 119.

8. Stern, "Presidential Strategies," 783.

9. Eisenhower cited in his memoirs the appointment of E. Frederic Morrow as a presidential assistant, Lois Lippman as a secretary in the White House office, and J. Ernest Wilkins as Assistant Secretary of Labor. See Dwight D. Eisenhower, *The White House Years: Waging Peace, 1956–1961* (Garden City, N.Y.: Doubleday, 1965), 149. However, Morrow's account of the tortuous progress of his appointment to a White House position should be read as well. See E. Frederic Morrow, *Black Man in the White House* (New York: Coward-McCann, 1963).

10. Morrow Files, Box 10, Dwight D. Eisenhower Library (hereafter DDEL), Abilene, Kan.

11. Herbert S. Parmet, *Eisenhower and the American Crusades* (New York: Macmillan, 1972), 444.

12. Legislative Meetings Series, Box 1, DDEL.

13. Cabinet Series, Boxes 6 and 7, DDEL.

14. Robert F. Burk, *The Eisenhower Administration and Black Civil Rights* (Knoxville: University of Tennessee Press, 1984), 214.

15. Alfred Steinberg, *Sam Rayburn: A Biography* (New York: Hawthorn Books, 1975), 313.

16. Burk, *Eisenhower Administration*, 217.

17. Eisenhower, *Waging Peace*, 154.

18. Legislative Meetings Series, Box 2, DDEL.

19. *Congressional Quarterly Almanac* (Washington, D.C.: Congressional Quarterly Press, 1957), 84.

20. Senate Boxes 289–291, Lyndon B. Johnson Library (hereafter LBJL), University of Texas, Austin.

21. Here is an unusually vivid example of conflicting interpretations. In attempting to assess Johnson's role in the passage of the act, two Sam Rayburn biographers write the following:

1. "Johnson, in one of the most agile parliamentary performances ever witnessed in the Senate, kept debate moving. Cajoling colleagues, assuaging reluctant southerners, he salvaged most of the bill. . . . The compromises Johnson had to strike with southern opponents diluted the bill's enforcement provisions—a price many thought was too high for southern acquiescence. But the heart of the legislation remained" (D. B. Hardeman and Donald C. Bacon, *Rayburn: A Biography* [Austin: Texas Monthly Press, 1987], 422).

2. "Just as he had done in 1956, Johnson, with the help of Senator Richard Russell, tried to ship the bill to Eastland's committee and certain death. But this year, . . . his point of order failed. . . . A filibuster followed—sixty-six speeches in eight days—and when the force of the wind abated, the advocates of the Eisenhower bill had not been traumatized. Johnson was left with no alternative except to put through the weakest bill possible, and he did so with the aid of

lawyers Dean Acheson and Ben Cohen from the Roosevelt-Truman administration'' (Steinberg, *Sam Rayburn*, 314).

22. Senate Box 290, LBJL.

23. Burk, *Eisenhower Administration*, 222.

24. Emmet John Hughes, *The Ordeal of Power: A Political Memoir of the Eisenhower Years* (New York: Atheneum, 1963), 242.

25. DDE Diary Series, Box 25, DDEL.

26. Legislative Meetings Series, Box 2, DDEL.

27. *Ibid.*

28. Burk, *Eisenhower Administration*, 223.

29. See also Brownell Oral History Interview, January 31, 1968, DDEL.

30. In a private letter to Captain E. E. Hazlett of July 22, Eisenhower summarized what he called the obvious truths. See DDE Diary Series, Box 25, DDEL.

31. Eisenhower, *Waging Peace*, 58.

32. Senate Box 418, LBJL.

33. George Reedy, *Lyndon B. Johnson: A Memoir* (New York: Andrews and McMeel, 1982), 16.

34. *Ibid.*, 117.

35. *Ibid.*

36. Burk, *Eisenhower Administration*, 224.

37. Legislative Meetings Series, Box 2, DDEL.

38. Steven F. Lawson, *Black Ballots: Voting Rights in the South, 1944–69* (New York: Columbia University Press, 1976), 193.

39. Senate Papers, Reedy Files, Box 418, Civil Rights Folder, LBJL; Robert L. Branyan and Lawrence H. Larsen, eds., *The Eisenhower Administration, 1951–61: A Documentary History* (New York: Random House, 1971), 1113.

40. *Congressional Quarterly Almanac* (Washington, D.C.: Congressional Quarterly, 1957), 86.

41. Steinberg, *Sam Rayburn*, 314; Hardeman and Bacon, *Rayburn*, 422.

42. Anthony Champagne, *Congressman Sam Rayburn* (New Brunswick, N.J.: Rutgers University Press, 1984), 150.

43. Eisenhower, *Waging Peace*, 159.

44. Cabinet Series, Box 9, DDEL; Legislative Meetings Series, Box 2, DDEL.

45. DDE Diary Series, Box 26, DDEL.

46. Senate Boxes 289–91, LBJL.

47. Senate Box 408, Horowitz files, LBJL.

48. Rogers Papers, Box 50, DDEL.

49. Senate Box 418, LBJL.

50. U.S. Commission on Civil Rights, *Report* (Washington, D.C.: U.S. Government Printing Office, 1959), 131–32.

51. Lawson, *Black Ballots*, 205.

52. It should be noted that by the time the 1961 report was written, Congress had passed the 1960 Civil Rights Act, which gave the Justice Department additional civil rights authority and responsibility. U.S. Commission on Civil Rights, *Report* (Washington, D.C.: U.S. Government Printing Office, 1961), 79.

53. U.S. Commission on Civil Rights, *Report* (Washington, D.C.: U.S. Government Printing Office, 1963), 23.

54. Lawson, *Black Ballots*, 203.

55. Reedy, *Lyndon B. Johnson*, 15.

56. George Reedy Oral History Interview, December 20, 1983, 23–24, LBJL.

57. Reedy, *Lyndon B. Johnson*, 15.

58. *Ibid.*, 119.

59. Materials in the Johnson Library covering this period reveal no clear evidence of long-term programmatic commitment to civil rights. In other instances Reedy claims Johnson had excellent tactical skills but no strategic sense of politics.

60. See note 58.

61. Stern's conclusions about the first years of the Eisenhower administration include the following:

Quietly, and most importantly with the constraints of his own vision of a limited Federal role and the need to avoid inflaming the passions of the white South, Eisenhower moved to aid the black rights cause. He argued with his southern white friends and pleaded with them to accept the changes that were occurring. He temporized and commiserated with his southern friends as they bemoaned their fear of the Negro tide. But he moved primarily in a positive direction in civil rights policy during the first years of his administration.

Stern, "Presidential Strategies," 789.

62. Richard F. Fenno, *The President's Cabinet: An Analysis of the Period from Wilson to Eisenhower* (Cambridge, Mass.: Harvard University Press, 1959), 110–11.

63. Lester G. Seligman and Cary R. Covington, *The Coalitional Presidency* (Chicago: Dorsey Press, 1989).

6

EISENHOWER: LEADERSHIP IN SPACE POLICY

Giles Alston

It is often assumed that because President John F. Kennedy committed America to landing a man on the moon before the end of the 1960s, his administration was the first to face the issue of establishing a space policy for the United States. In fact, as early as 1955 President Eisenhower had divided American space activity into two distinct and separate programs. During his presidency, the military space program developed the intercontinental ballistic missiles that would form the backbone of American strategic strength and the first of the reconnaissance satellites that were to prove so crucial for the success of arms control negotiations. At the same time, its civilian sibling, an altogether smaller and less hurried undertaking, was constructed around a scientific agenda designed to carry out a steady and considered examination of this new environment.

When the Soviet Union launched Sputnik 1 on October 4, 1957, there was intense pressure on the president from his political opponents to respond to this terrible blow to American prestige. A rushed and expensive space program was demanded, one that would allow the United States to catch up with the Soviets. Eisenhower, however, refused to believe that prestige was something that the U.S. government needed to purchase in this way and was convinced that a costly orbital race for prestige was no alternative to the calm scientific exploration of outer space. Using his leadership skills, and supported by the continuing trust of ordinary Americans, he diverted the calls for unlimited spending on space into a debate on the future of education and, buoyed by a close relationship with his science advisers, ensured that science remained the main rationale for the civilian space program.

Knowing now how American space policy has developed over the last thirty years, one is struck by the astuteness of Eisenhower's low-key position on space. Although the president was much criticized at the time for being parsimonious, overly cautious, and uncomprehending of the threat to American prestige posed by Sputnik, his refusal to regard the exploration of space as in any way a race can now be seen as imparting a crucial element of stability to the program that subsequent space policy has sorely lacked. His successor was persuaded to take a diametrically opposing view—much to Eisenhower's private disapproval— and, removing the scientific element completely, made the Apollo project a straight prestige race to the moon. From then on, the civilian space program has progressed in fits and starts, not driven by a steadily evolving scientific agenda but rather a hostage to the shifting requirements of foreign and domestic politics. (Kennedy himself tried to dismantle Apollo in the last months of his presidency.) In space, as in so much else, Eisenhower's steady approach seems to have been vindicated by the contrary actions of those who came after him.

SPACE POLICY BEFORE SPUTNIK

A prelude to Eisenhower's concern with the exploration of space came as early as the summer of 1953, when the White House received a report that had been commissioned in the dying days of the Truman administration. This urged the president to regard the development of the satellite as a vital component in the cold war, not for its negligible military potential but for its propaganda value. The report noted that:

Since the Soviet Union has been following us in the atomic and hydrogen bomb developments, it should not be excluded that the Politburo might like to take the lead in the development of a satellite. . . . If the Soviet Union should accomplish this ahead of us it would be a serious blow to the technical and engineering prestige of America the world over. It would be used by the Soviets for all it is worth.[1]

The report appears to have made no impact at all on a new administration that had swiftly found its hands full at home and abroad. But it is interesting to note that this, the first of several appeals to the president to invest in space activity for the sake of American prestige, coincided with an early and relatively rare top-level assessment of the status of America's prestige abroad.

In July 1953, the National Security Council (NSC) was disturbed by reports of waning U.S. prestige in Europe—many of which had been brought back by prominent Americans who had been touring the continent at the height of the McCarthy excesses. C. D. Jackson, a writer and executive at *Time* whom Eisenhower had asked to coordinate his administration's psychological warfare activities, was asked by the NSC to use his Psychological Strategy Board to produce a study of the problem. Completed in mid-September 1953, the board's report on "Reported Decline in US Prestige Abroad" provided almost unremitting criticism of the administration's attitude toward Moscow and McCarthy.[2]

It emphasized that the White House's hard line toward the former and soft line toward the latter was underscoring European distrust of the Republican Party's approach to foreign affairs and alarm at the president's own inexperience. Eisenhower was furious at the report. He told the NSC that he had almost blown his top after reading it and blamed its conclusions on data submitted to Washington by renegade New Deal Democrats, "traitors" who remained in the far-flung reaches of the State Department.[3] From his wartime experience, and from his more recent stint as NATO commander, he was convinced that the report maliciously misconstrued America's standing (and his own) in Europe.

Moreover, Eisenhower was not convinced that U.S. prestige rested on the lavish activities of government; rather, he believed, it rested on the prosperity and contentment of its citizens. For Eisenhower, in an image he would later use to criticize his successor's reason for racing to the moon, America's ability to impress the rest of the world with the achievements of its political and economic system lay in the abundance of its supermarkets rather than the swiftness of its space program.[4] It was simply America's way of life that radiated the superiority of its political and economic system. Given this attitude, attempts to convince him of the necessity for an expensive space program on the grounds of buttressing national prestige were unlikely to succeed—and indeed, they did not.

During 1954, Eisenhower approved the intercontinental ballistic missile (ICBM) development program that would yield both the Atlas and the Titan missiles and began research work on a reconnaissance satellite. Both projects were regarded as being of the highest national priority. In the same year, support for the launching of a satellite began to coalesce in the scientific community. It centered around the idea of incorporating such a project within planning for the International Geophysical Year (IGY), which was due in 1957–1958. As the U.S. IGY Committee decided to back the satellite proposal, the question then became one of providing the launch vehicle. By the spring of 1955, all three military services had put forward a proposal: Project Orbiter, a joint Army-Navy undertaking to be led by Wernher von Braun; an improved Viking sounding rocket to be built by the Naval Research Laboratory; and a late entry from the Air Force, which would be based on the as yet untested Atlas ICBM. It was left to the NSC to decide the criteria by which the winner would be chosen, giving it the chance to set the course for space exploration for the rest of the Eisenhower administration.

When the NSC met in May 1955 to discuss the IGY satellite proposal, expected to cost some $20 million, a number of considerations emerged. The Pentagon saw the project as having militarily useful spinoffs and supported it, provided that it took no men or material away from its current missile and reconnaissance satellite projects. Nelson Rockefeller, who had replaced C. D. Jackson in the White House, submitted a paper stressing the propaganda value of launching the first satellite: "The stake of prestige that is involved makes this a race that we cannot afford to lose."[5] The most important point for Eisenhower, though, seems to have been the enthusiasm for the program within the scientific community.

This had been conveyed to him personally by Detlev Bronk, president of the National Academy of Sciences, and National Science Foundation director Alan Waterman, from whose funds the budget for the IGY would have to come. They found that Eisenhower viewed the project with genuine interest. Eisenhower's regard for scientists, already high from his military experience, had recently been heightened by the work of the Technologies Capabilities Panel in 1954–1955 (under the chairmanship of James Killian of MIT), which had provided an impressively impartial and unself-serving contrast to the usually expensive and partisan Pentagon recommendations. The IGY satellite proposal, Project Vanguard, appealed to him as a program with clear scientific value.[6]

The NSC's decision, set out in NSC 5520, was to go ahead with Project Vanguard, with science as its central rationale. This was underlined by the choice of the experimental but all-civilian Viking rocket as the satellite's launch vehicle, and then placing management of the whole project with Alan Waterman's National Science Foundation rather than with any of the military services. Although Vanguard's costs began to escalate almost immediately, Eisenhower remained committed to the project. He later told a NASA historian:

Dr. Waterman came back and said the cost would be at least $60 million and again I agreed that we should go ahead. Very shortly thereafter he warned that the cost could easily reach $150 million, and I called in the Director of the Budget to tell him that we would have to find or obtain the money because I believed that it was the kind of experimentation that would have real value for the United States.[7]

But because the prestige value of launching the world's first satellite was not the driving force behind the project, and because to give Vanguard the highest priority would encroach on the resources needed for the ICBM and reconnaissance satellite programs, speed was not of the essence. The only deadline was that imposed by the finish of IGY at the end of 1958, and there was no pressure from the scientific community to move faster. Nor did domestic or foreign opinion seem to require that the United States expend additional effort on Vanguard—if only because there seemed no doubt that America would be first in space. Thus when von Braun and his Army team informed the Pentagon that they would be able to orbit a satellite significantly earlier than the Viking, they were reprimanded for fostering interservice rivalry rather than welcomed for offering to speed the program. Despite this, in September 1956 the Army team did launch a vehicle capable of orbiting a satellite, although without such a payload, and managed to hold a second such vehicle in reserve should the call from Washington finally come.[8] Had the administration at any stage felt the need to ensure that a satellite was launched quickly, then the option was there from mid–1956. But there continued to be little reason to alter Vanguard from a civilian-led, scientific undertaking to a military project whose goal was speed, even when the USSR, which had also declared its intention to launch a satellite for IGY, began to issue ever more optimistic progress reports during 1957.

THE RESPONSE TO SPUTNIK DURING FALL 1957

"The near-hysterical reactions to Sputniks 1 and 2 deserve more attention than they have so far received," writes James Killian in his memoirs.[9] Certainly it would seem that the launching of Sputnik on Friday night, October 4, 1957, produced an instantaneous crisis of self-confidence in the United States that called into question American technological prowess, educational standards, political leadership, and even national moral fiber. The comments of many notable people immediately following the launch convey a deep sense of shock and apprehension; several draw an analogy with Pearl Harbor.[10] In light of the recent work attesting to Eisenhower's political astuteness, one interesting question here is why he was taken so unaware by the response of ordinary Americans. While headline writers and politicians talked of the satellite in apocalyptic terms, the administration continued to appear unperturbed. This suggests that it was badly out of touch with the public and has on occasion been used to illustrate the idea that Eisenhower was losing his grip in the second term.

Yet despite later impressions, it is by no means certain that the near hysteria conveyed in the media was shared, at least initially, by the public at large. Only two specific opinion studies concerning the development of space technology were made in the United States before 1960, and their earliest questions about reactions to Sputnik 1 came several weeks after the launch. However, one attempt to gauge the immediate public response was made by Samuel Lubell, noted student of electoral trends at Columbia University.[11] On October 5, as the newspapers carried banner headlines about Sputnik, he was surveying voters on Long Island. Expecting respondents to share his own reaction of utter dismay, and the resultant feeling that a more intensive defense effort was needed even at the cost of higher taxes, he was surprised by the first dozen people he met. "Their reaction to Sputnik seemed to be shaped by their own economic outlooks. Those whose concern over unemployment led them to favor more government spending voiced considerably more concern over Sputnik than those who were untroubled by fears of economic recession or who were eager to see taxes reduced."[12]

Intrigued, Lubell added questions about Sputnik to his subsequent interviews. Surveying areas experiencing economic booms and others suffering from unemployment, he attempted to correlate reactions to the satellite with attitudes toward taxes, government spending, desegregation, and other issues.

My complete findings can be summarized as follows:

1. There was no evidence at all of any panic or hysteria in the public's reactions.

2. Thus many men and women dismissed the satellite as having no military significance and as only a propaganda defeat for this country.

3. Others argued we have something just as good which we're not showing because of secrecy.

4. Still others added "we're ahead in other things."

5. That deeper misgivings stirred beneath this desire to put up a good front was indicated

by the fact that most people interviewed thought that we ought to do everything necessary to catch up, even pay higher taxes if necessary.

6. A sizable part of the public, though, felt that no more money would be needed if the rivalry among the armed forces were stopped.[13]

While clearly not a full-scale statistical survey, Lubell's findings do have the advantage of immediacy. They were made during the period before the launch of a second Sputnik carrying a live dog, before Lyndon Johnson's televised Senate hearings on shortcomings in the American space program, and before the failure of the first Vanguard launch. During this time Lubell noted a strong identification with, rather than against, President Eisenhower. Lubell noted:

One thing that I found especially striking was how closely the public's reactions corresponded to the explanatory "line" which was coming from the White House. Relatively few persons repeated the criticisms which were being printed in newspaper editorials or were being made by members of Congress or by scientists. In talking about [S]putnik, most people tended to paraphrase what Eisenhower himself had said. . . .

Much of this, I suppose, reflected the natural tendency to look to the President for guidance in a novel situation. Fairly often, in the first days following [S]putnik when I asked what this country should do, the reply would be, "I'd leave that to the President. He ought to know." As the headlines out of Washington told of urgent presidential conferences and the appointment of missile expediters, a new note began to enter the interviews. "The President will do all that needs to be done" was one typical comment; or "He's taking action now"; or "We may be behind, but we'll be on top again soon."[14]

In the light of Lubell's findings, Eisenhower does not appear as out of touch with general public opinion as the headlines and editorials of the period might suggest; nor did confidence in his judgment and ability evaporate overnight. But this willingness to follow presidential leadership did not by itself guarantee that such leadership would be forthcoming. Eisenhower's strength lay in emphasizing moderation and conciliation rather than in taking decisive, and possibly divisive, action. While generally a popular virtue, particularly during a period of international tension, it had led him into much criticism on two specific issues. One was his refusal to take a public stand against McCarthy, even as the senator attacked the president's own friends and administration. The second was his refusal in the fall of 1957 to push the southern Democrats harder on desegregation. The sight of hundreds of paratroopers from the 101st Airborne Division surrounding the Central High School in Little Rock, Arkansas, in order to enforce a Supreme Court ruling suggested a cracking of the national consensus that had seemed to typify the middle years of the decade. In particular, the extent to which the Little Rock problem had been allowed to develop also suggested that the president's apparently noninterventionist style of leadership was of questionable relevance to current problems.

White House correspondents were already making this point at the news conference Eisenhower gave on October 3. The president's management style was clearly an issue. As one reporter put it: "Sir, you are probably aware that some of your critics feel you were too slow in asserting a vigorous leadership in this integration crisis. Do you feel, sir, that the results would have been any different if you had acted sooner instead of, as your critics say, letting the thing drift?" Another reminded Eisenhower that he had previously stressed the need for patience: "We saw that patience did not work. Now, what will you do? Many people are asking, what will you do?" To the latter he replied, "I don't know really much more that can be done." To the former he defended his policy of preaching patience, tolerance, and the need for understanding both sides before you move.[15]

Thus to those who felt that the dispute with Arkansas Governor Orval Faubus had shown Eisenhower's style of leadership to be insufficiently assertive in the face of the nation's troubles, Sputnik offered an opportunity to snatch the political initiative from an apparently hesitant White House. To those Democrats who were hamstrung in their ability to criticize Eisenhower's inaction on desegregation by their southern constituents, it was no less than a godsend. But Eisenhower would not be rattled. On his return from spending the weekend at his farm in Gettysburg, Pennsylvania, he conferred with both his military and scientific advisers. At a morning meeting on October 8, 1957, it was confirmed that the Army could have launched a satellite the previous September had it not been for the clear policy of maintaining a separate and civilian satellite program. Eisenhower reaffirmed his belief in that original decision to make science rather than timing the prime concern of the project but agreed that consideration should be given to the Army's offer to provide a backup launch vehicle for Vanguard should it run into long-term problems.[16] That afternoon, he saw Bronk from the National Academy of Sciences, who agreed that the Soviet success should have no bearing on the pace and progress of Vanguard. "We can't always go changing our program in reaction to everything the Russians do," noted Eisenhower. Bronk also confirmed for the press that the scientists had been given adequate responsibility and opportunity to develop the IGY satellite.[17]

Armed with this assurance, Eisenhower faced his regular press conference the following day. As had been the case with the previous week's session, from the first question the focus of the conference was on his leadership. "Russia has launched an earth satellite. They also claim to have had a successful firing of an intercontinental ballistic missile, none [sic] of which this country has done. I ask you, sir, what are we going to do about it?" Eisenhower replied with the three points that formed his consistent public position on the relevance of Sputnik. First, he noted that attempts to yoke together satellite and missile development were misleading; Vanguard and the ICBM program had been deliberately separated in order that the former should not hinder the latter. The lower priority given to the IGY satellite had allowed missile development to proceed faster.

Second, he emphasized that Vanguard was a scientific undertaking and in no way embodied a competitive element. The program's costs had continued to rise, from an initial $22 million to the current $110 million, and had been met because of its scientific rather than its political importance. "There has never been one nickel asked for accelerating the program. Never has it been considered a race; merely an engagement on our part to put up a vehicle of this kind during [IGY]." The psychological advantages of being the first to launch a satellite had been discussed, he continued, "but that didn't seem to be a reason, in view of the real scientific character of our development . . . to grow hysterical about it."

Finally, he endorsed the line followed by the administration since the launching that Sputnik was a laudable scientific achievement, which also presented a formidable lifting capacity for Soviet boosters, but did not in itself represent an immediate threat. Asked whether "in the light of the great faith which the American people have in your military knowledge and leadership" the Soviet satellite did not raise his concern about the nation's security, he replied: "As far as the satellite is concerned, that does not raise my apprehension, not one iota. I see nothing at this moment, at this stage of development, that is significant as far as security is concerned."[18]

This line was confirmed at a meeting of the NSC on October 10. While CIA director Allen Dulles reported that Khrushchev had "moved all his propaganda guns into place," Bronk urged that Sputnik not lead to a scientific race with the Soviets, and Alan Waterman outlined the successes to come if Vanguard maintained its steady course. Concluding the meeting, Eisenhower underlined the importance, for domestic political purposes as well as for the success of Vanguard, of "adhering to the U.S. scientific satellite program under NSC 5520 as being well-reasoned and well-placed."[19] Although the reaction to Sputnik had exceeded White House expectations, the flight of this satellite had done little to alter the arguments put forward during the discussion of NSC 5520 two years earlier. The Atlas ICBM program still demanded unhindered access to human and material resources, the more so since the failure of its first test flight earlier in the year. It was agreed that the Army's persistent offer to assist with Vanguard could be taken up without jeopardizing other military programs. But as Eisenhower remained at pains to point out, neither Vanguard's scientific utility nor its price tag would be improved by rushing into a launching.

The criticism of the president's response to Sputnik has long been identified with Senator Lyndon Johnson, although, as Robert Divine shows, it took some prodding from Senator Richard Russell and chief aide George Reedy before he fully realized its political potential. On October 7 Johnson began preparations for hearings on the state of the American satellite program, but not until October 18 and 19 did he make the speeches that attempted to wrest the political high ground on space away from the White House.[20] Meanwhile, Eisenhower's awareness of the dangers that a crash space program posed to the health of the economy was reinforced on October 14, when the chairman of the Federal Reserve Board warned him that "the economy is making a sideways movement with a slight tendency to decline"—or as Eisenhower translated, "a recession could be in the offing."[21] This increased the pressure to keep down taxes, and thus the need to resist calls for additional spending on a prestige race in space. In order to help assuage the public alarm that the media was now suggesting, if not reflecting, it was decided that the president should make a stirring yet reassuring speech to the nation at the earliest possible moment. As Under Secretary of State Christian Herter wrote to his boss John Foster Dulles, who had missed the immediate post-Sputnik discussions through illness,

> From the echoes of the satellite launching have come to me and others from many sections of the country a strong sentiment that the President alone can give the leadership which will restore a feeling of reasonable security and faith in the competence of the Administration. This leads on every side to the desirability of his finding a suitable date in the not too distant future to make a strong, fighting speech.[22]

Much of the content of that speech resulted from a White House meeting between Eisenhower and fourteen leading scientists on October 15. The president asked if they believed that American science was being "outdistanced" by the Soviet Union, and from that discussion two points emerged. The first was the advantage of appointing a full-time White House science adviser, with complete access to the president, who could advise on the technological aspects of defense and security policy. The second was the long-term need to rekindle the popular appeal of science within America. Edwin Land, the inventor of the Polaroid camera and a leader in the development of reconnaissance satellites, argued that in the current age of mass production, Americans had lost the pioneering spirit of building for the future. According to Killian, Land told Eisenhower that

> American science acutely needed the help of the president. Better than anyone else, he could kindle among young people an essential enthusiasm for science and teach people to understand it was a joyous and creative adventure. . . . [Eisenhower] was impressed by Land's plea that he could, as an act of intellectual leadership, create a more widespread understanding of science. He said, in fact, that he could help.[23]

But before the president could deliver the first in a proposed series of national addresses on the subject of science and national security, known within the White House as the chins-up speeches, the Soviet Union orbited its second Sputnik. This was a much larger satellite and carried the first living being into outer space, a dog named Laika. Reaction to this flight was far more subdued than that which had greeted Sputnik 1. There was little to say by November 2 that had not been said during the previous month, and the imminence of the first Vanguard launch offered at least the chance to pull even in the space race with the Soviet Union. It was to a calmer audience that Eisenhower made the first of his televised addresses on November 7.

His first point during the speech was to stress that America's defenses remained sound: indeed, "as of today, the over-all military strength of the free world is distinctly greater than that of the communist countries." Then came the announcement that the scientific advice available to the White House was to be improved by the appointment of MIT President James Killian as the first Special

Assistant to the President for Science and Technology. In conclusion, he underlined again the folly of allowing a campaign of unchecked spending to serve as the response to the Soviet challenge:

> It misses the whole point to say that we must now increase our expenditures on all kinds of military hardware and defense as, for example, to heed demands recently made that we restore all personnel cuts made in the armed forces.
>
> Certainly, we need to feel a high sense of urgency. But this does not mean that we should mount our charger and try to ride off in all directions at once. We must clearly identify the exact and critical needs that have to be met. We must then apply our resources at that point as fully as the need demands. This means selectivity in national expenditures of all kinds. We cannot, on an unlimited scale, have both what we must have and what we would like to have. We can have both a sound defense, and the sound economy on which it rests—if we set our priorities and stick to them and if each of us is ready to carry his share of the burden.[24]

A week later, speaking from Oklahoma and fortuitously in the middle of National Education Week, he emphasized the importance of science education as part of the nation's long-term security. School boards and PTAs were urged to check their curricula to see whether they met "the stern demands of the era we are entering." Eisenhower added:

> As you do, remember that when a Russian graduates from high school he has had five years of physics, four years of chemistry, one year of astronomy, five years of biology, ten years of mathematics through trigonometry, and five years of a foreign language.
>
> You know, I think that many of us have been a little slow in realizing that it is possible for almost everybody to share in science and engineering as an adventure. If we start early enough in school . . . and if our teachers can make our young pupils see the real satisfaction in working at science, then our young people, even if they do not become scientists and engineers, will experience a real excitement out of growing up in America.[25]

This channeling of the emotion generated by Sputnik into the debate on education strikes one as a typically deft move by Eisenhower. Before the end of October 1957, he was already stressing that the challenge posed by Sputnik was educational rather than military and was linking the best way to respond to the current debate over the desirability of federal aid to education. Seeing Sputnik as a way to redefine the terms of that debate, the administration joined forces with those supporting such aid to ensure passage of the National Defense Education Act in 1958, which, while limited in scope, did manage to produce something positive from the Sputnik crisis without threatening the budget with wasteful spending.[26]

However, these speeches did not deter Senator Lyndon Johnson from holding his televised hearings into the space and missile programs from late November to the end of January. One point that emerged from the testimony of the many witnesses was the need to be clear about whether the administration of the nation's space program should be in military or civilian hands. The administration's solution was to build a new, civilian National Aeronautics and Space Administration on a base carved out of the venerable National Advisory Committee for Aeronautics (or, as one astute observer put it at the time, transform NAcA into NA$A). In the Senate, Johnson tried to add into the draft bill a National Aeronautics and Space Council, modelled after the National Security Council, which would coordinate all executive space policy making from inside the White House. Although the president was unhappy with what he saw as an unnecessary congressional demand, a personal meeting with Johnson in early July smoothed the way for his signing into law the act creating the new space administration on July 29, 1958.

SPACE POLICY AFTER THE ESTABLISHMENT OF NASA

The legislative process that led up to this point has been recorded in detail, perhaps most definitively by Enid Curtis Bok Schoettle, but Eisenhower's attitude toward space policy during the remainder of his term is rather less well known.[27] One of NASA's first tasks was to construct a civilian-controlled man-in-space program (soon christened Project Mercury) out of several proposals put forward by the military services. Eisenhower had accepted the need for such a program in August when he gave his approval to a new NSC policy document on space policy. NSC 5814/1 gave several reasons for developing manned spaceflight:

In addition to satisfying man's urge to explore new regions, manned exploration of outer space is of importance to our national security because:

a. Although present studies in outer space can be carried on satisfactorily by using only unmanned vehicles, the time will undoubtedly come when man's judgment and resourcefulness will be required fully to exploit the potentialities of outer space.

b. To the layman, manned exploration will represent the true conquest of outer space. No unmanned experiment can substitute for manned exploration in its psychological effect on the peoples of the world.

c. Discovery and exploration may be required to establish a foundation for the rejection of USSR claims to exclusive sovereignty of other planets which may be visited by nationals of the USSR.

The first step in manned outer space travel could be undertaken using rockets and components now under study and development. Travel by man to the moon and beyond will probably require the development of new basic vehicles and equipment.[28]

Placing a man in space, this suggested, would increase the effectiveness of military reconnaissance and scientific research, fire the imagination of the world, and keep Soviet legal claims at bay. Moreover, it could be done using equipment already in development without a further commitment to an expensive and ambitious long-term program. These arguments are reminiscent of those put forward in NSC 5520, the NSC's previous statement of space policy in May 1955, which supported the IGY satellite program.

But by December 1959, when NSC 5814/1 was superseded by NSC 5918, the earlier rationale for Mercury had changed somewhat. Satellite missions in earth orbit by both the United States and the USSR had not resulted in legal problems. Nor had the crash landing on the lunar surface of Lunik 2, a Russian probe complete with red flag, led the Soviet Union to claim sovereignty over the moon. As a result, the legal imperative for placing an American in space was no longer so pressing, and it is missing from the section on manned space-flight in NSC 5918. This now left two primary reasons for carrying out manned space activities:

a. To the layman, manned space flight and exploration will represent the true conquest of outer space. No unmanned experiment can substitute for manned exploration in its psychological effect on the peoples of the world.

b. Man's judgment, decision-making capability, and resourcefulness will ultimately be needed in many instances to ensure the full exploitation of space technology.[29]

Thus by the end of 1959, the main motives for Mercury were seen as its international political importance and the human element it would bring to space-based scientific and surveillance work. However, the following year the success of the joint Air Force/CIA Discoverer satellite reconnaissance program showed that film packages could be ejected and retrieved from orbiting satellites, thereby allowing swift terrestrial analysis of information without the expense and risk of involving a man in orbit. This now left the human contribution to scientific study in space and the importance of his presence there for American prestige as the mainstays of the Mercury program.

But while the apparent rationale for space activity was fading, NASA itself was growing more ambitious. In July 1960, the agency outlined to the aerospace industry its tentative plans for the next ten years. These centered around Project Apollo, which would use large new boosters to send a three-man spacecraft around the moon in 1970 as preparation for a lunar landing. The ambitious nature of the program led Eisenhower to request from the President's Science Advisory Committee (PSAC, a Killian innovation) a report "to clarify the goals, the missions and the costs of this effort." George Kistiakowsky, who had succeeded James Killian as Eisenhower's science adviser the previous year, in turn coopted six PSAC members onto an Ad Hoc Panel on Man-in-Space.

The panel's report made four main points about the developing manned space-flight program, none of them favorable. First, it called the current Mercury project a marginal effort in which "it is difficult to achieve a high probability of a successful flight while also providing adequate safety for the Astronaut. A difficult decision will soon be necessary as to when or whether a manned flight should be launched."[30] Building on the success of Mercury, NASA's ten-year plan then called for the Apollo circumlunar flight in 1970. This might be achieved with the new Saturn C–1 booster that the von Braun team, now at NASA, was currently developing. But the panel's second point was that the amount of equipment needed for a lunar landing demanded the development of yet another booster, up to six times more powerful than the C–1. As a new rocket was indispensable to a moon landing, "it must be pointed out that this new, major step is implicit in the present Saturn program, for the first really big achievement of the man-in-space program would be the lunar landing."

The report's third and most resounding finding concerned the extent to which man's presence in space could contribute to its scientific exploration. Deliberately echoing the wording of NSC 5918, the panel accepted the value of human judgment, decision-making capability, and resourcefulness but pointed out that constantly evolving communications technology now allowed such mental capabilities to be performed for a spacecraft by experts working safely on earth with the benefit of computers. The panel found that when compared to the high safety margins, heavier booster requirements, and longer development time needed for manned spaceflight, unmanned spacecraft were capable of collecting scientific information about both the earth and the moon more easily, more effectively, and more swiftly. Asserting that man-in-space cannot be justified on purely scientific grounds, it stated that even if there were no manned program, the unmanned program might yield as much scientific knowledge and is justified in its own right.

The report concluded with an appraisal of the costs involved. Achieving the first major goal of the program—placing one man in orbit—was going to cost $350 million; to send three men round the moon would cost $8 billion, or roughly twenty times as much. The lunar landing, the second major goal after the first manned orbit and which would be reached in about 1975 using the necessary heavy booster, would cost somewhere between $26 billion and $38 billion, although booster development costs could push the figure as high as $46 billion.

These conclusions came as no surprise to Kistiakowsky. Meeting with the panel at the end of October, he discussed the probable costs of the earth orbit and lunar circumnavigation missions and the huge cost of the launcher needed for a manned lunar landing. Kistiakowsky noted:

In executive session of the panel, we talked about these things and I emphasized the need to spell out in our report what cannot be done in space without man. My opinion is that that area is relatively small and that, therefore, building bigger vehicles than Saturn has to be thought of as mainly a political rather than a scientific enterprise. The panel seemed to agree with me.[31]

The scientists' line was that while NASA's figures for its long-range plans were carefully calculated and realistic, they could not be justified by any expected scientific return. Kistiakowsky could be sure that the president would place a great deal of weight on a PSAC report. In his memoirs, Killian describes Eisenhower as having "an exaggerated confidence in the unbiased judgment of the scientists whom he had called upon to help him," and he would be likely to accept from the PSAC a conclusion that manned spaceflight could not claim a scientific justification.[32]

Kistiakowsky presented the panel's findings to the NSC on December 20. He noted later that, "the President was shocked and even talked about complete termination of man-in-space programs."[33] The minutes that would reveal the full nature of Eisenhower's reaction remain unreleased, but a "privileged source" participant has provided at least a sense of the meeting's response to NASA's proposals. In the ensuing discussion, the lunar journey was compared to Columbus's discovery of America, a voyage financed by Spain's Queen Isabella. Eisenhower reacted to this argument by asserting that he was "not about to hock his jewels" to send men to the moon. The general reaction of the meeting was one of "almost sheer bewilderment—or certainly amusement—that anyone would consider such an undertaking." Somebody said, "This won't satisfy everybody. When they finish this, they'll want to go to the planets. There was a lot of laughter at that thought."[34]

The PSAC report effectively removed the last nonpolitical motivation for putting a man into space. From Project Vanguard onward, Eisenhower had measured space projects by their scientific utility, and now he found himself all but committed to an undertaking of incomparable expense for no reason other than its "psychological effect on the peoples of the world." With a new administration waiting in the wings, Eisenhower was no longer in a position to take such a policy decision, but he did feel free to make his own views known. The partially declassified Draft Record of Action from the meeting records that after discussion of Kistiakowsky's presentation, the NSC "[a]greed that there appeared at this time to be no psychological or scientific reason for carrying on the 'Man in Space' program beyond the completion of Project MERCURY, and that ways might be sought publicly to disclose this administration's views on the subject."[35]

Two opportunities to do just that arose in the final week of the transition period. One was his final budget message, sent to Congress on January 16, 1961, in which he refused to include the funds NASA had requested for post-Mercury projects. He had originally intended to go further and state that no more manned flights should be undertaken after Mercury, but a last minute appeal by NASA administrator Keith Glennan changed his mind. He instead gave his successor the grounds for canceling any subsequent programs by saying that further work "will be necessary to establish whether there are any valid scientific reasons for extending manned spaceflight beyond the Mercury program."[36]

The other opportunity to display the administration's views was Eisenhower's farewell address to the nation. In it, he called on Americans, enjoying unmatched progress and riches, to resist "the recurring temptation to feel that some spectacular and costly action could become the miraculous solution to all current difficulties." Just as the new postwar experience of an immense military establishment required a guard against the unwarranted influence of the military-industrial complex, so the recent technological revolution also posed twin dangers. One was the "domination of the nation's scholars by federal employment, project allocations, and the power of money"; the other was "that public policy could itself become the captive of a scientific-technological elite."[37] For Eisenhower, a mammoth moon landing program that undertook to direct the labor of many scientists toward the purpose of demonstrating the nation's superior technological ability threatened to hasten both dangers.

As we know, Kennedy chose to ignore Eisenhower's views and begin an expensive moon landing program whose central aim was the enhancement of American prestige. Whilst this gave us the great space successes of the late 1960s, it transformed NASA from a scientific research agency into a goal-oriented bureaucracy, which found itself losing both its political constituency and its own sense of purpose once that goal was achieved. Neither the space shuttle, justified to the American people on the grounds of economy, nor the space station, which has yet to find a true *raison d'être*, has given the space program a sense of purpose. Meanwhile, scientific investigation, which for Eisenhower was so important, has consistently been left at the end of the queue for funding and support—even while giving us some of the greatest returns from space in the last two decades. It is tempting to think that had Eisenhower's attitude toward space policy prevailed, we might be seeing today a lower-profile but more productive space program in the United States, funded at a constant level by a public that recognized its value.

NOTES

1. A. V. Grosse, "Report on the Present Status of the Satellite Problem," August 25, 1953, Grosse Biography file, NASA History Office, NASA Headquarters, Washington, D.C. (hereafter NHO).

2. "Reported Decline in US Prestige Abroad," report of the Psychological Strategy Board, September 11, 1953, *Declassified Documents Series* (hereafter *DDS*), CIA (85) 000850.

3. Summary of Discussion, NSC Meeting, October 1, 1953, *DDS*, NSC (85) 002743.

4. Eisenhower comments,

If we must compete with Soviet Russia for world "prestige" why not channel the struggle more along the lines in which we excel—and which mean so much to the mass of ordinary citizens? Let's put some other items into this "prestige" race: our unique industrial accomplishments, our cars for almost everybody instead of just a favored few, our remarkable agricultural productivity, our supermarkets loaded with a profusion of appetizing foods.

Dwight D. Eisenhower, "Are We Headed in the Wrong Direction?" *Saturday Evening Post*, August 11–18, 1962, 19–25.

5. Memorandum from Rockefeller to NSC members, May 20, 1955, NSC file, NHO.

6. Eisenhower's role in the instigation of the project is well recounted in Constance McLaughlin Green and Milton Lomask, *Vanguard: A History*, NASA SP–4202 (Washington, D.C.: U.S. Government Printing Office, 1970).

7. Letter from Eisenhower to Lloyd Swenson, University of Houston, August 5, 1965, Eisenhower interview file, NHO.

8. See United States Senate, Committee on Armed Services, Preparedness Investi-

gating Subcommittee, *Inquiry into Satellite and Missile Programs: Hearings Before the Preparedness Investigating Subcommittee*, 85th Congress, First and Second Sessions, Part 1, November 1957, 544–45; and Part 2, January 1958, 1700–1701.

9. James R. Killian, Jr., *Sputnik, Scientists and Eisenhower: A Memoir of the First Special Assistant to the President for Science and Technology* (Cambridge, Mass.: MIT Press, 1977), xvii.

10. These have been compiled in Lynne L. Daniels, "Statements of Prominent Americans at the Opening of the Space Age," NASA Historical Note No. 21, July 1963, NHO.

11. The previous year, interestingly, Lubell had been one of the few to discern the depth of Eisenhower's political ability, referring to him as "one of the most masterful politicians in American history" and concluding "there is little question that Eisenhower must be rated as a highly skilled professional, as complete a political angler as ever fished in the White House pond." Samuel Lubell, *The Revolt of the Moderates* (New York: Harper Bros., 1956), 24–25.

12. Samuel Lubell, "Sputnik and American Public Opinion," *Columbia University Forum* 1, no. 1 (Winter 1957): 15.

13. *Ibid.*, 17.

14. *Ibid.*, 18.

15. Presidential News Conference, October 3, 1957, *Public Papers of the Presidents of the United States: Dwight D. Eisenhower, 1957* (hereafter *PPP: DDE 1957*) (Washington, D.C.: U.S. Government Printing Office, 1958), 707, 709.

16. Memorandum of a Conference, President's Office, White House, Washington, D.C., October 8, 1957, 8:30 A.M., *Foreign Relations of the United States, 1955–1957: Volume XI—United Nations and General International Matters* (Washington, D.C.: U.S. Government Printing Office, 1988), 755–756.

17. Dwight D. Eisenhower, *The White House Years: Waging Peace 1956–1961* (Garden City, N.Y.: Doubleday, 1965), 210–11; Killian, *Sputnik, Scientists, and Eisenhower*, 13.

18. News Conference, October 9, 1957, *PPP: DDE 1957*, 719–32.

19. Memorandum of Discussion at the 339th Meeting of the National Security Council, Washington, D.C., October 10, 1957, *Foreign Relations of the United States, 1955–1957: Volume XI*, 757–64.

20. Robert A. Divine, "Lyndon B. Johnson and the Politics of Space," in Robert A. Divine, ed., *The Johnson Years, Volume Two: Vietnam, the Environment and Science* (Lawrence: University of Kansas Press, 1987), 218–21.

21. Eisenhower, *Waging Peace*, 213.

22. Memorandum from Herter to Dulles, State Department, October 14, 1957, *DDS*, STATE (85) 000357.

23. Killian, *Sputnik, Scientists and Eisenhower*, 15–16.

24. *Congressional Quarterly Weekly Report*, November 15, 1957, 1250–51.

25. *Ibid.*, 1253–54.

26. For Eisenhower's role here, see Barbara Barksdale Clowse, *Brainpower for the Cold War: The Sputnik Crisis and the National Defense Education Act of 1958* (Westport, Conn.: Greenwood Press, 1981).

27. Enid Curtis Bok Schoettle, "The Establishment of NASA," in Sanford A. Lakoff, ed., *Knowledge and Power: Essays on Science and Government* (New York: Free Press, 1966).

28. "Preliminary US Policy on Outer Space," NSC 5814/1, August 18, 1958, NSC file, NHO.

29. "US Policy on Outer Space," NSC 5918, December 17, 1959, NSC file, NHO.

30. President's Science Advisory Committee, "Report of the Ad Hoc Panel on Man-in-Space," November 14, 1960, PSAC file, NHO.

31. George B. Kistiakowsky, *A Scientist in the White House: The Private Diary of President Eisenhower's Special Assistant for Science and Technology* (Cambridge, Mass.: Harvard University Press, 1976), 409.

32. Killian, *Sputnik, Scientists, and Eisenhower*, 228.

33. Kistiakowsky, *A Scientist in the White House*, 409.

34. John M. Logsdon, *The Decision to Go to the Moon: Project Apollo and the National Interest* (Cambridge, Mass.: MIT Press, 1970), 35.

35. Draft Record of Action, 470th NSC Meeting, December 20, 1960, *DDS*, NSC (87) 001670.

36. *PPP: DDE 1960–61*, 972.

37. *Ibid.*, 1036–40.

7

EISENHOWER AND THE BALANCED BUDGET

Iwan W. Morgan

Eisenhower's fiscal record can be better understood if put in historical context. Despite Republican mythology, deficits were not unknown prior to Franklin D. Roosevelt's presidency, but they were never the norm. One in three budgets were unbalanced between 1789 and 1932, usually during wartime or when recessions depressed tax revenues. Since 1932, however, only seven budgets have been balanced. Three of these were by Harry S. Truman, though this feat was arguably less impressive than the three also scored by Eisenhower. Two of Truman's balanced budgets predated 1950, before huge defense spending became a permanent budgetary feature. The only balanced budget since 1960 was Lyndon B. Johnson's fiscal 1969 budget.[1]

Eisenhower's budgetary policy was shaped by political and economic factors. It conformed with the traditional belief, dating from the Jeffersonian era, that balanced budgets symbolized commitment to limit the size and functions of the federal government, to protect states' rights, and to safeguard free enterprise. In other words, balanced budget convictions were entwined with the antigovernment bias inherent in American political culture.

However, the New Deal broke with this tradition and launched the United States into six decades of big government and almost perpetual deficit finance. Coming to power when this process was two decades old, Eisenhower saw the reestablishment of fiscal responsibility as the essential prerequisite for halting federal expansion. Possessing a well-defined conservative political philosophy, Eisenhower deemed big government a threat to free enterprise and individual endeavor, which his value system regarded as the core elements of American democracy. Domestic programs were not his sole concern in this respect. He also feared that a constantly expanding military budget would eventually require an excessive level of federal economic management to channel national resources into defense. The result would be a garrison state in which high taxes, monetary restrictions, and economic controls would throttle private enterprise.[2]

Such convictions did not mean that Eisenhower wanted a return to the past. In his view any party that attempted to dismantle the Roosevelt legacy would be committing political suicide. Moreover, he personally believed that the federal government should maintain a basic welfare state, sustain prosperity, and undertake public programs that were beyond the scope of private enterprise. In essence, Eisenhower looked to develop a modern Republicanism that assimilated much of the New Deal–Fair Deal legacy while drawing the line against its extension. He accepted the need to spend money on a wide range of programs, though always within a balanced budget. Recognizing that government had many responsibilities, Eisenhower deemed it essential to have clearly established priorities so that scarce public funds could be allocated based on the fiscal facts and to meet the requirements of a nation that operated on a free enterprise system.[3]

Eisenhower's budgets were also shaped by considerations of economic management that had been an inherent feature of fiscal policy since the 1930s. His recognition of federal responsibility to counteract recession through compensatory deficits was shaped in part by the political realities of the post–New Deal era, but he also recognized that individuals had no redress against the cyclical swings of the complex, interdependent modern economy. Paradoxically, Roosevelt had never formally sanctioned the legitimacy of deficit finance as a vital antidote against recession. The first president to do so was Truman. Eisenhower went further than FDR in this respect. Acknowledging that balanced budgets and stabilization were sometimes contradictory aims, he declared in 1954 that if the nation's economic condition required it, he would not hesitate to subordinate the first goal for the second.[4]

At best Eisenhower was a passive and half-hearted Keynesian who mainly relied on automatic stabilizers—in other words, falling tax receipts and increased payouts for unemployment insurance—to counteract economic decline.[5] Discretionary tax cuts and expenditure increases were not part of his fiscal armory during the three recessions of his administration. Nevertheless, four of the five Eisenhower deficits were incurred during recessions. His response to the 1953–1954 recession, in particular, put a bipartisan seal of approval on compensatory deficits for the first time. It also eradicated the albatross of Hooverism that had hung around the Republican Party's neck since the Depression.

Eisenhower's presidency therefore marked an important stage in the development of the fiscal revolution that had begun in the 1930s. Arguably, this is his most significant fiscal legacy. All his Republican successors have utilized deficits as instruments of economic stabilization.

Nevertheless Eisenhower's economic policy placed more emphasis on controlling inflation than on combatting unemployment. His insistence that the nation faced ruin unless balanced budgets became the operative rule rested on the conviction that inflation was the greatest economic threat facing the nation. To contemporary analysts, whose views are shaped by the very high inflation rates of the 1970s, inflation in Eisenhower's era appears remarkably low. The average rate was around 2 percent per annum. The Consumer Price Index rose by only 14 points from 1953 to 1961.

Yet creeping inflation of this kind was unacceptable to the president and his economic advisers, who feared that it would produce a serious cumulative devaluation of money if sustained for long and that inflation was likely to accelerate as inflationary psychology took hold of consumers. They viewed price stability as the main prerequisite for orderly economic growth, high employment, and effective national security. Typifying this outlook, Council of Economic Advisers (CEA) chairman Raymond Saulnier avowed that control of inflation had to be "the first imperative" of economic policy, and that when inflationary pressures were present, there was "no viable alternative" to a conservative budget policy.[6]

The erudite views of his advisers confirmed rather than inspired the president's horror of inflation. Historian Robert Griffith depicts Eisenhower's vision of an ideal American society as a "corporate commonwealth," in which all groups worked together in the national interest and forwent sectional gain. Price instability was the bane of such consensus because it created divisions among business, labor, and consumers. It also discouraged thrift and saving. In Eisenhower's view these were the foundations for sustained investment and economic growth. Most important of all, a stable dollar was vital for the United States to fulfill its role as world banker and leader in the global struggle against communism.

Underlying Eisenhower's fear of inflation was his concern about the nation's capacity to sustain the cold war. Early in 1953, he vowed that the nation could only combat communism in the longer term if its economy were healthy. This was a warning that he probably repeated more often than any other during his presidency. Cabinet minutes for November 27, 1959, record his admonition that keeping the economy strong enough for America to lead the free world had to be the top priority in every legislative and budget program.[7]

The effect of inflation on America's balance of payments problems also worried Eisenhower. The gold exchange standard, devised at Bretton Woods in 1944, underpinned the postwar international financial system. This valued the dollar in terms of gold, and other currencies in relation to the dollar. The United States had operated a virtually continuous international balance of payments deficit since 1945. This benefited other western nations who built up dollar reserves to alleviate their foreign exchange problems during the process of postwar reconstruction.

By the late 1950s these countries had largely achieved economic recovery and were becoming increasingly concerned about the dollar's stability. During the 1957–1958 recession foreigners began converting their excess dollars into gold, with the result that America's gold reserves fell by 10 percent in 1958. In reality the dollar was now overvalued in light of western Europe's postwar recovery and could not be defended in the long run. At the time, international concern centered on the supposedly harmful effects of deficit budgets on inflation and the value of the dollar.

Foreigners were horrified by the size of the record fiscal 1959 deficit and expected further deficits to follow in its wake. Some expressed fears that the United States would become trapped in an inflationary spiral. Accordingly, the need to restore foreign confidence in the dollar became the principal motive for the balanced budget strategy that the administration pursued so vigorously in its last two years.[8]

The Eisenhower administration perceived an explicit connection between big federal spending, particularly deficit budgets, and inflation. As the president noted in 1957, when the budget was too high, inflation occurred, which in effect cut the value of the dollar. This meant that nothing was gained and that the process was essentially self-defeating. In the administration's view, big budgets and deficit spending during periods of strong economic activity generated excessive aggregate demand for goods and services, which put pressure on scarce economic resources. This had the effect of nominally increasing gross national product (GNP), but with little capacity for output to expand; the real result was to increase prices. Deficits were also viewed as a threat to monetary restraint. Government borrowing to finance its debts competed with private demand for investment. This tended to force up interest rates, thereby putting the Federal Reserve under pressure to ease the situation and making an orderly antiinflationary monetary policy difficult to achieve. The Federal Reserve purchase of Treasury securities, issued to finance the deficit, also served to increase the money supply.[9]

The antiinflationary course pursued by the administration required it to do more than merely balance the budget. During the prosperous mid–1950s, it aimed for budgetary surpluses that could be used to retire portions of the national debt. This had the effect of curbing federal demand for goods and services and reducing government borrowing needs. The drive for surpluses took on new urgency following the sharpest recession of the Eisenhower era in 1957–1958. Owing to a combination of declining revenues, antirecession measures, and increases in other programs, the federal deficit for fiscal 1959 skyrocketed to a peacetime record of $12.4 billion.

To compensate for this, the administration aimed for large surpluses when the economy began to recover. The goal was to balance the budget over the course of the business cycle—in other words, to balance cumulative surpluses achieved when the economy was prosperous with the deficits incurred when it declined. Fundamental to this strategy was the notion that deficits incurred in future recessions should accrue wholly from the automatic stabilizers rather than from discretionary measures.

In theory, therefore, the size of surpluses achieved when the business cycle was on the upswing would not be affected by spending programs enacted during the preceding recession. This so-called stabilizing budget strategy was promoted by new Treasury Secretary Robert B. Anderson and had Eisenhower's strong support. It was immediately implemented in fiscal 1960 when a balanced budget was recorded, even though such a rapid turnaround from a large deficit was unprecedented in peacetime fiscal history.[10]

Balancing the budget was not purely a matter of fiscal strategy, of course. It was also a political process. The president had to ensure that federal department heads complied with his goals, had to make difficult decisions about the allocation of scarce resources, and had to win congressional approval for his proposals. As such, the pursuit of fiscal responsibility was a searching test of Eisenhower's leadership skills and of his determination to follow through on his objectives. His record in this stands in marked contrast to the traditional depiction of him as a weak president, lacking in political skill and uninvolved in policy making.

In the 1952 campaign Eisenhower had promised to balance the budget and cut spending to about $60 billion within four years, provided the cold war did not intensify. The fiscal 1954 budget inherited from Truman proposed expenditure of $78.6 billion and a deficit of nearly $10 billion. Security expenditures had sky-rocketed since fiscal 1950, when they amounted to just $13 billion, and were now put at $55 billion. To make matters worse, the Truman administration had made COD purchases worth some $80 billion, mainly for defense contracts, which were not covered by budget revenues. Claims for payment would occur predominantly during the first two fiscal years of Eisenhower's presidency. This would coincide with the scheduled termination of numerous temporary taxes that Truman had levied to help finance the Korean War and to curb wartime inflation. Meanwhile the national debt was only some $8 billion short of its legal limit of $275 billion. Arguably, none of Eisenhower's successors took office in circumstances less conducive to pursuing a balanced budget policy. His feat of moving the budget into the black within three years from this position was a signal achievement.

Defense cuts were the main reason for this early success. The Korean War armistice provided political justification for these cuts. Nevertheless, the scope of the military cutbacks went beyond a mere peace dividend. Eisenhower seized the opportunity to put national security on a more cost-effective basis. The New Look program restructured America's defense strategy by emphasizing the buildup of atomic air power at the expense of conventional strength. It was Eisenhower's solution to what he called the "Great Equation"—how to balance the nation's security with its need for a sound economy.

The Truman administration had implicitly followed the recommendations contained in the 1950 defense policy document known as NSC–68. This estimated that an annual national security budget of some $50 billion was necessary for the global containment of communism. It assumed that the economy could bear the strain, even if 20 percent of the GNP went to cold war needs.

By contrast the New Look recognized economic limits to America's military power. "Effectiveness with economy" was Eisenhower's slogan for the New Look, which others more pithily depicted as "more bang for the buck." The program projected a steady Air Force buildup, with compensatory savings on the other services. The aim was to get the defense budget down to a plateau of $33–34 billion by fiscal 1957. The program was quickly inaugurated. Total national security spending (defense, foreign aid, and atomic energy) was cut from $50.3 billion in fiscal 1953 to $40.6 billion in fiscal 1955, a 20.5 percent reduction. Military retrenchment accounted for $8.1 billion of this. To date, no other administration has made defense economies remotely close to this scale. Cuts made while American involvement in Vietnam was being decreased were slight by comparison.[11]

Security savings in combination with buoyant tax receipts from a prosperous economy brought the budget into the black in the mid–1950s, but Eisenhower's success proved short-lived. Domestic and international circumstances were conducive to presidential economizing during the first term. Party strength was evenly balanced in the Congress. Through its atomic superiority, America's military power relative to the Soviet Union's was at its peak. Finally, strong recovery from the 1953–1954 recession boosted federal revenues and bred confidence in the economy. All this changed during the second term, when only one Eisenhower budget was balanced. The launch of Sputnik aroused deep concern that the Soviets had the rocket technology to attack the United States, which generated political pressure to expand the defense budget. Also, the sharp recession of 1957–1958 depressed federal funds and provoked demands for expansionary fiscal policies. The political beneficiaries of Sputnik and the recession were the Democrats, who won a landslide victory in the 1958 congressional elections and grew more assertive in demanding bigger defense and domestic expenditures.

Retrenchment was politically impossible from late 1957 onward. Instead Eisenhower found himself in a desperate battle to hold the line against big spending increases, a struggle from which he eventually emerged victorious. Defense was the most contentious issue. After Sputnik the president came under attack from the Democrats, many Republicans, and prominent defense experts, all of whom claimed that short-sighted presidential penny-pinching had allowed the Soviets to gain the lead in space and missile technology.

The pressure increased after part of the Gaither Committee report was leaked. This secret study of deterrence alleged that American military superiority would be recovered only if defense funding was increased immediately by some 25 percent and sustained at this high level for five years. While accepting that this expansion would have to be financed by unbalanced budgets, the Gaither report predicted that deficits would be modest and that increased defense spending would boost economic growth.

Eisenhower's resistance to big post-Sputnik defense increases was based on economic and military considerations. His own economic advisers were adamant that Gaither's recommendation would mean big deficits and a higher inflation rate that might require economic controls. The result would be to bring the garrison state closer to reality. Eisenhower also considered Soviet missiles technologically crude and inferior to the B–52s as a means of bomb delivery.

Though widely condemned at the time, his restrained response to Sputnik was, as Stephen Ambrose notes, one of Eisenhower's finest hours as president.[12] It was entirely justified from a military viewpoint and caused no harm to national security. It also prevented a dangerous escalation of the arms race and saved the nation from many billions of dollars of unnecessary military expenditure.

Admittedly, the defense budget was increased after Sputnik, partly on congressional initiative and partly because Eisenhower sanctioned small increases to reassure public opinion. Military costs stood at around $41 billion by 1960. Though some $7 billion higher in current dollars than the initial New Look target, the increase was relatively small when inflation was taken into account. In fact, total national security outlays were lower in real terms in 1960 than in any year since 1951.

Eisenhower also refused to be panicked into big spending compensatory measures during the 1957–1958 recession, when unemployment crossed the five million mark for the first time since 1940. The Democrats put forward their own recovery measures in what amounted to the first effort by Congress to mount its own economic program since the emergence of the modern presidency. In reality the program was ill-conceived and contained few quick-acting stimulants. If enacted it would have had little compensatory effect and would have generated deficits for several years to come.

However, only one of the six main Democratic proposals made it onto the statute books. Eisenhower's effective use of the legislative weapons available to the president, particularly the veto and the threat of one, secured the enactment of more modest administration bills.

The president was utterly determined to balance the postrecession budget for fiscal 1960 but faced strong opposition from Congress. The Democrats had huge majorities in the Eighty-sixth Congress and were intent on legislating big increases in defense and domestic spending. Though the odds seemed against Eisenhower, he was the clear victor in his toughest budget battle with Congress. By skillful use of the presidential podium he convinced public opinion that deficits were ruinous and that the Democrats were inflationary spenders. Effective legislative liaison by the White House ensured sufficient Republican and conservative Democratic votes to support presidential vetoes. After early defeats, Democratic congressional leaders threw in the towel and went along with Eisenhower's budgetary ceilings. Only once could they overcome the veto, on a public works bill with a strong pork barrel flavor. As a tribute for performing "the political miracle of making economy popular," *Time* magazine made the president the 1959 "Man of the Year."[13]

Nevertheless Eisenhower's budgetary stand had political and economic costs for his party in 1960. Democratic charges that administration budgetary principles endangered national security became increasingly vehement as the 1960 election approached. "Missile gap" allegations were a potent issue for John F. Kennedy, who defined the choice facing the nation as: "which gamble . . . we take, our money or our survival."[14] In fact the missile gap was illusory, as Eisenhower knew from the secret U–2 spy flights. Kennedy learned the truth after taking office, but his accusations had hurt Richard Nixon in the close-fought 1960 presidential election.

Probably more damaging to Nixon were the economic consequences of the restrictive economic policy pursued in tandem by the administration and the Federal Reserve in 1959–1960. Many economists believe that Eisenhower's drive for a balanced budget so soon after the sharp 1957–1958 recession was the greatest fiscal policy mistake committed by any administration between 1945 and the Americanization of the Vietnam War. Raymond Saulnier had advised the president to run a small deficit in fiscal 1960 in order to strengthen recovery, but Eisenhower rejected this counsel because of his overriding concern with inflation.[15]

This decision ultimately did much to thwart Nixon's election prospects. The administration moved too rapidly to balance the budget after the recession. Denied adequate fiscal stimulus, the economy went into decline in the preelection months of 1960. The expansionary economic cycle that began in 1958 has proved the shortest of the entire postwar period. While many factors affected the outcome of the 1960 presidential election, the recession was certainly an important one. Significantly, Nixon ran worst not in areas with the highest concentration of Catholics, as initially predicted, but in places with the highest number of jobless.

A review of Eisenhower's balanced budget policies inevitably begs the question of why none of his successors has followed his example. A substantial answer is beyond the scope of this chapter, but three broad reasons can be put forward. First, Eisenhower's immediate successors—John Kennedy, Lyndon Johnson, and Richard Nixon—did not share his concern about big government. Recent presidents—Gerald Ford, Jimmy Carter, Ronald Reagan, and George Bush—have been conservative in political and fiscal terms, but the domestic legacy they inherited made budget balancing far more difficult than was the case for Eisenhower in dealing with the New Deal—Fair Deal legacy. Second, none of Eisenhower's successors has shown the same concern to control the growth of the military budget (though George Bush may have proven the exception to this rule). Last, and perhaps most important, none of his successors shared the fundamental assumption underlying Eisenhower's economic policy that perpetual deficits caused ruinous inflation.

Kennedy's New Frontier and, more particularly, Johnson's Great Society programs substantially increased federal domestic expenditures. Paradoxically, this trend intensified during the Nixon presidency when spending on social services increased sevenfold. This was partly the work of congressional Democrats, but the Republican administration also made major innovations. As vice president, Nixon had adopted a pragmatic outlook on budgetary matters and often supported higher domestic expenditure than Eisenhower for reasons of partisan advantage. As president, his aspiration to become an American Disraeli motivated him to expand many social programs, notably health insurance, food stamps, and cost-of-living adjustments for Social Security recipients.[16]

The programs of these three presidents changed the structure of the budget.

In the Eisenhower years, national security expenditures accounted on average for 55 percent of total federal spending (unified budget). By fiscal 1974 they made up only 29.5 percent, compared with 50.4 percent for human resource programs. In other words, domestic programs, particularly those involving transfer payments, had become far more expensive in total than the military budget.

Whereas Eisenhower was able to balance the budget largely through cutting national security costs, the post-Nixon presidents would have had to cut domestic as well as military costs to achieve the same goal. In political terms this was a more difficult task than Eisenhower's. Many transfer payment programs, such as Social Security, disability insurance, food stamps, and Medicare, have relatively uncontrollable expenditures because eligibility for benefit levels is established by the authorizing legislation. Moreover, many of the programs benefit the aged, and increased outlays have reflected the growth in this sector of the population.

There is no scope for presidential or congressional discretion over transfer payment programs, other than to amend the authorizing legislation. However, these are popular programs with a large number of direct beneficiaries, so Congress has been loathe to cut them. The best evidence of this was the Senate's unanimous rejection of President Reagan's 1981 attempt to amend the Social Security program, the most important and the fastest growing in costs of the transfer programs. By 1988 human resource programs still accounted for half of total budget expenditures, with relatively uncontrollable transfer programs making up some 43 percent.[17]

The growth of the military budget in the 1960s and the 1980s has also contributed significantly to perpetual deficits. Eisenhower took considerable political risks in holding the line on defense spending. Probably only a president of his immense military prestige could have resisted the post-Sputnik clamor for bigger national security outlays. Eisenhower was uniquely equipped to decide just how much security was enough.

Other presidents have felt a greater need to protect themselves against charges of weakening national security. They have also had to operate in a different international context than Eisenhower's. Soviet military power has grown in relative terms since the 1950s, and there has been nuclear parity since 1969. National security expenditures did decline by some 8 percent, from 1969 to 1974, as a result of the winding down of the Vietnam War, and were held under control for most of the 1970s.

In the late 1970s, however, Jimmy Carter became convinced that America's relative strength had fallen to unacceptable levels as a result of this restraint and began a substantial defense buildup. This turnaround came too late to protect him from Reagan's damaging charges of American weakness in the 1980 election. In office Reagan accelerated the buildup started by Carter but hoped to finance this through compensatory reductions in domestic expenditures. This strategy fell foul of congressional determination to protect social programs. Despite the military expansion of the Reagan era, national security programs only accounted for 29 percent of the budget in fiscal 1988, compared with 22.7 percent in 1980.

It is fair to say that all of Eisenhower's successors have aspired to balance the budget, but they have not seen their failure as economically harmful. Events have not borne out Eisenhower's conviction that deficits necessarily generate serious inflation, as the Reagan era has shown. Even when inflation was high in the 1970s, many economists put the blame on excessive monetary expansion and rising oil prices rather than spiralling deficits.[18] Eisenhower's fiscal policies, which prioritized balanced budgets to control inflation, did not become economic symbols that guided later presidents. Apart from Jimmy Carter during his last two years in office, all of President Eisenhower's successors have used fiscal policy to maximize economic growth and—sometimes explicitly, sometimes implicitly—have accepted deficits as useful for this purpose.

In prioritizing inflation, Eisenhower tolerated relatively low economic growth. The economy grew by 2.5 percent a year on average from 1953 to 1960, barely half the rate that had been achieved in 1947–1952 and that would be achieved in 1963–1968 and in the post–1983 Reagan economy. Soon after Kennedy took office, he determined to use fiscal policy to stimulate demand and promote economic expansion. Going beyond orthodox Keynesianism, Kennedy policy accepted the necessity for deficit spending when the economy was not in recession. The mechanism for what became known as the "new economics" was the so-called "full employment budget." Under Kennedy, it became conventional to calculate the budget on the basis of what deficit or surplus would accrue if the economy were operating at full capacity. More emphasis was placed on balancing the budget at the hypothetical full-employment level than at the actual level of economic activity.

Johnson, Nixon, and Ford continued this practice in pursuit of economic expansion. It yielded full employment "surpluses" in the early and mid–1960s and smaller deficits than the actual budget ran up in the 1970s. Thus Carter's fiscal 1981 budget could be calculated on a full-employment basis as operating a small deficit of $0.8 billion.[19]

In fact Carter was the first president since Eisenhower to seek a traditional budget balancing approach. The real deficit was substantially reduced during his first three years in office, but economic decline in 1979–1980 prevented him from achieving his stated goal of balancing the budget by the end of his term. Reagan's election brought to office a president whose devotion to balanced budgets nearly matched Eisenhower's, though with one crucial difference: Reagan believed that tax reduction held the key to balanced budgets in conjunction with domestic spending cuts. The massive supply-side tax cut of 1981 embodied this strategy.

The Republican administration accepted the inevitability of short-term deficits but assumed that tax cuts would generate rapid economic growth, which would produce sufficient extra revenue to balance the budget by the end of Reagan's first term. Whether the strategy could have worked is debatable, but it was never fully implemented, because domestic retrenchment was inadequate. Instead of balanced budgets, the combination of tax cuts and defense increases would produce skyrocketing deficits in the 1980s.

Whereas Reagan saw tax cuts as a prelude to a balanced budget, Eisenhower preached the opposite gospel because of his antiinflationary priorities. In the 1952 presidential campaign he insisted that a balanced budget should precede tax reduction. Two small tax cuts granted in 1954 marked a slight deviation from this principle. More significantly, however, Eisenhower resisted strong pressure from congressional Republicans for substantial tax reduction in 1953–1954 and rejected Treasury Secretary George Humphrey's pleas for probusiness supply-side tax cuts in 1955–1956. In addition, the temporary corporate tax increase levied by Truman during the Korean War was extended throughout Eisenhower's presidency.

President Eisenhower also stood firm during the 1957–1958 recession, when he was under immense pressure from Democrats and many Republicans for an expansionary tax cut. His final State of the Union message recommended that tax reduction should be deferred until several debt-reducing surpluses had been recorded. "Once we have established such payments as normal practice," he declared, "we can profitably make improvements in our tax structure and thereby truly reduce the heavy burdens of taxation."[20] This statement, better than any other, encapsulates the difference between the Eisenhower and Reagan approaches to budget balancing.

Present-day Americans should, at the least, be grateful that Eisenhower's prudent custody of federal finances did not enlarge the burden of debt that future generations would have to pay. This restraint had its costs, of course. Without doubt, it stymied development of new federal programs, particularly in education, health care, and welfare, which improved the lives of many Americans after their eventual introduction in the mid–1960s.

Yet Eisenhower's domestic parsimony has to be viewed alongside his military restraint. Had he loosened federal purse strings, the lion's share of new funds would almost certainly have gone into bigger defense programs that the nation did not really need. Eisenhower's fiscal policy was also linked with slow economic growth and recurrent recessions. Nevertheless, the eminent economist Herbert Stein suggests that the economic record of the Eisenhower era "was probably superior to that of any other eight-year period in this century."[21] Whether or not one accepts this verdict, it is true that inflation and unemployment were comparatively low, and economic growth, though sluggish, was steady. At the very least, the administration deserves some credit for contributing to this well-being. Despite this economic success, the fiscal course charted by Eisenhower was not followed by American government during the next three decades. Today, however, the White House and Congress are facing up to the difficult problems of balancing the budget through phased reductions of the deficit and of reducing a national debt that is heading beyond $4 trillion. In these circumstances Eisenhower's fiscal legacy may gain new relevance as a guide to the nation's budgetary decision makers.

NOTES

1. References in this chapter to pre–1969 budgets are to the administrative budget, unless stated otherwise. All references to budgets from 1969 onwards are to the unified budget.

2. For Eisenhower's philosophy of political economy, see Robert Griffith, "Dwight D. Eisenhower and the Corporate Commonwealth," *American Historical Review* 87 (February 1982): 87–122; Alonzo L. Hamby, *Liberalism and Its Challengers: F.D.R. to Reagan* (New York: Oxford University Press, 1985), 118–28; and Iwan W. Morgan, *Eisenhower versus "The Spenders": The Eisenhower Administration, the Democrats and the Budget, 1953–60* (New York: St. Martin's Press, 1990), especially 15–23.

3. Eisenhower to I. S. Ravdin, September 19, 1959, Eisenhower Presidential Papers (EPP), Ann Whitman File, DDE Diary Series (AWF–DDE DS), box 44.

4. Eisenhower to R. C. Leffingwell, February 16, 1954, *ibid.*, box 5.

5. Herbert Stein, *The Fiscal Revolution in America* (Chicago: University of Chicago Press, 1969), 298–308.

6. Raymond J. Saulnier, *The Strategy of Economic Policy* (New York: Fordham University Press, 1962), 27, 29–30.

7. Eisenhower to General Alfred Gruenther, May 4, 1953, EPP, AWF-DDE DS, box 3; Cabinet Minutes, November 27, 1959, *ibid.*, box 45.

8. Robert B. Anderson, "The Balance of Payments Problem," *Foreign Affairs* 38 (April 1960): 419–33.

9. Memorandum of Conference with the President, October 30, 1957, EPP, AWF–DDE DS, box 27; Arthur F. Burns, *Prosperity Without Inflation* (New York: Fordham University Press, 1957), especially 6–7, 74–81.

10. Stein, *The Fiscal Revolution in America*, 355.

11. Morgan, *Eisenhower versus "The Spenders,"* 51–56.

12. Stephen E. Ambrose, *Eisenhower: The President* (London: George Allen & Unwin, 1984), 426–35.

13. *Time*, January 4, 1960, 12.

14. *New York Times*, March 1, 1960.

15. Raymond J. Saulnier, Memorandum for the President, November 5, 1958, EPP, AWF–DDE DS, box 36; Memorandum for the Record, "Budgetary Struggles and the Outlook for Refinancing," December 6, 1958, *ibid.*, box 37.

16. Joan Hoff-Wilson, "Richard M. Nixon: The Corporate Presidency," in Fred I. Greenstein, ed., *Leadership in the Modern Presidency* (Cambridge, Mass.: Harvard University Press, 1988), 192–93.

17. James A. Thurber, "Budgetary Continuity and Change: An Assessment of the Congressional Budget Process," in D. K. Adams, ed., *Studies in US Politics* (Manchester, England: Manchester University Press, 1989), 95–97.

18. See, for example, Michael J. Boskin, *Reagan and the Economy: The Successes, Failures and Unfinished Agenda* (San Francisco: ICS Press, 1989), 14.

19. James D. Savage, *Balanced Budgets and American Politics* (Ithaca, N.Y.: Cornell University Press, 1988), 175–95.

20. *Public Papers of the President: Dwight D. Eisenhower, 1960–1961* (Washington, D.C.: U.S. Government Printing Office, 1961), 113.

21. See Stein's foreword in Boskin, *Reagan and the Economy*, xiii.

8

EXECUTIVE-LEGISLATIVE RELATIONS: EISENHOWER AND HALLECK

Henry Z. Scheele

On September 17, 1966, from his retirement home at Gettysburg, former President Dwight D. Eisenhower uncharacteristically wrote a laudatory tribute for a long-time professional politician. "Because of the unremitting claims against the fleeting hours of every day," wrote Eisenhower,

it has been my rule since entering public life to avoid writing prefatory remarks or an endorsement of another person's publication. Here I deliberately and happily break that rule. I do so out of an abiding personal affection, a high respect, and a deep sense of obligation to the able, hard-working and loyal Charles A. Halleck, whose counsel and leadership in his field I found indispensable throughout my service in the presidency.[1]

In the foreword of former U.S. House Majority and Minority Leader Charles A. Halleck's political biography, Eisenhower revealed that he first became acquainted with the Indiana congressman during the late stages of World War II. "From that period until I departed the White House in January, 1961, my estimation of this member of Congress increased. I salute him as one of the finest men I have known in the top councils of government."[2] The retired president continued his tribute by saying that Charles A. Halleck "demonstrated many times not only political courage but a higher order of selflessness in service to our nation. He has been faithful to friends, a hard-hitting but fair partisan, a dynamic and effective leader, and always a respected advocate of his views."[3]

Eisenhower's foreword suggests that a unique relationship existed between the president and the House leader. The words denote a close friendship and a deep admiration. It is the contention of this chapter that the executive-legislative relationship between the former president and the powerful House leader helps to define Eisenhower the man, Eisenhower the president, and Eisenhower the politician.

THE GENERAL AND THE CONGRESSMAN: PRIOR TO 1952

Although history will record that Dwight D. Eisenhower was a masterful politician, the gentleman from Abilene, Kansas, spent the first six decades of his life avoiding political identification. Biographer Herbert S. Parmet reports that there is no early record of Eisenhower's involvement in partisan politics.[4] When he did speak publicly, he spoke as a nonpartisan.[5] When President Harry S. Truman conferred with the heroic general at Potsdam in 1945, he told him that there was "nothing that you may want that I won't try to help you get. That definitely and specifically includes the Presidency in 1948."[6] Later Truman told him that his offer to step down and become vice president so Eisenhower could be president "still held good in 1952."[7]

Eisenhower recorded in his diaries that he was first approached about the presidency in June 1943 and again in the middle of 1945.[8] In a June 15, 1945, letter to his wife, Bess, Truman wrote that he had just pinned a medal on Eisenhower. "He's done a whale of a job. They are running him for President, which is O.K. with me. I'd turn it over to him now if I could."[9] Medals and awards were showered on the celebrated hero.

As World War II ended Eisenhower was internationally revered. On December 13, 1947, he was presented the Gold Medal for Distinguished Achievement at the annual dinner of the Pennsylvania Society held at the Waldorf-Astoria in New York. U.S. House Majority Leader Halleck shared the distinction of being guest of honor with the general that evening. The Indiana congressman delivered an address that evening that played a significant role in Eisenhower's political future.[10]

Halleck's presence was explained by the fact that, as majority leader in the House of Representatives, he was one of the top two or three Republican elected officials in government. He had first achieved national attention with his celebrated nomination speech in behalf of Wendell Wilkie in 1940. He later played a prominent role in the passage of the Taft-Hartley Labor Act, the Marshall Plan, and the Truman Doctrine. Halleck pointed out in his New York speech of December 13, 1947, that "under the bold and brilliant military leadership of General Eisenhower . . . we fought and won a bloody and costly war to preserve the American way of life."[11]

However, the House leader complained that during the previous fourteen years under the Democrats' leadership the federal government had expanded from 521 agencies and bureaus to 1,141, and the number of employees had grown from 582,000 to 2 million. He said: "Our American way of life . . . depends in large measure on local home rule. The closer the government is to the people . . . the better it is likely to be. A nation of forty-eight states . . . cannot be . . . governed from Washington alone.''

In calling for fiscal responsibility on the part of the federal government and encouragement of individual initiative, it struck a responsive chord with Eisenhower. The general called the House leader over to the side after the program and indicated that he identified strongly with Halleck's enunciation of Republican ideology. The majority leader was pleased with the general's reaction and firmly believed the speech had had an impact on Eisenhower's latent Republican convictions.[12]

A few months later Eisenhower addressed a Columbia University audience and utilized some of the same themes employed by Halleck at the Pennsylvania Society meeting. "Danger," asserted the general, "arises from too great a concentration of power in the hands of any one individual or group." He added that too much power in the hands of a few "is fully capable of destroying individual freedom."[13] Although Eisenhower's speeches reflected some Republican themes, the general persisted during the late forties and early fifties in concealing his own political preference. Sherman Adams recalled that shortly before the 1952 election he had difficulty finding any evidence that Eisenhower had ever voted Republican.[14]

Eisenhower announced on January 7, 1952, that he was indeed a Republican and that he would challenge the candidacy of Senator Robert A. Taft for the Republican presidential nomination. Senator Henry Cabot Lodge became the national chairman of the Eisenhower drive for the nomination.[15] Congressman Halleck played a prominent role in the 1952 presidential campaign. After being selected as a favorite son candidate for president at the 1948 Indiana Republican state convention, and narrowly missing the vice presidential nomination awarded to Governor Earl Warren of California, Halleck was locked out of his own state convention in 1952 by the controlling Taft forces.[16] The aggressive Hoosier had refused to make a pro-Taft speech several weeks prior to the Indiana state convention, and political insiders suspected correctly that he favored Eisenhower.

In spite of the severe setback dealt him by his state party, the fifty-two-year-old congressman went to the GOP convention in Chicago in an unofficial capacity and worked behind the scenes for Eisenhower. Few people realized that when Eisenhower received the nomination in 1952 he kept in his billfold a handwritten list of desired running mates. According to Eisenhower's memoirs, Senator Richard Nixon headed the select group and Charles Halleck was second, followed by Representative Walter Judd and Governors Dan Thornton and Arthur Langlie.[17]

Representative Halleck and Senator Carl Mundt were selected to head the GOP Speakers' Bureau. Eisenhower approved this and the two lawmakers arranged the speaking schedule for the presidential campaign.[18] Halleck had the additional responsibility of managing the Eisenhower campaign train. However, most of his time was spent at Republican headquarters in Washington making campaign arrangements.[19] One of the initial Eisenhower campaign addresses of

1952 was scheduled in Halleck's home state of Indiana. Skeptical state Republican leaders, mostly Taft supporters, suggested that Eisenhower would be fortunate to attract 3,000 spectators. However, when he stepped to the rostrum in Butler Fieldhouse in Indianapolis he was cheered by an overflow crowd of 20,000 avid Hoosiers, some of whom were hanging from the rafters.[20] Although Eisenhower's vigorous campaign speech produced cheers, appearing on the same stage with right-wing U.S. Senator William Jenner of Indiana was distasteful to him. Jenner, an outspoken supporter of the controversial U.S. Senator Joseph McCarthy of Wisconsin, was the antithesis of the general's more moderate political philosophy.[21] While Eisenhower's address praised Indiana's political ticket, he refused to mention Jenner's name. However, whenever the crowd cheered, Jenner would grab Eisenhower's arm and raise it high for all to see. When the address was over, Jenner further embarrassed the candidate by placing his arm around him and smiling broadly for the cameras. Eisenhower, repelled, turned to Halleck, and in a state of anger yelled, "Charlie, get me out of here!"[22] They left before anyone realized what had happened. Eisenhower, in reference to the Jenner incident, recalled that he "felt dirty from the touch of the man."[23]

Eisenhower was one of the last of the whistle-stop campaigners. His campaign train traveled over 50,000 miles through 230 towns and cities and 45 states.[24] Biographer Stephen Ambrose wrote that Eisenhower spoke with so much vigor and addressed so many people along the route that Adlai Stevenson's supporters were reluctant to make an issue of his age.[25]

THE PRESIDENT AND THE CONGRESSMAN: 1953–1961

The well-organized GOP campaign produced a landslide victory in 1952. Eisenhower received almost 34 million votes to Adlai Stevenson's 27 million. The electoral vote was 442 for Eisenhower and 89 for Stevenson.[26] Eisenhower's memoirs explain that he sought the presidency in 1952 because after two consecutive decades of Democratic rule the nation "sorely needed a change from one-party domination."[27] Concerned about excessive centralization of power in Washington, he believed that "a change was almost mandatory . . . to sustain our long cherished two-party political system."[28]

Dwight Eisenhower was inaugurated president of the United States on January 20, 1953. He had been in the public eye for many years and had previously acquired valuable administrative experience in Washington. He seemed comfortable in his new office, and, as historian Robert H. Ferrell noted, "When Eisenhower sat down in the chair behind the desk, he felt at home."[29] He recorded in his diary upon the first day at the president's desk that he had plenty of worries and difficult problems. "But such has been my portion for a long time—the result is that this just seems (today) like a continuation of all I've been doing since July 1941—even before that."[30]

Eisenhower's vast experience in the military had sharpened his leadership abilities, political acumen, and organizational talents. President Franklin D.

Roosevelt, who selected him to be Supreme Allied Commander, believed Eisenhower to be "the best politician" among the high-ranking military men: "He is a natural leader who can convince men to follow him."[31]

Eisenhower's keen sense of organization may have been one of his main strengths as chief executive. His efficient White House staff was responsible for coordinating the activities of the presidential office. They kept the president well informed on important policy matters and sought the successful execution of his initiatives. According to Purdue University's Donald Paarlberg, administrative proposals originated in the various departments of government. They were subsequently reviewed by the Bureau of Budget and "their economic feasibility was determined. When a given proposal took clear shape, the President's staff got on it." This was done independently of the Cabinet officers. After a small group of five or six experts looked at a given proposal from the standpoint of the president's attitude and its political appeal, it moved forward. Eisenhower did not concern himself with the intricate details of a given proposal, "but when it reached a point of decision, he was strong and decisive. Final decisions were made by Eisenhower himself."[32]

One new organizational feature of the Eisenhower White House that greatly enhanced executive-legislative relations was the creation of a congressional liaison office. The president gathered together an experienced legislative liaison team consisting of men such as Bryce Harlow, Jerry D. Morgan, General Wilton Persons, and former Congressman Jack Z. Anderson.[33] This congressional liaison group met once a day among themselves to formulate administration positions and plans. They met at the White House on Tuesdays to exchange ideas with Eisenhower and the Republican congressional leaders and on Thursdays with Republican and Democratic congressional leaders for bipartisan discussions. Phillip Henderson, in his book *Managing the Presidency*, indicates that all major Eisenhower initiatives were discussed with congressional leaders prior to submission to Congress.[34] Henderson's nine-page reproduction of the president's weekly appointment schedule provides abundant documentation that Eisenhower met frequently and on a routine basis with Republican and Democratic congressional leaders and was actively involved in the affairs of congress.[35] These legislative meetings, wrote Eisenhower, were "the most effective mechanism for developing coordination with Congress."[36]

In his memoirs, Eisenhower recalled the very first of these executive-legislative meetings held in the Cabinet Room of the White House on January 26, 1953:

Around the long table sat, from the Senate, Vice-President Nixon: the Majority Leader, Senator Robert Taft; the President Pro Tempore, and chairman of the Committee on Appropriations, Senator Styles Bridges; the chairman of the Republican Policy Committee, Senator William Knowland; the chairman of the Finance Committee, Senator Eugene Millikin; and the Majority Whip, Senator Leverett Saltonstall. From the House there was Speaker Joseph W. Martin; Majority Leader Charles Halleck; Majority Whip Leslie Arends; and, from my staff, Governor Adams, General Persons, and General

Persons' assistants. I knew all of these men. Among the senators I knew Bob Taft best. . . . On the House side, I knew Charlie Halleck best.[37]

This initial meeting with the Republican congressional leaders was an eye opener for Eisenhower. He was amazed that they were unable to agree upon the need to fulfill some of the stipulations of the party platform. He expected, after twenty years of Democratic control, some solidarity among the Senate and House GOP leaders, but that was not the case. "It was clear," wrote Eisenhower, "that habitual, almost instinctive opposition to the Chief Executive, as well as differences in political convictions, would create difficulties in Executive-Legislative relations."[38]

The president recorded in his diaries that the Republican Party must be known "as a progressive organization or it is sunk." He felt that "far from appeasing or reasoning with the dyed-in-the-wool reactionary fringe, we should completely ignore it and when necessary repudiate it."[39] Eisenhower encountered various challenges and hostile reactions from Congress. In 1952 the American people elected a Republican Senate and House of Representatives. The Eighty-third Congress constituted the last session in which Republicans controlled the House of Representatives during the twentieth century. Republicans gained a slight 49–47 edge in the Senate and an equally slim 221–214 margin in the House.[40] The victory ensured that important leadership positions in Congress would go to Republicans.

Eisenhower's opponent for the Republican presidential nomination, Robert Taft, agreed to serve as majority leader in the Senate and worked diligently for the administration until his untimely death in the summer of 1953. California's Senator William Knowland took Taft's place, but he seemed less communicative than his predecessor and less inclined to work harmoniously with the administration.[41] Eisenhower circumvented Knowland and dealt informally with Everett Dirksen instead. Dirksen later supplanted Knowland as Senate minority leader.

In the House, Speaker Joe Martin, Majority Leader Halleck, and Whip Leslie Arends made up the Republican hierarchy. The aging Martin, although friendly and supportive of the administration, appeared "lackadaisical and uninspired."[42] Halleck quickly emerged as the president's key leader in the House and was recognized as his chief legislative lieutenant on Capitol Hill.[43] In his intensive study of the Eighty-third Congress, Gary Reichard observed that "the most important leader in the lower house was Charles Halleck, who came closer than anyone else to filling Taft's shoes after mid–1953."[44]

Halleck very likely consulted on legislation with the president more often during his two terms than any other lawmaker. According to Reichard: "The floor leader's credentials as an administration loyalist were nearly impeccable. He took a leading part in the floor fight on virtually every major piece of administration sponsored legislation to come before the House in 1953–1954 and registered an overall support score of .92; in no issue area did he score below .86 in support of the President's position."[45]

At an early February 1953 conference with the president, the congressional leadership planned the strategy for implementing Eisenhower's eleven-point program. Some of the major items proposed by the administration were Social Security extension, reciprocal trade extension, temporary aid to depressed-area schools, submerged-land bills, defense controls, the Hawaiian statehood bill, and appropriations measures. Halleck's goals for the new Republican-controlled Eighty-third Congress were reduction in the cost of government, reduction in taxation, and budget balancing.

His first battle with the Democratic opposition was over the installation of the Twenty-one-Day Rule provision in the House Rules Committee. Liberals favored adoption of the proposal, which provided that legislation tied up in the Rules Committee could be brought to the House floor after twenty-one days. Conservatives, led by Halleck, knew that this would work to their disadvantage, and so they fought to defeat the measure.[46]

As majority leader, Charlie Halleck used his influence adroitly and supported almost all Eisenhower initiatives. He backed the president in his efforts for foreign aid, extension of reciprocal trade agreements, and the Tidelands Oil Bill. His tactics defeated a heavy protectionist tariff opposed by the administration.[47] His loyalty to the president was put to the test during the administration's 1953 tax fight with House Ways and Means Committee Chairman Daniel A. Reed of New York. As a guest on "Meet the Press" Majority Leader Halleck, representing the president, said that Republicans would cut taxes after a balanced budget was achieved. However, Congressman Reed felt that Republicans, who controlled Congress, were bound by their campaign promises to trim taxes without delay, and he drove through the House Ways and Means Committee an 11 percent tax cut bill without administration approval. Reed's proposal passed in committee by a twenty-one-to-four vote despite the objections of the president who felt that world tensions warranted delay of a tax reduction for a year.

Eisenhower also wanted Reed's committee to extend the excise tax and the excess profits tax on corporations, but the powerful Ways and Means Committee chairman was uncooperative. Eisenhower believed Reed's tax reduction proposals would cost the government more than $2 billion in needed revenue.[48] Eisenhower joined with congressional leaders to find a way to circumvent Reed. Halleck, expert on the subtleties of parliamentary procedure, was selected to plan and direct the task of bypassing Chairman Reed's committee. Halleck realized that the Democrats on the Ways and Means and the Rules Committees favored, in principle, excise tax extension; Democrats had supported such tax legislation for years. However, in their determination to frustrate and embarrass the Eisenhower administration they would not cooperate in committee. Halleck claimed in a later interview that "those hammerheads wouldn't give me the votes in either the Ways and Means Committee or the Rules Committee . . . not a one. . . . I knew damn well that if you ever called a roll on the floor of the House they'd all flock to support it."[49]

Halleck won the deciding vote from war hero Carroll Reece, and the Eisenhower administration succeeded in forcing a floor vote on the excise tax. "Getting that rule," said Halleck, "was the roughest day of my life ever . . . up there alone. . . . God, it was tough. It was the roughest deal I was ever in or ever hope to be in again."[50] Once the measure to prolong the tax went to the House floor an Eisenhower victory was certain; it passed with a triumphant vote of 325–77. Halleck reflected, "In all my nineteen years in Congress this has been the most burdensome thing of all."[51]

On May 14, 1953, Eisenhower entered in his diary the names of men who had established themselves as "competent, capable, and dedicated public servants." The list consisted of several Cabinet members, including Secretary of State John Foster Dulles, some advisers, and Charles Halleck, Republican leader in the House of Representatives.

Significantly, Halleck was the only member of Congress to be mentioned.[52] Eisenhower's diary entry noted that Halleck was different:

He is a Phi Beta Kappa, which means at least that he is highly intelligent and mentally adept. He has had a reputation as being a ruthless politician, but I find him not only considerate and kind but a real team player. He does believe in discipline in an organization, and he has no patience whatsoever with the individuals that "stray off the reservation" when it comes to a matter of Republican regularity. He is charming company and, so far as I can determine, of exemplary tactfulness. Perhaps my opinion can be best expressed by merely stating the fact that he was high on my list of acceptable vice-presidents when my opinion was asked last July, and since that time, he has steadily grown in my estimation.[53]

While Halleck was cognizant that the administration had not achieved all its goals during the first session of the Eighty-third Congress, he was pleased with what it had accomplished. He noted that the teamwork between the executive and legislative branches helped contribute to peace in Korea. The general housecleaning in federal positions, the removal of wage and price controls, and the cuts from the final Truman budget were significant achievements. The $14 billion cut from the Truman budget was the largest reduction made up to that time by any Congress in American history.[54] During the second session of the Eighty-third Congress Secretary of Agriculture Ezra Taft Benson conferred with congressional leaders to reach agreement on the administration's farm program. Democrats were determined to maintain 90 percent parity, but the Eisenhower administration wanted to substitute flexible farm price supports at 75 to 90 percent parity. On three occasions this administration plan had been rebuffed. Defeat seemed inevitable, but as Secretary Benson described, "That was when the generalship of Charlie Halleck came into play."[55]

Benson said that Halleck had decided that he had just one chance—that he might possibly be able to put over a compromise by splitting the difference right down the middle and offering, instead of 75 to 90 percent, an amendment establishing flexible support for 1955 at 82.5 to 90 percent for all of the basic crops except tobacco, which would continue at 90 percent. Maybe in this way he could swing some tobacco votes and pick up some other wavering votes.[56] The amendment was approved 179 to 165 and, according to Benson, "Under Halleck's shrewd floor management only seventeen Republicans voted against the amendment." The president was pleased.

Halleck's persuasive efforts had attracted several key Democratic votes from urban area congressmen when he reminded them that 90 percent parity prices to farmers could be thought of as a vote against the interests of urban constituents.[57] The establishment of the principle of flexibility by the Eighty-third Congress was precedent-setting and was considered to be one of the crucial votes of the legislative session.[58] The personal relationship between the president and his legislative lieutenant grew stronger during Eisenhower's two terms. Occasionally the president invited Halleck for a round of golf at Burning Tree Country Club. A scorecard found in Halleck's scrapbooks showed that on one outing the majority leader shot an even 90, Eisenhower an 88, and Sam Snead, a 2-under par 70.[59]

Democrats regained control of the House of Representatives during the 1954 off-year elections. Sam Rayburn superseded Joe Martin as House speaker, and John McCormack replaced Halleck as majority leader. Martin became House minority leader, and Halleck served as an assistant party leader without official title. Les Arends remained GOP House whip, though Halleck was considered to be second in command in the House Republican hierarchy. Eisenhower insisted that he attend the weekly legislative leadership meetings at the White House.[60] As Martin's unofficial assistant, Halleck continued to serve as the most aggressive and most vocal proponent of Eisenhower's programs in the House.

The president made a significant effort to work cooperatively with Democratic congressional leaders. He continued his weekly meetings at the White House with legislative leaders of both parties. The agenda was prepared in advance by General Persons. Most Republican legislative leadership meetings usually consisted of reports given by Halleck and Knowland as to the status of administration proposals in the House and Senate.[61] Eisenhower fostered a vigorous exchange of viewpoints and welcomed intense discussion. His weekly leadership conferences developed into "a sort of forum in which everyone has a chance to unburden himself in an orderly fashion."[62]

Eisenhower endeavored to improve executive-legislative relations by trying to meet all members of Congress, not just the leaders. He invited every one of the 531 members of Congress for meals in relatively small groups at the White House. For most congressmen these informal meals represented the first time they had dined with a president of the United States.[63]

Halleck, who had graduated first in his law class at Indiana University, was an able and unrelenting tactician in Congress. Eisenhower would discuss a bill with Halleck before sending it to the lower chamber. The veteran congressman would apprise the president of how members of Congress could be expected to respond to specific issues. In suggesting strategies for securing legislative approval he enlightened the president with information about day-to-day congressional operations. If Halleck told the president that he could get a bill through Congress, Eisenhower informed White House aides that "Charlie guaranteed it."[64] In his diary Eisenhower recorded that Halleck "is smart, capable and courageous . . . so great are his powers of persuasion that it is rarely indeed that he cannot produce for us a good showing on any proposition that is important to us."[65]

Eisenhower was recovering from a serious illness on July 10, 1956, when Republican leaders met at his Gettysburg, Pennsylvania, farm. Eisenhower gave reassurance to party leaders that he would remain in the race and that he planned to lead an energetic campaign.[66] Within a few days of that he met at Gettysburg with his press secretary James Hagerty and Republican national chairman Leonard Hall to determine strategy for his reelection. They decided that Halleck should give the presidential nomination speech at the Republican national convention in August.[67]

Halleck was elated when the president himself telephoned to invite him to deliver the nomination address. Eisenhower said, "Charlie, the boys tell me I have to choose someone to give my nomination speech. Would you do it?"[68] In his memoirs Eisenhower claimed that he himself had chosen Halleck as his nominator because he was an "effective leader in the House of Representatives, helping to enact into law the proposals the Administration laid before the Congress."[69] In the 1956 presidential nomination speech in San Francisco Halleck enumerated the Eisenhower administration's accomplishments. He highlighted: the Korean peace, a large tax cut, a balanced budget, reduced federal deficits, reduced inflation, an end to wage and price controls, higher employment, improved pay for workers, fewer strikes, higher minimum wage, increased Social Security benefits, broadened medical care, increased military strength, unequaled highway construction, and better farming conditions.[70] Answering critics who had asserted that Eisenhower's illness had curtailed his time spent in the Oval Office, Halleck confronted the issue head-on when he asked his audience, "Are these amazing achievements the work of a part-time President?" "No!" roared the crowd in the Cow Palace.[71] Approximately 40 million people viewed or heard the convention proceedings on television or radio.[72]

Once nominated, Eisenhower was reelected by an even larger landslide victory over Stevenson in 1956 than in 1952. Democrats, however, remained in control of Congress. Furthermore, as a result of the 1958 off-year elections, House Democrats gained an almost two-to-one majority over Republicans. In the wake of their severe election losses in 1958, concerned House Republicans such as Gerald Ford, John Byrnes, and Don Jackson strongly encouraged Joe Martin to leave his post as minority leader and become "leader emeritus."[73] According to Tip O'Neill, "party members viewed Martin as pretty well over the hill."[74]

Martin was unwilling to step down, so Ford and his followers banded behind Halleck, the only man who appeared to have the votes needed to topple the aging leader.[75] Eisenhower recalled that in 1954 and again in 1956 when Democrats won control of the House, Representative Halleck went to the White

House to inform him that he planned to oppose Martin for the post of minority leader. On both occasions the chief executive, in the spirit of party harmony, refused to give his blessing. When Halleck returned for a third time in 1958 to request White House cooperation in the move to unseat Martin, the president said: "As you know, I've done my best to unify the Republican members in the House and try to get them to pull together. But now, . . . while I shall make no attempt to influence any congressman's vote, I shall no longer stand in your way."[76]

Upon assuming the top GOP leadership post in the House, Halleck, referred to as the "Gut Fighter" by some, quickly prodded his outnumbered party members into line. His assertive style of leadership was based on his conviction that party discipline was a necessity. *Congressional Quarterly's* average party-unity score for House Republicans increased by 11 percent, from 66 percent to 77 percent, during the first year of Halleck's minority leadership.[77]

By the end of the 1959 congressional session, the Eisenhower administration had won approximately twenty victories against no out-and-out defeats on major legislation in the House.[78] Though Halleck consistently denied the existence of a Republican–southern Democrat coalition, that mythical symbiotic alliance accumulated a 91 percent success ratio on legislation sought in the House as opposed to a 65 percent ratio in the Senate. "It soon became obvious," reported the *New Republic*, "that the dominant figure in the House was not (Speaker Sam) Rayburn but Minority Leader Halleck."[79]

Sherman Adams claimed that Halleck's bold support for the president's programs was a major factor in Eisenhower's renewed interest in legislative activity.[80] Eisenhower referred to Halleck both as a "political genius" and as "a master in the science of government."[81] One of the major contributions of the Eisenhower administration was the passage of two civil rights bills: the 1957 Civil Rights Act and the 1960 Voting Rights Act. Eisenhower had worked for adoption of civil rights legislation in the summer of 1956. Halleck's role was primarily one of providing the president with procedural information concerning passage. Upon introduction of the first bill on Capitol Hill a bitter congressional battle ensued; more than eighty southern Democrats signed a manifesto to fight the legislation.[82] In spite of their massive effort to block passage, the first federal civil rights bill since the Reconstruction era was enacted into law in 1957. The 1960 bill, which according to Mark Stern "mainly allowed judges to appoint federal voting registrars under very selective conditions," also angered and mobilized southern Democrats.[83] Again, despite their opposition the bill became law. Halleck helped guide both successfully through the House.

The 1957 and 1960 acts seen in retrospect appear only to have inched forward in addressing an unmet need of major proportion, but indeed they represented a momentous breakthrough that had not been achieved by any previous administration. In addition, they paved the way for the Civil Rights Act of 1964.

Toward the end of his presidency Eisenhower became more conservative in regard to legislation for domestic and military spending. His intention was to balance the budget, reduce the national debt, and produce a surplus. As this surplus manifested itself Democrats attempted to use their congressional majority to pass additional social legislation. Minority Leader Halleck urged Eisenhower to use the veto and its threat to halt the surge.[84] Eisenhower preferred to shun public confrontation with Congress, but as his administration progressed, he did not hesitate to use the veto; he employed it 181 times during his presidency, and it was overridden only twice.[85]

Though the prevailing wisdom of the time perceived him to be less politically active than Presidents Roosevelt and Truman, Eisenhower was an adroit politician who, according to Fred Greenstein, only appeared to be uninvolved with the political process, a style which allowed him to succeed in his purpose.[86] According to Michael Mayer, the Civil Rights Act of 1957 and the Voting Rights Act of 1960 show that "historians have failed to give sufficient credit to the Eisenhower administration either for what it attempted to do or for what it actually achieved."[87]

Perception of the executive-legislative relationship during the Eisenhower years gains acuity through the benefit of new information and the vantage point of historical perspective. R. Gordon Hoxie reports that recent researchers have shown that "bipartisan consensus with the White House, in both houses of Congress, peaked at nearly 70% during the two terms of Dwight D. Eisenhower." From Kennedy through Reagan, bipartisan consensus dropped "nearly 30 percentage points."[88] The quality of the executive-legislative relationship during Eisenhower's years in office was enhanced by the administration's aggressive and loyal support rendered by House Leader Halleck.

THE FORMER PRESIDENT AND THE MINORITY LEADER: 1961–1965

As early as 1954, Eisenhower pondered about his successor. He wrote that Bob Anderson of Texas would make a splendid president. "Another fine man is Herbert Hoover, Jr. In addition there are Dick Nixon, Cabot Lodge, Herb Brownell and Charles Halleck."[89] Richard Nixon emerged with the nomination in 1960 but lost the election in one of the closest presidential contests in American history. Furthermore, both houses of Congress maintained Democratic majorities.

Ever conscious of the need for a viable two-party system, President Eisenhower met with Republican congressional leaders on the day he left office to discuss formulating a structured, unified communication vehicle that would permit the party out of power to publicly disseminate positions on issues.[90] What emerged from that meeting became an "extension of Eisenhower's leadership."[91] Upon Eisenhower's recommendation it was decided that the GOP would create a new policy-making group called the Joint Senate-House Republican Leadership. The group was to consist of nine congressional leaders who would hold weekly meetings to discuss important legislative matters and formulate party policy. A press conference would follow the meetings to "put out the news."[92]

It was Eisenhower's understanding that when the GOP had been out of power in the past, the party floor leaders in Congress had assumed the role of spokesmen. Consequently, it was decided that Senate Minority Leader Everett Dirksen and House Minority Leader Charlie Halleck would appear jointly in press conferences designed to provide Republicans with an effective opposition voice.[93] Although the televised appearances of the top two elected Republican officials were satirically labeled the "Ev and Charlie Show" by the press, their transcripts provide rich material about GOP positions on issues during the Kennedy and Johnson administrations.

An analysis of the transcripts reveals the significant role and input of Eisenhower. In their April 6, 1961, news conference Senator Dirksen informed the media that the Joint Senate-House Republican Leadership meetings and press conferences were conducted "at the express suggestion and request of President Eisenhower."[94] He then announced that the Republican leadership group would go to Gettysburg to confer with the former president to "examine the problems and the legislative proposals that come along." Asked when the May 1 meeting had been arranged, Halleck replied, "It was set up . . . over the phone last night."[95]

After opening statements at Gettysburg on May 1, 1961, by Dirksen and Halleck, the former president met with the press. He expressed pleasure at conferring again with the congressional leaders and said that he hoped they would continue their weekly meetings. He invited them to return to Gettysburg on occasion for future sessions.[96] In typical Eisenhower fashion the former president answered questions about Cuba, Laos, Chile, Japan, and President Kennedy's first hundred days. Regarding the final question concerning President Kennedy's New Frontier proposals, Eisenhower responded: "I support the proposals that were made before I left the White House. . . . [T]hey are very definitely different in their scope and their cast. . . . [N]o matter how much we like to say that we can afford to do something we want to do, let us not forget that a sound currency is the first backstop to a free enterprise."[97]

Eisenhower visited again with the Joint Senate-House Republican Leadership on May 10, 1962, and was the sole interviewee at the news conference afterward. He said: "The real threat to liberty in the republic will not come from any sudden, calculated onslaught; rather, the threat to our liberties will be primarily found in a steady erosion of self-reliant citizenship . . . resulting from an ever-growing federal bureaucracy."[98]

Reflecting his strong belief in checks and balances, Eisenhower went on to declare "that the problem of the Presidency is rarely an inadequacy of power. Ordinarily the problem is to use the already enormous power of the Presidency temperately, judiciously, and wisely."[99] In response to a question about a Senate seat for former presidents, he asserted that since "any ex-President . . . can have or find a pretty good political platform from which to make a statement whenever he desires, and since he's not voting, I don't see how his influence could be greater in the Senate than it is right now."[100] He did agree that the amendment limiting the president to two terms was wise.[101] Reporters used the occasion to ask Eisenhower about his farewell address and what he had meant by the military-industrial complex. Eisenhower explained that a great portion of America's gross national product is dedicated to the military and its procurement of materials. "Now, let us think of the vast power, the vast influence that this kind of thing brings to our lives and to the deliberations of Congress. . . . I would dare say there are very few districts and no states—that don't have some strong, prominent and important military facility. . . . Now, that's one kind of influence that you can understand."[102]

Eisenhower reckoned that with approximately $25 billion involved in military spending, "That's a very strong inducement to all of our procurement plants that are going to make these things, and of course, they come to the Congress and they come to the Executive Department and everybody else to sell their gadgets."[103] He mentioned that the Joint Chiefs of Staff assured him that the military budget was already ample for the defense of the country, "but the strange thing was that each thought that it [sic] personally should have more."[104] Dwight Eisenhower's continued influence can be readily seen as his name appears in 73.4 percent of the Joint Senate-House Republican Leadership press conferences held during the Kennedy administration. He or his administration was either present, mentioned, or quoted in 47 of the 64 verbatim transcripts. He was consulted by the leadership, especially by Halleck, on numerous occasions throughout the Kennedy presidency. Eisenhower's continued involvement in political activity during his retirement years was also evident when he traveled to Halleck's district during the 1962 congressional campaign. A crowd of 30,000 people, 5 times the size of Halleck's hometown of Rensselaer, gathered in an open field adjacent to St. Joseph College to hear Eisenhower praise the House minority leader.[105]

Eisenhower's dislike for the New Frontier proposals advanced by the Kennedy administration was shared by Republican congressional leaders Halleck and Dirksen. Again and again they marshaled the opposition to defeat what they considered to be costly, repetitive spending bills, which they felt would threaten the future financial solvency of the government.

In the House, Halleck frequently helped engineer a joint front consisting of the Republican minority in combination with many southern Democrats to impede passage of Kennedy's programs. That "coalition" was notably successful in checking President Kennedy's programs in the House, but because of Halleck's frequent opposition stance to the administration's proposals, he was widely perceived as an obstructionist. Resentment grew over Halleck's brusque leadership style and his close association with Howard Smith of Virginia. His demand for rigid adherence to party discipline aroused indignation. His television appearances on the controversial "Ev and Charlie Show" revealed an old-fashioned politician whose image contrasted sharply with that of the younger and more charismatic president.

The climate for social change in America intensified during the 1960s. The Civil Rights Movement manifested the internal strife of the nation. Although the first two Civil Rights Acts since Reconstruction had been enacted during the Eisenhower administration, the need for additional legislation was evident. Though the Democratic Party platform of 1960 had promised additional civil rights legislation, President Kennedy delayed in submitting an administration civil rights bill to Congress. Finally the president submitted a bill to the House Judiciary Committee in 1963. Committee and subcommittee activity was intense with feelings running high, but progress on the bill was slow.

Halleck felt strongly that the situation was "getting out of hand" and that additional legislation was needed to relieve the civil strife that was building.[106] He met with civil rights leaders and assured them of his support when they rallied in Washington that summer. Halleck worked personally with President Kennedy in constructing a compromise civil rights bill that softened the much stronger but, in all likelihood, unpassable version developed by Democrats on the Judiciary Subcommittee. Lawrence F. O'Brien, Kennedy's congressional liaison, credited Halleck's work on the compromise measure and claimed the House GOP leader was "the unsung hero" of the Civil Rights Act that finally was enacted into law in 1964.[107]

Southern Democrats were angered over Halleck's prominent role in the successful passage of a compromise bill. Some Republican Policy Committee members were disturbed that Halleck had not communicated adequately with them as he worked with the president in rewriting the bill. Furthermore, the Young Turks of the Republican Party were becoming increasingly dissatisfied with the image Halleck conveyed as cospokesman for the party. This ambitious group of younger politicians felt that the sometimes irascible Halleck was not sufficiently responsive to their input. The seeds for Halleck's demise as GOP leader had been planted.

The Goldwater defeat in November 1964, which accounted for dozens of Republicans being swept out of office, severely altered Halleck's power base in the House. Many of the senior members of the House, the majority of whom were Halleck supporters, did not return to Washington. Thomas P. "Tip" O'Neill confided that the reduction in membership of Republicans in the House following Goldwater's defeat was matched in his time only by the Watergate fallout a decade later.[108] Of the 140 Republicans left in the House, 100 had less than 10 years of congressional experience.

The Young Turks, displeased with November's election results, maneuvered to change the party leadership in the House. It is significant to note that during the ensuing intraparty politicking, Eisenhower's close associate and former Postmaster General Arthur Summerfield submitted a resolution giving Halleck a vote of confidence. It had been signed by twenty members of the Republican National

Finance Executive Committee. However, Halleck's eighteen-year tenure as a top party leader in the House had run its course. After a seventy-three-to-sixty-seven House Republican caucus vote on January 4, 1965, Halleck was unseated as minority leader by Gerald Ford.

CONCLUSION

Through speech appearances, press conferences, telephone conversations, leadership meetings, golfing engagements, banquets, and tributes of various kinds, Eisenhower and Halleck developed over three decades a cordial personal and professional relationship. On Capitol Hill Halleck's leadership tactics were designed to attain Eisenhower's programs and their shared philosophy of government. The House minority leader's rigorous support of administration initiatives greatly helped the Executive Branch accomplish most of its objectives.

The study of the relationship between the president and his legislative lieutenant reveals an enduring friendship. It also lends definition to a president of great organizational ability and political astuteness. Eisenhower's December 24, 1953, letter to "Swede" Hazlett outlined his plan to achieve an effective executive-legislative relationship. He wrote that it was important to get together with legislative leaders for several purposes.:

a. To gather from the legislative leaders their impressions of the sentiment of the country. Compare their reactions with ours, and thus arrive at an order of procedure or priority in the presentation of the program.

b. Under the principles and purposes laid out by the administration, to work out applicable legislative methods, as well as modifying small details to add to the attractiveness or popularity of the particular program.

c. To renew the habit of cooperative effort between the executive and legislative departments.

d. To bring out that the Republican Party, headed by the president, had reached that point where a combined, concerted effort to put over a progressive, enlightened legislative program was mandatory.[109]

Eisenhower strove to carry out his plan partially through his administration's organizational structure. Permanent weekly meetings were developed to provide a framework for regular two-way communication between the chief executive and congressional leaders of both political parties. These sessions, and lawmakers' anticipation that the president would continue to take part in them, nurtured better understanding and helped maintain the balance between the executive and legislative branches of government. Additionally, Eisenhower worked closely with Republican floor leader Halleck to achieve his goals in the House. Halleck's knowledge of House practices and members' voting behaviors provided the president with a fairly accurate view of what he could hope to accomplish in the lower chamber. The president had reason to feel confident if "Charlie guaranteed it."

Eisenhower found Halleck able, hard-working, and loyal. His advice and political leadership were indispensable. A reexamination of the Eisenhower-Halleck relationship reveals a president actively engaged in political matters and deeply involved with legislative activity.

NOTES

1. Henry Z. Scheele, *Charlie Halleck: A Political Biography*, foreword by Dwight D. Eisenhower, introduction by Everett McKinley Dirksen (New York: Exposition Press, 1966), 1.

2. *Ibid.*

3. *Ibid.*, 2. Senator Everett M. Dirksen was the author's first choice to write the foreword to the Halleck biography. Halleck replied, "Fine, but what about Dwight D. Eisenhower?" It was agreed that Senator Dirksen's statement would be used as an introduction if Representative Halleck could arrange the Eisenhower foreword. According to Halleck, Bryce Harlow produced a draft for Eisenhower, "but he didn't like it and tore it up." Halleck reported that Eisenhower then "wrote the tribute in his own hand."

4. Herbert S. Parmet, *Eisenhower and the American Crusades* (New York: Macmillan, 1972), 23.

5. *Ibid.*

6. John Gunther, *Eisenhower: The Man and the Symbol* (New York: Harper and Brothers, 1952), 134.

7. Peter Lyon, *Eisenhower: Portrait of the Hero* (Boston: Little, Brown and Co., 1974), 455.

8. Robert H. Ferrell, ed., *The Eisenhower Diaries* (New York: W. W. Norton, 1981), 369.

9. Robert H. Ferrell, ed., *Dear Bess: The Letters from Harry to Bess Truman, 1910–1959* (New York: W. W. Norton and Co., 1983), 516.

10. *Philadelphia Bulletin*, December 14, 1947.

11. Charles A. Halleck, Radio address before the Annual Dinner of the Pennsylvania Society, New York, December 13, 1947. Subsequent quotations are taken from the manuscript provided by the office of the House minority leader.

12. Robert Allett, administrative assistant to U.S. House minority leader, interview with author, Washington, D.C., June 13, 1961.

13. Robert Griffith, ed., *Ike's Letters to a Friend: 1941–1958* (Lawrence: University Press of Kansas, 1984), 8.

14. Sherman Adams, *Firsthand Report: The Story of the Eisenhower Administration* (New York: Harper and Brothers, 1961), 13. Eisenhower did say "I had always been a Republican in leanings and had always voted that way when given the opportunity to do so." See Ferrell, *The Eisenhower Diaries*, 374.

15. *Ibid.*

16. Thomas E. Dewey, letter to the author, December 12, 1961.

17. Dwight D. Eisenhower, *The White House Years: Mandate for Change, 1953–1956* (Garden City, N.Y.: Doubleday, 1963), 46.

18. *New York Times*, August 5, 1952.

19. Blanche White Halleck, "On Being a Politician's Wife," in James M. Cannon, ed., *Politics U.S.A.* (Garden City, N.Y.: Doubleday, 1960), 55.

20. Charles A. Halleck, interview with the author, February 15, 1965.

21. Parmet, *Eisenhower*, 128.

22. *Ibid.*

23. *Ibid.*

24. Stephen E. Ambrose, *Eisenhower: Soldier, General of the Army, President-Elect, 1890–1952* (New York: Simon and Schuster, 1983), 551.

25. *Ibid.*

26. Emmet John Hughes, *The Ordeal of Power: A Political Memoir of the Eisenhower Years* (New York: Atheneum, 1963), 228.

27. Dwight D. Eisenhower, *The White House Years: Waging Peace, 1956–1961* (Garden City, N.Y.: Doubleday, 1965), 651.

28. *Ibid.*

29. Ferrell, *The Eisenhower Diaries*, 225.

30. *Ibid.*

31. Blanche Wiesen Cook, *The Declassified Eisenhower: A Divided Legacy* (Garden City, N.Y.: Doubleday, 1981), 64.

32. Donald Paarlberg, Special Assistant to the President for Economic Affairs and Assistant Secretary of Agriculture, interview with the author, West Lafayette, Ind., April 23, 1990.

33. Phillip G. Henderson, *Managing the Presidency: The Eisenhower Legacy—From Kennedy to Reagan* (Boulder, Colo.: Westview Press, 1988), 27.

34. *Ibid.*, 28.

35. *Ibid.*, 189–98.

36. Eisenhower, *Mandate for Change*, 194.

37. *Ibid.*

38. *Ibid.*, 195.

39. Ferrell, *The Eisenhower Diaries*, 288.

40. Gary W. Reichard, *The Reaffirmation of Republicanism: Eisenhower and the Eighty-Third Congress* (Knoxville: The University of Tennessee Press, 1975), 14.

41. *Ibid.*, 195.

42. *Ibid.*, 196.

43. George B. Galloway, *History of the House of Representatives* (New York: David McKay Co., 1963), 112–13.

44. Reichard, *The Reaffirmation of Republicanism*, 196.

45. *Ibid.*

46. *New York Times*, February 10, 1953.

47. *New York Times*, June 16, 1953.

48. Eisenhower, *Mandate for Change*, 201.

49. Halleck, interview, February 15, 1965.

50. *Ibid.*

51. *New York Times*, June 30, 1953.

52. Ferrell, *The Eisenhower Diaries*, 236–40.

53. *Ibid.*, 239.

54. *Washington Star*, September 21, 1953.

55. Ezra Taft Benson, *Cross Fire: The Eight Years with Eisenhower* (Garden City, N.Y.: Doubleday, 1962), 204.

56. *Ibid.*, 205.

57. *Ibid.*

58. *St. Louis Post-Dispatch*, July 18, 1954.

59. Charles A. Halleck, personal scrapbooks, scorecard of golf match between Dwight D. Eisenhower, Sam Snead, and Charlie Halleck. Halleck's scrapbooks, speeches, hunting rifles, shotgun shells, and other personal items were placed in a storage room in the basement of the Capitol Building.

60. Eisenhower, *Mandate for Change*, 442.

61. Merlo J. Pusey, *Eisenhower the President* (New York: Macmillan, 1956), 207.

62. *Ibid.*

63. *Ibid.*, 211.

64. "These Are the Men Ike Listens To," *Newsweek*, June 14, 1954, 27.

65. Ferrell, *The Eisenhower Diaries*, 270.

66. *New York Times*, July 11, 1956.

67. Earl Mazo, *Richard Nixon: A Political and Personal Portrait* (New York: Harper and Brothers, 1959), 170.

68. Halleck, interview with the author, Rensselaer, Ind., April 12, 1984.

69. Eisenhower, *Waging Peace*, 13.

70. Charles A. Halleck, presidential nomination speech, Republican National Convention, San Francisco, August 22, 1956. See *New York Times*, August 23, 1956, 14, for complete text.

71. Henry Z. Scheele, "The 1956 Nomination of Dwight D. Eisenhower: Maintaining the Hero Image," *Presidential Studies Quarterly* 17 (Summer 1987): 459–71.

72. William B. Prendergast, director of research for Republican National Committee, letter to the author, February 5, 1962.

73. Gerald R. Ford, *A Time to Heal* (New York: Harper & Row, 1979), 72.

74. Thomas P. O'Neill, Jr., former Speaker of the U.S. House of Representatives, interview with the author, Boston, November 12, 1988.

75. Ford, *A Time to Heal*, 72.

76. Eisenhower, *Waging Peace*, 374.

77. "Chairman Halleck Is Major GOP Spokesman in Congress," *Congressional Quarterly Weekly Report*, July 15, 1960, 1269.

78. *New York Times*, September 6, 1959.

79. "Halleck Rides High," *New Republic*, December 14, 1959, 7.

80. Adams, *Firsthand Report*, 26.

81. "The Gut Fighter," *Time*, June 8, 1959, 15.

82. *New York Times*, July 14, 1956.

83. Mark Stern, "John F. Kennedy and Civil Rights: From Congress to the Presidency," *Presidential Studies Quarterly* 19 (Fall 1989): 805.

84. *New York Times*, April 6, 1960.

85. R. Gordon Hoxie, "Dwight David Eisenhower: Bicentennial Considerations," *Presidential Studies Quarterly* 20 (Spring 1990): 260.

86. Fred I. Greenstein, *The Hidden-Hand Presidency: Eisenhower as Leader* (New York: Basic Books, 1982), 230.

87. Michael S. Mayer, "The Eisenhower Administration and the Civil Rights Act of 1957," *Congress and the Presidency* 16 (Autumn 1989): 137.

88. Hoxie, "Eisenhower," 263.

89. Griffith, *Ike's Letters to a Friend*, 138.

90. A record of press conference statements made by Senator Everett McKinley Dirksen and Representative Charles A. Halleck for the Joint Senate-House Republican Leadership, Senate Document no. 63, 87th Congress, First Session, Washington, D.C., 11.

91. R. Gordon Hoxie, "About This Issue," *Presidential Studies Quarterly* 19 (Fall 1989): 701.

92. Henry Z. Scheele, "Response to the Kennedy Administration: The Joint Senate-House Republican Leadership Press Conferences," *Presidential Studies Quarterly* 19 (Fall 1989): 825–46.

93. *Ibid.*, 827.

94. Official transcript, the Joint Senate-House Republican Leadership press conference, April 6, 1961, 4. Copies of transcripts of the press conferences were obtained from the offices of House Minority Leader Charles Halleck and staff consultant Robert Humphreys.

95. *Ibid.*, 8.

96. Press conference, May 1, 1961, 9.

97. *Ibid.*, 21.

98. Press conference, May 10, 1962, 1.

99. *Ibid.*, 2.

100. *Ibid.*, 5.

101. *Ibid.*, 7.

102. *Ibid.*, 14.

103. *Ibid.*, 15.

104. *Ibid.*

105. *Rensselaer Republican*, September 14, 1962.

106. Halleck, interview, February 15, 1965.

107. Lawrence F. O'Brien, *No Final Victories* (Garden City, N.Y.: Doubleday, 1974), 147.

108. O'Neill, interview, November 12, 1988.

109. Griffith, *Ike's Letters to a Friend*, 116.

9

EISENHOWER AND THE SUEZ CRISIS OF 1956

Michael Graham Fry

Presidents are Janus-like. They face outward to the world and inward to society in everything they do that is policy relevant and politically significant. Thus, when a president looks in the mirror he can say, without fear of contradiction, that there are two of him. In this respect, presidents are typical of leaders in modern, complex, industrial societies around the world.

It follows, axiomatically, that every presidential decision of consequence, every policy of significance, every agreement of importance negotiated and bargained over with foreign leaders must be politically acceptable at home. That is why presidents must explain, justify, and seek support for decisions, courses of action, and agreements in and through acts of legitimation. That is also why they must persuade and communicate effectively to make their propositions clear, straightforward, and unexceptionable.

Yet the vast majority of the scholarly literature on decision making about foreign policy tends either to ignore the proposition itself or to intellectualize it excessively. Theodore Sorenson's book, *Decision Making in the White House* (New York: Columbia University Press, 1963), elegantly written, crafted from the inside and ringing true because of that, will continue to be read when most of the "scientific" literature has disappeared. That literature will become largely irrelevant because John Steinbruner's conundrum, "the hard task of integrating the abstract paradigms of decision theory into the realities of political life," remains largely unsolved.[1] George Reedy, press secretary to Lyndon Johnson, attempted to address this in his breezy, sobering, but not necessarily impeccable way:

I have participated in more studies of the decision making processes of the White House and I don't think any of them, in terms of the White House, are worth the paper they are written on. What they've gotten is a study of the decision making processes of a particular president, whereas decision making can vary tremendously from president to president. I think Eisenhower was probably the closest model to a well organized president, for that was closer to the military model than it was to modern management structures.[2]

Something fundamental has been either largely ignored or clouded over by scholars in pursuit of other puzzles. The problem is that scholars have not brought together theoretical perspectives—on the presidency, legitimacy (support), decision making with an adequate reexamination of rationality, and communication—and archival research—for example, the firsthand reading of the records of decisions made by a presidential policy community. The archives of President Eisenhower's predicaments in the second half of 1956 are particularly rich sources for addressing this issue.

Eisenhower could not have lost to Adlai Stevenson in 1956 as long as the universe unfolded in any normal way. Yet even Eisenhower was governed by the legitimation imperative, and the Republicans failed to gain control of either house of Congress. The campaign was fought in the midst of the Suez and Hungarian crises. The former carried with it domestic political considerations of the utmost importance, and it fell to Eisenhower's communication specialists to ensure domestic support. James Hagerty, Eisenhower's press secretary, is recognized to have been the most complete and successful of presidential press secretaries. Emmet Hughes, Eisenhower's speech writer, and Sherman Adams (a former governor of New Hampshire), his Chief of Staff, were central actors in a way that Charles Wilson, the Secretary of Defense, for example, was not. In addition, Eisenhower stood on the threshold of the television age.

Eisenhower was the first president to have to deal with television, a challenge which John Foster Dulles, his Secretary of State, also had to face. What was novel for them is now routine, if not easy, to master. Presidents cannot ignore the imperative to legitimate; the political risk is too great. Therein lies a further risk—that substance is undermined as images are created and preserved.

It is not possible in a single chapter to set out the broader themes of the legitimation imperative that faced Eisenhower and Dulles in 1956 *and* analyze the decision sessions that demonstrated in detail that they managed the crises with an eye to both international and domestic considerations. (Only the former task is attempted here.) The driving force behind their legitimation campaign was that they felt they were behaving rationally as they did so. This conviction was aided by the fact that, while Eisenhower may have had a sense of his limited intellectual skills, he was not a humble or timid man. He was self-confident. He did not see his equal among the Democrats.

THE SUEZ CRISIS, JULY TO NOVEMBER 1956

The Middle East policies of the Eisenhower administration were the most sensible and judicious of any American administration since 1945. Eisenhower and Dulles made a sustained and serious attempt to craft balanced policies—to address the Arab-Israeli dispute and to cooperate with Britain, the foremost NATO ally, while refusing to support and even countering specific acts of imperialism.

They agreed that the United States, as the leader of the free world, must play a larger role in the Middle East. Eisenhower and Dulles regarded Egypt as the key Arab state and President Nasser as the most important Arab leader. They decided, in March 1956, in view of his unfriendly actions, to seek to reduce his influence and produce a more cooperative attitude toward Israel on his part, while not driving him into the Soviet Union's arms and leaving a bridge for Nasser to cross back into the western camp.

The Suez crisis began on July 26, 1956, with President Nasser's dramatic announcement of the nationalization of the assets of the Suez Canal Company. Nasser's decision followed the Anglo-American refusal to fund the construction of the Aswan High Dam in collaboration with the World Bank. Dulles had conveyed that decision to the Egyptian ambassador on July 19. The crisis passed through seven phases, with France and Britain and their coconspirator Israel, finally snatching aggression out of negotiation with an escalating series of military moves between October 31 and November 5 (the Israeli attack into the Sinai, the Anglo-French bombing of Egyptian airfields, and the Anglo-French invasion of the canal zone). The United Nations and the United States primarily, with Canada particularly prominent, arranged a cease fire that went into effect in November.

The Suez affair was the second Middle East crisis following the creation of the state of Israel, and it remains the only crisis involving Israel for which adequate archival evidence is available. By that time U.S. Jews were organized and powerful if not united; the city of New York had developed a foreign policy on the Middle East. Very few American politicians and aspirants for office could risk disengaging Middle East policy from domestic political calculations. Some members of Congress objected to national policy being subject to Jewish dictation at election times. U.S. policy in the Middle East must be independent, not jeopardize relations with the oil-producing states, and not risk damage to European security and the integrity of NATO. Others pressed Dulles to supply defensive arms to Israel and to conclude a treaty with Israel, guaranteeing its borders.

In 1956 the incumbent Republicans, Dwight D. Eisenhower and Richard Nixon, faced Adlai Stevenson and Estes Kefauver. Thus a Middle East crisis in the last days of the election raised urgent questions about policy legitimation, involved quite fundamental political calculations, and required skillful communication strategies. That was the case even though Eisenhower was widely respected and trusted and despite the fact that a Republican president had less to lose than a Democratic president or aspirant in challenging Israel and risking alienating Jewish voters.

It was already apparent in 1956 that the issue was not merely one of seeking to affect Israeli policy directly but also to convince the leaders of the American Jewish community to accept U.S. policy and to work to convince the government of Israel to conform. Israeli governments, in turn, were adept at going their own way and calling on the American Jewish community to support their policies.

The Jewish community was not the only relevant presidential constituency. Unavoidably, the management of Middle Eastern policy was bound up with the maintenance of a bipartisan foreign policy; Eisenhower's Middle East policy required all the bipartisan support it could muster. In the fall of 1955, for example, Dulles pointed out that Middle Eastern problems were intractable, that they had to keep looking over their shoulders at political consequences at home, and that bipartisan positions had to be established or the entire Arab world would be lost. The administration felt that they should appoint a representative from the Democratic Party to help diffuse a situation that could be as dangerous as the loss of China. Mike Mansfield came to mind as liaison between the Senate and the administration because he was least likely to insert a partisan note into Middle Eastern policy.[3] By April 1956, both U.S. membership in the Baghdad Pact and a new security treaty with Israel guaranteeing its borders faced close congressional scrutiny.

Eisenhower and Dulles preferred to manage business in small, trusted decision groups. There were twenty-nine recorded decision sessions on the Suez crisis between July 27 and November 6. The decisions made concerned both substance and legitimation. Predictably, no decisions were made at the Cabinet meetings though Dulles briefed its members on July 27 and August 3.[4]

The NSC met nine times during the Suez crisis with the crisis itself or other Middle Eastern questions on the agenda. No substantive decisions of significance were made, except perhaps on November 1.[5] The election may have interfered with its schedule and certainly made attendance somewhat erratic, especially that of Dillon Anderson, Eisenhower's Special Assistant for National Security Affairs. Dulles's meetings in London and at the United Nations had a similar effect. Anderson was present at only two of the nine meetings. At a private meeting on August 6, Eisenhower, Dulles, and Anderson discussed a memorandum from the Joint Chiefs of Staff requesting that the National Security Council provide for the early implementation of appropriate courses of action to resolve the Suez Canal crisis. Eisenhower agreed with Dulles's view that the United States' course of action should not become a council action but should continue as part of the president's day-to-day decision making. Eisenhower also agreed with Dulles that an effort to chart a course by Council might unduly freeze the U.S. position and thereby destroy needed flexibility, and that the NSC was not the vehicle to resolve the issue of the need to use force against Egypt.

Eisenhower went on to rule that while formal decision making by the NSC would not be appropriate, a general discussion of the situation by the NSC would be beneficial. He asked Dulles to brief a very small group of NSC members at the upcoming August 9 meeting. Eisenhower would decide, aided by his trusted advisers; the NSC would meet in rump form.[6] Eisenhower and Dulles also agreed that the United States should not disclose its position beforehand should another state intervene militarily in the crisis and that any U.S. military action must be approved by Congress. At times Eisenhower opted for confidentiality. At an inner group meeting on July 31 without Sherman Adams or James Hagerty present, Eisenhower insisted on secrecy.[7]

EISENHOWER AND DULLES

The relationship between Eisenhower and Dulles was relatively straightforward. Eisenhower made the major decisions in consultation with Dulles. The president decided, authorized, and approved. Dulles implemented decisions, handled negotiations, conducted diplomacy, and practiced statecraft. No one matched him as a trusted adviser to Eisenhower; no one got between them, though Herbert Hoover, Jr., at the State Department, a reputed Anglophobe, stood tall with Eisenhower. He was acceptable as a substitute when Dulles was away.

In contrast, Eisenhower felt very much in command of defense issues and, as a result, kept Secretary of Defense Charles Wilson on a tight rein. The Suez crisis is remarkable in many ways, one of which is the prominence of the State Department and the virtual irrelevance of the Department of Defense. Wilson contributed to his own problems with Eisenhower and did not enhance his position by irritating the British ambassador with comments that the Suez affair was a relatively minor incident.

The Eisenhower-Dulles relationship was not without its dangers. Eisenhower perhaps left too much to Dulles's discretion, did not challenge sufficiently his conduct of negotiations, and was too reluctant to force Dulles to reassess his preferences. Eisenhower delegated a great deal to Dulles and expected him to make routine decisions and actions. But Dulles checked his own understanding of decisions and agreements faithfully with Eisenhower before launching major initiatives. He ensured that he had the president's approval before acting. He acquiesced in Eisenhower's use of personal envoys and emissaries such as Robert Anderson. He acknowledged that the president could seek information and policy suggestions informally and should at times involve himself in personal diplomacy.

However, Eisenhower and Dulles did not always share the same views, even on supremely important issues such as the conduct of Soviet-American relations. But they shared many central beliefs, on colonialism for example; serious differences of opinion were rare and did not result in conflict. Dulles had full access to Eisenhower and, thus, had every opportunity to place his views privately before him. They were in touch daily, and more than that if necessary.

Eisenhower, in contrast, met only weekly with Wilson and developed a more formal relationship with Dulles's successor, Christian Herter. If Eisenhower were reelected in 1956, Dulles would stay on. Eisenhower told Arthur Krock how Dulles's death had affected him more than it was possible to describe.[8]

LEGITIMATION STRATEGIES

Both Eisenhower and Dulles, in their respective ways, were sensitive to the politics of decision making. Effective communication strategies, particularly during an election, had to be constructed so as to educate, inform, and convince. Andrew Goodpaster, Eisenhower's staff secretary, recalled that Arthur Minnich of the White House staff played a significant role in alerting Eisenhower to the political content of various policies. On such matters Dulles would defer to Eisenhower. The president must judge the public mind. Whatever the reservations and challenges, Eisenhower felt that he could explain and justify policies and convince the public of their legitimacy. Indeed, Robert Bowie, head of policy planning at the State Department, sensed a certain confidence on Eisenhower's part in this regard.

Dulles, for example, feared that western opinion, pacifistically inclined, fearing war, and wanting to believe that coexistence was possible and that the international system was not pathological, would grasp at a dangerous accommodation with the Soviet Union. The Soviet Union would exploit such sentiment. Eisenhower disagreed. He felt he could cooperate with the Soviet Union to some extent, get a satisfactory working relationship with its leaders, and legitimate the policy to the American public.[9]

The Suez crisis was the last Middle East crisis not subject to television coverage, thus reducing public exposure to its unfolding and public awareness of its final, dramatic military events. Eisenhower, on the threshold of the television era, hired Robert Montgomery to advise him on use of the medium. He would not allow his office or himself to be used to sell policy in any crass way.

In that sense he was modest and restrained and had to be convinced that media devices and techniques were becoming. But he understood the power he had to persuade through the press. On September 24, 1956, for example, Eisenhower called Arthur Sulzberger of the *New York Times*, and they talked at length the next day. Ann Whitman, Eisenhower's secretary, recorded the conversation. Her notes indicate that President Eisenhower noted, not only in the papers but from friends in the political campaign, that Sulzberger's staff had not made a decision on whom to support. As a result, Mrs. Whitman noted, Eisenhower was urged by friends in New York to make an appeal directly to Sulzberger. However, Eisenhower assured Sulzberger that because they had been long-time friends, he did not want Sulzberger to feel that their friendship would be damaged by the paper's decision on whom to support.[10]

When Sulzberger responded that he was bothered by the presence of Richard Nixon on the ticket, Eisenhower replied that "he sometimes wishes he could

put him clear before the public.'' The president then invited Sulzberger down
"for lunch and a little talk" or for an informal supper including their wives.
They decided to meet the next day for an off-the-record lunch.[11]

The communication strategies of Eisenhower's presidency were designed
largely by James Hagerty, who had been with him since the 1952 Republican
National Convention.[12] After a briefly troubled initial relationship, they became
an accomplished team. Hagerty was competent and loyal; Eisenhower trusted
him and his judgment. Hagerty's strategies were generally effective. Eisenhower
held regular half-hour press conferences that Eisenhower did not always enjoy;
his somewhat tangled syntax occasionally produced amused embarrassment.

Hagerty handled relations with the media during the Suez crisis, particularly
in the final, dramatic days. He recalled his long hours at the White House,
sleeping there or getting away only after the first editions of the eastern press
had gone in and being back at his desk by 7:00 A.M. Often his announcements
were dictated or written out personally by Eisenhower; when he spoke he knew
that he was reflecting Eisenhower's views.

It was characteristic of Eisenhower, and became routine, to brief his press
secretary and anticipate questions before Hagerty met the press. It reflected
accurately their relationship. Hagerty established the right to be informed on a
need-to-know basis. He was not present at any meetings of the NSC during the
Suez crisis, but he had the right to attend not only NSC but also Cabinet meetings.
In addition, he regularly received meeting agendas and minutes. As the crisis
matured, Hagerty was present at the small group decision sessions on October
29 and 30 and November 3, 4, and 5. He was concerned, predictably, with
legitimation rather than substance and had kept an eye throughout the crisis on
political considerations.

Early in October, for example, he urged the president to take decisive action
to solve the crisis if efforts at the United Nations failed. Stevenson must not
benefit from promising to go to Egypt if elected, thus imitating Eisenhower's
1952 pledge to go to Korea. Eisenhower's letter to Hoover of October 8, listing
several feasible policy steps, was in part a reaction to Hagerty's initiative.[13]
Eisenhower was also well aware of the international dimensions of a successful
communication strategy. What appeared in the American media was consumed
abroad, including in the Middle East.

The United States Information Agency, under Abbot Washburn and Theodore
Streibert, was given a role in the Middle East. Its pamphlet in Arabic on communism, distributed in the winter of 1956–1957, sold well in Egypt but poorly
in Syria. Early in April 1956, Eisenhower warned Air Chief Marshall Dickson,
head of the British Chiefs of Staff, of the importance of the information, propaganda, and political warfare activities in the area. He cautioned Dickson that
the propaganda from Cairo and Moscow was quite significant but that we had
not been as aggressive in doing the same. Naturally, Eisenhower understood
that allies and antagonists used the American media and the United Nations to
influence domestic opinion.

British politicians, for example, like all politicians, had to secure reelection, even at the cost of "demagoging against a friend."[14] Hagerty, Sherman Adams, Robert Cutler (Dillon Anderson's predecessor), Goodpaster, and W. B. "Jerry" Persons (when he became head of the White House staff) monitored Dulles's relationship with the press. Dulles had his own press secretary, Carl McCardle and later the somewhat more effective A. Berding. They cooperated with Hagerty on press relations and consulted with him before press conferences and on statements to the press. Dulles, Hagerty recalled, believed in public knowledge and public information.[15] He kept his press secretary fully informed. Robert Bowie agreed with that assessment. Dulles felt it very important to inform the public and Congress fully, to simplify and make issues understandable, to maintain the public's confidence in the administration, and to demonstrate the dangers of Soviet propaganda. Bowie noted that Dulles was deeply concerned that public opinion might be misled or that it might be tempted to drop its guard or stop supporting the necessary measures to combat communism.[16]

In Nixon's judgment, Dulles did not decide policy for political reasons. Once policy was made, however, Dulles would check the polls, see what was possible, weigh the controversial issues, and turn to the task of educating the public, of convincing them of what might be done. Dulles was a creative speech writer and an effective speaker. Nixon thought that Dulles had the ability to communicate and sell the ideas that he thought should be sold, but he also developed new ideas in the course of writing his own speeches.[17]

Dulles had a good press sense, although he often made errors in press conferences and apologized to Hagerty for the slips. It was understandably difficult, in Hagerty's opinion, for either Eisenhower or Dulles always to recall what had been agreed upon as to what should be kept secret and what should be made public, and to be able to judge whether a particular comment would be politically embarrassing or internationally damaging. Hagerty described Dulles as having a passion for the *New York Times*, which led him to give special access to its reporters, a practice which Hagerty deplored.[18]

Dulles found the challenge of television a somewhat daunting one. In April 1956, Lawrence Spivack urged Dulles to appear on "Meet the Press" because he regarded him as adept in using the media and expected him to be effective in reaching the public. Dulles was doubtful. He had reservations about the propriety of the Secretary of State going on television and worried about the international repercussions of a misspoken word. Once something had been said on television, it had been said; one had to prepare very carefully. Spivack pointed out that Eisenhower was permitting the filming of his press conferences and the use of those films on television. But Dulles was extremely reluctant; he would review the matter, consult McCardle, and reserve his decision.[19] By September 1956, Helen Reid of the *New York Herald Tribune* was congratulating Dulles on a superb performance on "Meet the Press."

Sherman Adams and Richard Nixon could be relied upon to raise political considerations during discussions of policy. Adams attended Cabinet meetings and sessions with legislative leaders routinely. He was present at the NSC on August 9; September 6 and 20; October 4, 12, and 26; and November 1. He participated in the decision sessions of October 29 and 30 and November 5 and 6. Nixon was present only at the NSC meeting on August 9. He was on the campaign trail and not involved in any decision sessions. However, he was in touch regularly with Eisenhower and Dulles; he was more involved once the election was over; and his views on political matters were respected even though he was, in some ways, a political liability.

On July 27, for example, Eisenhower phoned Nixon to bring him up to date on the Suez situation and asked him to keep Senators William Knowland and Lyndon Johnson informed. There could be serious developments, but he did not want the United States to be "out in front in being tough." At the NSC meeting on August 9, Nixon argued that they must ensure that the Democrats, at their national convention, did not adopt a position that would embarrass the negotiations over Suez. A Democratic recommendation to sell arms to Israel, Nixon suggested, could have an impact on the Middle East situation. Dulles tended to discount that. Dulles assured him that he had the matter in hand since he had been working indirectly through Senator Mike Mansfield. The Arab states took it for granted that if the Democrats won the election, the United States would back Israel, and the Democratic Party platform would not materially affect Arab attitudes.

Subsequently, Hagerty explained that Eisenhower's seemingly deprecatory remarks about Nixon, in 1960 for example, were attempts neither to ridicule nor to trivialize Nixon's role, but to emphasize the singular responsibility of the president to make command decisions. Dillon Anderson testified to Nixon's influence. Anderson noted that Nixon usually commented on the domestic political feasibility of a policy and the support that the policy would have in Congress. Anderson thought that Nixon's judgment was usually right since he had been in both the executive and legislative branches.[20]

The sensitivity of Eisenhower and Dulles to the need for the legitimation of policy is demonstrated particularly by the careful, effective, even superb way they courted Congress, massaged individual senators and members of the House, and played on the merits and morality of a bipartisanship, all without surrendering their control over foreign policy and leaving them virtually free to seize credit and dole out blame. It was axiomatic to Eisenhower and Dulles that there must be a bipartisan foreign policy and close cooperation between Congress and the administration, but the Executive Branch conducted foreign policy. They did not want the Hill to make excessive demands on the time and resources of the State Department. They regarded consensus as necessary to conduct foreign policy effectively; they knew it was also smart politics. Dulles's skills in fostering a bipartisan spirit, securing broad support, and encouraging members of both parties either to defend him or to avoid recrimination over policy failures were truly remarkable.[21]

Dulles, accepting the enhanced role of Congress in the foreign policy process,

was able to raise bipartisanship to the level of principle. He was indefatigable
in his efforts to inform, consult, and negotiate with Congress and to involve its
leaders in the policy process. He invited Democrats onto international delega-
tions, to conferences, and to the United Nations. He offered, often unsuccessfully, appointments to important Democrats; provided prompt information to
congressional committees; and took care of chairmen and ranking minority members through meetings, private conversations, telephone calls, letters, and hos-
pitality.

His relations with Republican Senators William Knowland and H. Alexander
Smith of New Jersey and with Democratic Senator Walter George, chairman of
the Foreign Relations Committee in 1955, were particularly close. Knowland
was the key Republican. Dulles made a practice of keeping him informed and
fully in support of Middle East policy. He was a man to cultivate, for he had
his own ideas and was by no means a puppet of the administration. Dulles was
generally very frank with Senator George. Dulles extended the courtship to the
House of Representatives and particularly to Congressman James P. Richards,
Democrat from South Carolina and chairman of the Foreign Affairs Committee
from 1955. Democrats did not want this process to go too far. But Dulles put
the State Department's relations with Congress on a new footing, particularly
with the lower house.

Eisenhower was equally adept at congressional relations, creating the first
White House congressional liaison staff, under Persons and later Bryce Harlow,
and had assistants for both legislative and intergovernmental affairs. He presided
over regularly scheduled meetings with Republican congressional leaders and
chaired, as established practice, several bipartisan congressional leadership briefings on foreign policy. These briefings were dominated by Dulles. Eisenhower
held many private meetings with individual congressional leaders. Senators
Knowland and Lyndon Johnson, particularly, and Speaker Sam Rayburn frequently received such personal attention.

Eisenhower regarded Johnson as the key Democratic senator and as decisively
influential with those senators committed to the state of Israel. He was a man
to court, to keep informed, and to be made to feel that his ideas were decidedly
valuable and welcome. Eisenhower made a point of consulting congressional
leaders and securing their opinions before an event and before the possibility of
crisis and disarray, even when national security issues were involved. He accepted the risk that Democrats might leak information to the likes of Drew
Pearson. Fruitful contacts made were kept up as a matter of routine. In these
ways he won the confidence of and established credibility with members of
Congress, demonstrating the significance of sober, bipartisan judgment about
foreign and defense issues.

STEVENSON'S OPPORTUNITIES

Eisenhower was a formidable political opponent, skilled in the ways of legitimation. But Adlai Stevenson had, in 1956, certain weapons at his disposal. Stevenson could seek to undermine the bipartisan support of foreign policy that Eisenhower and Dulles had so assiduously and successfully created. In fact, Stevenson failed to disrupt the consensus to any significant degree. During the campaign, Eisenhower and Dulles handled congressional leaders with their customary skill. They agreed that it would be wise to consult promptly with a bipartisan group of congressional leaders—Senators Johnson, George, Mansfield, Knowland, Wiley, and Smith and Speaker Rayburn—and to include a prominent Democrat in the delegation that Dulles would lead to the first London Conference in late August.

Dulles told the NSC on August 9 that they must act without regard to the political situation. On August 12, in the midst of the Democratic National Convention in Chicago, they convened a meeting of congressional leaders.[22] Dulles and Arthur Flemming, director of the Office of Defense Mobilization, briefed them. Dulles was particularly critical of Nasser, "an extremely dangerous fanatic with a Hitler-ite personality." Both he and Eisenhower compared Nasser's aggressive statements to those of Hitler, and Dulles referred explicitly to *Mein Kampf*, no doubt with the pro-Israeli senators in mind. Dulles was supportive of Britain and France and yet eager to bring about a peaceful solution that retained a free hand for the United States.

Eisenhower emphasized the need both to ensure the flow of oil to Western Europe and to ensure that the United States would not have to underwrite its economy permanently. He also emphasized that the loss of oil revenues would undermine the economies of the Arab states and provide an opportunity for Soviet mischief. Vigorous diplomacy outside the United Nations seemed to be the best course of action. Dulles's delegation to London must be impressive and effective. A treaty might result, and Eisenhower expressed the hope, therefore, that one senator from each party would accompany Dulles.

The arguments were sound enough, but no leading Democrat went with Dulles to the first London Conference. Dulles had earlier identified Mike Mansfield as the most likely Democratic colleague. By late September, however, the enthusiasm for Mansfield cooled distinctly because of his discussions in Paris with Christian Pineau, the French foreign minister. Mansfield, apparently, was playing politics, suggesting that the United States should subsidize the cost of shipping oil round the Cape to western Europe if that proved necessary, and seeking to convince the French that the Suez affair would be handled better by a Democratic than a Republican administration. Eisenhower and Dulles, it should be noted, did not have a high opinion of the French government, preferring the opponents of Prime Minister Guy Mollet. It was exactly the reverse with regard to Britain. They did not relish dealing with a Labor government. Nixon and George Humphrey were not alone in fearing the prospect of Aneurin Bevan in high office.[23]

When it became clear that the mission to Cairo, headed by Sir Robert Menzies, the prime minister of Australia, to present the Eighteen Power proposals to Nasser was likely to fail, and that Dag Hammarskjold, the U.N. secretary general, was not able to secure Israel's cooperation to strengthen the armistice agreements, Dulles, on September 6, met with the leaders of the Senate Foreign Relations Committee and the House Foreign Affairs Committee. He emphasized the seriousness of the Anglo-French threat to use force, the "evil game" being played by the Soviet Union, and his own role in seeking a settlement.[24] The meeting was cordial and unifying and without a trace of criticism of Dulles's actions.

Two days later Dulles briefed Knowland. The senator emphasized that the country would not support the use of force by Britain and France. He wanted the United Nations to handle the crisis, He was well satisfied with Dulles's assurances. Efforts were made throughout September to keep congressional leaders fully informed of the Suez affair, a strategy reconfirmed in mid-October as the crisis seemed temporarily closer to a settlement, only to deteriorate rapidly as the election drew near. State Department spokesmen gave regular briefings on the Hill, the last one on October 30. Knowland had little but praise for the way Eisenhower and Dulles were handling Middle Eastern affairs. He was particularly content with the response made on October 22 to Nicolai Bulganin's note of the previous day, which an angry Dulles had taken to be a personal attack on the president and himself and an offensive gesture in support of Stevenson.

Dulles briefed Knowland on October 29 and 30 before leaving for New York to handle policy at the United Nations. He assured Knowland that the administration was not party to the Anglo-French ultimatum, In fact, Britain and France had broken their word and were using Israel as a decoy. Knowland was content; going to the United Nations was a sound step as far as the people were concerned.[25] Dulles pointed to the pending discussions at the United Nations and emphasized that the divided governments of Britain and France were not keeping the United States fully informed. In any case, the United States could not give them a blank check.

Lyndon Johnson assured Dulles, after the election, that he remained loyal to the idea of a bipartisan foreign policy, that he was doing all he could to preserve the consensus, and that he fully understood the problems associated with seeking a balanced policy in the Middle East and not simply backing Israel against the Arab states. He suggested a series of informal breakfasts involving himself, Dulles, and Mansfield, and that Dulles keep Senator George in the picture. Dulles was careful to point to seemingly insoluble problems; the United States was identified with Israel, Britain, and France and was seen to be in contest with the Arab states supported by the Soviet Union.

The administration wanted to launch a dramatically new and balanced Middle Eastern policy, and yet its only weapons were oil purchases and Arab dependence on oil exports. These flimsy tools were the reverse side of western dependence on Arab states to cut off oil supplies to Europe.[26]

Dulles did not need reminding to stay in touch with Senator George and marshal his continuing, if diminishing, influence in Congress. On October 30, he told George that it was almost certain that the British and the French were working in collusion with the Israelis. There would be, however, no need to call Congress back into special session unless either U.S. military action or massive aid were planned, which they were not.

The British and the French had defied American advice and faced probable disaster. The United States would act in compliance with the U.N. resolution which called upon Israel to withdraw its forces and would withhold economic assistance to Israel as long as it was in violation of the resolution.[27] But more perhaps had to be done to neutralize Stevenson. On October 31, John Hanes, Jr., one of Dulles's special assistants, informed Dulles that in the opinion of John Vorys, a respected Republican:

1. the president should make a speech in Philadelphia, or at an earlier time, speaking not as a candidate but as a leader of the people to report on the Middle Eastern situation;
2. Stevenson should be called in and specifically briefed on the Middle East situation (apparently Vorys had in mind a further or higher level briefing than was presumably taking place once or twice by the CIA); and
3. to protect the administration's bipartisan position, Rayburn and Lyndon Johnson should be telephoned and asked if they want a foreign policy briefing and if so when.

Another of Dulles's aides felt that there was merit in calling Lyndon Johnson and putting the matter squarely on the backs of the Democrats. But the aide also felt that Eisenhower should clear this strategy with Senator Knowland beforehand. Dulles's aides conferred with Persons; he wanted no action until he had consulted with Sherman Adams.[28] On October 31 Eisenhower educated a shocked Senator Knowland. They should try and put themselves in England's shoes and not be bitter, despite the enormity of the error in British policy, which he called the biggest error of our time besides that of losing China. They must not condemn Britain too severely but should pursue a settlement in the General Assembly and keep ahead of the Soviet Union on this. He was, himself, about to lose h is "British citizenship."[29]

Stevenson, clearly, had not seriously threatened the bipartisan consensus, and no doubt he took a sensible and long-term view of the matter. Bipartisan support for foreign policy was desirable; it was unwise to tamper unduly with it. This did not mean, however, that the conduct of policy and the issues of competence, effectiveness, and vision could not be made politically relevant. Stevenson could point to the Suez affair as an extremely dangerous problem for which the administration's policy, faltering and misguided, was largely responsible. Stevenson, reportedly taking Dexterene to combat fatigue and sleeping pills to get some rest, told Arthur Krock at breakfast on September 21 that he was convinced that the administration's policies in the Middle East were directly responsible for the Suez crisis. He also felt that the United States was encouraging the Egyptians in their anti-British policy. Stevenson said he planned a play-by-play speech on this subject and would not be hampered by the confidential reports he received from the CIA. He wanted to rein in Kefauver, handle the foreign policy speeches himself, and prevent his running mate from making further "unbaked comments" on Egypt and Israel. Krock was close to Eisenhower, he had access to the president and Dulles. Perhaps he passed on this information.

Two days later Dulles told Eisenhower about his conversation with Anthony Eden about possible military measures to be employed. Eisenhower doubted that they would be decisive. Four days later, Harold Macmillan, the British Chancellor of the Exchequer, met with both Eisenhower and Dulles.[30] Eisenhower, well and in a robust mood but rambling as always, according to Macmillan, told him that he understood the British predicament but emphasized that he was currently in the position in which the Conservative Party had been in May 1955. Eisenhower was campaigning hard but feared for the outcome of the election. Surprisingly, he attacked the United Nations for undermining the leadership of the great powers and called for a resurrection of something like the old Concert of Europe.

Macmillan concluded that Eisenhower was determined to bring Nasser down, understood the economic problems that would follow from the pursuit of a protracted settlement, and accepted the fact that the British must win on the canal issue or face economic collapse. Dulles, in their private conversation on September 25, still upset about Britain's independent approach to the United Nations, spoke of the Suez Canal Users Association (SCUA) scheme as a way to be rid of Nasser within six months and that Nasser, meanwhile, was growing in prestige.

Dulles stated that he realized that they might have to use force and that the threat of the use of force might bring Nasser to heel. He wanted to keep alive the alternative of using the Cape route to ship oil to Europe. It would frighten the Arabs as they faced loss of royalties. Dulles went on to point out that the Suez, affair, while not a major election issue at that time, could become so. It would be disastrous if anything happened before the election. He pointed out that Eisenhower had helped the conservatives in May 1955 by agreeing to a four-power conference. He hoped, therefore, that Britain would not act before November 6. Congress would not vote aid for Britain and France, feeling that they should be on their own feet by now, but, Dulles suggested, there was a possibility that a loan could be negotiated or that the terms of the existing loan could be modified. Such a step would have to be kept secret because of the election; it would be fatal if the information leaked out.

From one perspective the historical significance of these conversations is the extent to which they encouraged Eden to risk the use of force and undermined the opposition to such a step. From another it is the extent to which the election and consideration of congressional opinion affected U.S. policy in 1956. If Stevenson could demonstrate that Eisenhower was not vigorous enough in his support of the United Nations and had not turned to it to handle the Suez affair, he had an election issue of some potency. The polls showed that the majority of Americans, Republican and Democrat, overwhelmingly supported the United Nations and wanted to see it managing major, threatening problems. But the evidence of neglect of the United Nations in 1956 was flimsy. Dulles's attendance in New York and his record at the United Nations undercut criticism. They could not be made a major election issue. On September 8, as noted above, Knowland insisted that the country would not back Britain and France in military action and would expect the United States to use the United Nations to prevent aggression. Dulles assured Knowland on that score and made it clear that he had refused an Anglo-French request to block a U.N. resolution against the use of force should such a resolution be introduced.[31]

Dulles's well-publicized anger at the Anglo-French initiative in late September to move the dispute to the United Nations was a possible opportunity for Stevenson, but not one easily turned to his own advantage. The Anglo-French case was suspect and their motives highly questionable. Eden mishandled the incident, even going back on his word to Dulles, and those Anglophiles hostile to Dulles could not damage him seriously over the incident. Dulles's opposition to the initiative could be pictured as tactical, suitably cautious, and thoroughly justified, his outrage as perfectly understandable.

That incident, and others, pointed to a further potential issue—the charge that Eisenhower and particularly Dulles were neglecting the "special relationship" with Britain, the most popular and trusted ally of the United States. In addition, by failing to support Britain and France, it could be said that they were threatening the unity of NATO and undermining the position of the west in the Middle East, with all the potentially disastrous consequences—the loss of oil, the estrangement of certain Arab states, and providing a golden opportunity for the Soviet Union. At that time, the Anglo-American "special relationship" had its devotees, its own informal lobby, with Anglophile representatives of the east coast establishment, old foreign policy hands, leading Democrats, and powerful members of the press such as the brothers Alsop prominent. The Alsops, through their own influence and later through instruments such as Herman Finer's book on the Suez crisis, Eden's memoirs, and the reminiscences of Winthrop Aldrich, the U.S. ambassador to Britain, could turn the Suez crisis into an assault on Dulles that was largely unjustified and inadequately documented, alleging incompetent and duplicitous behavior culminating in the double cross of Britain and France. Aldrich showed little loyalty, felt badly treated, and delighted in the cutting story—Churchill, during the U–2 incident, was heard to remark, "They tell me that there is another *Dulles. Can* that be *possible?*" Aldrich's assessment of Eisenhower's conduct in the Suez crisis was very critical.

The British embassy in Washington was adept at using the American press to deplore any deviation from the "special relationship" and to assert pressure on the Eisenhower administration to support British policy, both during and in the aftermath of the Suez crisis. To the Anglophile Eisenhower, this was both puzzling and difficult to take. On April 10, 1956, for example, Eisenhower called Dulles on the telephone to "talk . . . about constant references in the press to the effect that the British press is getting awfully sore with you and me and saying that we are vacillating around about the Middle East. I don't know what they are talking about." He had had a query in a recent press conference about a letter from Eden on the subject; "of course almost every letter from Eden has referred to it. . . . It looks like the British government was handing out something to the papers about us. Apparently some question if Ambassador Makins was doing it here. . . . The President suggested that he might write Anthony Eden something to the effect—here, if you want policies published, we have been trying to [get] together on policy so we could make a public statement, they want our support of the Baghdad Pact, they will have to make certain concessions." Despite the less than clear transcript and the somewhat confused prose, Eisenhower's irritation was plain.[32]

The British in particular attempted to indict Dulles, blaming him for the ill-fated decision on the Aswan Dam and his reported failure to consult adequately with the British. This attempt gathered strength with attacks on his supposedly unwarranted restraint on British attempts to bring Nasser down, accompanied by his rumored disingenuous conduct toward Eden and British Foreign Secretary Selwyn Lloyd, and on his bewildering oratory. The indictment culminated with an assault on what was regarded as a pro-Arab and even pro-Soviet response to the Anglo-French-Israeli military operations against Egypt.

Dulles's statements of September 13, which confirmed that the United States would not use force to ensure passage through the canal for American ships, and of October 2, which distanced the United States from European colonialism, seemed particularly reprehensible, even treacherous. The charge was extended to Eisenhower with the accusation that his public statements in early September on the need to balance the rights of Egypt against those of the international community with regard to the Suez Canal had been instrumental in undermining the Menzies mission. He had encouraged Nasser to be obdurate. Menzies certainly paraded this interpretation of his failure in Cairo to confidants in London and elsewhere. It was picked up in official British and French circles and turned into a very broad hint that Eisenhower had acted in part to influence the election. The former charge is unsound, the latter preposterous. Lloyd described Eisenhower's statement of October 13 as deplorable and let Dulles know that he was disgusted by the way that the British position was weakened at every stage by what was being said in the United States.[33]

Whatever the treatment of Eisenhower, Dulles became, on the tongues and under the pens of his critics, a fatal combination of high principle and deviousness. He was considered a self-righteous, ruthless liar who did not understand the Middle East and Arab nationalism and who was playing a dangerous game. According to the critics, Dulles was, in fact, both treacherous and incompetent. Eden was, on occasion, frank. Writing to Lloyd on October 6, he warned that Dulles's purpose was different from that of the British. The canal, he noted, was not vital to U.S. interests, and he might string the British along until Election Day.

The early days of October brought some evidence of the prospect of Anglo-American cooperation without erasing the irritation and distrust. Dulles told Lloyd on October 7 that he was in full agreement on every point except the ultimate use of force. Dulles said that Lloyd had been absolutely right to maintain the threat of force and that he did not rule out force at a later stage. Dulles further assured Lloyd that he could rely on him to secure the essence of the Eighteen Power proposals. Eden, in response to this report from Lloyd, seemed somewhat assured but cautioned that the British had been misled by Dulles before and that they could not afford to risk another misunderstanding. Time was not on Britain's side; they must stand firm with France and stifle Dulles. Defense of Dulles—by George Humphrey and Herbert Hoover, Jr., for example, the latter dismissed as a petty and incompetent Anglophobe, insisting that there had been no double-cross of Britain—cut no ice in London.[34]

The indictment of Dulles was fed by the British Embassy in Washington; the Washington and New York press were enlisted to undercut Dulles's reputation. In a conversation on October 19 about the SCUA and the payment of dues to it, Henry Cabot Lodge, the ambassador to the United Nations, asked Dulles whether the British understood the American position. Dulles assured Lodge that they did, that Drew Middleton's recent article was wrong, and that the British were using him to point out what they wanted U.S. policy to be.[35] No one was more enthusiastically vitriolic than newspaper columnist Joseph Alsop.

Of course when the thing actually happened, Dulles was downhill from the first round, and that fool, Herbert Hoover, Jr., was in charge and literally believed that it was a plot to deprive Eisenhower of the election. It was very distasteful. We were anything but loyal and true and forthright. And it was of all the episodes in the Dulles time . . . most deeply colored by domestic politics, including the famous speech about Nasser that touched off the whole thing.

Alsop reported that at Dulles's first meeting with Britain's new ambassador, Harold Caccia, Dulles said that he disapproved of what the British did and that he could not condone it. However, Dulles added that he was puzzled why the British stopped once they had started. Caccia was sufficiently outraged that he felt like jumping across the desk and attacking Dulles.[36] Eisenhower's care in handling these gentlemen of the press was laced with a certain contempt. In a letter to his old friend Captain E. E. Hazlett about solutions to the Suez crisis, Eisenhower wrote that Walter Lippmann and the Alsops had many ideas, most of which were not particularly good. Eisenhower drew the analogy that these ideas were similar to those that would be developed by one's youngest grandchild.[37]

There were those on Eisenhower's staff, including James Hagerty, who did not share the president's Anglophilia. Goodpaster came to the conclusion that the British, French, and Israelis had timed their actions to coincide with the American election, assuming that Eisenhower would not act, and that his hands would be tied because of the Jewish vote. They had made a terrible mistake. Lodge described a meeting on October 29 with Sir Pierson Dickson, the British ambassador to the United Nations, as one where Dickson's true colors were seen. Lodge described Dickson as helping Dulles and Herbert Hoover, Jr., to undermine the "special relationship" the United States had with Britain. Eisenhower and Dulles themselves did not rule out the assumption that Eden and Mollet were willing to present the United States with a *fait accompli*, gambling that Eisenhower would, in the final analysis, stand by them.[38]

Eisenhower liked Eden personally and respected him as Churchill's aide and successor. Assisted, if not always productively, by Dulles, and despite the many irritants and the sharpest disagreement on the validity of the use of force, he had made a sincere and sustained effort to work with Eden, both at the London conferences and at the United Nations. He had looked for ways to bring Nasser to heel and even to bring him down while avoiding war.

Eisenhower was correct in his view that a resort to force would antagonize the Arab states, threaten the supply of oil, undermine the prospects for an Arab-Israeli settlement, and provide an opportunity for Soviet influence. It might also damage American interests in Saudi Arabia as well as severely complicate the election. Eden, his close senior colleagues, and the French were bent on snatching aggression out of negotiation. They seemed to feel that Eisenhower's policies were framed for election purposes and that once the election was over he would acquiesce in the use of force. Their collusion with Israel to attack Egypt was not the only aspect of policy kept hidden from the United States. Even then, when Eisenhower sensed that Eden was being less than frank, he tended to attribute it more to confusion than ill will. And why had Eden risked a campaign he could not win, Eisenhower asked, without the support of a united country, and one which made Britain out to be the bully—surely sheer desperation mixed with anachronistic reasoning.

Ultimately, Dulles and Eisenhower, each in his own way, were angry, out-raged, and bitterly disappointed with Anglo-French behavior. They felt deceived and shabbily treated by friends and allies, let down personally, and manipulated. Yet, they worked with Canada and at the United Nations to extricate Britain and France honorably from their folly. After November 6, while being brutally firm with Britain and France, insisting that a settlement be made on the terms laid down by the United Nations and the United States and using the formidable financial weapons at their disposal, they were instrumental in ensuring that Britain and France left the fiasco in Egypt with as little damage as possible. They worked to restore Anglo-American relations to something like normality as rapidly as was decent and wise.

On November 2, Eisenhower and Hoover discussed the problem of acting in the United Nations in ways that would both maintain Afro-Asian support and promote moderation. Yet they wanted to maintain an unyielding firmness toward

Britain and France, while, at the same time, extricating these allies from their predicament.

It was a difficult challenge made more so by Stevenson's criticism that Eisenhower had thrown over America's allies and stood against them alongside the Soviet Union. Eisenhower felt that this charge was both unfair and incorrect. He had broken with Britain and France only over the use of force and had kept American troops out of the conflict. Eden and Mollet had behaved irrationally, irresponsibly, and stupidly. They had used the wrong issue to challenge Nasser. Eisenhower took comfort from the fact that at least part of the British Commonwealth stood with the United States on these issues. He remained determined to work vigorously to settle the crisis through and in the United Nations.[39] In any event, neglect of the "special relationship" and of America's allies had not proven to be an issue that Stevenson used with any great effect. He preached largely to the converted, the partisan, and, on that occasion, to those of flawed judgment and unworthy sentiment.

Nothing matched the Jewish vote in Stevenson's arsenal if a major Middle Eastern crisis erupted and reverberated in the election campaign. Candidates felt compelled to calculate the political significance of every major policy decision affecting Israel.

Earlier in the year Israel had requested a $75 million loan for irrigation projects from the export-import bank. The State Department refused to take a position on the politics of the loan until it received the bank's economic assessment of the project. The matter was still pending in August 1956. There were, however, other more pressing and politically significant issues. The government of Israel and its Jewish supporters in the United States had, for much of 1955 and into 1956, pressed the Eisenhower administration for arms, particularly for F-86 fighter planes. The administration's strategy was clear; in line with the policy of not rearming either Egypt or Israel, it would refuse to sell planes to Israel but ask Canada and France to fill the requests.

Eisenhower agreed that it would be acceptable for France to sell twelve Mystere jet fighters to Israel but wanted the tightest possible constraint placed generally on arms transfers. In that way the Arab states would be reassured and embarrassing complications avoided. Israeli anger would be deflected, even though the United States had evaded Israel's attempts to achieve de facto alliance status through arms transfers. The administration would insure against political damage in an election year by privately assuring the leaders of the Jewish community that Canadian and French arms sales reflected American influence and policy.[40]

But arms sales to the Israelis could, as Hoover pointed out, bring further complications. The French were willing to oblige and, indeed, deliberately armed Israel in 1956 beyond agreed levels. The French also pressed Canada to support the policy, but the Canadian government, even with Lester Pearson, a gentile Zionist, as Minister for External Affairs, was, for good reason, less sure. The Canadian government was willing to help arm Israel as part of an agreed, public western policy and, in 1955, had supplied both fighter and training aircraft to Israel. But they were extremely reluctant to act in a way that Dulles wished and the French advised. Yet Dulles seemed satisfied. He told Senator George in late March 1956 that the United States would continue to deny export licenses for major military items to Israel but would not object if other states such as France, Italy, and Canada provided arms.

Israeli pressure on the administration for arms lessened as they saw that they could probably get the arms they needed from their traditional suppliers in Europe.[41] Eisenhower could not avoid handling the correspondence with Ben-Gurion on the denial of arms, even though there were certain policy and political risks. As Dulles pointed out on April 23, secrecy was called for. He believed that it was unwise to make any reference to the more recent exchange, which had not been given to the press for fear that the Israeli government would utilize it.[42] And, as justified as the policy was, it was not one that could either entirely satisfy Israel or be palatable to leading American Jews, with Senate aspirant Jacob Javits and Rabbi A. H. Silver prominent. Eisenhower used Silver as a conduit to Ben-Gurion, and, very reluctantly, he and Dulles met with Silver, recently returned from Palestine, on April 26.[43] As Dulles recorded, Rabbi Silver made a very strong plea for arms for Israel along the conventional lines, picking up all the arguments of Abba Eban in answering the counterarguments made to Eban.[44]

Silver was anything but deferential, and his devotion to the cause was unyielding, but he cut little ice. Eisenhower remained committed to established policy, although he wanted neither to perpetuate any arms imbalance in the Middle East nor prevent allies from selling arms to Israel. The United States would not itself sell arms at that juncture and would not give blanket concurrence in advance to unlimited arms sales to Israel.[45] It was time for statesmanship, not commerce; arms sales could not preserve peace. Ben-Gurion's blandishments included favorable comments about American as opposed to British policy, his willingness to enter into a regional security agreement if Israel were rearmed, and the prospect of creating a U.S. base in case of trouble in the region if the United States built airfields, roads, and ports in Israel. He had little or no effect. U.S. arms shipments to Israel in 1956 were modest, entailing only the transfer of trucks, halftracks, spare parts, and ammunition and did not include aircraft. They were matched by the arms embargo on Egypt.

It is unusual to regard the Roman Catholic vote in the United States as a lobby, although there are today signs that there may well be consequences of some significance for both parties in how Catholics, led by the bishops, vote. The Pope recognizes neither the state of Israel nor Jerusalem as Israel's capital; he will not ignore the problem of the Palestinians. On June 18, 1956, Cardinal Spellman told Dulles that Jewish activities were becoming excessively demanding. Dulles responded that he felt it was very important to demonstrate that the Jewish population did not dictate the foreign policy of the United States. He also added that this was not an easy task.[46]

But, throughout 1956, Dulles argued that it would be wise to insulate the election as far as possible from Middle Eastern problems. He advised Eisenhower, on June 22, not to invite either Ben-Gurion or Nasser to Washington. Such visits would not help the peace process, which was best left to the United Nations. Dulles argued that there was the risk that a visit by Ben-Gurion would inject the Israeli issue into the presidential campaign. An invitation to Nasser, he felt, would almost certainly be misunderstood both at home and abroad in view of his recent acts supporting the Soviet bloc.[47]

The role of Jacob Javits in all this was fascinatingly delicate. Javits, Jewish and a self-styled progressive Republican, was seeking the Senate seat in New York in 1956. His contacts with Dulles went back to the early 1930s. Both were lawyers practicing in New York but, according to Javits, were on opposite sides of the fence professionally, socially, and instinctively. Javits had encouraged Eisenhower to run in 1952. He himself ran successfully for the position of attorney general of New York in 1954 and began to emerge as a Jewish spokesman on issues affecting Israel. In March 1956, he declared his availability for the Republican nomination. He was willing to run against either the incumbent, Senator Herbert Lehman, a respected liberal Jewish elder statesman of the Democratic Party, who was, however, seventy-eight years of age and ready to retire, or, in all probability, Robert Wagner, Jr., the Democratic mayor of New York City.

Javits took up the cause of rearming Israel and preventing the sale of arms to the Arabs, especially to Saudi Arabia, in representations to Eisenhower and Dulles beginning at least as early as February 1956. Dulles alerted Eisenhower to the situation on May 22. He pointed out that Javits would argue that he could not run successfully for the Senate unless they changed their Middle East policy because of the impact of that policy on Jewish voters in New York. The Democrats, predictably, were attacking the administration's policy to court Jewish voters, who, under the circumstances, were likely to rally to Wagner. Dulles felt, however, that the situation was manageable. The Israeli ambassador, Abba Eban, seemed satisfied. Israel was getting arms from various sources. The United States was shipping minor items such as munitions and spare parts and might increase the amounts as the discussions with Saudi Arabia, linked to the negotiation of a new air base agreement, matured.

Dulles advised Eisenhower to encourage Javits's political aspirations but to give him no details on arms transfers.[48] Dulles and Javits discussed the situation on the following day. Javits agreed that U.S.-Israeli relations were satisfactory but argued that the Jewish voters in New York had a different perception of the situation and were opposed to the administration's policies. He suggested using Vice President Nixon to present the administration's case and confirmed that he would run if the party nominated him.[49] He secured Eisenhower's support and the nomination, ran against Wagner, and faced the political dilemmas of the Suez crisis.

Arthur H. Dean, a Wall Street international and corporate lawyer and a fellow Episcopalian, had succeeded Dulles as senior partner in the law firm of Sullivan and Cromwell when Dulles became a U.S. senator in 1949. Dulles trusted him and had used him in the preliminary negotiations to end the Korean War. In 1956 Dean became involved in Middle Eastern issues and acted as a conduit between Eban, Golda Meir, various Jewish leaders, and Dulles. On June 7, Dean reported to Dulles that Philip Ehrlich had met with Eban who had confirmed that Israel was having difficulty obtaining arms from Canada. Eban asked Ehrlich to assist Israel in obtaining arms from other countries since Canada did not seem to be able to supply them.[50]

On July 11, Dean met with Eban and Reuven Shiloah, a political officer at the Israeli embassy in Washington, D.C., and promptly informed Dulles of their concern. Eban asked Dean to urge Dulles to give his personal attention to such issues and reiterated the feeling of frustration in Israel about the deterioration of their relations with the United States and the feeling of hopelessness about the continued buildup of arms in Egypt by the Soviet Union.[51] Dulles was unmoved. He reported to Eisenhower on July 16, commenting on the Dean-Eban meeting, that Israel recognized that it was not good for them to have the Democrats try to capitalize on Israeli issues in the campaign. The president should hold his nerve, not be swayed by Jewish leaders, and pursue a balanced Middle Eastern policy based on substantive rather than political considerations.[52] All this, however, occurred before the confrontation with Egypt in late July.

Pressure on Dulles mounted from other sources. Helen Reid, the former publisher and chairperson of the *New York Herald Tribune*, questioned the apparent lack of State Department vigor in protesting the discriminatory practices of Arab states against Jews who were American citizens. She was concerned about the Jewish vote in the campaign and did not find Dulles's response entirely satisfactory. Dulles had neither informed American Jews about the position of the State Department nor spoken out himself. While recognizing that the State Department did not wish to be involved in the campaign, she felt that the administration's position on this matter should be made known to the public. As she emphasized to Dulles, there had been a great deal of bitterness as a result of the State Department's silence, and, as a result, Eisenhower may have lost a large majority of the Jewish vote. She further pointed out that this was not a matter of Zionism because all Jews were affected. She concluded by saying that the campaign was in jeopardy and she wanted to do something to reverse that trend.[53]

Reid had ample reason to be concerned. A Republican presidential candidate does not expect to win significant numbers of Jewish votes. In 1956, Eisenhower's national support was sufficiently broad to ensure that the Jewish vote was not pivotal to his own reelection. But the margin of victory concerned Eisenhower, and the vote in certain key states such as New York seemed critical. Hagerty recalled that they felt they would carry New York by 1.2 million votes. The Republican polls indicated that the Jewish electorate would decide that they were Americans first. In the end, Eisenhower carried New York by 1.6 million votes of which 400,000 were Jewish votes.[54]

Both Eisenhower and Dulles impressed on Harold Macmillan how tough the campaign and how close the race was in late September. Emmet Hughes, Eisenhower's speech writer, recorded that they were sure the president would be reelected, but, as Eisenhower told Eden in mid-October, they must win big. Merely to win was not enough. He could not be effective as president without a large personal majority. He must campaign vigorously, particularly in order to demonstrate that he was in sound health.[55]

Then there was Congress. The Democratic majority in the Senate was a mere forty-nine to forty-seven. A Republican victory, for example, in New York, without any offsetting losses, would give the vice president the deciding vote. In fact, eight seats changed hands, but the losses and gains were equally divided and the balance in the Senate did not change. The Democrats actually increased their majority in the House of Representatives.

Emmet Hughes recalled that the Suez affair and, indeed, the Middle East were something of a time bomb that could explode and affect materially the outcome of the election. If a Middle East war broke out, and the administration's policies seemed in part responsible, then Stevenson would have a powerful political weapon. Eisenhower saw little merit in and drew little comfort from speculation among certain members of Congress that the interruption of Middle East oil supplies, should the Suez Canal be closed or oil pipelines shut down, would boost United States oil exports to western Europe and Britain. The NATO allies could not pay in dollars, and they would be made vulnerable because the costs and problems of moving oil by the Cape route were enormous.[56]

In this situation, Dulles was something of a political liability. His commitment to the state of Israel appeared to some to be sufficiently lukewarm to make him a problem, if not an embarrassment. Javits recalled that although Dulles was not antisemitic and the conduct of relations with Israel was a challenging problem, and with 1956 being an especially difficult year because of Israeli assaults on Jordan, it was hard for him to work with Dulles on Middle East issues. Also, it was difficult for Dulles to dispel the impression that he was hostile to Israel. Dulles had to work at his image so as not to be a liability to the president. The Republicans knew that they had to show that Dulles was not an enemy of Israel and used Bernard Kutzen, a consultant to the Republican National Committee, to plan campaign strategy on that question. But the Suez crisis, in any case, marked the nadir of Dulles's standing with Jewish leaders in the United States. After that, in Javits's view, Dulles rebounded to the point where he became something of a hero of American-Israeli relations.[57]

Eisenhower was personally less vulnerable. Jewish leaders understood that he was committed to Israel's right to exist in peace and to the development of its political economy. During his presidency, Israel enjoyed a preferential position with regard to aid. Eugene Black, president of the World Bank, recalled that he, among others, urged Eisenhower to deal more even-handedly with the Middle East, to divide military aid equitably between Israel and the Arab states, and to be especially solicitous of relations with Egypt, the key Arab state. Black saw funding the Aswan Dam, a proposal opposed by Israel, as a major step in that direction.[58] Cancellation of the funding of the Aswan Dam project cannot have hurt Eisenhower's relations with Israel and American Jews, but he had in no sense abandoned Egypt and wanted lines kept open to Nasser. Much would depend, therefore, on how he and Dulles handled the third Middle Eastern crisis of the postwar era, the Suez affair.

CONCLUSION

This is not the place to attempt to assess why Eisenhower gained a landslide victory over Stevenson in 1956 while the Republicans failed to gain control of either the House or the Senate. Nor is it the appropriate place to assess what role foreign and defense policy generally, and the Suez crisis in particular, played in producing those results. The issue here is that the Suez affair gave Stevenson certain potential political weapons that Eisenhower had to counter and neutralize. Some contemporary observers tended to miss the dimension that was Eisenhower's concern for political legitimation and communication. To be sure, Eisenhower was determined to handle the Suez affair principally on substantive grounds. In fact, he felt, in retrospect, that he had done so. He told "Swede" Hazlett that they had realized that Ben-Gurion might think that he could take advantage of the United States because of the election and because so many politicians in the past had courted the Jewish vote. But Eisenhower emphasized to Hazlett that he had given strict orders to the State Department that they should inform Israel that the election did not influence U.S. foreign policy. He stated that the welfare of the United States was the sole criterion of the nation's foreign policy.[59]

But it would be naive to suggest that Eisenhower ignored the politics of the crisis. The mounting, if sometimes uneven and unclear, evidence of British, French, and Israeli intransigence brought the crisis to its military phase and spawned severe political complications. The week beginning Monday, October 29, the final week of the election, was the worst of Eisenhower's political life. Dulles, a former senator from New York, it must be recalled, was an intensely political person deeply involved in Republican Party affairs. He was the political orator of the Eisenhower-Dulles team, touching responsive chords with party conservatives and the general public. He was central to the formulation of the party planks on foreign policy in 1956, in touch with the campaign and with Republican candidates. He helped coordinate matters with Vice President Nixon.

Dulles was involved as a matter of routine, as was Hagerty, with decisions affecting both the handling of the Suez affair and the election. If, for example, Eisenhower was to attend the London Conference in late August, he would have to be back to address the Republican National Convention in San Francisco on its final evening, August 24. When Max Rabb, Cabinet secretary, wanted to go to Israel in August, ostensibly to dedicate the "Eisenhower Forest" but mainly "for political effect," Dulles was involved.[60] His advisers at the State Department strongly urged Dulles to disapprove the Rabb visit.

Emmet Hughes, no fan of Dulles, pictured him as harassed, irritated, improvising so as to stave off military solutions, and ultimately bitter that aggression against Egypt had deflected attention from Soviet behavior in Hungary. All that may be true, but no one in Eisenhower's entourage doubted that Dulles understood fully the domestic political implications of the Suez affair and the need to legitimate policy.[61] And in that, as in all important things, he was in tune with the president.

NOTES

All dates are in the year 1956 unless otherwise indicated. The location of materials is as follows: (1) Eisenhower papers are in the Dwight D. Eisenhower Library (DDEL); (2) Dulles papers, Dulles files are part of the Eisenhower collection in the DDEL; (3) Dulles papers are in Princeton University Library; (4) Krock papers are in Princeton University Library; and (5) Prime Ministers' files (PREM) are in the Public Records Office, London.

1. John D. Steinbruner, *The Cybernetic Theory of Decision* (Princeton, N.J.: Princeton University Press, 1974), 342.

2. Kenneth Thompson, ed., *Three Press Secretaries on the Presidency and the Press* (Lanham, Md.: University Press of America, 1983), 36.

3. Anna Kasten Nelson, "John Foster Dulles and the Bipartisan Congress," *Political Science Quarterly* 102, no. 1 (Spring 1987): 48–49; Dulles to Mansfield, April 2, Dulles papers, Dulles files, general correspondence and memoranda series, box 1, Dwight D. Eisenhower Library (hereafter DDEL), Abilene, Kan.

4. Minutes of cabinet meetings, July 27 and August 3, Eisenhower papers, Ann Whitman files, 1953–1961, cabinet series, boxes 6 and 7, DDEL. For a different view see Sherman Adams, *Firsthand Report: The Story of the Eisenhower Administration* (New York: Harper and Brothers, 1961), 4–11. Dulles briefed the cabinet on Middle Eastern questions six times in 1956, assisted by Herbert Hoover, Jr., George Humphrey, Herman Phleger, and Arthur Flemming.

5. Minutes of the nine NSC meetings, August 9 (292nd meeting), August 30 (295th meeting), September 6 (296th meeting), September 20 (297th meeting), September 27 (298th meeting), October 4 (299th meeting), October 12 (300th meeting), October 26 (301st meeting), and November 1 (302nd meeting), Eisenhower papers, Ann Whitman file, NSC series, box 8 and box 2 (records of actions by NSC, 1956, 2), DDEL; and Office of Special Assistant, National Security Adviser (OSANSA), NSC series, administrative subseries, box 2 (NSC agenda and minutes, 1956, 2, 4), *ibid.* On August 9, Dulles briefed the meeting, and Humphrey and Flemming were prominent in the discussions. Flemming was especially prominent on the oil question. Nixon introduced political considerations. Eisenhower called for a joint State and Defense Department study of contingencies, policy options, possible outcomes and implications, and coordination with the Office of Defense Mobilization. On August 30 Dulles, Admiral Radford, and Flemming briefed the meeting. Eisenhower emphasized the extreme gravity of the situation; they must prevent the spread of any war that broke out. It might be necessary, therefore, to consult Congress. On September 6, 20, 27, and October 4, General C. P. Cabell, acting director of the CIA, briefed the meeting. On October 12, Hoover and Cabell briefed the meeting, the former using mainly a report from Dulles who was at the United Nations. The French were the main obstacle to an agreement. Eisenhower stated

that he and Dulles agreed that "if the United States could just keep the lid on a little longer, some kind of compromise plan could be worked out." The issue was whether or not they had enough time. On October 26, Allen Dulles and Flemming briefed the meeting. The crisis in Jordan was of major concern, though it was confirmed that King Hussein had not been assassinated. Eisenhower expected "a donnybrook in this area." On November 1, John Dulles, Allen Dulles, and Radford briefed the meeting. Eisenhower instructed Dulles to draft action papers for his subsequent consideration. Eisenhower had forced attention on the Middle East, not Hungary, and raised the political significance of the crisis along with Harold Stassen. The discussions on August 9 and 30, October 12, and especially November 1 were the most significant. Of the nine meetings, three (September 20, 27, and October 4) were not centrally concerned with the Suez crisis. Eisenhower chaired all nine meetings. Dulles attended seven meetings, and Hoover represented the State Department in his absence. Charles Wilson, the Secretary of Defense, attended four meetings, and Reuben Robertson, the Deputy or Acting Secretary, represented the Defense Department in his absence. Flemming attended all nine meetings. Allen Dulles attended only two meetings, with Cabell generally representing the CIA. Sherman Adams was present at six meetings; W. B. Persons at five meetings; Theodore C. Streibert, director of the U.S. Information Agency, was at eight meetings; and Dillon Anderson at only two meetings. Anderson spent much of the fall speech writing and speaking in the election campaign.

6. Minutes of meeting, August 6, Eisenhower papers, OSANSA, special assistant series, subject subseries, box 9, DDEL.

7. Minutes of meeting, July 31, *ibid.*

8. Record of conversation between Eisenhower and Arthur Krock, Krock papers, box 1, Princeton University Library. Those who worked closely with Eisenhower and Dulles never doubted that their relationship was the one described here. James Hagerty, Andrew Goodpaster, Richard Nixon, Henry Cabot Lodge, Livingston Merchant, Robert Bowie, and Dillon Anderson agree on this in their oral history contributions as the Dulles and Eisenhower papers demonstrate. Emmet Hughes, Eisenhower's speech writer, saw their relationship as remarkably anomalous because of their very different personalities, methods, world outlooks, and reasoning processes. But Hughes's assessment does not seriously challenge the points made here about the policy-shaping and decision-making processes. Emmet John Hughes, *The Ordeal of Power: A Political Memoir of the Eisenhower Years* (New York: Atheneum, 1963), 206–8. See also Eisenhower to Dulles, January 10, Eisenhower papers, Ann Whitman file, diaries, January 1956, Dulles files; Dulles to Eisenhower, October 14, Dulles papers, chronological series, box 14, October 1956 (2), *ibid.*, Eisenhower to Dulles, August 19 and 20, *ibid.*, box 17, August 1956, misc. file 2; and Dwight D. Eisenhower, oral history, Dulles papers, Princeton Unversity Library. Yet scholarly analysis was often and for a long time very wide of the mark, and it was also excessively critical of both men. Richard H. Immerman's "Eisenhower and Dulles: Who Made the Decisions?" *Political Psychology* 1, no. 2 (Autumn 1979): 21–38, was the initial revisionist interpretation, taking us back to contemporary views.

9. Interview with Robert Bowie; and Fred I. Greenstein, *The Hidden-Hand Presidency: Eisenhower as Leader* (New York: Basic Books, 1982), 25–52.

10. Record of conversation between Eisenhower and Sulzberger, September 25, Eisenhower papers, Ann Whitman file, diaries, box 19, September 1956, phone calls, DDEL.

11. Kenneth Thompson, ed., *Ten Presidents and the Press* (Lanham, Md.: University

Press of America, 1982), 50–55 (comments by Ray Scherer); Andrew Goodpaster, oral history, Eisenhower papers; Hughes, *Ordeal of Power*, 64–66, 131–32.

12. Record of telephone conversation between Eisenhower and Dulles, December 31, Eisenhower papers, Ann Whitman files, diaries, box 20, file December 1956 phone calls, DDEL.

13. James Hagerty, oral history, Eisenhower papers, DDEL; and Donald Neff, *Warriors at Suez: Eisenhower Takes America into the Middle East* (New York: Linden Press/Simon and Schuster, 1981), 327; Eisenhower to Hoover, October 8, and record of telephone conversation between Eisenhower and Hoover, October 8, Eisenhower papers, box 14, misc. file 1, DDEL.

14. Memorandum of conversation between Eisenhower, Radford, and Dickson, April 3, Eisenhower papers, Ann Whitman file, diaries, box 15, April 1956, DDEL. See also Eisenhower to Churchill, March 29, *ibid*.

15. Hagerty, oral history, Eisenhower papers, *ibid.*; Bowie, oral history, Dulles papers, *ibid*.

16. Bowie, oral history, Dulles papers, *ibid*.

17. Richard Nixon, oral history, Dulles papers, *ibid*.

18. Dulles memorandum of conversation with Reston, December 26, Dulles papers, general correspondence and memoranda series, box 1, memos of conversations general, Q–S, *ibid*.

19. Record of conversation between Dulles and Spivack, April 13, Dulles papers, Eisenhower library, Dulles files, general correspondence and memoranda series, box 1, DDEL; and record of conversation between Dulles and Rountree (State Department), May 22, Dulles papers, telephone calls series, box 5, memoranda of telephone conversations, general, May 1–June 29, 1956 (3), *ibid*.

20. Hagerty, oral history, DDEL; and Anderson, oral history, Eisenhower papers; *ibid*. Anderson described Nixon's handling of the NSC during Eisenhower's illness as superb, done with consummate grace and taste, and without any trace of political ambition or fear.

21. Nelson "Dulles and the Bipartisan Congress," 43–64. Dulles had held 160 bipartisan meetings with congressional groups by May 1957. See also telephone conversation between Dulles and Senator George, March 30, Dulles papers, telephone calls series, box 4, memoranda of telephone conversations, general, January–March 1956, DDEL.

22. Minutes of NSC meeting, August 9, Eisenhower papers, Ann Whitman file, NSC series, box B, DDEL; meeting with bipartisan group of congressional leaders, August 12, Eisenhower papers, Ann Whitman file, legislative meetings series, box 2, legislative leaders meetings, 1956–1957, *ibid.*; Adams, *Firsthand Report*, 250–53.

23. Minutes of Cabinet meeting, August 3, Eisenhower papers, Ann Whitman files, 1953–1961, Cabinet series, box 7, DDEL; record of telephone conversations between Dulles and Eisenhower, September 25 and December 3, Eisenhower papers, Ann Whitman file, box 19, file September 1956, phone calls, and Dulles papers, Dulles files, White House memoranda series, box 4, file 2, DDEL. This preference for the Conservatives was clear despite the knowledge that Eden, Macmillan, and Lord Salisbury preferred to use force as soon as was politically feasible and that an approach to the United Nations by Britain was to be a preface to rather than removing the need for the use of force. Dillon to Dulles, September 19, Dulles papers, subject series, box 7, Suez problem, July–November 1956 (6), *ibid.*; Dulles to Eisenhower, August 19, Eisenhower papers,

Ann Whitman file, Dulles-Herter series, box 5, Dulles, August 1956 (2), *ibid.*; memorandum of conversation between Eden and Dulles, September 21, Dulles papers, subject series, box 11, misc. papers, U.K. (1), *ibid.*

24. Memorandum of conversation, September 6, Dulles papers, subject series, box 7, Suez problem, November 1956, *ibid.* Dulles; Senators Hubert Humphrey, Mansfield, and William Langer; and Representatives James Richards and A.S.J. Carnahan were present. See also record of conversation between Eisenhower and Dulles, October 14, Dulles papers, Dulles file, chronological series, box 14, *ibid.*

25. Record of conversations between Dulles and Knowland, September 8 and 22 and October 30, Dulles papers, Dulles file, telephone conversations, box 5, file 3, and general correspondence and memoranda series, box 1, *ibid.*

26. Record of conversations between Dulles and Johnson, October 4 and November 13, Dulles papers, Dulles file, telephone conversations 1956, box 5, file 4, *ibid.*

27. Memorandum of conversation between Dulles and George, October 30, Dulles papers, subject series, box 10, Israeli relations 1951–57, file 2, *ibid.*

28. Hanes to Dulles, October 31, Dulles papers, Dulles files, general correspondence and memoranda series, box 5, *ibid.*

29. Record of conversation between Eisenhower and Knowland, October 31, Eisenhower papers, Ann Whitman file, box 18, October 1956, phone calls file, *ibid.*

30. Krock memorandum, Arthur Krock papers, box 1, black notebook 1, *ibid.*, and Macmillan to Eden, September 26, prime minister's papers (PREM) 11/1102, Public Record Office, London; and record of conversation between Dulles and Eisenhower, September 22, Dulles papers, Dulles file, box 4, file 5, DDEL.

31. Notes of conversation between Dulles and Knowland, September 8, Dulles papers, Dulles file, general correspondence and memoranda series, box 4, *ibid.*

32. Record of conversation between Eisenhower and Dulles, April 10, Eisenhower papers, Ann Whitman file, Eisenhower diaries, April 1956, *ibid.*; Aldrich, oral history, Dulles papers, *ibid.* Aldrich applauded Finer's assessment of Dulles.

33. Adams, *Firsthand Report*, 253–54; Menzies to Eden, September 9, and Makins to Lloyd, September 15, PREM 11/1101, DDEL; and Lloyd to Eden, October 14, PREM 11/1102, *ibid.* Eisenhower was somewhat philosophical about the attacks. He had made his views clear to Eden in his letters of September 2 and 8. Now Pineau was upset. He regretted Nasser's rejection of the Eighteen Power proposals and denied that he was responsible. Dulles speculated about the influence of U.S. press reports that they had never expected the Menzies mission to succeed and that they had an amended plan "up our sleeves." Dulles wondered whether Eisenhower's last press conference had been interpreted as signaling that the United States was turning to appeasement. Eisenhower responded that he could not recall what he had said, exactly, but felt it had been clear. Record of two telephone conversations between Eisenhower and Dulles, September 10, Eisenhower papers, Ann Whitman files, diaries, box 18, file September 1956 phone calls, *ibid.*

34. Eden to Lloyd, October 6, Lloyd to Eden, October 8, and Eden to Lloyd, October 8, PREM 11/1102, DDEL; the brothers Alsop, George Humphrey, and Herbert Hoover, Jr., oral histories, Dulles papers, *ibid.*

35. Record of telephone conversation between Dulles and Lodge, October 19, Dulles papers, Dulles files, file 4, telephone conversations, box 5, *ibid.*

36. Joseph Alsop, oral history, Dulles papers, *ibid.* See also record of conversation between Dulles and Macmillan, December 12, Dulles papers, general correspondence

and memoranda series, box 1, memoranda of conversations, general L-M (2), and record of conversation between Dulles and Caccia, December 24, general A-D (3), *ibid.* For a different view of the Dulles-Caccia relationship, see Arthur Heeney, oral history, Dulles papers, *ibid.*

37. Eisenhower to Hazlett, November 12, Eisenhower papers, Ann Whitman file, diaries, box 20, miscellaneous file November 1956, *ibid.*

38. Hagerty and Goodpaster, oral histories, Eisenhower papers, *ibid.*, and record of conversation between Dulles and Lodge, October 30, Dulles papers, Dulles file, box 5, file 3, *ibid.*

39. Record of conversation between Eisenhower and Hoover, November 2, Eisenhower papers, Ann Whitman file, diaries, box 19, November 1956, phone calls file, *ibid.*, Eisenhower to L. W. Douglas, November 3, Eisenhower papers, Ann Whitman file, diaries, box 20, November 1956, misc. (4), *ibid.*

40. Record of conversations among Eisenhower, Goodpaster, and Hoover, March 5 and 6, Eisenhower papers, diaries, box 13, Goodpaster file, *ibid.*, Abba Eban, oral history, Dulles papers, *ibid.* Eban denounced this aspect of Dulles's policy as devious, in error, and in part responsible for Israel's attack on Egypt in October 1956. Eban's reasoning is demonstrably flawed. Edward Tivnan's *The Lobby: Jewish Political Power and American Foreign Policy* (New York: Simon and Schuster, 1987), is inadequately researched. Celler presented the views of the New York State Democratic Congressional Delegation to Dulles, insisting on a meeting with him and refusing to meet with mere subordinates such as Robert Murphy. Celler to Dulles, March 15, Dulles papers, correspondence files, 1953–1957, DDEL. See also Michael Fry, ''Canada, the United Nations and the North Atlantic Triangle,'' in William Roger Louis and Roger Owen, *Suez 1956: The Crisis and Its Consequences* (New York: Oxford University Press, 1989), 285–316.

41. Record of conversation among Dulles, George, and MacArthur, March 30, Dulles papers, subject series, box 10, Israel relations, 1951–1957, DDEL.

42. Eisenhower to Ben-Gurion, February 27 and April 9 and 30, Eisenhower papers, 1956–1957, diaries, box 13, February 1956, file 1, *ibid.*; and Ann Whitman file, international file and meetings, box 29, files 2, 5, and 6, *ibid.*; Hoover to Eisenhower, February 20, Ann Whitman file, international file and meetings, file 6, *ibid.*; record of conversation between Hoover and Eisenhower, April 23, Eisenhower papers, diaries, box 15, phone calls, file April 1956, *ibid.*, Dulles to Eisenhower, April 23 and 28, Ann Whitman file, international series, Israel (4), *ibid.* Ben-Gurion wrote to Eisenhower on March 16, requesting arms. Dulles met with Eban on March 28 and April 11.

43. Silver to Eisenhower, April 9, and Eisenhower to Silver, April 12, 1956, Eisenhower papers, Ann Whitman file, international file and meetings, box 29, file 5, *ibid.*, and Goodpaster to Eisenhower, n.d. (April 1956), *ibid.*

44. Record of meeting of Dulles, Eisenhower, and Silver, April 26, Dulles papers, Dulles files, general correspondence and speeches, box 1, memoranda of conversations, general Q-S (1), DDEL. Eisenhower was most reluctant to meet with Silver, knowing that he would make excessive demands that could not be met.

45. Silver to Dulles, April 27, Dulles papers, box 104, Israel file, *ibid.*; and Eisenhower to Ben-Gurion, April 30, Eisenhower papers, Ann Whitman file, international file and meetings, box 29, file 2, *ibid.*

46. Record of conversation between Dulles and Spellman, June 18, Dulles papers, Dulles files, general correspondence and memoranda series, box 1, *ibid.*

47. Dulles to Eisenhower, June 22, Dulles papers, chronological series, box 13, file 1, *ibid.*; and Goodpaster, oral history, Dulles papers, *ibid.*

48. Javits to Dulles, February 21, Dulles papers, box 104, Javits file, *ibid.*; Dulles to Eisenhower, May 22, Dulles papers, Dulles file, White House memoranda series, box 3, general correspondence 1956, *ibid.*; and Jacob K. Javits, *Javits: The Autobiography of a Public Man* (Boston: Houghton-Mifflin, 1981), 43, 191, 217–46, 251.

49. Record of conversation between Dulles and Javits, May 23, Dulles papers, Dulles files, general correspondence and memoranda series, box 1, DDEL.

50. Dean to Dulles, June 7, Dulles papers, Dulles files, subject series, box 10, Israeli Relations, 1951–1957 (1), *ibid.*

51. Dean to Dulles, July 11, *ibid.*

52. Record of conversation between Dulles and Eisenhower, July 16, Dulles papers, Dulles files, White House memoranda series, box 4, file 1, DDEL.

53. Dulles to Reid, September 17, and Reid to Dulles, September 25, *ibid.*, correspondence file 1953–1957. Dulles reported the steps taken to implement the Senate resolution, pointed to the principle of noninterference in the internal affairs of other states, and suggested that the settlement of the Arab-Israeli conflict would resolve such problems.

54. Hagerty, oral history, Eisenhower papers, DDEL.

55. Emmet Hughes, oral history, Dulles papers, *ibid.*; Hughes, *Ordeal of Power*, 190–91, 197; Macmillan to Eden, September 26, prime minister's files, PREM 11/1102, DDEL; Eisenhower to Eden, October 12, *ibid.*

56. Emmet Hughes, oral history, Dulles papers, DDEL; Hughes, *Ordeal of Power*, 177–78; record of conversation between Eisenhower and Dulles, September 7, Eisenhower papers, Ann Whitman file, diaries, box 18, September 1956, phone calls file, DDEL.

57. Jacob Javits, oral history, Dulles papers, DDEL.

58. Eugene Black and Goodpaster, oral histories, Dulles papers, *ibid.*

59. Eisenhower to Hazlett, November 1 or 2, Eisenhower papers, Ann Whitman file, diaries, box 20, November 1956, miscellaneous file, *ibid.*

60. Hanes memorandum, July 31, Dulles papers, Dulles files, special assistants chronological series, box 10, *ibid.*; record of telephone conversations between Dulles and Eisenhower, August 6 and 8, Eisenhower papers, Ann Whitman file, diaries, box 16, August 1956, phone calls file, *ibid.*

61. Hughes, *Ordeal of Power*, 219.

10

PRESIDENTIAL PERSONALITY AND IMPROVISATIONAL DECISION MAKING: EISENHOWER AND THE 1956 HUNGARIAN CRISIS

Kenneth Kitts and Betty Glad

Our goal in this chapter is to delineate the American response to one of the key events in the early phases of the cold war. In response to the Soviet intervention in Hungary in 1956, the United States backed off from the rollback rhetoric that the Republican Party had embraced in the early fifties. When confronted with the realities of actually trying to dislodge the Soviet Union from areas on its borders where it had previously established political and military dominance, the United States did not undertake risky policies but adjusted to the very real limits on American power. American policy making during the crisis was marked by a remarkable degree of ad hoc personal interaction and informality. The president's political objectives, his skills, and his personality determined to a great extent the arena in which decisions would be made and who the key players would be. In short, there is considerable evidence here to support Fred Greenstein's theory of Eisenhower's deft "'hidden-hand'' leadership ability.[1]

Domestic factors and historical accidents also came to affect American policy. The way in which decisions were made not only helped determine the policy outcome the president wanted but also served a domestic political purpose. The sharing in public of some of the responsibility for the management and explanation of policy made it more difficult for critics of the policy to target the president and undermine his political authority.

PHASES OF THE CRISIS

In analyzing the American response to the situation in Hungary, it is useful to differentiate the three phases of the crisis as it confronted administration policy makers. The first phase, October 23 through October 31, covers the initial uprising in Budapest to Imre Nagy's proclamation of intent to break with the Warsaw Pact. The United States during this period did not have clear information on Soviet intentions or Nagy's political orientation, and consequently made no overt policy responses. The second phase, from Nagy's announcement that Hungary would withdraw from the Warsaw Pact to the full-scale Soviet invasion on November 4, was the crucial period in which the administration decided that it could not take military action. Finally, the third and final phase deals with the American effort to control the damage and salvage some benefit from the whole affair.

The First Phase

On October 23 over 200,000 demonstrators marched in Budapest to call for the election of Imre Nagy as premier. That call was soon transformed into an increasingly radical protest against Soviet control. Responding to these events, the Soviets acceded to the installation of Imre Nagy as premier on October 24 in an effort to satiate the demonstrators' demands. Sporadic violence and demonstrations continued, however, throughout the following week. Unofficial reports soon had the casualty figure in Budapest alone at 5,000 and climbing. Finally, on November 1 Nagy announced that Hungary would withdraw from the Warsaw Pact. That event brought an entirely new set of concerns into the picture and is thus used as the line of demarcation between the first and second phases of the crisis.

Confronted with these unprecedented challenges, the Soviet leadership wavered. After initially resisting the rebellion, the Soviets began withdrawing from the capital on October 28. Budapest Radio proclaimed victory for the rebels. On October 30, the Kremlin issued a statement of nonintervention and hinted that Soviet advisers might be withdrawn from Rumania, Poland, and Hungary.[2] According to one highly placed Hungarian official, that assurance was the primary catalyst behind Nagy's decision to withdraw Hungary from the Warsaw Pact.[3]

The United States at the time of the crisis was entering into the final two weeks of its presidential campaign. Though the situation in the Soviet satellite nations naturally became a campaign issue, there was no significant divergence of opinion on the fundamentals of U.S. policy. On the Democratic ticket neither Adlai Stevenson nor Estes Kefauver suggested the use of American military force in Hungary but were content to grumble that an administration so "caught off guard" by the uprising could hardly claim credit for creating the dissent in the Soviet bloc. The Republicans countered by emphasizing the need to retain a proven leader. At an October 29 speech in California, Vice President Nixon launched a particularly sharp attack, criticizing Stevenson as being a "confused, weak, and vacillating man."[4]

During this period the national security apparatus played a decidedly minor role in the decision-making process. Neither Secretary of Defense Wilson nor chairman of the Joint Chiefs of Staff Radford figured prominently in either the formal or informal decision-making process. Moreover, at the National Security Council meeting on October 26, Eisenhower bought time and limited debate by simply ordering that a comprehensive position paper (NSC 5616) be prepared by the council's planning board. There was a briefing on developments in eastern Europe by Allen Dulles. But when Harold Stassen suggested that a special meeting of the NSC be called to deal with the problem, the president said this would not be the best "initial step" to take. The president warned the defense agencies to be "unusually watchful and alert."[5]

At the NSC meeting on November 1 (the day Imre Nagy announced the withdrawal of Hungary from the Warsaw Pact) the president explicitly took the Hungarian issue off the agenda. According to the minutes of that meeting, "the President informed the members of the council that, except in so far as it was the subject of the DCI's [Director of Central Intelligence] intelligence briefing, he did not wish the council to take up the situation in the Soviet satellites."[6] Action on NSC 5616—"U.S. Policy Toward Poland and Hungary"—was deferred until the NSC meeting on November 15. By that time the Red Army had substantially crushed the Hungarian rebellion.

The reason for this evasion of the National Security Council, one can surmise, may have been to limit access to discussion about possible covert operations. The possibility that the United States was engaged in some operations along these lines is discussed later. Our focus here, however, is on Eisenhower's strategy of limiting the decision-making arena to better contain pressures within his administration for more overt military operations in Hungary. We know from other studies that Eisenhower did not see his Secretary of Defense as a strategist and that he often made up his own mind on strategic matters apart from the recommendations of the Joint Chiefs of Staff.[7] Certainly his final policy choices were more politically restrained than those proposed by the Joint Chiefs of Staff or the CIA's directorate of plans. The Joint Chiefs, for example, criticized the conciliatory tone of NSC 5616. They argued that the administration should keep its options open and not give the Soviets any assurances that might operate to the military disadvantage of the United States.[8]

The president made the crucial decisions during this phase of the crisis without significant formal consultation with key administration insiders. Though John Foster Dulles, Allen Dulles, and staff aide Colonel Andrew Goodpaster all met with Eisenhower frequently, none of these men seemed to harbor serious reservations about his final decisions. John Foster Dulles carried a heavy burden in implementing the policy. When Vice President Nixon issued an October 25 policy statement on the Hungarian issue, it was Dulles he turned to for advice.[9]

The overt American policy response during this first phase of the crisis was limited in scope and cautious in nature.[10] Despite strong rhetorical denunciations of the Soviet action, no concrete action was taken in the U.N. Security Council. Some initial discussions were held regarding the possibility of circulating letters among the council's members to mobilize support for a critique of the Soviet suppression. On October 28, just before their attack on Egypt over Nasser's seizure of the Suez Canal, the British and French had helped the United States place the Hungarian matter on the agenda of the U.N. Security Council. But their suggestion on November 3 that the United States join them in condemning Soviet actions in Hungary was brushed aside by the president as an "absurdity," given their own violations of the U.N. charter in the Middle East.[11]

Neither did the United States respond to the lobbying of the Hungarian National Council. This group of emigrés wanted the issue to be taken to the General Assembly where it would be immune to the Soviet veto.[12] U.N. Ambassador Henry Cabot Lodge would later argue that technical difficulties prevented this move to the General Assembly.[13] But it was also clear that the blockage in the Security Council effectively enabled the United States to dodge the sensitive issue of a possibly more interventionist stance at this time.

There was not even any attempt to contact the new Hungarian government, as later reported by Nagy's Deputy Foreign Minister.[14] Indeed, Peter Lyon suggests that American diplomatic personnel at the United Nations were active in opposing the Nagy government within that organization. Nagy's would-be representatives to the U.N., the American representatives apparently suggested, had appalling communist records.[15] Radio Free Europe (RFE) echoed the administration's distrust of the Nagy regime. On October 29, the military expert of Radio Free Europe compared the cease-fire order of the Nagy government to a "Trojan-horse episode." They "need a cease-fire so that the present Government in power in Budapest can maintain its position as long as possible." On October 31, another RFE broadcast beamed into Hungary went as follows: "Freedom Fighters. Do not hang your weapons on the wall. . . . Not a lump of coal, not a drop of gasoline for the Budapest government, until [the ministries of] Interior and Defense are in your control."[16] It was not until Nagy's declaration of independence from the Warsaw Pact on November 1 that a perceptible shift in the American attitude was evident.

Whatever the administration might have been doing behind the scenes, the president's public condemnations of the Soviet actions were relatively mild. He rejected especially threatening phrases. In a speech to the United Brotherhood of Carpenters and Joiners on October 23, he noted that: "the day of liberation . . . may be postponed where armed forces for a time make protest suicidal."[17] In his speech to the nation on October 31, the president toned down some of the stronger phrases Dulles had suggested to him in a working draft, including a statement about the "irresistible force of liberation in Eastern Europe."[18] His allusions to the "wounds inflicted by the guns of Imperialist Communism" did not come until November 8, by which time the outcome of the rebellion was apparent.[19]

Indeed the president was the one who seemed to emphasize most the importance of assuring the Soviet Union of the limited goals of the United States in eastern Europe.[20] Thus at Eisenhower's behest, Dulles noted in his speech in Dallas on October 27 that the United States did not look at the new government in Budapest as a potential military ally; nor would it be required to renounce communism.[21] The president himself, when meeting with the new U.S. ambassador, Tom Wailes, on October 30, told the ambassador that the U.S. objective in eastern Europe was simply a neutral tier of states there.[22] In his nationwide address on October 31, he stressed the lack of any U.S. "ulterior purpose" in supporting the rebellion and affirmed again that the United States did not look upon these new governments in eastern Europe as potential military allies.[23]

Aside from Eisenhower's desire not to provoke the Soviet Union into a war, there were other reasons for his relatively mild response. Partly, the administration could not take strong action because it simply did not know what was going on. The CIA gave the administration no advance warning of the rebellion and had no clear information to present on what was happening in the earliest phases of the rebellion.[24] At the time of the revolt the State Department was in the midst of shuffling ambassadors as the administration's first term drew to a close. The new ambassador, Tom Wailes, did not reach Budapest until November 12, thus leaving the American delegation leaderless during the most critical days of the crisis.[25] The result, as veteran diplomat Robert Murphy later recalled candidly, was that "the State Department did not know what was going on behind the scenes."[26] Eisenhower himself later noted the frustration of having to rely on news ticker reports for information.[27]

American intelligence regarding Soviet intentions was no better. An unusually heavy burden was placed on U.S. Ambassador Charles Bohlen to provide some insight on Soviet motives. By his own admission, however, the ambassador was forced to rely on hearsay and innuendo gleaned over cocktail party conversation.[28]

With such ambiguity, it is not surprising to find that prior predispositions influenced the administration's perception of events. The distrust of Nagy stemmed from his past association with the Hungarian Communist Party and the fact that the Soviets had themselves agreed to his appointment as premier.[29] As late as October 29 Secretary Dulles was still speaking of the "bad people" in the Nagy government.[30] Ambassador Bohlen's cable to Washington that same day revealed a similar sentiment: "it would appear Nagy's statement on the . . . Soviet troop withdrawal from Budapest was nothing more than a trick, with Soviet connivance, to cause the insurgents to cease fire."[31] According to Lyon, several administration officials saw Nagy's differences with the Soviets as a "falling out among thieves."[32]

Wishful thinking also seems to have led several administration officials to make mistakes in assessing Soviet intentions. The widespread support within Hungary for the rebels, the partial Soviet withdrawal, and the October 30 Kremlin statements suggesting policies of nonintervention led some policy makers to jump to premature conclusions. Ambassador Bohlen reported on October 27, for example, that "the Soviet Union will not use overt force against a Commie regime no matter whether the policies it is pursuing are contrary to Soviet wishes."[33]

The Soviet silence following Nagy's proclamation left him wondering if the

Kremlin might have "decided . . . to cut its losses and accept a high degree of independence for the satellites."[34] Vice President Nixon noted on October 29 that the uprising in Poland and Hungary had proved how correct the administration's "liberation position" was.[35] In the National Security Council meeting on November 1, Allen Dulles spoke of the "miracle" taking place in Hungary and argued that the Kremlin pledge of nonintervention was "one of the most significant [statements] to come out of the Soviet Union since the end of WW II." These events, he continued, "have disproved that a popular revolt can't occur in the face of modern weapons." Even the normally reserved John Foster Dulles was not immune to the contagious optimism. In a phone conversation with the president on October 30, he opined that "the whole Soviet fabric is collapsing."[36]

The administration's failure to act at this time, in short, would be best interpreted as a decision to ride out the affair, hoping that a government even more desirable from the U.S. perspective than the suspect Nagy regime would come to power. That there was some thinking along these lines is evident in Allen Dulles's review of events in eastern Europe on November 1. According to Eisenhower, he called the situation as follows: "The problem in Hungary . . . was the lack of a strong guiding authority for the rebels; Imre Nagy was failing and the rebels were demanding that he resign. Cardinal Mindzenty, if supported by the Roman Catholic ardor of the Hungarian people, was a possible leader; newspapers that morning were reporting his release from house arrest and his return to Budapest."[37]

The Second Phase

The second phase of the crisis runs from November 1 through to the Soviet intervention on November 4 and 5. With Nagy's announcement on November 1 that Hungary would withdraw from the Warsaw Pact, much of the uncertainty and speculation surrounding his government was eliminated. This act, however, represented a clear threat to the balance of power in Europe. The Soviet Union initially suggested that it would absorb this loss. The silence that greeted Nagy's proclamation left many American policy makers wondering with Ambassador Bohlen if the Kremlin had decided to cut its losses. But then on November 3, Khrushchev warned Bohlen at a diplomatic reception in Moscow that "the Soviet Union was going to be just as strong as it needed to be." The ambassador immediately cabled Washington that an invasion was now imminent.[38] The next day, November 4, over 200,000 troops and nearly 6,000 tanks swept into Hungary from the Ukraine and Romania to quell the rebellion. Within two hours, the Soviets were in control of Budapest, and Janos Kadar was named the new premier of an all-Communist government.

At the same time that this crisis was coming to a head, events in the Middle East seemed to be spinning out of control. On October 28 Israel seized the Suez Canal, and two days later Great Britain and France, without any advance notice to the United States, joined Israel in the attack on Egypt. On November 5 the Kremlin called for joint U.S./USSR military action to resolve the conflict. Fearful of what he saw as a Soviet attempt to extend Soviet influence in the region, Eisenhower pressed America's allies to accept a cease fire. This was accomplished on November 6, although the withdrawal of foreign forces from the Suez would not occur until December.

These events in the Middle East not only increased the workload of Eisenhower and the whole national security establishment; they greatly hindered the ability of the west to construct a unified response to the Hungarian crisis. Eisenhower had long been committed to collective action in the face of security threats. With the split among the NATO members and the U.S. sponsorship of a vote in the Security Council condemning the actions of the allies, the possibility of constructing a unified western response to the Hungarian crisis was severely limited. As the president later observed: "armed assistance could not have succeeded without the full cooperation of all NATO countries and you know as well as I do that . . . would not have been possible."[39]

Domestically the president at this time faced a certain restiveness within the right wing of the Republican Party. Senator William Knowland informed Secretary Dulles on November 2 that the Senate Internal Security Committee was interested in "something over and beyond the statements (of support)." Dulles responded by declaring that the administration was "doing a lot but perhaps not dramatizing it enough."[40] Moreover, the Democratic presidential candidate, Adlai Stevenson, now linked the two crises together, charging that Eisenhower's neglect of the western Alliance—as signified by the Suez imbroglio—had crippled the American ability to act in Hungary. Yet Eisenhower was not forced by these critiques to take a weaker stand *vis à vis* Israel in the Middle East or a tougher one regarding Hungary in eastern Europe. Catholic and Jewish voters who might have been influenced by these critics of administration foreign policy were predominantly Democratic and thus not crucial to the Republican coalition.[41] On November 5, the president won a second term by capturing 57.4 percent of the popular vote—a slight increase over his 1952 total—though he lost control of the Congress. The electorate seemed to be moved by the Republican promise that experienced leadership would be more likely to keep the peace. Indeed the Gallup poll revealed an extraordinary amount of public faith in Eisenhower's ability to deal with the Soviets during the crisis.[42]

In this middle phase of the crisis, decision making remained informal and ad hoc. There were no meetings of the NSC from November 2 through November 6. Moreover, there were only a limited number of sessions with military leaders in the Oval Office. The sole meeting with both Secretary of Defense Wilson and chairman of the Joint Chiefs of Staff Radford occurred on November 3 and lasted for less than half an hour. In fact, that meeting was Secretary Wilson's only significant appearance during the entire crisis. Meetings with his special assistant for national security affairs, William Jackson, were held only infrequently and, again, lasted only for short periods of time.[43]

There was, however, a shift among the key civilian players. On November 2 (two days before the massive Soviet intervention in Budapest), Secretary of State John Foster Dulles was hospitalized in Washington for emergency surgery, a condition which would keep him away from his department for the remainder of the crisis. Under Secretary Herbert Hoover, Jr., temporarily filled in for the State Department, and Allen Dulles began to play a more central role. Similarly, U.N. Ambassador Lodge recalled that, in Dulles's absence, he began meeting with the president more frequently.[44] During the period of the secretary's hospitalization, however, Eisenhower maintained regular contact with John Foster Dulles, both by phone and by visit.[45]

Dulles's absence from the inner circle of decision making meant that Eisenhower was forced to carry an unusually heavy foreign-policy-making burden. The chronological convergence of two foreign policy crises and the strains of a reelection campaign only added to his problems. At the same time, his heart attack the previous fall made it necessary for him to pace his schedule and avoid unnecessary stress. The president maintained his tranquillity, as well as his health, by consciously seeking diversions to minimize the strain. Two hours before his nationwide address on October 31, for instance, he took time to practice golf on the White House lawn. On November 2, he set aside an hour in the middle of the day to swim and relax. When Ellis Slater visited the White House on November 3, he found the president watching a college football game on television. Later, the two men and their wives spent the evening playing bridge.[46] Emmet Hughes later observed that, even when presented with the confounding British-French attack on Suez, Eisenhower was "more calm than either the White House staff or State Department."[47] Slater echoed the sentiment marveling at the president's "equanimity during periods of stress."[48]

In contrast to the earlier period, the administration's political response to these events was swift and clear. At 3:13 A.M. on November 4, shortly after word of the Soviet attack reached New York, Ambassador Lodge brought a resolution before the Security Council calling for the withdrawal of all Soviet forces from Hungarian territory and an on-the-spot U.N. investigation of events in that country. When the measure was vetoed by the Soviet Union, it was moved to the General Assembly, where it passed that same day by a vote of fifty to nine with India, Indonesia, and certain representatives from other Asian and Arab nations abstaining.[49] That same day Eisenhower wrote Premier Nikolai Bulganin of his shock of the Soviet intervention after pretending to be yielding to Hungarian pressure, and he urged their withdrawal.[50]

Bulganin's suggestion on November 5, that the United States join with the Soviet Union to oppose British and French troops in the Middle East, was dismissed as "unthinkable" in a White House statement issued the same day. The most important step the Soviet Union could take to insure world peace, the United States noted, would be for it to "observe the United Nations resolution to cease its military repression of the Hungarian people and withdraw its troops."[51]

The alternatives open to the administration, at least up to the massive Soviet intervention beginning on November 4, included the possibility of providing overt military assistance to the rebels. NSC 5616, the position paper ordered by Eisenhower at the October 26 National Security Council meeting, was being prepared at this time, and the president must have been informed of the alternatives it would eventually delineate. These included courses of action ranging from covert support of the rebels to overt support of them, such as open recognition of their status and even military support.[52]

Outside of Eisenhower's immediate circle of advisers, certain individuals pressed for military action to aid the rebels in eastern Europe.[53] In the CIA, director of plans Frank Wisner argued forcefully for the United States to support the rebellion through conventional arms as well as covert means. Deputy director of intelligence Robert Amory would go even further. He wrote a memorandum calling for a surgical nuclear strike of the railroads near the Soviet-Hungarian border to deny the Red Army easy access to Budapest. The U.S. advantage in strategic weaponry, he argued, would prevent the Soviets from expanding the conflict.[54] Yet the president was not inclined to provoke the Soviet Union at this time.

At a meeting in his office with his top advisers on Monday, November 5, Eisenhower expressed his concern that the Russians might overreact. The Soviets, he noted, are concerned about losing hold over their satellites and might start a world war. "Those boys are both furious and scared. Just as with Hitler, that makes for the most dangerous possible state of mind." The letter from Bulganin urging joint action by American and Soviet naval units in the Mediterranean against the Anglo-French-Israeli military operations in Egypt had arrived earlier that day, and he saw it as possibly the "opening gambit of an ultimatum." In those circumstances, he noted, "we have to be positive and clear in our every word, every step." But, he continued, "if those fellows start something, we may have to hit 'em—and, if necessary, with everything in the bucket."[55]

The president, however, realized that there was little he could do to prevent the Russians from reincorporating Hungary into their empire.[56] In this instance, as in many others concerning military strategy, he relied on his own judgment rather than calling on the Secretary of Defense or the Joint Chiefs of Staff to recommend a course of action. Discussing the situation with his brother and confidante Milton, he argued: "Look at a map. Hungary is inaccessible to any western force. Austria is a neutral country. . . . [T]he main fighting would have taken place on Austrian soil and most of the killing would have occurred there. A non-communist force could not have reached Hungary through Yugoslavia. . . . The difficulty would have been as great or greater in trying to get through Czechoslovakia."[57] The president even rejected proposals to give less visible military support to the rebels in Hungary, refusing the CIA permission to airdrop supplies to the anti-Soviet forces.[58]

In these decisions the president was supported by Secretary of State Dulles. Known for his advocacy of hard-line policies, Dulles was convinced that any military action in Hungary would inevitably result in a wider war.[59] Allen Dulles also went along, telling Wisner and Amory that electoral considerations alone proscribed the use of force.[60] (There is no indication that the director ever passed along Amory's memorandum to the president.) Both brothers also felt that the Allied invasion of Egypt had made a stronger military response impossible. Allen Dulles argued that the United States could ill afford to act against Soviet imperialism in Hungary while its allies were engaged in much the same activity in Egypt. John Foster Dulles also was reluctant to cooperate with British and French efforts to coordinate a unified western response to Hungary in the United Nations, deeming any such collaborative efforts a mockery.[61]

The Third Phase

Phase three presented different problems for the United States. The Soviets quashed the uprising in the city of Budapest in a few days, and by November 14, Nagy had taken refuge in the Yugoslav embassy in that city.[62] Yet many Hungarians continued to resist the Soviet crackdown. Several Budapest trade unions remained on strike throughout the early days of November, and after Hungarian police and Soviet troops prevented the National Council of Workers from meeting in the Budapest Sports Hall, a new general strike declaration was issued. On December 11, 5,000 women and young girls, supported by 10,000 other demonstrators, marched onto Hero's Square in Budapest to put flowers on the tomb of the Hungarian Unknown Soldier. They were fired upon by Russian soldiers. Meanwhile, electric and coal production in the nation plummeted and rebel groups roamed the countryside. Some freedom fighters were hung on lamp posts, evidently in retaliation for the severe measures taken by them against some members of the Hungarian security police in the earliest days of the rebellions. Many rebellious youths were put on trains bound for Siberia.

In the meantime, refugees poured out of Hungary into Austria. When Soviet forces countered by closing the borders and shooting those who tried to escape, the flight slowed down a bit. But by the end of the year approximately 155,000 refugees had fled Hungary, and an average of 800 per day were still crossing the border. Austria could not care for all these refugees, and it became clear that the United States and other western nations would have to help accommodate the outflow.

Around the world, the Soviet measures evoked protests. In France, the offices of the Communist Party and of the communist newspaper *L'Humanité* were sacked by anti-Soviet demonstrators. Similar protests occurred in other capitals around the world. In the United States, the Communist Party newspaper, *The Daily Worker*, criticized the Soviet use of force against Hungary as an action that "retards the development of socialism."[63]

The president was eager to capitalize on these reactions. At an NSC meeting on November 8, he suggested that films of Soviet tanks rumbling through Budapest be distributed to American embassies throughout the world. He was informed that the U.S. Information Agency (USIA) had already undertaken that task.[64] On November 9, three resolutions were adopted by the General Assembly. One proposal, submitted by Cuba, Ireland, Italy, Pakistan, and Peru, reiterated the call upon the Soviet Union to withdraw its forces from Hungary and recommended that free elections be held in that country under U.N. auspices as soon as law and order had been restored. The resolution was adopted by a vote of forty-eight to eleven. An Austrian proposal calling upon all member states to participate in relief efforts for the affected territories was adopted with no negative votes—the Soviet bloc, except Hungary, simply abstaining. A U.S. resolution called upon the USSR to cease its violence against the Hungarian population. Four other resolutions followed, culminating with an overwhelming December 12 General Assembly vote to condemn the Soviet violation of the U.N. Charter.

There were both varied sponsorship of and overwhelming support for each of the above measures. This was the result, in part, of the Eisenhower administration's decision to let other nations sometimes take the lead, as well as a sensitivity to their points of view.[65] The president was particularly concerned about the Indian response. He perceived Krishna Menon, the Indian ambassador to the United Nations, as arrogant and inflexibly procommunist.[66] Still, India's strategic importance as head of the nonaligned bloc piqued the president's interest in courting Jawaharal Nehru.[67] Through phone calls and letters to key administration officials, efforts were initiated toward that end. In a memo to John Foster Dulles on October 29, Eisenhower wondered if the situation in Eastern Europe and the Middle East "might not be creating in Nehru the feeling that he might, very wisely, begin to strengthen his ties with the West and separate himself more distinctly from the Communists." Any such proclivities on his part, he suggested, should be nurtured.[68] When films of the Soviet oppression became available, Eisenhower urged that one of the "best reels" be sent to Nehru.[69]

The president too, made special efforts to see things from the perspectives of the neutral states in an effort to understand why they acted as they did. At a meeting in his office on November 5, for example, State Department Chief Counsel Herman Phleger noted that the Indian and Arab abstentions on some of the Hungarian resolutions in the United Nations may have been the result of a deal with the Soviet Union to obtain support for their policy initiatives on the Middle East crisis, including the establishment of a neutral police force. When Vice President Nixon questioned India's motivations for these abstentions, the president suggested that Nehru thought of only one thing—colonialism, which he saw as the domination of whites over colored people. The president mused that it might be well for him to write Nehru, pointing out the nature of Russia's "colonialism by bayonet" in Hungary. His concern was persuasion, not propaganda. One must protect, he suggested, the ability to exchange such letters without having them released for such ends. He also wanted Nehru's forthcoming visit to the United States to be expedited.[70] There are indications that these combined efforts did have some impact on Nehru's stance.[71]

In addition to the U.N. actions described above, the administration took the initiative on several other diplomatic and cultural measures to show its displeasure at the Soviet actions. At a November 5 meeting in his office, Eisenhower suggested that the Soviet diplomatic reception celebrating the communist revolution be boycotted by American diplomats. On December 3, cultural exchanges with the USSR were suspended. The president and the Secretary of State also made several speeches condemning the Soviet violation of human rights in eastern Europe. In his statement on Human Rights Day on December 10, for example, the president noted that "the recent outbreak of brutality in Hungary has moved free people everywhere to reactions of horror and revulsion."[72] Relief efforts were undertaken to lessen the suffering of the Hungarian people, as well as to accommodate the growing refugee problem. The first American efforts were undertaken quietly and indirectly, many of them channeled through voluntary organizations. Secretary Dulles noted on October 28 that the administration was "actively concerned" with the plight of the Hungarian people and had offered aid through the International Red Cross. On November 2, the president went beyond these efforts, authorizing the expenditure of $20 million for food and other kinds of relief support.

The administration also opened up American doors to Hungarian refugees. On November 8, Eisenhower directed the Refugee Relief Administration to rush the process for admission to the United States of new refugees from the "brutal purge of liberty" carried out by "imperial communism" in Hungary.[73] Shortly thereafter the president requested emergency legislation to permit qualified refugees to obtain permanent residence in the United States. By January 1, 1957, over 15,000 people had been admitted.[74]

The president also had to deal with concerns that the United States had a moral responsibility for the fiasco in Hungary. Charges were circulating in the corridors of the United Nations, Ambassador Lodge informed the president on November 9, that the United States had encouraged the freedom fighters to rise up in the first place, only to abandon them when it became politically costly to give them aid.[75] The charge was repeated by Anna Kethly, the president of the Hungarian Social Democratic Party, who had been appointed a U.N. delegate by the Nagy regime before it was overthrown. In late November, as a refugee in Brussels, she charged that Radio Free Europe had "gravely sinned by making the Hungarian people believe that Western aid was coming when no such aid was planned."[76]

Eisenhower evidently had not been completely certain himself what the United States might have done along these lines, checking out the gossip in the United Nations with Secretary of State Dulles. When the latter assured him that he "had always been against violent rebellion," Eisenhower retorted that he had told Lodge that but was amazed that he "was in ignorance of this fact."[77] In his November 14 news conference, he affirmed that the United States "never has advocated open rebellion." Of course, he went on, "we . . . have always urged that the spirit of freedom be kept alive, that people do not lose hope. But we have never . . . urged or argued for any kind of armed revolt which could bring about disaster to our friends.''[78]

POLICY AND PROCESS: SOME ASSESSMENTS

The U.S. responsibility for the uprising was somewhat greater than the president suggested. Eisenhower had earlier embraced the doctrine that the United States should go beyond the mere containment of Soviet expansion, to the notion that it could roll back communism. In August 1952, for example, he had pledged that we can "never know peace until these (enslaved) people are restored again to being master of their own fate," and that "never shall we desist in our aid to every man and woman of those shackled lands who is dedicated to the liberation of his fellows." A month later he committed himself to use "every political, every economic, every psychological tactic" to keep alive the spirit of freedom in the nations conquered by communism.[79] These pledges, moreover, had been implemented in some ways.[80]

For several months, RFE broadcasts from Munich had called for the liberation of enslaved countries, and the United States had dropped leaflets containing similar messages from balloons floated over the satellite countries. The Committee for a Free Europe, a private group close to the government and led by former administration officials such as C. D. Jackson, had developed a full-scale plan envisaging the incorporation of liberated countries in eastern Europe into a united Europe.[81] The U.S. Senate in June 1956 had allocated $25 million for the purpose of financing secret activities behind the iron curtain.[82] The CIA-sponsored Red Sox/Red Cap training groups had plans for assisting eastern European rebels should the occasion present itself. Authorized earlier under NSC 5412/1, these groups had been training for such a contingency at a secret agency facility in Munich, West Germany.[83]

Once the rebellion began, it is true that the president pulled back from the full implementation of his earlier rollback policies. At his insistence, several statements were made in the initial phase of the crisis to assure the Soviets that the United States did not envisage Hungary joining in the western alliance. In the second phase of the crisis, the president turned down CIA requests that the United States use tactical nuclear weapons to bomb supply lines from the Soviet Union into Hungary, as well as requests that it be allowed to fly over Budapest and airdrop arms and supplies to the rebels. Subsequent studies of RFE broadcasts by the West German government and the Council of Europe suggest that the U.S. government itself sent out no explicit appeals for a Hungarian uprising.[84]

Yet, there is other indirect evidence suggesting that the United States may have continued to play an active covert role in the early phases of the rebellion. The president himself, at one meeting with Secretary of State Dulles, suggested that he should "explore the chances of helping to assist centrifugal, disruptive currents in the Iron Curtain countries."[85] The administration was initially suspicious of the Nagy government and gave it little support. Allen Dulles even suggested that the Nagy government could not last and that another government might eventually be formed by Cardinal Mindzenty.

In the first days after the uprising, as noted above, several administration officials thought that the Hungarians might succeed in their revolution. Given these assumptions, the encouragement of covert operations would have made a great deal of sense. Radio Free Europe broadcasts to Hungary, moreover, were far more hysterical in tone than the earlier RFE broadcasts to Poland, as Ranelagh notes in his careful study of the CIA. They carried, without comment, several local broadcasts from Hungary containing rumors of help and diatribes against the Gero regime.[86] Even after Nagy had come to power, at least two RFE Hungarian broadcasts contained suggestions that his government must be overthrown, as noted above. The president himself later expressed the fear that some of the RFE statements could be considered incitements to war.[87]

Indeed, a subsequent review of CIA policies in eastern Europe, conducted by General Lucian Truscott at the president's request, suggests the operations people in the CIA may have been more active in stirring up the rebellion than the president realized at the time.[88] Truscott questioned Red Sox/Red Cap operatives, Hungarian refugees arriving at Camp Kilmer, New Jersey, and sources within the military intelligence services in his inquiry. He discovered to his horror that the CIA was continuing operations in Czechoslovakia, hoping that the unleashing of massive discontent with life under Soviet control would lead to a mass uprising and the establishment of a prowestern regime. He concluded that the CIA had failed, conceptually, to distinguish between insurrectional violence, guerrilla mass uprisings, revolutionary action, and true guerrilla warfare in the twentieth century. The Hungarian experience, he concluded, suggests that it is not possible to succeed with an uprising in any country in which the police and security forces are solidly in the control of the government.[89]

The most important consequence of the Hungarian crisis, in retrospect, was the decision to abandon the liberation rhetoric and policies so crucial to the American right. Eisenhower was a man who could learn from experience, and when confronted with the actual costs of intervening in areas controlled by the Soviet Union, he quickly moved to dissociate his administration from that orientation.[90] Upon receiving the Truscott report, the president decided, with the support of the Joint Chiefs and a reluctant Allen Dulles, to end the Red Sox/Red Cap operations altogether.[91] Once it became clear that the Kadar government was in place, the administration adapted to this new reality and decided not to block that government from taking the Hungarian seat at the U.N. Later, prebroadcast control over all RFE scripts was reintroduced. (Jackson had originally abolished such "censorship".)[92]

This reversal of the rollback policy could have created domestic political problems for the president within both the administration and Republican Party circles more broadly. The plans people in the CIA were deeply disappointed at this policy reversal. "This [support for the Hungarian uprising] was exactly the end for which the Agency's paramilitary capability was designed,'' William Colby, then a junior CIA officer, notes.[93] Clare Boothe Luce, ambassador to Italy and the wife of the publisher of *Time* and *Life*, was also disillusioned with the administration. Prior to the Hungarian crisis she had sent the president a thirty-seven-page essay calling for a preventative war using tactical nuclear weapons.[94] During the Hungarian crisis, she met with the president to express her extreme concern over developments in Europe, suggesting the need for radical action.[95]

Outside the inner circle of decision making, certain members of the Republican right attempted to stir public opinion over the administration's handling of the crisis. A disgruntled C. D. Jackson, for example drafted an editorial for *Life* called "Grasping the Nettle." According to Cook he argued that the administration should confirm the policy of liberation during its second term in office.[96] Although that specific editorial seems not to have appeared in *Life*, an essay with a similar critique entitled "If There's a New Hungary . . . " appeared on March 4, 1957.

The administration, it was argued, did not act swiftly during the five days when Hungary was free and action might have "been able to forestall the subsequent Soviet invasion." Their proposals included the suggestions that U.S. Ambassador Lodge could have immediately asked for an emergency session of the General Assembly on November 2; that a Hungarian observation commission could have been created and flown to Hungary so that they would have been there before the massive Soviet intervention; and that Anna Kethly, Nagy's authorized representative, could have been installed as Hungary's accredited U.N. spokesman.

The president, however, was not the major target of such critiques. Partly this was due to his decision-making style. Eisenhower communicated, at least privately, with hard-liners in the government in an attempt to soften their opposition to his policies. Thus he saw Clare Boothe Luce during the crisis, as we have seen. He handled her concerns by suggesting to Under Secretary Hoover from the State Department that he also talk to her to set her ideas in a "little broader perspective."[97] Responding to C. D. Jackson's many calls for more aggressive action, Eisenhower, on November 19, 1956, empathized with Jackson's concerns, all the while suggesting why he could not go along with his suggestions. "I know that your whole being cries out for action. . . . I assure you that the measures taken there by the Soviets are just as distressing to me as they are to you. To annihilate Hungary . . . is in no way to help her."[98] He subsequently offered Jackson the position of Under Secretary of State to head up the administration's disarmament efforts. Jackson rejected the offer.[99]

Equally important was Eisenhower's proclivity for delegating authority and sharing the spotlight with others in his administration—a central element of the hidden-hand presidency. Dulles, for example, made most of the initial statements of what the U.S. response would be to the Hungarian rebellion. Lodge carried the brunt of the effort within the United Nations, making most of the speeches and at the tactical level putting together coalitions for measures the United States favored. The result was that these men drew most of the fire as the administration retreated from its liberation policies. The direct target of Jackson's attack, as we have seen, was not the president but Henry Cabot Lodge, whom he accused of not being "prepared to do anything." In the *Life* editorial noted above, "the administration" and Lodge were critiqued, but the president was spared any direct assault. Moreover, the defense of the U.S. position, printed in a guest editorial in *Life* on March 11, 1957, came from Lodge and not the president.[100]

This hidden-hand presidency was not without its drawbacks.[101] Sometimes key players should have been shuffled, even if the president had to pay some relatively high political costs. This is evident in Eisenhower's dealings with Allen Dulles. The CIA had failed to predict the uprising in East Berlin in 1953 and in Hungary in 1956 and had not kept the president fully informed on British, French, and Israeli plans for the Suez attack that same year. These problems were due, in part, to Allen Dulles's fixation on covert operations and his lack of interest in the administration and the coordination of intelligence from other sources.[102]

Aware of Allen Dulles's failings along these lines, Eisenhower had earlier resorted to an administrative device he often used when not fully confident of a department head. He appointed someone else whose strengths would compensate for the failings of the department head. Lieutenant General Charles P. Cabell, U.S. Air Force, had been appointed in an effort to bring into that operation the management skills and finesse to deal with leaders in the House and Senate in ways that Dulles lacked.[103] As Eisenhower's personal eyes and ears at the CIA, he enhanced the president's oversight capabilities.[104] In January 1956, the president also created a Board of Consultants of Foreign Intelligence Activities to give him advice, from outside the lines of authority, on intelligence matters.[105] These arrangements, however, had not prevented the intelligence failures related to the Hungarian and Suez crises. As the president's Foreign Intelligence Advisory Board noted in December 1956, there was an imbalance in Dulles's role as director of Central Intelligence. They recommended the appointment of a chief of staff for the DCI to oversee the CIA's internal administration. Later, in 1960, the board suggested the possibility of separating the DCI from the CIA, having the director serve as the president's intelligence adviser/coordinator for all intelligence activities.[106]

Yet, nothing came from these recommendations.[107] Eisenhower was reluctant to curtail the responsibilities of less important people when such moves would have clearly created political problems for him.[108] Certainly he was not about to demote someone as important as Dulles, particularly when he valued some of his characteristics. As he noted in a statement cited in a CIA history, "I have two alternatives, either to get rid of him and appoint someone who will assert more authority or keep him with his limitations. I'd rather have Allen as my chief intelligence officer with his limitations than anyone else I know."[109]

THE POLICY, THE PROCESS, AND THE MAN

From this analysis of Eisenhower's response to the Soviet intervention in Hungary, several conclusions may be drawn as to Eisenhower's role in the policy-making process. Eisenhower was a political realist who had the moral and political strength to change his policies when external events suggested they were no longer viable. He played a central and active role in the formulation of crucial foreign policies and maintained control over the administration of these policies. Once the Soviet Union intervened in Hungary, he informally consulted with his inner circle and decided against military countermeasures and overt support for the rebels. He took the initiative in devising and implementing a variety of economic and political actions against the Soviets. And he showed considerable sensitivity to how the situation might be used to wean India and others from too close a coalition with the Soviet bloc. He did not want to heat up the political climate to the point that the Soviet Union might feel threatened by the United States. He was the one who showed the greatest concern over assuring the Soviet Union that the United States did not seek to make military allies out of the newly independent regimes. His moral condemnations of the Soviet action never took him to such lengths that there would be an irrevocable break with that nation. The president, in short, managed this crisis as he evidently did others, "without overreacting, without going to war, without increasing defense spending, without frightening people half out of their wits."[110]

His approach to the Hungarian crisis also supports broader revisionist interpretations of his decision-making style.[111] Earlier in his presidency, Eisenhower had created a formal, hierarchical apparatus to maximize rationalization of decision making in the national security arena.[112] It was a system that he used in his handling of the Suez crisis and many other situations. Yet, as this account suggests, the president knew how to use this system in a flexible manner. In dealing with the Hungarian crisis, practically no use was made of the National Security Council as a deliberative body. Eisenhower handled the strategic issues involved pretty much on his own. Policy decisions were made mainly in informal meetings in the Oval Office. Yet he delegated the implementation of policy to key aides he trusted and shared public responsibility for the policy with them.[113] His reluctance to use the more formal policy-making mechanism, we suggest, stemmed from his fear that political and bureaucratic pressures there could have mounted in favor of a more active—and more dangerous—policy.

In some hands this kind of improvisational approach to decision making could have certain negative effects. Broad discussions in which a full array of alternatives are formally presented and considered make it less likely, as Janis and George have pointed out, that the president will opt prematurely for one preferred but ill-considered option.[114] But structures are only safeguards, and a wise leader may disregard them if he senses that the process itself could create political obstacles to achieving what he sees as the policy best for the nation. As some recent scholarship has suggested, an enhanced "personal capacity to test reality" may indeed permit a president greater policy-making flexibility.[115]

The quality of the policy pursued in this fashion, we suggest, will depend to a great extent on the vision, ideological bent, strategic skills, political capabilities, and personality characteristics of the leader who chooses to improvise in such a manner. In the case at hand it is clear that the president clearly had pursued covert interventionist policies and gone along with the anticommunist bent of his times prior to the crisis. During the crisis he seems to have been aware that a bureaucratic momentum for intervention could easily have grown out of control. But he also had the military knowledge and command experience that gave him the confidence to assess, on his own, what he would and could do in a high-risk situation such as that presented in the fall of 1956. Where less self-confident men might have been pushed by the recommendations of the Joint Chiefs of Staff and the operations people in the CIA into a more interventionist posture, he was able to resist their advice.[116] The hidden-hand style he used in this crisis gave him a "free hand" in exerting his influence over political affairs. The sharing of detailed policy implementation and public explanations with other key members of his administration diluted the extent to which he, himself, would become the target of the right wing in his own party, unhappy at this reversal of the rollback theories it had so strongly embraced.

His ultimate policy choices, however, cannot be understood fully without a closer look at Eisenhower's political skills and deeper values. He could change direction when he made a mistake. In this case, he reversed a whole policy direction and set of bureaucratic commitments.[117] He had the political skills to navigate this policy reversal through the decision-making process in ways that would cause the least resistance.

Most important, he knew that major-power warfare was not simply a game and should not be undertaken lightly.[118] He was a man who could take risks and had done so earlier in his life at the D-Day landing, when the fate of the free world was at stake.[119] But he was a man who at times seemed to feel for those lives that had been lost, and he realized that his family could have suffered as others did. Twenty years after the D-Day landing, for example, he looked again upon those rows of crosses on Normandy Beach, and he knew what those crosses meant. Touring the area with Walter Cronkite, he brought the issue home:

My mind goes back to the fact that my son was graduated from West Point on D-Day, and on the very day he was graduating men came here—American, British, and our other Allies, and they stormed these beaches, not to fulfill any ambitions that America had for conquest but just to preserve freedom, to establish systems of self-government in the world. Many thousands of men died for ideals such as these.

Now, my own son has been very fortunate. He has had a very full life since then. But these young boys, many of them whose graves we have been looking at, contemplating their sacrifices—they were cut off in their prime. They had families who grieved for them. But they never had the great experience of going through life like my son.[120]

He also saw war as a very clumsy political instrument. That process, as he noted in his memoirs, "has produced notable victories and notable men, but in temporarily settling international quarrels it has not guaranteed peace with right and justice. War is stupid, cruel, and costly. Yet wars have persisted. In the name of self-defense, nations have paid the human price and, spurred on by fear and competition, have continued to accept the burdens of armaments, the size and cost of which grow ever more fantastic.''[121]

But men must have hope. ''Humanity,'' he argued, is not prepared to ''spinelessly . . . accept the cynical conclusion that war is certain to recur, that the law of the jungle must forever be the rule of life.'' One of his major goals as president, as he also noted in his memoirs, was to prevent such wars from happening. None of the tasks to which he had devoted himself as president transcended in importance that ''of trying to devise practical and acceptable means to lighten the burdens of armaments and to lessen the likelihood of war.''[122] That commitment, we suggest, played a central role in his decision not to confront the Soviet Union militarily in Hungary in the fall of 1956.

NOTES

1. Fred I. Greenstein, *The Hidden-Hand Presidency: Eisenhower as Leader* (New York: Basic Books, 1982).

2. U.S. Ambassador Charles Bohlen reported from Moscow that there appeared to be a power split pitting Khrushchev and Bulganin against the more reactionary elements in the Kremlin. The available evidence, however, suggests that the decision to invade Hungary in force was made at a meeting of the Presidium on October 29, one day after the withdrawal from Budapest. Charles Bohlen, *Witness to History* (New York: W. W. Norton and Co., 1973), 412–15. See also ''Text of Soviet Statement of October 30,'' *Department of State Bulletin* 35 (November 12, 1956): 745–46.

3. Telephone interview with First Deputy Foreign Minister under Nagy, Dr. Georgi Heltai, by Kenneth Kitts, Charleston, S.C., May 14, 1990.

4. *New York Times*, October 30, 1956, 27.

5. ''Minutes of the 301st Meeting of the National Security Council,'' October 26, 1956, Whitman National Security Council files, Dwight David Eisenhower Library, Abilene, Kan. (hereafter DDEL). All NSC minutes cited in this work are from the same location. For ''unusually watchful'' order see Louis Galambos, *Diaries of Dwight D. Eisenhower*, entry for October 26, 1956 (Washington, D.C.: University Publications of America, 1980) (hereafter Galambos, *Diaries of DDE*).

6. ''Minutes of the 302nd Meeting of National Security Council,'' November 1, 1956, Whitman National Security Council files, DDEL.

7. See Douglas Kinnard, *President Eisenhower and Strategy Management* (Lexington: University of Kentucky Press, 1977), 123.

8. Joint Chiefs of Staff, ''Memorandum for the National Security Council on U.S. Policy Toward Developments in Poland,'' November 6, 1956, DDEL. For earlier document they would revise, see Planning Board Document, ''U.S. Policy Toward Developments in Poland and Hungary,'' October 31, 1956, *NSC 5616/1, ibid.* The Joint Chiefs of Staff suggested deleting from the original proposal such items as these assurances. A proposal for the partial withdrawal of U.S. forces from western Europe in exchange for a complete Soviet withdrawal from Hungary was also criticized. The Joint Chiefs recommended that the United States inform the Soviet Union that an ''immediate military action would follow any Soviet use of military force to reimpose its control in Poland.'' Joint Chiefs of Staff, ''Memorandum for the Secretary of Defense on U.S. Policy Toward Developments in Poland and Hungary,'' October 31, 1956, *ibid.* They also stated that

it would be feasible to intervene in Poland even though this could lead to a general war. "Memorandum for the Secretary of Defense on U.S. Policy Toward Developments in Poland," December 1956, *ibid.*

   9. William Rogers to J. F. Dulles, October 25, 1956, *Minutes of the Telephone Conversations of J. F. Dulles and Christian A. Herter* (Washington, D.C.: University Publications of America, 1980) (hereafter *Telephone Conversations of J. F. Dulles*).

   10. Ambassador Lodge, for instance, referred to the Soviets as the "murderers of innocent women and children." "Second Statement," October 28, U.S./U.N. press release 2481, *Department of State Bulletin* 35 (November 12, 1956): 759.

   11. "Memorandum of Conference with the President," November 3, 1956 (Hoover, Phleger, Rountree, Hagerty, and Goodpaster attending), in Galambos, *Diaries of DDE*; Peter Lyon, *Eisenhower: Portrait of the Hero* (Boston: Little, Brown and Co., 1974), 718.

   12. Telephone call from Ambassador Hughes to president, November 2, 1956, in Galambos, *Diaries of DDE.*

   13. "Inquest on Hungary (cont.): Ambassador Lodge's Defense of the U.S. Role Shows There Is a Gap in U.S. Policy," *Life*, March 11, 1957, 41.

   14. Heltai, interview with Kitts, May 14, 1990.

   15. Lyon, *Eisenhower*, 709–10.

   16. Tibor Meray, *Thirteen Days that Shook the Kremlin* (New York: Frederick A. Praeger, Publishers, 1959), 140–69. For a similar view, see Blanche Wiesen Cook, *The Declassified Eisenhower: A Divided Legacy* (Garden City, N.Y.: Doubleday, 1981), 202.

   17. "Communist Imperialism in the Satellite World," *Department of State Bulletin* 35 (November 5, 1956): 702–3.

   18. Emmet John Hughes, *The Ordeal of Power: A Political Memoir of the Eisenhower Years* (New York: Atheneum, 1963), 220.

   19. "Statement by the President Concerning the Admission of Refugees from Hungary," November 8, *Public Papers of the President: Dwight D. Eisenhower, 1956*, 1093.

   20. "Minutes of the 301st Meeting of the National Security Council," October 26, 1956, DDEL.

   21. "Task of Waging Peace," address by Secretary Dulles before Dallas Council on World Affairs, *Department of State Bulletin*, 35 (November 5, 1956): 697.

   22. "Memorandum of Conference with the President, October 30, 1956, 11:15 A.M.," in Galambos, *Diaries of DDE.*

   23. "Radio and Television Report to the American People on Developments in Eastern Europe and the Middle East, October 31," *Public Papers of DDE 1956*, 1062.

   24. Rhodri Jeffreys-Jones, *The CIA and American Democracy* (New Haven: Yale University Press, 1989), 108–9. The agency was reported to have better intelligence on events in Poland. Robert Amory later recalled that the CIA kept way ahead of the wire services and the diplomatic cables on events in that country. Jolm Ranelagh, *The Agency: The Rise and Decline of the CIA* (New York: Simon and Schuster, 1986), 304.

   25. A fuller discussion of these circumstances may be found in Robert Murphy, *Diplomat Among Warriors* (Garden City, N.Y.: Doubleday, 1964), 428.

   26. *Ibid.*, 429.

   27. Dwight D. Eisenhower, *Waging Peace: The White House Years* (Garden City, N.Y.: Doubleday, 1965), 64.

   28. For details, see Bohlen, *Witness to History*, chapter 23.

   29. On October 27 Under Secretary of State Robert Murphy met with Tibor Zador,

first secretary of the Hungarian legation. During the course of their conversation Murphy directly asked Zador what Nagy's position was regarding the Soviet troops in Hungary. "Conversation Between Mr. Murphy and Mr. Zador, October 27," *Department of State Bulletin* 35 (November 5, 1956): 701.

30. Eisenhower, *Waging Peace*, 69.

31. Bohlen, *Witness to History*, 415.

32. Lyon, *Eisenhower*, 709.

33. Bohlen, *Witness to History*, 411–12.

34. *Ibid.*, 416, chapter 23.

35. Lyon, *Eisenhower*, 710.

36. *Telephone Conversations of J. F. Dulles*, October 30, 1956.

37. Eisenhower, *Waging Peace*, 82.

38. Bohlen, *Witness to History*, 416–18.

39. As recalled by Milton S. Eisenhower, *The President Is Calling* (Garden City, N.Y.: Doubleday, 1974), 355. According to deputy foreign minister George Heltai, the Nagy government felt that Eisenhower would seek a tradeoff in which the United States would force its allies out of Egypt in return for a Soviet promise to respect Hungarian sovereignty. Heltai, interview with Kitts.

40. Phone call from William Knowland to John Foster Dulles, November 2, 1956, *Telephone Conversations of J. F. Dulles*.

41. A Gallup poll in early October showed Stevenson leading Eisenhower among Jewish voters 65 percent to 21 percent, while with Catholics the margin was 50 percent to 43 percent. A poll just before the election also shows that there had been no substantial change in the voting proclivities of either Catholics or Jews between the 1952 and 1956 presidential elections. See George A. Gallup, *The Gallup Poll: Public Opinion 1935–1971* (New York: Random House, 1972), 1450, 1453.

42. "Reasons for Voting," November 9–14, 1956, in George A. Gallup, *The Gallup Poll* (New York: Random House, 1977), 1457.

43. Daily calendar, October 24–November 7, 1956, in Galambos, *Diaries of DDE*.

44. Henry Cabot Lodge, *As It Was: An Inside View of Politics and Power in the 50's and 60's* (New York: W. W. Norton and Co., 1976), 94.

45. Eisenhower's daily schedule shows that the two visited at Walter Reed hospital on November 4. Galambos, *Diaries of DDE*.

46. Ellis D. Slater, *The Ike I Knew* (Ellis D. Slater Trust, 1980), 140–43.

47. Hughes, *The Ordeal of Power*, 216.

48. Slater, *The Ike I Knew*, 143.

49. For text of resolution, see *NSC 5616/2*, Annex B, November 19, 1956, DDEL.

50. "Letter from President Eisenhower to Premier Bulganin, November 4," *Department of State Bulletin* 35 (November 19, 1956): 796–97.

51. "White House Statement, November 5," *Department of State Bulletin* 35 (November 19, 1956): 795–96. Eisenhower was infuriated by Bulganin's November 5 proposal. He saw the suggestion as an opening wedge to be used by the USSR to extend its influence in that area. The public statement noted above was drafted in his office at a meeting including Hoover and Phleger from State and speech writer Emmet Hughes. See Eisenhower, *Waging Peace*, 89–90; Lyon, *Eisenhower*, 719; and Hughes, *The Ordeal of Power*, 223.

52. "U.S. Policy Toward Developments in Poland and Hungary," *NSC 5616/1*, October 31, 1956, DDEL.

53. Former head of the Psychological Strategy Board C. D. Jackson had suggested in the summer of 1956 that he thought it desirable for the United States to make as many crises at once as possible. "If the summer passes without our having made some intelligent moves toward the East European satellite countries, we will really have exhibited idea bankruptcy." He wrote Henry Luce that his psychological warfare education had taught him that "international psychological activity" must be accompanied by "little bits of cold, hard, action." Cook, *The Declassified Eisenhower*, 201.

54. Ranelagh, *The Agency*, 287, 305–7.

55. Hughes, *The Ordeal of Power*, 222–23. See also Stephen Ambrose, *Eisenhower: The President* (New York: Simon and Schuster, 1984), 368.

56. Ann Whitman makes note of this realization in her diary entry of November 15. Cook, *The Declassified Eisenhower*, 371.

57. Milton S. Eisenhower, *The President Is Calling*, 355. For Milton Eisenhower's role as Dwight Eisenhower's confidante, see 308–16. The White House was Milton Eisenhower's weekend home for eight years. The two men would sit in the president's bedroom for hours, as the president worked out his ideas on various matters. Milton's role was to provide a sounding board, enabling the president to clarify his ideas. He was no advocate. Dwight Eisenhower never lost his temper with his younger brother.

58. At least two such appeals were rejected by Eisenhower. Ambrose, *Eisenhower*, 356.

59. According to Andrew H. Berding, Dulles referred to such proposals as "madness." See his *Dulles on Diplomacy* (Princeton, N.J.: Van Nostrand and Co., 1965), 115.

60. Ranelagh, *The Agency*, 307.

61. Phone call from Allen Dulles, November 2, 1956, *Telephone Conversations of J. F. Dulles*.

62. Nagy left the Yugoslav embassy on November 22 with a safe conduct pledge and an understanding that he would be permitted to go to Yugoslavia. He was nevertheless seized, deported to Rumania, and eventually killed.

63. *New York Times*, November 5, 1956, 23.

64. "Memorandum of Discussions at 303rd Meeting of the National Security Council," November 8, 1956, DDEL.

65. The fruit of the administration's efforts along these lines was even clearer in the initiatives taken by India and other Afro-Asian powers concerning the establishment of a peacekeeping force in the Middle East. See "Memorandum of Conference with the President, November 5, 1956, 10:20 A.M.," in Galambos, *Diaries of DDE*.

66. Eisenhower, *Waging Peace*, 107.

67. Interview with Andrew Goodpaster, 1967, Oral History Program, Columbia University, 106.

68. Letter to Dulles, October 29, 1956, Galambos, *Diaries of DDE*. Eisenhower's sensitivity to the Indian situation was also evident in his discussions with Treasury Secretary Humphrey when they were debating the problem of aid to India. Humphrey did not think that the United States should be taxed to support a Socialist economy. Eisenhower jumped in and reprimanded Humphrey and explained that India did not have the resources to operate a free enterprise society like the United States. It was unfair to judge the Indian situation by examples that were relevant to the United States but not to the Indian economy. From interview with Robert Bowie, 1967, Oral History Program, Columbia University, 8–9. At the NSC meeting on October 26, CIA Director Allen Dulles

was also concerned about the effect of the events in Hungary and Poland on neutral nations such as India. See "Minutes of the 301st Meeting of the National Security Council," October 26, 1956, DDEL.

69. 303rd NSC Meeting, November 8, 1956, in *Foreign Relations of the United States, 1955–1957*, vol. 9 (Washington, D.C.: U.S. Government Printing Office), 595–96.

70. "Conference with the President, November 5, 1956, 10:20 A.M.," in Galambos, *Diaries of DDE.*

71. India, Ceylon, and Indonesia, for example, sponsored a resolution urging Hungary to permit U.N. observers to enter their country so that they could check reports that Hungarian nationalists were being forcibly deported from their country. Nehru himself, along with the prime ministers of Burma, Indonesia, and Ceylon, issued a communiqué expressing regret that Soviet troops had been reintroduced into Hungary after Moscow had indicated that they would leave. "In the course of 10 years, the Hungarian people could not be converted to Soviet ideas," he noted. *Facts on File* 16 (November 14, 1956), 388. Also, Anthony Eden in his memoirs notes that Nehru was much more inclined to condemn the British and French operations in Egypt, while pleading that he could not follow "the very confusing situation in Hungary." See Anthony Eden, *Full Circle: The Memoirs of Anthony Eden* (Boston: Houghton Mifflin Co., 1960), 610. Eisenhower's press secretary, James Hagerty, suggests that Eisenhower, too, may have experienced the same confusion. Interview with James Hagerty, 1969, Oral History Project, Columbia University, 200.

72. "Statement by the President: Human Rights Day in the Light of Recent Events in Hungary, December 10," *Public Papers of DDE, 1956*, 1119–20.

73. "Statement by the President Concerning the Admission of Refugees from Hungary," November 8, 1956, *Public Papers of DDE, 1956*, 93.

74. Austria was the primary place of refuge for the Hungarians. By early 1957, there were still 37,000 Hungarians awaiting resettlement. Vice President Nixon argued that the Hungarians should be admitted to the United States under the parole procedure then in effect until Congress could act to make the resettlement permanent. See Eisenhower, *Waging Peace*, 97–98; and "Providing for the Needs of the Hungarian Refugees, Report by Vice President Nixon, January 1, 1957," *Department of State Bulletin* 36 (January 21, 1957): 94–99.

75. Ambrose, *Eisenhower*, 372.

76. Lyon, *Eisenhower*, 710.

77. Ambrose, *Eisenhower*, 372.

78. "The President's News Conference of November 14, 1956," *Public Papers of DDE, 1956*, 1096. Studies of RFE's broadcasts during this period suggest that it had not called for armed rebellion. A CIA officer, Cord Meyer, head of the International Organization division responsible for RFE, cleared the Hungarian section of the CIA operation, as did a West German and a Council of Europe investigation. Ranelagh, *The Agency*, 308–9.

79. Quotes from Lyon, *Eisenhower*, 708.

80. Khrushchev's speech to the Twentieth Party Congress in the Soviet Union was secured by the CIA and released to the *New York Times* in early June 1956. Broadcast by Radio Liberty and Radio Free Europe, it played a central role in creating the unrest in the Eastern Bloc countries. Stephen Ambrose with Richard H. Immerman, *Ike's Spies: Eisenhower and the Espionage Establishment* (Garden City, N.Y.: Doubleday, 1981),

236–38; William R. Corson, *The Armies of Ignorance* (New York: Dial Press, 1977), 367–77.

81. Cook, *The Declassified Eisenhower*, 199. See also Ambrose with Immerman, *Ike's Spies*, 235–36.

82. See *The New York Journal American*, June 30, 1956, cited in Cook, *The Declassified Eisenhower*, 370, n.101.

83. The dissemination of Khrushchev's secret speech in the summer, due in large part to Wisner's efforts, had done much to provoke the unrest. After the Polish uprising, leaders in the plans division apparently pushed ahead with plans for operations in Hungary, Czechoslovakia, and Rumania, in that order. Groups were inserted into those nation's capitals for the purpose of fermenting and cultivating discontent. Corson, *The Armies of Ignorance*, 369.

84. Ranelagh, *The Agency*, 30–39.

85. See Eisenhower, *Waging Peace*, 64–65.

86. Ranelagh, *The Agency*, 309.

87. Ann Whitman diary, January 7, 1957, Box 8, DDEL; Ranelagh, *The Agency*, 305–7.

88. Corson, *The Armies of Ignorance*, 371. One cannot document covert operations from NSC records. More than thirty years later, several items on the agenda are still blocked out as national security sensitive. Moreover, much CIA activity at this time was reported only to the 5412 committee for approval. The NSC was considered too big and likely to engender leaks. Gordon Gray, Eisenhower's Special Assistant for National Security Affairs, was also chairman of this committee. The proposal, once approved by this committee, would then usually be presented to Robert Murphy, John Foster Dulles's deputy, for his approval. Gray would then bring the decision privately and informally to the president. Ambrose with Immerman, *Ike's Spies*, 240.

89. Corson, *The Armies of Ignorance*, 370–71.

90. Allen Dulles was already distancing himself from the more extremist liberation rhetoric by this time. The East German riots of 1953 had, moreover, convinced Eisenhower of the need to address such issues cautiously. See H. W. Brands, Jr., *Cold Warriors* (New York: Columbia University Press, 1988), 123–24.

91. Corson, *The Armies of Ignorance*, 371.

92. The role of the president's Special Assistant for Psychological Warfare had earlier been redefined. Rather than overseeing a broad array of active psychological warfare operations, that official would now simply assure the coordination and timing of the execution of foreign policy involving more than one department or agency. See Cook, *The Declassified Eisenhower*, 369–72. For the organizational framework for psychological warfare see Jeffreys-Jones, *The CIA and American Democracy*, 92–93; and Corson, *The Armies of Ignorance*, 342.

93. William E. Colby, *Honorable Men: My Life in the CIA* (New York: Simon and Schuster, 1978), 134; Ambrose, *Eisenhower*, 355. Wisner went into a manic-depressive reaction and was institutionalized for a few months. Ranelagh, *The Agency*, 307.

94. Clare Booth Luce, "Russian Atomic Power and the Lost American Revolution," August 21, 1954, copy in C. D. Jackson papers, Box 57, DDEL, cited in Cook, *The Declassified Eisenhower*, 195.

95. Eisenhower noted that she expressed these views to him in a meeting on the morning of November 19. "Memorandum of Conference with the President, Secretary Hoover and Colonel Goodpaster Present. November 19, 1956," in Galambos, *Diaries*

of DDE, 1956. C. D. Jackson continued to pepper administration officials with exhortations to keep the rollback orientation alive. He opposed the seating of the Kadar government's representative in the U.N., as well as the efforts to establish automatic prebroadcast review of RFE's political news. Cook, *The Declassified Eisenhower*, 200–201, 204, 369–72.

96. C. D. Jackson Papers, Box 56, DDEL, quoted in Cook, *The Declassified Eisenhower*, 371.

97. "Memorandum of Conference with the President, Secretary Hoover and Colonel Goodpaster Present, November 19, 1956," in Galambos, *Diaries of DDE*.

98. Quoted in Cook, *The Declassified Eisenhower*, 203.

99. *Ibid.*, 205. Jackson's interest in the Hungarian case (and in "hotting up" eastern Europe generally) lasted well into 1959, though his influence in the administration on such matters waned. See Brands, *Cold Warriors*, 132–36.

100. "Inquest on Hungary (cont.)," 41.

101. Greenstein, *The Hidden-Hand Presidency*, 93–208.

102. Jeffreys-Jones, *The CIA and American Democracy*, 108; Ray Cline, *Secrets, Spies and Scholars: Blueprint of the Essential CIA* (Washington, D.C.: Acropolis Books Ltd., 1976), 183–84. The president also said that he had first read about the British, French, and Israeli attacks on Suez in the newspapers. Amory's liaison man in London, Chester Cooper, was summoned to Washington, D.C., to explain why he had not sent a warning about the British intention to attack the Suez (108–9).

103. Corson, *The Armies of Ignorance*, 336.

104. *Ibid.*, 359–60, 372.

105. *Ibid.*, 372.

106. *Ibid.*

107. Ibid.

108. When Chip Bohlen, for example, told Eisenhower that one man in the State Department had completely undermined morale, Eisenhower told him that he knew that person was Scott McLeod, the security man. Interview with Charles Bohlen, 1970, Oral History Program, Columbia University, 6–7.

109. Quoted in Corson, *The Armies of Ignorance*, 359. See also Cline, *Secrets, Spies and Scholars*, 184.

110. Ambrose, *Eisenhower*, 626.

111. For the revisionist interpretations see Greenstein, *The Hidden-Hand Presidency*; and Phillip G. Henderson, *Managing the Presidency: The Eisenhower Legacy* (Boulder, Colo.: Westview Press, 1988).

112. Henderson, *Managing the Presidency*, 74–99.

113. Eisenhower also did not go public very often during this crisis, letting John Foster Dulles and Lodge make many of the policy explanations needed. For Eisenhower this was not atypical. As King and Ragsdale's survey of presidential public appearances suggests, only Truman made fewer than Eisenhower did during his first term in office. In his second term, Eisenhower became the champion nonappearer, making a total of only forth-three public appearances, in contrast to Truman's fifty-three. See Gary King and Lyn Ragsdale, *The Elusive Executive* (Washington, D.C.: Congressional Quarterly, Inc., 1988), Tables 5.10 and 5.11.

114. Alexander L. George, "The Case for Multiple Advocacy in Making Foreign Policy," *American Political Science Review* 66 (September 1972): 751; Irving L. Janis,

Groupthink: Psychological Studies of Policy Decisions and Fiascoes (Boston: Houghton Mifflin Co., 1982).

115. See, for example, John P. Burke and Fred I. Greenstein, *How Presidents Test Reality* (San Francisco: Russell Sage Foundation, 1989), 292–93.

116. His bureaucratic political skills, moreover, had been honed to a high point as Supreme Allied Commander during World War II, and on this occasion as others, he used those skills to good effect. Kinnard has argued elsewhere that Eisenhower often relied on his own expertise in his strategic choices in the military arena. "His aggressiveness, confidence and success in handling his adversaries, especially the service chiefs, comes through quite clearly in the numerous meetings in his office." Kinnard, *President Eisenhower and Strategy Management*, 127.

117. On November 7, he agreed to meet with Anthony Eden and Guy Mollet in the United States. When his staff and leaders in the State Department suggested that it would have a bad effect on Dag Hammarskold's efforts to restore peace to the Middle East and could be misinterpreted by the Arab world, he reversed his decision. See Eisenhower, *Waging Peace*, 93. For his superior ability at "testing reality," see Burke and Greenstein, *How Presidents Test Reality*, 261–68. For the argument that Eisenhower was generally quite well read, see Arthur Larson, *Eisenhower: The President Nobody Knew* (New York: Scribner and Sons, 1968), 172–73.

118. At a fundamental level, he was a man who both valued life and confronted his own mortality. This is evident in how he responded to the demands placed on him during fall 1956. Relaxing with speech writer Emmet Hughes on election eve he wearily remarked on his own health and the need to "take it a bit easy." Hughes, *The Ordeal of Power*, 227–28.

119. These risks included the decision to invade on June 6, a day when the weather might have proved to be worse than predicted and thus disastrous for the landing. Another risky decision was to land airborne troops on one side of Utah Beach to obtain command of the causeways crossing the marshlands on the other side. Air Chief Marshall Leigh Malloy objected strongly, but Eisenhower persisted. He knew that there was no way to break out from the beaches if those causeways were not taken. See "With Weather Still Risky Ike Called for Invasion," *Washington Post*, June 8, 1964, A3; and "Extreme Security Measures Kept Invasion Secret," *Washington Post*, June 11, 1964, A3. Both are edited versions of Eisenhower's interview with Walter Cronkite broadcast on CBS on June 5, 1964.

120. The conversation with Cronkite was viewed by Betty Glad in a replay of the film on the fortieth anniversary of D-Day. The quote is taken from Merle Miller, *Ike the Soldier: As They Knew Him* (New York: G. P. Putnam's Sons 1987), 618–19.

121. Eisenhower, *Waging Peace*, 466.

122. *Ibid.*, 467.

Bibliographic Essay: Eisenhower Revisionism, 1952–1992, a Reappraisal

John Robert Greene

"Revisionism" has long been a dirty word in many literary and historical circles. Much of this is the result of the fact that most revisionists, particularly those who toil in the vineyard of presidential history, tend to develop theses which paint the president under consideration in a much more unflattering light than was previously believed. When such a view is published, there are inevitably a score of defenders of the original thesis—most notably those who served in the administration under scrutiny. The battle between revisionist historians and the defenders of the faith has been one of the most important and interesting debates in the literature of the modern American presidency. The presidency of Dwight D. Eisenhower is no exception. However, in the realm of Eisenhower historiography, there is a rather singular difference: in few areas of modern presidential scholarship do the revisionists disagree among themselves as rabidly as do the Eisenhower revisionists. In a sense, then, there are several definable schools of Eisenhower revisionism, a division that has been, for the most part, missed by students of the Eisenhower years, and is the subject of this chapter.[1]

EISENHOWER AS POLITICAL GRANDFATHER: THE SHANNON/CHILDS SCHOOL

As has been the case with every president, works appeared during the Eisenhower administration that glorified both the man and his achievements to date. As a genre, these hagiographies are dismissible, as they have no historical distance from their subject and often were written as the result of projects guided either by the White House or the Eisenhower campaign apparatus. John Gunther's

1952 campaign biography, *Eisenhower: The Man and the Symbol* (New York: Harper and Brothers, 1952), is the best known of this genre. A glowing tribute, Gunther's main purpose was to convince the reader that Eisenhower was, indeed, a Republican. He also emphasized Eisenhower's "civilian-mindedness," a key theme in the upcoming presidential campaign.[2] Other laudatory works of the period include Merlo J. Pusey, *Eisenhower the President* (New York: Macmillan, 1956); Merriman Smith, *Meet Mr. Eisenhower* (New York: Harper and Brothers, 1954); and Marty Snyder, *My Friend Ike* (New York: F. Fell, 1956).

One early favorable treatment of Eisenhower deserves special mention. *New York Herald Tribune* reporter Robert J. Donovan was approached early in 1955 by the White House and asked to write a book on Eisenhower's first term. After agreeing to do so, Donovan was given an office in the White House and unprecedented access to executive office documents, which included a "Q clearance" to see National Security Council memoranda. The result, *Eisenhower: The Inside Story* (New York: Harper and Brothers, 1956), is a fascinating narrative, a progenitor of the insider journalism of the 1970s and 1980s. However, the tone is clearly a laudatory one, and a careful reading makes clear the information that Donovan was denied by the White House as he did his research.[3]

However, it was inevitable that thoughtful critics of the hero-in-politics image would soon surface. They were the first Eisenhower revisionists, and their work reflected Robert Griffith's salient 1982 definition of that group of revisionist scholars who "share a willingness to treat Eisenhower seriously and who see in the Eisenhower presidency an important subject for historical consideration."[4] These early revisionists unquestionably took Eisenhower and his administration with much more substantive seriousness than did the hagiographers. They did, however, paint a drastically antithetical portrait of a president who, rather than being a competent military leader in the White House, was merely a passive figure who just barely maintained control over his own administration. As a politician, he was depicted as the tool of the moderate Republicans—a human response to Taftian conservatism. As president, his domestic policy was seen as a direct response to the demands of big business, while his foreign policy was treated as the exclusive creation of John Foster Dulles. Treated as a man who relied on others but rarely initiated anything, the early revisionists treated Dwight Eisenhower with the same amount of deference that one would reserve for an aged relative in a nursing home.

The first of these early critics was William V. Shannon, whose November 1958 article for *Commentary*—undertaken to coincide with what would be, from the point of view of the administration, the disastrous Democratic landslide in the congressional elections of 1958—produced quite a stir. A thoughtful and detailed analysis of the administration to date, Shannon's "Eisenhower as President: A Critical Appraisal of the Record," concluded that Eisenhower's "place in history and the significance of his presidency are already becoming clear. Eisenhower is a transitional figure. He has neither shaped the future nor tried to repeal the past. . . . The Eisenhower Era is a time of great postponement."[5]

Shannon was followed the next year by journalist Richard H. Rovere's *Senator Joe McCarthy*. Engagingly written and still a primary source for the debacle that was McCarthyism, Rovere was quite critical of Eisenhower's role in handling of the crisis, noting that McCarthy held both Truman and Eisenhower "captive."[6]

The most substantive accomplishment by an early revisionist writer was the work of Marquis Childs, whose 1958 book *Eisenhower: Captive Hero* offered the first monograph of any import on the Eisenhower administration. Childs's portrait of Eisenhower as a man who fulfilled America's desire to have a hero in charge, particularly in the wake of Korea, and his overall criticism of Eisenhower were both devastating and trend setting. For Childs, Eisenhower was a president detached from his own presidency: "if he was concerned over the state of the nation or the world he showed no sign of it." In foreign affairs, Childs observed that "no president in history delegated so much of his constitutional authority over the conduct of foreign policy as Eisenhower." One of Childs's final conclusions: "Eisenhower's face betrayed a seeming indifference to the office he held."[7]

This thesis of an aloof, grandfatherly Eisenhower gained instantaneous credence with the election of John F. Kennedy. The distinction between the two men and the two administrations was treated as seismic—the vigor of the "New Frontier" versus the passivity of the country-club Republicans. Kennedy himself joined the ranks of the Shannon/Childs school on the day of his inauguration, when in his first address to the nation he reminded his audience—which included the seventy-year-old Eisenhower—that his would be the first administration led by men "born in this century." The seeming "vigor" of the Kennedy administration led most observers of the first half of the 1960s to side with the early revisionists and view the Eisenhower years as did scholar Norman Graebner: "Never has a popular leader who dominated so completely the national political scene affected so negligibly the essential historical processes of his time. . . . The recent past is interlude."[8]

EISENHOWER ENGAGED: THE IN-HOUSE REVISIONISTS

The works of these early revisionists sent the alumni of the Eisenhower administration into fits of apoplexy. In their memoirs—including Eisenhower's own two volumes—all of them positioned Eisenhower as being in command of his presidency. These in-house revisionists countered the Shannon/Childs conclusions with portraits of an engaged leader who delegated much less authority than the early revisionists believed, and whose presidency was far from a holding pattern but rather one of substance.

This is not particularly surprising. As a genre, memoirs of White House intimates had been, to this point at least, glowing tributes to their leader and his accomplishments. The memoirs of advisers E. Frederic Morrow (who pronounced himself as being "awed" in the presence of Eisenhower)[9] and Arthur Larson[10] were both spirited attacks against the "Grandpa Ike" thesis and animated defenses of both the man and his administration. Eisenhower himself wrote a work that belongs to this genre. In the early preparation for the writing of his memoirs, Eisenhower's son John was quoted as saying that "one thing this book is going to demonstrate" was the key theme of the in-house revisionists—"that Dad knew what was going on."[11] In a nutshell, this was the thesis of both *Mandate for Change, 1953–1956* and *Waging Peace, 1956–1961* (Garden City, N.Y.: Doubleday, 1963, 1965). While not particularly well written, and more self-serving than any other presidential memoir with the possible exception of Nixon's, Eisenhower's memoirs continued the theme of himself as an engaged president, particularly in the area of foreign affairs—an area where, during the period of his writing, Eisenhower was enduring some rather unflattering comparisons to Kennedy.

However, the majority of the memoirs produced by the alumni of the Eisenhower administration, while equally dismissive of a passive Eisenhower, surprised virtually everyone by painting the administration as a failure. Eisenhower's first Chief of Staff, Sherman Adams, provided the mildest of the rebukes, arguing in *Firsthand Report* that while the president was actively engaged, "the goals to which Eisenhower gave his finest efforts have yet to be reached."[12] Somewhere in the middle were the observations of Vice President Richard M. Nixon, whose first set of memoirs, *Six Crises* (1962), included the rather cryptic assessment of Eisenhower as "a far more complex and devious man than most people realized, and in the best sense of those words." It also included a not-too-subtle criticism of Eisenhower's refusal to strongly back Nixon either during the Fund Crisis or the election of 1960.[13] On the far end of the spectrum was the rather shrill criticism of speechwriter Emmet John Hughes, who concluded that Eisenhower's "political naiveté" led to an administration besmirched by "intellectual and moral confusion."[14]

EISENHOWER AS CAMOUFLAGED MACHIAVELLIAN: THE KEMPTON/WILLS SCHOOL

Thus it can be seen that despite the conclusions of most Eisenhower students, Eisenhower revisionism did not begin in 1967 with the startling appearance of Murray Kempton's devastating portrayal of Eisenhower in the pages of *Esquire* magazine. However, Kempton did indeed usher in a new phase of Eisenhower scholarship. As did both the Shannon/Childs and the in-house revisionists, Kempton took the Eisenhower years seriously. However, Kempton took the conclusions of Adams and Hughes to a higher plane, concluding that the Eisenhower that all previous scholars had been analyzing was merely a media-enhanced image— a carefully concocted fraud. The first page of Kempton's "The Underestimation of Dwight D. Eisenhower" is accompanied by a rather unflattering cartoon of Eisenhower as a grinning Cheshire cat. This character, who grins and disappears at will, offers the perfect characterization of Kempton's Eisenhower. Rather than being an up-front, middle-class, regular guy—as all previous writers, both hagiographers and revisionists, had portrayed him—Eisenhower was no more than a regular politician: "It was the purpose of his existence never to be seen in what he did. . . . [T]he mask he contrived for his comfort has already become the reputation."[15] In this portrayal, Kempton had articulated the "hidden hand" thesis some fifteen years before the publication of Fred Greenstein's influential work (see below).

In a somewhat more positive vein, the work of a second journalist, Garry Wills's *Nixon Agonistes* continued this theme. In his portrait of the relationship between Nixon and Eisenhower, it is easy to sense an almost begrudging respect that Wills held for Eisenhower's political abilities. Nevertheless, the hidden hand is there. Typifying Eisenhower as "a master of the essentials," Wills observed that he "had the true professional's instinct for making things look easy. He appeared to be performing less work than he actually did. And he wanted it that way. An air of ease inspires confidence."[16]

What made the observations of Kempton and Wills so singular was the spirit with which they were accepted by the scholarly community. Students of the presidency began to crow about an Eisenhower revisionism that had finally discovered an engaged Eisenhower. The fact that they had ignored the contributions of the in-house revisionists and had so quickly embraced the theses of two journalists is easy to explain: by the late 1960s, a country engulfed in the losing effort in Vietnam and a scholarly community that held Lyndon Johnson responsible for that debacle was now ready to accept Eisenhower as a hidden-hand leader. Given the temper of the times, particularly on the college campuses, it made sense to believe that, at heart, all presidents were somehow crooked—even Ike.

This is not to say that either the views of the in-house revisionists or of Kempton and Wills completely destroyed the allure of the Shannon/Childs thesis of passivity. Richard Rovere, himself one of the early revisionists, challenged both Kempton and Wills in the pages of the *New York Times Magazine* in 1971. Rovere sniffed: "A Political Genius? A Brilliant Man? Who ever said or thought that about Eisenhower in his own time?"[17] This view was echoed by presidential scholar James David Barber, whose 1972 work *The Presidential Character*, which labelled Eisenhower as a "passive-negative president," kept the thesis of the early revisionists alive.[18] It would be the release of the papers of Eisenhower and his administration that would give scholars the fodder with which to bury the passive theory.

EISENHOWER AS MAN OF THE MIDDLE: THE EISENHOWER PAPERS AND THE PARMET SCHOOL

On May 1, 1962, the Dwight D. Eisenhower Presidential Library was dedicated in Eisenhower's hometown of Abilene, Kansas. Staffed with archivists of the National Archives and Records Administration (NARA), the library began the lengthy process of cataloguing and classifying the thousands of documents that had been donated both by Eisenhower and by members of his administration. The White House Central File (WHCF) was made immediately available to scholars, and throughout the decade of the 1960s Eisenhower continued to send to the library his personal memoranda, diaries, and files, which he had kept at Gettysburg to aid in the writing of his memoirs. A veritable treasure trove of material was found in the files of Ann Whitman. While Eisenhower's secretary at the White House, Whitman would review any material that had been sent by a staff member to the WHCF, remove documents that were sensitive or important in any way, and place them into a separate file that she maintained throughout the life of the administration. This file was taken to Gettysburg, and it passed to the library after Eisenhower's death in 1969. Archivists began work on the Whitman files in 1972, and the first of them were released to scholars in May 1975. The opening of these extraordinary files gave ample evidence of Eisenhower's control over his own administration.[19]

The opening of the Eisenhower Library was complemented by a project that would eventually lead to the publication of a multivolume edition of those papers. In the summer of 1963, Eisenhower agreed to a proposal by David Donald, a historian at Johns Hopkins University, to have his papers edited and published by the Johns Hopkins University Press. Eisenhower's brother Milton, then the president of Johns Hopkins, raised the money for the project and hired Dr. Alfred D. Chandler, Jr., as the project editor. In 1970, the first five volumes of *The Papers of Dwight D. Eisenhower* (Baltimore: Johns Hopkins University Press, 1970–) were published. Many historians criticized Chandler's decision to publish "only those documents that Eisenhower had either signed or initialed." Nevertheless, the release of the volumes gave even further evidence that Eisenhower was far from a passive leader.[20]

The opening and the publication of the Eisenhower Papers led to the publication of a book that many scholars have labelled the most influential work on the Eisenhower administration yet written. Herbert S. Parmet's *Eisenhower and the American Crusades* was truly a landmark effort. It was the first book-length piece to seriously utilize the Eisenhower Papers; as such, it stands as the first work of scholarly sophistication on Eisenhower. Both balanced and gracefully written, Parmet's work accepted the thesis of both the in-house revisionists and the Kempton School, but he moderated their tone with his judicious use of archival evidence. No less convinced that Eisenhower was in charge of the destiny of his administration, Parmet paints a picture not of a closet Machiavellian, but rather of a consensus builder—a man that he tags "the centrist from Mid-America."[21]

Parmet's work ushered in a series of books that painted Eisenhower as a man of the middle, actively striving to keep the actions of his administration from rocking too many boats. Peter Lyon's *Eisenhower: Portrait of the Hero* (Boston: Little, Brown, and Co., 1974), offers a picture of an Eisenhower whose entire career was built upon his success in making disparate groups—be it the planners of Operation Overlord, or the Civil Rights Bill of 1958—come to an acceptable consensus. Lyon's was also the first biography to utilize the Ann Whitman files, and although the book was tediously written, his research made a serious contribution. Not so Charles C. Alexander, *Holding the Line: The Eisenhower Era, 1952–1961* (Bloomington, Ind.: Indiana University Press, 1975), or Elmo J. Richardson, *The Presidency of Dwight D. Eisenhower* (Lawrence: University Press of Kansas, 1979), both of which expanded upon the view of Eisenhower as a consensus builder, but neither of which made serious use of the available archival material.[22]

EISENHOWER AS NEGATIVE SUCCESS: THE DIVINE SCHOOL

As the third decade of Eisenhower scholarship opened, Eisenhower revisionists added another piece to the growing picture of the activist Eisenhower. It was a theme that, not surprisingly, was first voiced by Eisenhower in his memoirs. He clearly stated that what was important in his administration was what he did not do in terms of foreign policy. Summarizing, Eisenhower declared that during his administration "the United States lost no foot of Free World to Communist aggression, made certain that the Soviets and China understood the adequacy of our military power, and dealt with them firmly but not arrogantly."[23] The key development in the Eisenhower historiography of the 1980s centered around this point. Agreeing that he was an activist leader looking to move his administration toward consensus, Eisenhower revisionists began to examine—and ultimately praise—Eisenhower for the decisions that he made that avoided disasters.

The dean of the negative revisionists was Robert A. Divine. His *Eisenhower and the Cold War* treated Eisenhower as a man in control of his own foreign policy—one of the first books to suggest that Dulles worked for Eisenhower and not the other way around. As important, however, was how Divine interpreted the results of Eisenhower's foreign policy—"nearly all of Eisenhower's foreign policy achievements were negative in nature."[24] Eisenhower had gotten the United States out of Korea and kept the country out of Vietnam; there had been no World War III over Suez and no military showdown over Berlin; and there had been a halt in the explosion of nuclear weapons in the atmosphere. This is high praise from Divine, who concludes that "in the aftermath of Vietnam, it can be argued that a President who avoids hasty military action and refrains from extensive involvement in the internal affairs of other nations deserves praise rather than scorn."[25]

The two major works of the first half of the decade concurred with Divine. William Bragg Ewald's survey of the Eisenhower presidency, *Eisenhower the President: Critical Days, 1951–1960* (Englewood Cliffs, N.J.: Prentice-Hall, 1981), concluded that "many terrible things that could have happened, didn't." The overall thesis of Stephen E. Ambrose's superb two-volume biography, *Eisenhower* (New York: Simon and Schuster, 1984) followed the same tack: "Eisenhower gave the nation eight years of peace and prosperity. No other president in the twentieth century could make that claim. No wonder that millions of Americans felt that the country was damned lucky to have him."[26]

THE HEIRS TO THE REVISIONISTS: 1982–1989

Since the publication of Divine's book in 1982, there has been no noticeably new school of thought in Eisenhower revisionism. The continued opening of the Eisenhower Papers, as well as the willingness of Eisenhower administration alumni to talk with scholars (a willingness which, from the experience of this writer at least, is unparalleled in the administrations of any of Eisenhower's predecessors or successors), produced several works that expanded upon the seminal works of Kempton, Parmet, and Divine. Kempton's heir was Princeton University's Fred I. Greenstein. His *The Hidden-Hand Presidency: Eisenhower as Leader* stunned the academic world, being the first scholarly monograph to concentrate solely upon Eisenhower as a political operator who "often camouflaged his participation not only in political activity . . . but also in more commonplace political leadership."[27] Parmet's legacy could be seen in Robert Griffith's brilliant 1982 essay for the *American Historical Review*, "Dwight D. Eisenhower and the Corporate Commonwealth." Based upon prodigious archival research, Griffith observed that Eisenhower had a view of how society ought to operate—a "corporate commonwealth," a "non-coercive, self-disciplined, harmonious society."[28] The work of George C. Herring and Richard H. Immerman expanded upon Divine's treatment of Vietnam and served to cement the validity of the thesis of the negative revisionists. Using the archival record, their "Eisenhower, Dulles, and Dien Bien Phu: 'The Day We Didn't Go to War' Revisited" criticized press reports at the time that concluded that the day after Dien Bien Phu, the administration had committed itself to a massive air strike (Operation VULTURE). Instead, Herring and Immerman show that "VULTURE was not discussed seriously at the top levels, and the administration never made a commitment to it."[29]

The works of Greenstein, Griffith, and Immerman and Herring kept the flame of an engaged Eisenhower alive. Younger scholars working on the Eisenhower years began to produce specialty works that continued to expand upon these themes. These works, written in the intellectual doldrums of the Reagan years, tended to be quite critical of the Republican Eisenhower's personality, method, and administration. Griffith's consensus argument has profoundly affected students of the civil rights movement under Eisenhower, such as Robert F. Burk, who argued in his *The Eisenhower Administration and Black Civil Rights* (Knoxville: University of Tennessee Press, 1984) that "the administration sought forms of racial change that were more symbolic than substantial." Greenstein's hidden-hand model has been the basis of any discussion of Eisenhower's politics since its publication. John Robert Greene, *The Crusade: The Presidential Election of 1952* (Lanham, Md.: University Press of America, 1985), argued that both Eisenhower and Stevenson actively sought the nominations of their respective parties but did so covertly, as they hid their true ambitions from the American public and quietly cooperated with "draft" efforts that were set up in their names—what Greene called "Non-Participant Politics." The hand of Herring and Immerman is evident in the interest seen in new studies of Eisenhower's military and security policies. John Prados's critical *"The Sky Would Fall":* *Operation Vulture, the U.S. Bombing Mission in Indochina, 1954* (New York: Dial Press, 1984), Stephen G. Rabe's superb *Eisenhower and Latin America: The Foreign Policy of Anticommunism* (Chapel Hill: University of North Carolina Press, 1988), and Michael Beschloss's riveting recounting of *Mayday: The U– 2 Affair* (New York: Harper & Row, 1986) all demonstrated beyond a shadow of a doubt that Eisenhower was in complete control of covert operations from start to finish—including taking the lead in any deceptions of the American people that he might deem to be necessary.

THE RESURGENCE OF THE DEBATE: THE CENTENNIAL CELEBRATION

One would be tempted to conclude that the literature of the second half of the 1980s forever buried the Shannon/Childs viewpoint. However, as the 1990 centennial of Eisenhower's birth approached, the debate triggered anew. Several scholarly articles of substance argued once again that Eisenhower was not the master of his administration but rather the caretaker of a flawed and ultimately inconsequential moment of history. H. W. Brands began the discussion. His 1989 piece for the *American Historical Review*, "The Age of Vulnerability: Eisenhower and the National Insecurity State," was a scholarly piece of substance, utilizing a wide breadth of archival evidence. His conclusion was that the administration was full of "confusion . . . at times approaching paralysis," which led to the nation's becoming "alarmingly vulnerable" during that period.[30] Alan Brinkley followed with a detailed op-ed piece for the *Wilson Quarterly* in the spring of 1990. Brinkley's "A President for Certain Seasons," which concluded, somewhat in spite of his own evidence, that "nothing in Dwight D. Eisenhower's uneventful presidency ensures him an important place in political history. . . . [H]is reputation, it seems safe to predict, will remain what it has been now for thirty years: a hostage to Americans' fluctuating expectations of their leaders and their state."[31]

The reaction against these new proponents of the early revisionism was swift. Brands was countered by name in R. Gordon Hoxie's lead article for the Eisenhower centennial issue of *Presidential Studies Quarterly*. Hoxie's concluding observation, that "more and more of Eisenhower's career and his Presidency will be compared with those of Washington and Lincoln,"[32] might well have been the theme of the October 1990 Symposium on the Eisenhower presidency held by Gettysburg College, the subject of this book. Panel members—scholars, journalists, administration intimates, and friends alike—found themselves spending three days attacking the view of Eisenhower as passive. It is quite possible that the most lasting legacy of this conference, of this volume of scholarly works, and of its sister publication from the conference, Shirley Anne Warshaw, ed., *The Eisenhower Legacy: Discussions of Presidential Leadership* (Silver Spring, Md.: Bartleby Press, 1992), will be to bury the Shannon-Childs school forever.

Eisenhower would have understood all of this. As he wrote in the conclusion to his memoirs, "the judgement of history, to some degree, will always be altered by the events that followed upon the life of the subject attracting the historian's interest, whether or not these events were directly related to the person under scrutiny."[33] The debate over the successes and failures of the Eisenhower years will continue to rage—such is the nature of presidential scholarship. On one point, however, this author must agree with former president Gerald R. Ford, a participant in the Gettysburg Eisenhower Conference: "We owe Dwight Eisenhower a great deal."[34]

NOTES

1. Scholarly evaluation studies of the literature of the Eisenhower administration include: Vincent P. DeSantis, "Eisenhower Revisionism," *Review of Politics* 38 (April 1976): 190–208; Anthony Jones, "Eisenhower Revisionism: The Tide Comes in," *Presidential Studies Quarterly* 25 (Summer 1985): 561–71; Mary S. McAuliffe, "Commentary: Eisenhower, the President," *Journal of American History* 68 (December 1981): 625–32; and Gary W. Reichard, "Eisenhower as President: The Changing View," *South Atlantic Quarterly* 77 (Summer 1978): 265–81. Other valuable appraisals include: Katharine Seelye, "History Is Liking Ike, Again," *Philadelphia Inquirer*, October 14, 1990, 7–C; and Karen J. Winkler, "Eisenhower Revised: From a 'Do-Nothing' to an Arch-Manipulator, a Low-Key Leader," *Chronicle of Higher Education*, January 30, 1985, 5–9.

2. John Gunther, *Eisenhower: The Man and the Symbol* (New York: Harper and Brothers, 1952), 2.

3. Donovan told the story of his research and writing experience at the Gettysburg Symposium on the Eisenhower presidency. See Shirley Anne Warshaw, ed., *The Eisenhower Legacy: Discussions of Presidential Leadership* (Silver Spring, Md.: Bartleby Press, 1992), 58–61.

4. Robert Griffith, "Dwight D. Eisenhower and the Corporate Commonwealth," *American Historical Review* 87 (February 1982): 87.

5. William V. Shannon, "Eisenhower as President: A Critical Appraisal of the Record," *Commentary* 26 (November 1958): 390.

6. Richard H. Rovere, *Senator Joe McCarthy* (New York: Harper & Row, 1969).

7. Marquis Childs, *Eisenhower: Captive Hero* (New York: Harcourt Brace, 1958), 259, 281, 286.

8. Norman A. Graebner, "Eisenhower's Popular Leadership," *Current History* 39 (October 1960): 230, 244.

9. E. Frederic Morrow, *Black Man in the White House* (New York: Coward-McCann, 1963).

10. Arthur Larson, *Eisenhower: The President Nobody Knew* (New York: Scribner, 1968).

11. Quoted in William Bragg Ewald, *Eisenhower the President: Critical Days, 1951–1960* (Englewood Cliffs, N.J.: Prentice-Hall, 1981), 310.

12. Sherman Adams, *Firsthand Report: The Story of the Eisenhower Administration* (New York: Harper and Brothers, 1961), 454.

13. Richard M. Nixon, *Six Crises* (Garden City, NY: Doubleday, 1962).

14. Emmet John Hughes, *The Ordeal of Power: A Political Memoir of the Eisenhower Years* (New York: Atheneum, 1963), 267–69.

15. Murray Kempton, "The Underestimation of Dwight D. Eisenhower," *Esquire* 68 (September 1967): 108.

16. Garry Wills, *Nixon Agonistes* (New York: New American Library, 1979), 118, 129.

17. Richard Rovere, "Eisenhower Revisited: A Political Genius? A Brilliant Man?" *New York Times Magazine*, February 7, 1971, 14–15.

18. James David Barber, *The Presidential Character: Predicting Performance in the White House* (Englewood Cliffs, N.J.: Prentice-Hall, 1972), 156–73.

19. Robert Ferrell of Indiana University would publish several volumes of collected material from the Eisenhower Papers, including *The Eisenhower Diaries* (New York: W. W. Norton, 1981), a valuable collection of both diary and memoranda from the Eisenhower Diary Series (although some of the editorial comments are debatable—"For all thinking Republicans the prospect of a Taft candidacy was horrifying," 203); and the extremely valuable *The Diary of James C. Hagerty: Eisenhower in Mid-Course, 1954–1955* (Bloomington: Indiana University Press, 1983).

20. Alfred D. Chandler and Louis Galambos, eds., *The Papers of Dwight D. Eisenhower*, vol. 1 (Baltimore: Johns Hopkins University Press, 1970–), vii, xii, xv; Stephen E. Ambrose, *Eisenhower: The President* (New York: Simon and Schuster, 1984), 653–54.

21. Herbert S. Parmet, *Eisenhower and the American Crusades* (New York: Macmillan, 1972), 22.

22. Richardson's work was markedly improved when a revised edition, drafted by Chester J. Pach, Jr. (Lawrence: University of Kansas Press, 1991), made a much broader utilization of both the available literature and archival sources.

23. Dwight D. Eisenhower, *Waging Peace, 1956–1961* (Garden City, N.Y.: Doubleday, 1965), 624.

24. Robert A. Divine, *Eisenhower and the Cold War* (New York: Oxford University Press, 1981), 154.

25. *Ibid.*

26. Ambrose, *The President*, 627.

27. Fred I. Greenstein, *The Hidden-Hand Presidency: Eisenhower as Leader* (New York: Basic Books, 1982), 59.

28. Griffith, "Eisenhower and the Corporate Commonwwealth," 100.

29. George C. Herring and Richard H. Immerman, "Eisenhower, Dulles, and Dien Bien Phu: 'The Day We Didn't Go to War' Revisited," *Journal of American History* 71 (September 1984): 349.

30. H. W. Brands, "The Age of Vulnerability: Eisenhower and the National Insecurity State," *American Historical Review* (October 1989): 963–64.

31. Alan Brinkley, "A President for Certain Seasons," *Wilson Quarterly* (Spring 1990): 119.

32. R. Gordon Hoxie, "Dwight David Eisenhower: Bicentennial Considerations," *Presidential Studies Quarterly* 20 (Spring 1990): 263.

33. Eisenhower, *Waging Peace*, 653–54.

34. Warshaw, *The Eisenhower Legacy*, viii.

Name Index

SUBJECT INDEX

About the Contributors

SHIRLEY ANNE WARSHAW is associate professor of political science at Gettysburg College. She has published extensively in the field of presidential politics, including works on the Nixon and Carter presidencies. She was the director of the Eisenhower Symposium at Gettysburg College and is the author of the recently published *The Eisenhower Legacy: Discussions of Presidential Leadership*. Warshaw received her B.A. from the University of Pennsylvania, M.G.A. from the Wharton School of Finance and Commerce, and her Ph.D. from Johns Hopkins University.

GILES ALSTON is a lecturer in the government department at the University of Essex, England. He graduated with combined honors from the University of Exeter where he received his B.A. in history and politics. He earned both his M.Phil. and his D.Phil. from Saint Antony's College, Oxford University, where his areas of specialization included international relations and strategic studies. Dr. Alston also held the distinguished Oxford-Yale Scholarship. He has held the positions of regional editor and contributing editor for the *Oxford Analytical Daily Brief*, for which his responsibilities included coverage of developments in American, Soviet, and Asian civil and commercial space programs. Currently, he teaches American government at all levels, including M.A., along with international relations.

MICHAEL GRAHAM FRY is professor of international relations at the University of Southern California. He is a graduate of the London School of Economics. He books include *Illusions of Security: North Atlantic Diplomacy 1918–*

1922 (1972); *Lloyd George and Foreign Policy, Volume I: The Education of a Statesman, 1890–1916* (1977); *Dispatches from Damascus: Gilbert Mackereth and British Policy in the Levant, 1933–1939 (1985); and Statesmen as Historians: History, the White House and the Kremlin,* editor (1991). He is editing the Festschrift for Donald Cameron Watt, which will be published this year.

LOUIS GALAMBOS is professor of history and editor of *The Papers of Dwight David Eisenhower* at Johns Hopkins University. His area of research includes economic history, and he has published extensively in various newspapers, magazines, and scholarly journals. Galambos is the coauthor (with Joseph Pratt) of *The Rise of the Corporate Commonwealth: U.S. Business and Public Policy in the Twentieth Century* (1988). He is a graduate of Indiana University, where he received his B.A. in history, and Yale University, where he earned both his M.A. and Ph.D. in history.

BETTY GLAD is professor of government and international affairs at the University of South Carolina, where she has taught since 1989. She graduated magna cum laude with a B.S. from the University of Utah and received her Ph.D. from the University of Chicago. She is the author of numerous books and articles concerning the American presidency, including *Jimmy Carter: In Search of a Great White House* (1980). She has also authored and edited various works on foreign policy and political psychology, including her most recent book, *The Psychological Dimensions of War* (1990).

JOHN ROBERT GREENE is professor of history and communication at Cazenovia College, Cazenovia, New York, where he has taught since 1979. His research focuses on the twentieth-century American presidency. His books include *The Crusade: The Presidential Election of 1952* (1985) and *The Limits of Power: The Nixon and Ford Administrations* (1992). He is presently at work on *The Presidency of Gerald R. Ford* for Greenwood Press. Greene received his undergraduate degree from St. Bonaventure University and his Ph.D. in modern American history from Syracuse University.

DONALD W. JACKSON is the Herman Brown Professor of political science at Texas Christian University. He previously served as a judicial fellow at the Supreme Court of the United States. His teaching and research interests include the protection of human rights in domestic and international law and the contributions of U.S. presidents to civil rights policy. His most recent publications include *Even the Children of Strangers: Equality under the U.S. Constitution* and *Comparative Judicial Review and Public Policy* (coedited with C. Neal Tate).

TRAVIS BEAL JACOBS, the Fletcher D. Proctor Professor of American history at Middlebury College, graduated from Princeton University and received his Ph.D. in history from Columbia University in 1971. He began teaching at Middlebury in 1965 and has served as department chair from 1976 to 1988 and since 1991. He is the author of *America and the Winter War, 1939–1940* and coedited with Beatrice Bishop Berle *Navigating the Rapids, 1918–1971: The Papers of Adolf A. Berle*. He has contributed to professional journals and is preparing a manuscript on Dwight D. Eisenhower's presidency of Columbia University.

KENNETH KITTS is assistant professor of political science at Francis Marion College in Florence, South Carolina. He is a graduate of Appalachian State University, where he received both his B.A. and M.A. in political science, and is currently working on his Ph.D. at the University of South Carolina. Kitts's current research includes "The Elusive 'Third Way': Eduardo Frei and the Search for a Centrist Foreign Policy."

MICHAEL MAYER is assistant professor of history at the University of Montana. His research endeavors have included U.S. history with a particular emphasis on the role of the president. He has published extensively in this area, especially with regard to President Eisenhower and his role in civil rights. Mayer's books include *Merrill Proudfoot, Diary of a Sit-In* and *Simon E. Sobeloff*. He is a graduate of Duke University where he earned his B.A. in history and english. He earned both his M.A. and Ph.D. from Princeton University.

IWAN W. MORGAN is principal lecturer in politics and government at London Guildhall University, England. His research and teaching focuses on postwar American political history and contemporary American politics. He has published extensively in this area, including the following books: *Eisenhower versus "The Spenders": The Eisenhower Administration, the Democrats and the Budget, 1953–1960*; *America's Century: Perspectives on United States History Since 1900*; and *Beyond the Liberal Consensus: A Political History of the United States Since 1965* (forthcoming, 1994). Morgan is a graduate of the University of Wales where he earned his B.A. in history. He earned his Ph.D. in international history from the London School of Economics.

BRADLEY H. PATTERSON, JR., received his B.A. and M.A. from the University of Chicago. He was a federal executive for thirty-two years, fourteen of which were on the White House staff including seven as the assistant Cabinet secretary with President Eisenhower. He won the 1960 Arthur Fleming Award as "One of the Ten Outstanding Young Men in Federal Service." Later, he served seven years with Presidents Nixon and Ford and twelve years with the Brookings Institution. He was the national president of the American Society for Public Administration, is a member of the National Academy of Public Administration, and authored the book *Ring of Power: The White House Staff and Its Expanding Role in Government*.

JAMES W. RIDDLESPERGER, JR., is associate professor of political science at Texas Christian University. He teaches in the field of American politics with an emphasis on the presidency. His current research interests include analyzing the administrative presidency and the role of presidents in the field of civil rights. He has published articles in *Journal of Politics*, *Social Science Quarterly*, *Legislative Studies Quarterly*, and *Social Science Journal*, among others.

HENRY Z. SCHEELE is an associate professor at Purdue University. He has researched and published extensively in the field of the American presidency. His book *Charlie Halleck: A Political Biography* was nominated for citation as "most distinguished book of the year" in 1966. Scheele is a graduate of Lake Forest College where he received his B.A. in speech and history. He earned both his M.S. and Ph.D. from Purdue University.

MICHAEL WALA, who was educated at the University of Wisconsin–Madison (M.A.) and Universität Hamburg (Ph.D.), teaches at the Universität Erlangen-Nürnberg. He is the author of *Winning the Pace: Amerikanische Außenpolitik und der Council on Foreign Relations, 1945–1950* (1990) and editor of Allen W. Dulles, *The Marshall Plan* (1993).